# PISA, Power, and Policy:
## the emergence of global educational governance

# PISA, Power, and Policy:
## the emergence of global educational governance

Edited by
## Heinz-Dieter Meyer & Aaron Benavot

*Oxford Studies in Comparative Education*
**Series Editor: David Phillips**

SYMPOSIUM
BOOKS

**Symposium Books**
PO Box 204, Didcot, Oxford OX11 9ZQ, United Kingdom
www.symposium-books.co.uk


Published in the United Kingdom, 2013


ISBN 978-1-873927-96-0


This publication is also available on a subscription basis
as Volume 23 Number 1 of *Oxford Studies in Comparative Education*
(ISSN 0961-2149)

Printed and bound in the United Kingdom by Hobbs the Printers, Southampton
www.hobbs.uk.com

# Contents

POLICY

# Acknowledgements

The idea for this book took shape during a conference at the University at Albany (the State University of New York) in December 2011. The conference's theme was 'Who succeeds at PISA and why? The role of PISA in global educational benchmarking'. The conference was supported by grants from the University at Albany, its School of Education, and the Department of Educational Administration and Policy Studies, which we gratefully acknowledge.

Under the excellent leadership of Jessica Siracusa, the department's doctoral students provided essential assistance in organizing the conference. In addition, SueHye Kim, Tom Enderlein, and Taya Owens provided valuable assistance in getting the manuscript into shape.

INTRODUCTION

# PISA and the Globalization of Education Governance: some puzzles and problems

## HEINZ-DIETER MEYER & AARON BENAVOT

ABSTRACT Over the past ten years the assessment of the Programme for International Student Assessment (PISA) sponsored by the Organisation for Economic Co-operation and Development (OECD) has risen to strategic prominence in international education policy debates. Through PISA, the OECD is poised to assume a new institutional role as arbiter of global education governance, simultaneously acting as diagnostician, judge and policy advisor to the world's school systems. The goal of this book is to problematize this development and to question PISA as an institution-building force in global education. The authors scrutinize the role of PISA in an emerging regime of global educational governance, which has the potential to induce changes in how nations and states organize public education, to what ends, and in what spirit – and whether to so according to emergent international standards. They question the presumption that the quality of a nation's school system can be evaluated through an assessment that claims to be politically and ideologically neutral, presumably producing disinterested data. They propose that PISA's dominance in the global educational discourse runs the risk of engendering an unprecedented process of worldwide educational standardization for the sake of hitching schools more tightly to the bandwagon of economic efficiency, while sacrificing their role of preparing students for independent thinking and civic participation.

Over the past ten years the assessment of the Programme for International Student Assessment (PISA) sponsored by the Organisation for Economic Co-operation and Development (OECD) has risen to strategic prominence in international education policy debates. Organized and administered by the OECD – an organization whose mission is to further the growth of global economic markets – PISA seems well on its way to being institutionalized as the main engine in the global accountability juggernaut, which measures, classifies and ranks students, educators and school systems from diverse cultures and countries using the same standardized benchmarks. The OECD, in turn, begins assuming a new institutional role as arbiter of global education governance, simultaneously acting as diagnostician, judge and policy advisor to the world's school systems.

For the creators and sponsors of PISA to assume a role of such prominence and strategic influence on the international stage of educational discourse should be viewed as a momentous occasion and a historic caesura of first importance in the social history of public education.

Not surprisingly, PISA has prompted a range of reactions from the scholarly and policy communities. Some characterize PISA as a step towards global transparency in educational policy, in terms of facilitating evidence-based decision-making, aiding national movements of education reform, and spurring productive labor markets and international competitiveness. PISA has also raised hopes that its reports and research will advance knowledge of what works in education, based on truly international and comparable databases. Scholars in this vein focus their efforts on analyzing the data to find ways to improve school performance, by, for example, identifying what schools and educational leaders in high-achieving countries do in a different way from their lower-ranking peers (see Owens, this volume).

Other researchers raise serious doubts about the tests' validity and reliability (Prais, 2003; Bracey, 2004, 2009; Dohn, 2007).[1] Critics also question the possibility of a culturally neutral educational platform in which the same tests and test questions are used in countries whose social, economic, cultural and colonial backgrounds are so vastly different. Some critics expressed concerns (even fear) that a non-educational organization is assuming a global standardizing role in the name of accountability despite a lack of accountability to any of its members or affiliates. And still others raise questions as to the OECD's ability to prove its commitment to the kind of professional standards to which the organizations of peer-controlled academics typically adhere.

Each of these concerns and responses to the growing prominence of PISA is echoed throughout this book. But this book's distinct contribution lies elsewhere. Its focus is on the role of PISA in advancing a new mode of global education governance in which state sovereignty over educational matters is replaced by the influence of large-scale international organizations, and in which the very meaning of public education is being recast from a project aimed at forming national citizens and nurturing social solidarity to a project driven by economic demands and labor market orientations. We thus focus on the OECD's international assessment program as the harbinger of changes in both the political frameworks and the educational objectives, by which public education is governed.

We approach this task from the perspective of institutionalist researchers who see institutions emerging through political contestation and cultural forces – national, regional and international – as they seek to establish taken-for-granted principles governing our daily lives (Meyer & Rowan, 2006). Our goal is to problematize PISA as an institution-building force by subjecting many of its 'taken-for-granted' assumptions and beliefs to critical scrutiny. We scrutinize the role of PISA in an emerging regime of global educational governance, which has the potential to induce changes in how nations and states organize public education, to what ends, and in what spirit – and whether to do so according to emergent international standards. We question the presumption that the quality of a nation's school system can be evaluated through an assessment exercise claiming to be a politically and ideologically neutral undertaking – an act of technocratic rationality – which produces disinterested data to galvanize education reforms around the world. Thus there is a critical need to pay attention to PISA's ideological foundations and the politically contingent factors of its institutionalization.

The leading questions addressed in this volume include:

- How, and through which interested actors, is PISA being institutionalized as a global mode of education governance?
- What key legitimizing beliefs and assumptions are being established, and to what extent are they contested?
- What historical, political and cultural processes have contributed to the emergence and institutionalization of PISA?
- What are the organizational and policy consequences of this new political regime for education being ushered in worldwide?

These critical questions raised in this volume follow not only from a conceptual commitment to an institutionalist mode of research, but also from puzzles and paradoxes inherent in the expanding reach of PISA and its publications. The next section provides a brief account of the theoretical-methodological framework animating this project. Section three discusses major puzzles and paradoxes taken up by this book and then surveys the main ideas and arguments in each book chapter.

## Changes in the Institutional Environment and Conceptual Framework

### Shifts in Education Governance: growing markets, shrinking states

It has become commonplace that in an increasingly knowledge-dependent economy, schools and colleges take on a more central role in society's institutional fabric where their performance has definite repercussions throughout the economy and society. A key result is that schools are no longer shielded from the pressures of accountability and efficiency. As the once airtight education monopoly of national governments is invaded by explicitly efficiency-oriented auditors and providers, the previously dominant state-controlled forms of schooling no longer serve as unrivalled models for emulation.

This shift from a government-controlled condition of education governance to one that is subject to control from markets and civil society must be reflected by a corresponding shift in the dominant mental models, policies and management tools. As market forces are inherently international, the pressure for accountability and the shift to market-based governance mechanisms leaves the states, which once controlled education in the name of nation-building, loyalty and patriotism among its citizens, increasingly dependent on global forces. The gap left by the state's withdrawal from many areas of social life, housing and health, social services and education (Strange, 1996; Bourdieu, 1998a, b) is filled by international organizations (IOs) which stand ready with a well-defined package of policies and management methods.

## The Standard Global Reform Package

In this new globalizing political landscape, IOs are able to socialize states to accept new political goals and new social values (Finnemore, 1996; Barnett & Finnemore, 1999). Like all bureaucracies, they make rules, and, in so doing, they create social classifications that frame and reframe our understanding of social practice. IOs define tasks, create new social actors (like auditors and consultants), form new interests for actors, and transfer new models of political organization around the world (Haas, 1992).

These international organizations have managed to give global legitimacy to a contingent collection of policies as the default method of social reforms. These policies include decentralization, choice, privatization, expanded use of market mechanisms, centralization of goal setting and curriculum, and regular audit assessments (Chabbott, 2003; Steiner-Khamsi, 2003; Daun, 2005). The audit explosion is recasting public education as primarily a bureaucratic organization, subject to the imperatives of efficiency, calculability, predictability and control, and ruled by numbers and league tables (Power, 1999; Apple, 2005).

The orientation of public education is changing from what used to be a focus on cultural and civic socialization, to preparation for the workforce. Given that education is at the heart of a nation's social and civic reproduction, and is crucial for its civic coherence, this is a far-reaching shift indeed. We learn democracy by learning to think independently via deliberation and contestation. To the extent that education is sacrificed to economic imperatives, the civic function is neglected, and the political-democratic fabric of societies is bound to loosen (Olssen, 2004).

As we impose a utilitarian education agenda (Grubb & Lazerson, 2006, p. 301) in which education is harnessed to the goal of economic fitness, we lose sight of education as a practice of and for democratic participation. This conforms to the outlook of Weber's 'specialist types' – uniform-minded technocrats and statisticians, who have de facto unseated the traditional humanities-based experts in ministries of education.

*New Public Management*

The need for efficiency in public-sector institutions has brought to global dominance an innocuous set of ideas about replacing bureaucratic rule by market mechanisms. By approaching public-sector activities like education, health, welfare and social security first and foremost from an efficiency standpoint, the civic role of these activities becomes subordinated to an economic calculus. In developed economies the urge to apply New Public Management to any and all public services is increased due to slowing economic growth rates. As high-growth manufacturing activities are outsourced overseas, service-intensive segments, like education and health care, represent an increasing share of economic activity. Thus, First World economies are increasingly dominated by sectors with little growth in productivity. Hence the need to treat public institutions as 'industries' and to revolutionize them through the application of market principles.

The result is the instrumentalization of education for the purpose of economic productivity. Bourdieu puts it as follows: 'Education is never taken account of as such at a time when it plays a determining role in the production of goods and services as in the production of the producers themselves' (Bourdieu, 1998b).

*Shifts in Institutional Analysis: economic embeddedness, history and power*

From the pioneering studies of sociological founders like Durkheim (1977 [1911]) and Weber (1947), to early critics like Veblen (1993 [1918]) and Waller (1932), to writers like Bidwell (1965), Archer (1984 [1979]), Bourdieu and Passeron (1977) and Collins (1979), sociologists have recognized the importance of education and its institutional configurations for a host of structural and cultural characteristics, from social mobility, to equality, to innovation, and a country's cultural values. These sociological perspectives have been notably enriched by work on the nature and functioning of education by institutional historians like Ravitch (1974), Kaestle and Vinovskis (1980), Katznelson and Weir (1985), Tyack (1974), Tyack et al (1987), and Meyer et al (1992), to name a few.

Following the influential statements of the sociological new institutionalism (e.g. Meyer & Rowan, 1977, 1978; Meyer & Scott, 1983; Powell & DiMaggio, 1991; Rowan & Miskel, 1999), institutional theory has been extended into other social scientific disciplines. Authors like March (1980) and March and Olsen (1989) applied institutional theory to the study of politics broadly. North (1990) and Campbell and Pedersen (2001) applied it to the study of economic change and development.

Earlier institutional perspectives, in which institutional forces were seen as operating mainly in non-economic social sectors, left the market-education nexus largely to economists to analyze education as 'human capital' (Schultz, 1961). New institutionalists, by contrast, view economic markets as institutionally embedded (Granovetter, 1985) and thus affected by institutionalized forms of property, security, and modes of enforcing contracts that are developed by states and enacted in civil society (Meyer & Rowan, 2006). Depending on the specific institutional arrangements, the relative efficiency and distributional consequences of economic behavior may vary widely. Like traditional economic actors, the parties to economic transactions are seen as motivated by the potential costs and benefits of an exchange. But unlike rational choice notions of economic behavior, the new institutionalism does not see individuals as autonomous authors of their preferences. Rather, their preference formation takes place within the constraints imposed by the institutional settings (Weber, 1947; Immergut, 1998). New institutionalists recognize the futility of trying to explain human behavior without reference to history, tradition, culture and idiosyncratic institutional configurations. As Powell and DiMaggio (1991, p. 187) put it, 'institutional processes help shape the very structure of economic arrangements'. New institutionalists 'place interests and power on the institutional agenda' and 'deepen the conversation about the form that a theory of institutional change might take' (Powell & DiMaggio, 1991, p. 27). Thus, institutionalists today emphasize the possibility and need for sociologists and other social scientists, notably economists, to collaborate (DiMaggio, 1998).

Importantly, institutionalists make no assumption that institutional arrangements garnering the support of powerful actor coalitions necessarily produce the most efficient institutional arrangements. In fact, dominant coalitions may precisely act to delay or prevent institutional change toward more optimal solutions. Institutional arrangements are seen as path dependent – that is, emerging as a result of pre-existing institutional formations and the affordances and constraints provided therein (Meyer, 2003, 2011). This may be true for forms of educational governance like the OECD's PISA model, which makes it important to inquire into the interests of the coalition of actors pushing the model.

### Puzzles and Paradoxes in the Globalization of Education Governance: the organization of this book

Processes of institutionalization are rarely without internal inconsistencies, conflicts and unanticipated consequences that tellingly speak to the contestations of institution building. To uncover these internal fault lines, institutionalists have found comparative and historical perspectives particularly useful. Consequently, our approach to analyzing the emerging OECD/PISA regime is organized in three sections, around four puzzles and paradoxes.

1. The first paradox is that PISA has thrown a country to the top of the international ranking charts that *least* follows the OECD's 'standard global reform package' – i.e. an accountability-driven and standardized-test based model of global education (Sahlberg, 2011).

2. The second paradox is that PISA is a key instrument in the construction of a new governance regime that is widely embraced by the very governments that it disempowers.

3. The third paradox is that PISA outcomes are widely read as indicative of intentional educational policies and practices, despite evidence that out-of-school or non-educational factors rival or overshadow school-internal ones.

4. The fourth paradox is that similar PISA outcomes may trigger very dissimilar policy responses on the ground.

### The Finland Paradox

According to PISA, the education system of the small Finnish nation state is the most successful in the world – and has been for more than ten years running. Such is the power of PISA that it has produced unprecedented streams of visitors to this country of five million inhabitants. To control the avalanche of visitors, the Finnish government has finally decided to regulate the flow by applying market principles: visitors now have to pay a fee to sit in a Finnish classroom. Ironically, Finland is the *one* country in the world that most distinctly deviates from the OECD's standard reform package. Finland succeeds not by following the policies recommended by the OECD, but by ignoring them. So what accounts for Finland's success, and what are the prospects for the Finns being able to continue to resist the OECD's charming embrace?

Global policy reforms have a tendency to diffuse around the globe and reshape different societies with dissimilar histories where they interact with locally embedded policies. **Janne Varjo, Hannu Simola and Risto Rinne** notice a contradiction between international acceptance and a deeply rooted entrenchment of traditional social democratic and agrarian egalitarianism. This contradiction means that in official rhetoric the New Public Management reform discourse is fairly prominent, whereas at the local level a silent consensus based on antipathy and resistance against national tests and ranking lists prevails. Municipalities have restrained themselves from implementing studies that could be used to create public school-specific ranking lists.

In their chapter, **Tiina Silander and Jouni Välijärvi** note that Finland has not followed the Anglo-Saxon accountability movement in basic education, which believes in making schools and teachers accountable for learning outcomes. There are consequently no inspection systems or centrally organized examinations or nationwide tests in basic education. Only in very few cases are teachers evaluated – for example, by the principal or school authorities for accountability purposes. Finns have never been enthusiastic about making schools compete with each other, although parents can now freely choose the school their child goes to.

A key feature of Finnish success is the historically explained high status of teaching, causing the most intelligent and ambitious students to go into teaching, and providing universities with an opportunity to only select the best. **Paul Andrews** compares the two most successful European educational systems – Finland and Flanders – from the perspective of the mathematics achievement of their students. He is interested in how the two systems construe and, through the practices of their teachers, present mathematics to their students. He demonstrates that success on PISA is not necessarily a result of pedagogic quality, but rather is a consequence of cultural factors that extend substantially beyond the classroom.

## The Global Governance Paradox: stronger IOs, weaker states

A new institution is emerging – the institution of global education governance – and international organizations like the OECD are at its center. Nation states are ceding power over what used to be considered a 'sacred' part of their jurisdiction, which controlled the reproduction of dominant ideologies and the production of a country's power elites. How do we make sense of that? To address this question, the chapters in this section enter into a broad institutional, historical investigation. **David Kamens** relates the dramatic success of PISA to the general 'audit explosion' that has captured the world of formal organizations, a development that lends itself to interpretation through the lens of Max Weber's secular trend of rationalization. Measuring, assessing, comparing and analyzing are becoming 'taken for granted' in social domains from pre-school to universities, and from health care to old-age homes.

Kamens suggests that part of the explanation of the dramatic rise of accountability regimes is the uncontested spread of several new beliefs in which institutions are seen as self-directed and responsible actors, rather than mere 'arms of government'. Another such belief is that education has become a key institution not, as previously assumed, for the social integration and reproduction of society (Durkheim, 1977 [1911]; Bourdieu & Passeron, 1977), but as an economic lever of the knowledge economy. Innovation and accountability become the organizational mantras. Education is seen as one of the most important factors in the high-stakes international competition for economic and political power.

Another aspect of the rapid rise of the new regime of global education governance is the presumption that its core activities are politically and ideologically neutral. **Daniel Tröhler** disagrees. He challenges the idea that governance regimes like PISA are institutions of technocratic rationality that are deployed in the uncontestable interest of efficiency and productivity. He argues for the need to place PISA in the larger context of the history of the OECD – an organization that was created under the leadership of the United States to advance American interests, as it assisted war-torn Europe in its post-World War II development. His argument revolves around the provocative thesis that many of the institutional characteristics that US leadership attributed exclusively to the Soviet Union – centralization, standardization, uniformity, training (in the sense of 'drilling'), technocratic elitism – have increasingly become part of the western institutional practice. He asks us to reconsider the taken-for-granted juxtaposition of education for freedom in the West and education for indoctrination in the East and to view PISA in the context of an ideology to legitimize institutional structures that are increasingly unequal.

Part of the OECD's agenda of expansionism has been to extend PISA to the developing world. But here we encounter another paradox. While the OECD's motives in extending the radius of countries is fairly clear, why would relatively poor and economically less developed countries want to participate in an assessment in which they can only come in last? **Marlaine Lockheed** explores the reasons for developing country participation in international large-scale assessments and the impact of such participation on education policy or practice in developing countries. She reviews how multi-lateral and bi-lateral donor organizations contributed to the rise of international large-scale assessments in developing countries. She also suggests reasons why the OECD's PISA program has come to dominate policy discussions, arguing that the educated elites that populate the ministries of developing countries see participation in international assessments as guidance for education and social reform. Their interests often dovetail with the interests of international organizations in strengthening the assessment capacities of their member states on the road to institutionalizing the expansion.

To give us a sense of the direction in which the new global regime of education governance is headed in the near future, it is useful to understand the programs the OECD currently has under development. **Sam Sellar and Bob Lingard** focus on how PISA has not only enhanced the OECD's role in global governance in education but also provided a policy prototype for the OECD to expand its global assessment to new areas – in particular, the assessment of a country's workforce skills and its higher education institutions. For Sellar and Lingard, the expansion into the domains of labor force and higher education assessment positions the OECD to become the global center of accountability and calculation.

## Educational Assessment, Non-educational Causes

PISA's expanding power depends in large measure on the simplicity and presumed clarity of its tri-annual global rankings. Governments and media editors are said to await the new rankings with the same anxious trepidation as that felt by deans at American colleges awaiting the annual *US News and World Report* rankings. In both cases, two or three ranks up or down from last year can mean the difference between jubilation or depression, promotion or demotion, pride or shame. But win or lose, the PISA results are read as valid and reliable gauges of a country's educational performance. They trigger thorough reassessments of policies, and floods of new regulations and memos to school administrators. But is this reading of PISA as a gauge of educational quality justified? Does a move up or down the global ranking reflect any real changes in the world of teachers and students? David Berliner (2011) points to the importance of 'out-of-school factors', as does Daniel Koretz, who points out that 'the impact of noneducational factors on test scores is widely ignored' (2008, p. 117). The chapters in this section of the book are likely to further these doubts. They deal, albeit from different angles and with different foci, with the theme of non-educational influences on PISA.

**Heinz-Dieter Meyer and Kathryn Schiller** ask how much of what happens in schools is the result of school-internal factors (teacher behavior, curriculum and testing, administration, etc.) and how much of it is the result of non-educational or 'out-of-school' forces. If the influence of those out-of-school factors is significant, then it is not warranted to attribute, without qualification, high scores on PISA to excellent schools and poor performance to weak schools. They consider PISA scores in the context of non-educational factors such as economic resources and cultural beliefs like individualism and power distance. Their analysis identifies two PISA success patterns: a western 'individualistic' pattern, and an eastern 'paternalistic' pattern. Taking the often dramatic differences in socio-economic and cultural patterns and resources of the 62 countries into account calls the PISA league table into question, in which Peru – a country with large amounts of child labor and little Internet access – is listed and compared with countries like Finland or Canada according to a single performance standard. More realistic and informative would be peer comparisons, in which countries of similar context factors are compared against each other.

Two aspects of non-educational factors are culturally shaped habits of self-efficacy and learning strategies and a country's ability to integrate diverse student populations, including immigrants from other countries. These are the focus of the next two chapters. As the two chapters make clear, both of these culturally shaped factors have a significant impact on PISA outcomes.

**Xin Ma, Cindy Jong and Jing Yuan** explore the role of student learning strategies and school disciplinary climate as overlooked factors explaining East Asian educational success. In contrast with factors like teacher quality or exit exams, student learning skills reflect culturally learned cognitive and meta-cognitive processes that are associated with more favorable learning outcomes. Relating their findings to the long-standing debate over 'effort versus ability', the authors suggest that learning strategies could provide a window on the interaction between the two.

In a globalizing world characterized by increasing migration, a country's ability to integrate diverse student populations and lead them to success has a significant influence on average learning outcomes. While it is clear that different countries have experienced large differences in their success in this matter, the governing causes are controversial. Does a migrant student's home culture matter more than the socio-cultural context of the host country? Focusing on the scientific literacy of migrant children, **Jaap Dronkers and Manon de Heus** look at features of migrant children's origin countries and destination countries and communities, and they show that the better educational performance of migrant children living in traditional immigration countries cannot be explained by these children's favourable background characteristics. They find that differences in PISA scores between migrant children from different origins and between children living in different destination countries cannot be fully explained by compositional differences. Contextual attributes of origin countries and destination countries and communities matter as well.

PISA has been introduced as a test measuring the literacy skills young people need to succeed in the workforce. **Yong Zhao and Heinz-Dieter** Meyer argue that high achievements on a standardized test like PISA may also reflect cultural traits like docility and obedience, as well as a school system's efficient functioning as a disciplinary mechanism, representing the absence of independent and creative thinking. To focus the debate, they concentrate on entrepreneurialism, a key indicator of a person's ability and willingness to take risks in the pursuit of innovation, and important for economic prosperity. They find that entrepreneurialism is not only unrelated to the attitudes and dispositions that may produce high scores on standardized tests like PISA, it is often its exact opposite. For illustration, they focus on East Asian countries often touted as paragons of high educational achievement.

**Stephen Heyneman's** chapter continues the exploration of cultural practices and attitudes, explaining that within Asia the view of Asian education is much less enthusiastic than it is abroad. Where Zhao and Meyer challenged Asian school systems' ability to stimulate creativity, risk taking, and entrepreneurialism, Heyneman points out that rankings that use narrow indicators like math and science test scores as criteria of success ignore important functions of schooling, such as civic responsibility and cohesion (where American schools do very well), which indirectly also affect economic productivity. Worse, these narrow comparisons mask the fact that Asian successes often come at a very high price of condemning the nation's young to spending their entire available time in low-level activities of learning drill and cramming. Using available data to compute 'efficiency' ratios (e.g. test score gains per unit of per-pupil expenditure), he finds that the much-maligned American education system looks significantly better than is often alleged to be. For example, when taking into account the extraordinary amounts of time and (private) money that countries like Korea spend on education, their educational achievements shine much less brightly. Heyneman also challenges the usefulness of averaging the test results across vast nation states, as it obscures the often very stark internal differentiation, where states like Massachusetts, Minnesota or Vermont perform at the highest levels of PISA countries.

Alexander Wiseman reflects on the causes and meaning of frequently dramatically different national responses to PISA, which run the gamut from shock to indifference. He suggests that the ways that educational policymakers respond to PISA and other international assessments is a product of local policy agendas, public opinion and local conditions. This chapter investigates the kinds of policy responses to PISA that are found in and across participating countries, and how they compare with one another. Wiseman does not see an end to the divergence of responses, seeing both globally convergent and divergent policy responses at work.

## Technocratic Standardization or Cross-cultural Innovation? Two Futures of the Globalization of Education Governance

For some 15 years, PISA has been making headlines around the world, comparable in impact only with the most pivotal leaps in the public's awareness, like the 1956 Sputnik Shock and the 1983 'Nation at Risk'. It has caused upheavals in many countries and prompted a re-grouping of policy priorities with reverberations down to schools and classrooms. PISA has shaped the Zeitgeist, finding some of its biggest fans in the editorial offices of national newspapers. It has produced headline-grabbing media content in many of its 60+ participating nations around the world, allowing journalists to make far-reaching pronouncements on the quality of their nation's education after spending ten minutes with the latest iteration of a single league table.

It is the task of critical scholarship to provide a counterweight to the Zeitgeist's insistent drum beat. It is our task to analyze and contextualize, to compare and to keep the horizons of our imagination open. Thus, we end this chapter by speculating on two possible futures of the emerging global governance of education.

### *Future 1: Worldwide Standardization, Uniformity and Surveillance of Education*

In less than 20 years the OECD has moved from think tank to policy actor with global authority. If only fifteen years ago the OECD was home to conflicting visions between US and European government regarding whether to approach education as a neo-liberal or social-democratic project, that tension has been resolved in favor of a US victory. Where previously there was respect and concern for the uniqueness of national educational traditions, the OECD has become the ideological leader of a shift towards culturally indifferent comparisons, moving from input to output orientation. In addition, the OECD has expanded its reach far beyond its thirty member states, and is well on its way to achieving full global coverage. Where is this juggernaut headed?

The most serious long-term result may be the creation of an apparatus of continuous, never-ending testing and reforming. The fact that this apparatus relies on numbers and statistics does not mean that it is anchored in transparent, objective, uncontestable truth. In fact, the 'cloud of data' produced by PISA may easily operate like a Rorschach in which anyone can find support for any preconceived idea. It creates the opposite of transparency because key assumptions and key decisions about categorization and the construction of measures are *black-boxed* by a complex array of behind-the-scene judgments and decisions.

More disastrous than mediocre results – which, on inspection, may not be all that mediocre to begin with – is if our conception of education narrows to a carbon copy of what an unaccountable elite in the headquarters of international organization agree it to be.

Those horizons may be further shrinking if we allow a single test to determine our collective standards and expectations of education. As those standards become more uniform the world over, we may gain comparability and transparency, but lose *diversity* – diversity of culture, traditions, beliefs and practices. Some of these may crystallize wisdom and experience that deserve to be conserved and cultivated, rather than marginalized and destroyed. It is as true for the evolution of species as it is for social and cultural evolution that diversity is the great reservoir of options that helps us weather unforeseen and unforeseeable storms. As we impoverish our natural and our cultural environments, as we accept the idea that we are in a race for competitiveness, as we accept the same definition of what the race is about, and as we all enter the race as set up, we may end up improving our speed on the track laid out, but lose our ability to adapt to radical changes.

Mindlessly accepting the myth of economic growth and economic competitiveness as a goal to which all other goals – in particular, education and education policy – are to be subordinated, we fail to ask 'growth for what?' Nor do we ask whether there are limits to economic growth, or whether growth for growth's sake is sustainable, or whether there are competing projects, like justice, civility, environmental stability, that might be similarly central to an agenda of prosperity and justice for all. In this future, PISA might become what Bourdieu (1998b) called a 'strong discourse'– 'impossible to refute and typically self-fulfilling, comparable to psychiatric discourse in an asylum'.

*Future 2: Cross-cultural Learning, Diversification and Innovation*

An as-yet-latent possible long-term result of PISA could be a rather different outcome, initiating, emphasizing and facilitating a tradition of rich cross-cultural learning, in which long-standing cultural practices are honored and taken seriously, even as countries innovate and selectively adopt best practices in light of the results of a set of 'peers' from whom they believe they can learn. In this future, the assessment process would be controlled by the governments in whose jurisdiction the tests are administered. The published results would not focus on meaningless global rankings, but on specific comparisons of specific practices and results. A lower result in a particular category would not lead to a rush to make policy changes, but to considered reflection and deeper probing. Instead of travelling troupes of IO test-makers and implementers, we would have groups of teachers and administrators visiting and perhaps interning in the school systems of their peers. Instead of narrow statistics and numbers, they would return with rich knowledge and stimulating experiences. And instead of competing for rank, the educators of different countries would collaborate, exchanging ideas and borrowing practices across borders and institutions. The result would be diversification and innovation instead of standardization and narrowing of education.

This future of the further globalization of education governance is no less 'realistic' than the one that currently seems to have the momentum of opinion, resources and taken-for-granted beliefs on its side. But that is, as we said, a contingent institutional phenomenon – subject to change.

### Notes

[1] Criticism of the methodology of OECD's Programme for International Student Assessment (PISA) has been widespread. Gerald Bracey, writing in *Phi Delta Kappan* (2004, 2009), has been a consistent critic. Here is a sampling of issues he reports from the literature:

– different assessments produce big differences for the same student populations; e.g. although both TIMSS-R and PISA look at UK students born in 1984, there is a much higher score for PISA for the UK (Prais, 2003; Dohn, 2007);
– cultural bias in the test items: test items may favor students along lines of gender or economic development. In one such item, requiring that the student imagine a car lapping around a race track, the scores of girls from southern Europe were vastly inferior to those of boys from the UK;
– cultural dispositions that inhibit guessing: French students displayed an unusual pattern of non-response, particularly for open questions which necessitate long answers calling for a personal experience. French students, when they do not know for sure, prefer not to answer at all. Also, they consider their own personal experience irrelevant to academic knowledge;
– age-based sampling may mean that students from three different grades are assessed (e.g. 8, 9, 10);
– selective (non-) participation of schools: countries may control test participation to make them themselves look good. This is true both for the types of schools that may or may not participate, as well as for the rate of participation. For example, special schools were excluded in England, but not in Germany. As to degree of participation, the PISA requirement was 85%

participation. Most countries managed this, and France, Germany, Hungary and Switzerland attained 95% participation. In Britain, it was a mere 61%. In the United States it was only 57%, and chances are that the participating schools were, on the whole, the stronger schools;

– selective (non-) participation of students: But not only do schools need to agree to participate, students must agree too, and it is not clear how local culture and school regimes may have produced differential degrees of participation. For example, there is anecdotal evidence that in some countries (e.g. Argentina), students handed in largely blank tests.

– external (non-) validity of tests: according to Bracey (2009), average test scores are mostly irrelevant as a measure of economic potential, while other indicators do matter. Bracey quotes Salzman and Lowell, who claim that 90% of the variance in scores is within countries, not between countries.

– A significant problem is that of black-boxing consequential decisions of test design and test evaluation in the statistical fine print that can hide a lot: 'Prais expresses dismay that the paper on how Rasch transformations were applied to get from raw scores to scaled scores "is not easy reading even for professional mathematicians and makes no concessions to those who are not fully adept research-psychometricians"' (Bracey, 2004, p. 478).

Daniel Koretz (2008), one of the foremost authorities on testing and test-design, gives an example concerning decisions about sampling of content: 'for example, what percentage of mathematics test items should be allocated to algebra?' TIMSS allocated 25%, PISA only 11%. On what basis? Another design decision that may be more far reaching than it looks: what percentage of items should be multiple choice versus open answer? TIMSS had two-thirds open answer, PISA only one third' (Koretz, 2008, p. 104). As a result, countries' math performance has fluctuated appreciably depending on whether it's measured by TIMSS or PISA. In the case of US math performance: both PISA and TIMSS show a clear difference to Korea and Japan, while the US performance relative to Europe is unclear, depending on what test you use (Koretz, 2008, p. 108).

A country's outcome relative to the mean is often the main thing focused on; but the mean is variable according to which countries decide to participate. The more poor countries participate, the lower the mean, and the better looking are the richer countries, without any change in actual quality (Koretz, 2008, p. 105).

Koretz cautions: 'But the low scores by themselves don't tell why achievement is low and are usually insufficient to tell us where instruction is good or bad ... Disappointing scores can mask good instruction, and high scores can hide problems that need to be addressed' (Koretz, 2008, p. 120).

## References

Apple, M.W. (2005) Education, Markets, and an Audit Culture, *Critical Quarterly*, 47(1-2), 11-29.

Archer, Margaret S. (1984 [1979]) *Social Origins of Educational Systems*. Beverly Hills, CA: Sage.

Barnett, M.N. & Finnemore, M. (1999) The Politics of Power, and Pathologies of International Organizations, *International Organizations*, 53(4), 699-732.

Berliner, David C. (2011) The Context for Interpreting PISA Results in the USA. Negativism, Chauvinism, Misunderstanding, and the Potential to Distort the Educational Systems of Nations, in Miguel A. Pereyra, Hans-Georg Kotthoff & Robert Cowen (Eds) *PISA under Examination: changing knowledge, changing tests, and changing schools*, 77-96. Rotterdam: Sense Publishers.

Bidwell, Charles (1965) The School as Formal Organization, in J.G. March (Ed.) *Handbook of Organizations*, pp. 972-1019. New York: Rand McNally.

Bourdieu, P. (1998a) *Acts of Resistance against the New Myths of our Time*. Cambridge: Polity Press.

Bourdieu, P. (1998b) The Essence of Neoliberalism, *Le Monde diplomatique*. http://mondediplo.com/1998/12/08bourdieu

Bourdieu, Pierre & Jean-Claude Passeron (1977) *Reproduction in Education, Society, and Culture*. London: Sage.

Bracey, Gerald W. (2004) International Comparisons: less than meets the eye? *Phi Delta Kappan*, 85(6), 477-478.

Bracey, Gerald W. (2009) PISA: not leaning hard on US economy, *Phi Delta Kappan*, 90(6), 450-451.

Campbell, J.L. & Pedersen, O.K. (2001) *The Rise of Neoliberalism and Institutional Analysis*. Princeton, NJ: Princeton University Press.

Chabbott, C. (2003) *Constructing Education for Development: international organizations and education for all*. London: RoutledgeFalmer.

Collins, Randall (1979) *The Credential Society*. New York: Academic Press.

Daun, H. (2005) Globalisation and the Governance of National Education Systems, in J. Zajda (Ed.) *International Handbook on Globalisation, Education and Policy Research*, pp. 93-107. Dordrecht: Springer.

DiMaggio, Paul (1998) The New Institutionalism: avenues for collaboration, *Journal of Institutional and Theoretical Economics*, 154(4), 696-705.

Dohn, N.B. (2007) Knowledge and Skills for PISA: assessing the assessment, *Journal of Philosophy of Education*, 41(1), 1-16.

Durkheim, Emile (1977 [1911]) *The Evolution of Educational Thought: lectures on the formation and development of secondary education in France*, trans. Peter Collins. London: Routledge & Kegan.

Finnemore, M. (1996) *National Interest in International Society*. Ithaca, NY: Cornell University Press.

Granovetter, Mark (1985) Economic Action and Social Structure: the problem of embeddedness, *American Journal of Sociology*, 91(3), 481-510.

Grubb, W. Norton & Lazerson, Marvin (2006) The Globalization of Rhetoric and Practice: the education gospel and vocationalism, in H. Lauder, P. Brown, J.A. Dillabough & A.H. Halsey (Eds) *Education, Globalization, and Social Change*, pp. 295-307. Oxford: Oxford University Press.

Haas, P.M. (1992) Introduction: epistemic communities and international policy coordination, *International Organization*, 46(1), 1-37.

Immergut, Ellen M. (1998) The Theoretical Core of the New Institutionalism, *Politics and Society*, 26(1), 5-35.

Kaestle, Carl F. & Maris Vinovskis (1980) *Education and Change in Nineteenth Century Massachusetts*. Cambridge: Cambridge University Press.

Katznelson, Ira & Weir, Margaret (1985) *Schooling for All: race, class, and the decline of the democratic ideal*. New York: Basic Books.

Koretz, Daniel (2008) *Measuring up: what educational tests really tell us*. Cambridge, MA: Harvard University Press.

March, James (1980) *Ambiguity and Choice in Organizations*. Oxford: Oxford University Press.

March, James G. & Olsen, Johan P. (1989) *Rediscovering Institutions: the organizational basis of politics*. New York: Free Press.

Meyer, Heinz-Dieter (2003) Tocqueville's Cultural Institutionalism, *Journal of Classical Sociology*, 3(2), 197-220.

Meyer, Heinz-Dieter (2011) Path Dependence in German and American Public Education: the persistence of institutional difference in a globalizing world, in Douglas E. Mitchell, Robert L. Crowson & Dorothy Shipps (Eds) *Shaping Education Policy: power and process*, pp. 189-212. London: Routledge.

Meyer, Heinz-Dieter & Rowan, Brian (2006) *The New Institutionalism in Education*. Albany: SUNY Press.

Meyer, John W., Kamens, David H. & Benavot, Aaron (1992) *School Knowledge for the Masses*. Washington, DC: Falmer Press.

Meyer, John W. & Rowan, Brian (1977) Institutional Organizations: formal structure as myth and ceremony, *American Journal of Sociology*, 83: 340-363.

Meyer, John W. & Rowan, Brian (1978) The Structure of Educational Organizations, in Marshall W. Meyer (Ed.) *Environments and Organizations*, pp. 78-109. San Francisco: Jossey-Bass.

Meyer, John W. & Scott, W. Richard (1983) *Organizational Environments: ritual and rationality*. Beverly Hills, CA: Sage.

North, Douglass C. (1990) *Institutions, Institutional Change, and Economic Performance*. Cambridge: Cambridge University Press.

Olssen, Mark (2004) Neoliberalism, Globalization, Democracy: challenges for education, *Globalization, Societies, and Education*, 2(2), 238-273.

Power, M. (1999) *The Audit Society: rituals of verification*, 2nd edn. Oxford: Oxford University Press.

Powell, Jr., Walter W. & DiMaggio, Paul (Eds) (1991) *The New Institutionalism in Organizational Analysis*. Chicago: University of Chicago Press.

Prais, S.J. (2003) Cautions on OECD's Recent Educational Survey (PISA), *Oxford Review of Education*, 29(2), 139-163.

Ravitch, Diane (1974) *The Great School Wars: a history of the New York City public schools*. New York: Basic Books.

Rowan, B. & Miskel, C.G. (1999) Institutional Theory and the Study of Educational Organizations, in J. Murphy & K. Seashore-Louis (Eds) *Handbook of Research on Educational Administration*. San Francisco: Jossey-Bass.

Sahlberg, Pasi (2011) *Finnish Lessons*. New York: Teachers College Press.

Schultz, Theodore W. (1961) Investment in Human Capital, *American Economic Review*, March, 1-17.

Steiner-Khamsi, G. (2003) The Politics of League Tables, *Journal of Social Science*, 1, 1-6.

Strange, S. (1996) *The Retreat of the State: the diffusion of power in the world economy*. Cambridge: Cambridge University Press.

Tyack, David (1974) *The One Best System*. Cambridge, MA: Harvard University Press.

Tyack, David, James, Thomas & Benavot, Aaron (1987) *Law and the Shaping of Public Education, 1785-1954*. Cambridge, MA: Harvard University Press.

Veblen, Thorstein (1993 [1918]) *The Higher Learning in America*. New Brunswick, NJ: Transaction.

Waller, Willard (1932) *The Sociology of Teaching*. New York: Wiley.

Weber, Max (1947) *The Theory of Social and Economic Organization*, ed. A.H. Henderson & Talcott Parsons. Glencoe, IL: Free Press.

CHAPTER 1

# Thinking Beyond League Tables: a review of key PISA research questions

## TAYA L. OWENS

ABSTRACT Since 2000, the Programme for International Student Assessment (PISA) data set has provided a resource of comprehensive information relating to cross-national educational achievement, describing socio-economic, cultural, programmatic and technology characteristics supplied through questionnaires to students, parents, and schools in over 60 countries worldwide. PISA offers social science researchers and policymakers an opportunity to explore perennial issues in education through these cross-national data. This chapter examines 74 peer-reviewed, published secondary analyses that look to uncover empirical links between student-, school- and system-level factors and educational success. Taken together, these articles provide a thorough examination of educational policy at the turn of the decade, spanning fifteen thematic categories. From gender gaps, socio-economic inequalities and immigration to classroom assessment practices, retention and large-scale system efficiencies, researchers have mined PISA data to address long-standing questions, moving beyond the league table to illuminate the contemporary understanding of the global state of education.

## Large-scale International Comparative Studies: a brief background

If custom and law define what is educationally allowable within a nation, the educational systems beyond one's national boundaries suggest what is educationally possible. The field of comparative education exists to examine these possibilities. (Foshay, 1962, p. 7)

The words Foshay penned to introduce the results of a pilot international mathematics assessment not only remind the reader of the origins of an emergent field of study, but foreshadow the exponential growth of comparative studies through the course of the following five decades. Far from outdated, his vision of the role of large-scale international surveys has developed yet deeper roots in the globalized world of the contemporary twenty-first century. In announcing the Programme for International Student Assessment (PISA) at the turn of the millennium, the Organisation for Economic Co-operation and Development (OECD) joined the company of other international and regional agencies involved in the production of a multitude of standardized assessments designed to measure various schooling outcomes. Beginning in 1959, the International Association for the Evaluation of Educational Achievement (IEA) piloted a conceptual and methodological framework for large-scale international studies. The pilot quickly grew into a formalized first (FIMS), second (SIMS) and third (TIMSS) study, all designed to measure the extent to which students are able to successfully solve problems based on a synthesis of national curricula (Howie & Plomp, 2005).

Through the course of the 1980s and 1990s, large-scale assessments proliferated in type and design. The IEA expanded the roster of surveys from math and science into reading, pre-primary education, classroom environment, second language acquisition, technology and civics. (For a complete table of international comparative surveys, see Howie & Plomp, 2005.) International, regional and national agencies such as the Institute for International Education Planning, the Southern African Consortium for Monitoring Educational Quality, and the Educational Testing Service have all tried their hand at developing systematic studies of various aspects of schooling, most with the intent to provide an evaluation of national educational quality. While PISA echoed the 1959-61 pilot mathematics study in the intent to evaluate student performance close to the end of schooling, the objective of the assessment had evolved distinctly from curriculum-based learning to *literacy*, a term employed by PISA to signify a mastery of broad concepts, applicable to life beyond the classroom (OECD, 1999). According to Barry McGaw, one-time OECD Director for Education, while TIMSS asks, 'What science have you been taught and how much have you learned?', PISA asks, 'What can you do with the science you have been taught?' (Schagen & Hutchison, 2007).

Since the introduction of PISA, researchers have questioned the distinction between the main surveys (the IEA family and PISA). Wu (2009) compares 22 common participants of the 2003 PISA and TIMSS cycle; the summary conclusion of her analysis suggests that despite differences of curricular or literacy intent, country results are comparable between the two surveys. Schagen and Hutchison (2007) underscore similarities between the tests as well, citing both methodological construction as well as applications for further research. In fact, the aggregated 'league table' results of these international surveys have caused more consternation than the psychometric underpinnings.

Wu, Schagen and Hutchison are joined by myriad voices, most of which opine that the intrinsic value of these surveys is overshadowed by superficial country rankings, comparisons that provide little substantive insight for results-based decision-making. Among others, Torrance (2006) calls for researchers to complete secondary analyses, putting the wealth of background and performance data collected by these international surveys to good use, stating that researchers have a responsibility to interpret and explain these results within a cogent theoretical framework. Bray (2007) echoes the call for rigorous research, distinguishing between the roles of various comparativists in their use of educational information: parents, practitioners, policymakers, international agencies and academics. Bray calls upon the academic to move beyond immediacy so as to postulate lasting conceptual contributions to the greater body of knowledge. PISA has completed one full rotation of assessments – reading (2000), mathematics (2003) and science (2006) – and is in full swing with the second rotation beginning in 2009. This chapter seeks to review the state of secondary analyses. To what extent have academic researchers used PISA data to enlighten interested parties beyond the league tables? What contributions have academic analyses added to these cursory national rankings? As such, the purpose of this chapter is to systematically review published, refereed research articles which use PISA data as a primary source of secondary analyses.

## Methodology Used for Selection and Analysis of Studies Reviewed

By their nature, articles published in peer-reviewed journals represent a standard of evidence evaluated by professional and scholarly experts, which in turn then serves as a baseline of comparison for future knowledge. Given the critical role of the peer-reviewed journal in disseminating accurate and high-quality knowledge, this systematic review includes only research articles that first appeared in journals identified as peer-reviewed by the Ulrichsweb Serials Analysis System, a catalogue of serials and academic journals. Of course, accurate and high-quality analyses are published in books and working papers and by national and international research organizations; nonetheless, these types of publications are not included in this review. As such, the search procedure for pertinent articles was conducted online, through several large databases and bibliographies. The author began by reviewing the *Comparative Education Review* bibliographies from 2000 to 2010, and then thoroughly searched WorldCat, a global catalog of library collections, in addition to Ebsco, WilsonWeb, and the Education Resources Information Center (ERIC), three comprehensive scholarly databases. Inclusion criteria for selected articles required that the article be written in

English and that variables from the PISA data set be used as the principal source of data for an original secondary analysis, either qualitative or quantitative. Articles that described the PISA survey, discussed the merits of national participation or analyzed the methodology of the survey were not selected. In total, 74 articles met the inclusion criteria (see Appendix).

| Theme | Year | | | | | | | | | | Total |
|---|---|---|---|---|---|---|---|---|---|---|---|
| | 2003 | 2004 | 2005 | 2006 | 2007 | 2008 | 2009 | 2010 | 2011 | 2012 | |
| *Student level* | | | | | | | | | | | 50 |
| gender | | | | | | 2 | 2 | 1 | | | 5 |
| immigration | 1 | 1 | | | 1 | 3 | 1 | 1 | | | 8 |
| learning outcomes | | | | | | | 2 | 3 | 1 | | 6 |
| motivation & affect | | | 1 | | | 1 | | 2 | 2 | | 6 |
| national overview | | 1 | 1 | | | | 1 | 1 | | | 4 |
| socio-economic background | 1 | 3 | | 1 | | 2 | | 6 | 2 | | 15 |
| technology | | 1 | | | | | 2 | 1 | 2 | | 6 |
| *School level* | | | | | | | | | | | 11 |
| autonomy & management | | | 1 | | 2 | | | 2 | | | 5 |
| teacher & classroom | | | 1 | | | 1 | 2 | 1 | | 1 | 6 |
| *System level* | | | | | | | | | | | 13 |
| accountability | | | 1 | | | | | | | | 1 |
| efficiency | | | | 1 | | | | | | | 1 |
| retention | | | | | | 1 | | | 1 | | 2 |
| school choice | | | | 1 | 1 | | 1 | | | | 3 |
| school entry age | | | | | | | 1 | 1 | | | 2 |
| tracking | | | 1 | 2 | | | 1 | | | | 4 |
| Total | 2 | 6 | 6 | 5 | 4 | 10 | 13 | 19 | 8 | 1 | 74 |

*Note*: 2012 includes only the month of January. This collection of peer-reviewed analyses is not comprehensive; rather, this review is limited by selection and inclusion criteria. See page 29 for details.

Table I. Peer-reviewed secondary analyses by theme, by year.

## Journals

The first of these articles was published in the fall of 2003 in the *Journal of International Migration and Integration*, while the most recent appeared in the January 2012 issue of *Quality & Quantity*. Overall, these analyses were published in 53 unique journals, representing the interdisciplinary nature of educational analyses by spanning academic interests ranging from psychology, economics and sociology to computers, labor and science. The majority of the journals are focused on educational topics: sociology of education, economics of education, educational policy, etc. Of these journals, three dedicated a special issue to PISA analyses: the *Scandinavian Journal of Education Research* (July 2004, vol. 48, no. 3), the *Journal of Research in Science Teaching* (October 2009, vol. 46, no. 8), and the *Journal of Science and Mathematics Education* (June 2010, vol. 8, no. 3).

*Themes*

The research presented by these authors has been synthesized into three overarching categories, defined by level of the principal question. Fifty studies explored questions at the student level, 11 investigated context and processes attributed to the school level, and 13 studies analyzed system-level policies and procedures. For the sake of simplicity, categorization of the theme was based on the most prominent thread of discussion; however, some articles provide insight that is valuable to multiple levels of investigation. As such, this systematic literature review has identified 15 unique and mutually exclusive sub-categories by theme (see Table I).

Of these themes, the most popular were student-level investigations (68%); about one-fifth of all papers focused on an aspect of socio-economic inequality, wherein authors explored the effects of student background antecedents on a dependent variable of interest, most often student achievement. Immigration status and student motivation or affect also proved to be popular themes. School-level and system-level themes were spread out more or less evenly, respectively comprising 15% and 17% of the total studies.

*Analyses of Data and Country Participation*

Taken together, these 74 articles applied social scientific methods of analysis to three PISA survey cycles (2000, 2003 and 2006), using data gathered from student content-area tests, as well as from the student, school and special topic background questionnaires. Of the three content areas, authors put reading data to the most use, followed by mathematics, then science. The overwhelming majority (71) of these studies employed quantitative methods of analysis, while the remaining three authors used case-study and survey methods to complete their investigations. Of the quantitative analyses, 80% of studies held student achievement as the dependent variable, although a few researchers used PISA data to estimate postsecondary enrollment, access and persistence, teacher shortage, social segregation or environmental awareness. Researchers analyzed data from a total of 60 participating nations or economies between 2000 and 2006, of which at the time 30 nations were

OECD members (see Figure 1). With regard to the comparative analysis, 24 articles investigated a research question within the constraints of one national border. The remaining compared at least two countries, while 30 articles compared data from at least 21 nations. Most authors confined themselves to data from a single-year survey, although 8 researchers put surveys from multiple years to use in one report. Figure 1 visually highlights the geopolitical representation included in these comparative analyses. Consequently, many of the results derived from these secondary analyses pertain to educational data representative of Europe, North America, Oceania, a portion of Asia and a portion of Latin America. Results from comparative analyses do not include educational data from Africa (except for Tunisia), India or China, to highlight a few notable non-participating regions or nations.

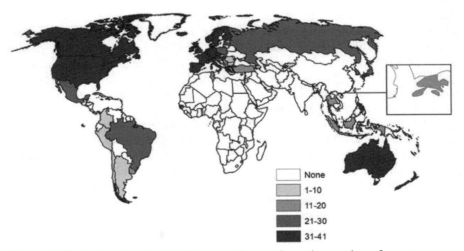

Figure 1. Nations/regions included in secondary analyses, by number of reports.

### Contributions to the Field

The great majority (67) of these articles have already been incorporated into the academic canon, as scholars have cited these works in different publications. According to metadata collected by Google Scholar citations, these articles have been collectively cited 1713 times by fellow researchers. (Google Scholar citations have been estimated to correlate significantly with Thompson Reuters ISI citations in eight fundamental academic disciplines [Kousha & Thelwall, 2007].) Although most studies looked at student-level effects, three of the top five most often cited articles reported on system-level effects – namely, tracking (Hanushek & Wößmann, 2006), efficiency (Afonso & St. Aubyn, 2006) and accountability (Wößmann 2005). Of these top five articles, the remaining two examined student-level effects: the gender gap in mathematics (Guiso et al, 2008) and the relationship between educational equity and social segregation (Gorard & Smith, 2004).

## Review of Secondary Analyses by Theme

Given the combination of critiques regarding the cursory aggregated country league tables and the calls for academic research to interpret and explain results of large-scale international assessments in a way that can facilitate evidence-based policy and practice, this review of 74 articles seeks to ascertain these results and interpretations. In order to facilitate a cogent comparison of analyses, these articles have been grouped into fifteen primary themes based on the main topic of investigation. These themes have been collapsed into three major groups: student-level, school-level and system-level analyses. The following review takes a look at results and interpretations within each theme.

### Student-level Analyses

*Gender.* Focused on the effects of gender on academic achievement, these articles all ascertained that, while perhaps diminishing, gender gaps are still pervasive between boys and girls. Girls tend to perform better at reading, while boys tend to perform better at math. Marks (2008) parsed out student aspirations from school composition and public spending effects on student performance in mathematics and reading in 31 countries. While a handful of countries presented notable differences, overall student aspiration and country-level policies were not related to the gender gap. In contrast, the study suggests that differences in school composition affect gender-based performance, confirming that while girls lag behind boys in math, they are at a comparative advantage in reading. Guiso et al (2008) detected the same subject-based differentiation in 40 countries; however, their study extended gender-gap estimations from adolescents to infer adult abilities using the World Economic Forum's Gender Gap Index. The results surmise that in gender-equitable societies, the advantage boys have over girls in math mostly disappears by adulthood. Furthermore, their analyses suggest that the gap in reading widens, as women progressively outperform their male counterparts.

Even though both these studies indicate that boys are lagging in reading, the remaining articles in this category focus on female underperformance in mathematics. Liu and Wilson (2009a, b) dig deep into the math gender gap to analyze test-item type, so as to shed some light on the domains of information where boys and girls differ. Focusing on the United States and Hong Kong, these articles both highlight international competition and pinpoint the gap in specific cognitive domains. Else-Quest et al (2010) provide a thorough investigation of gender stratification of learning outcomes by identifying 18 countries that participated in both PISA and TIMSS. Informed by a robust theoretical framework, this article sets out a detailed review of both international surveys as well as a comparison of common participants. What is notable is that these three articles evaluate female math performance rather than male reading performance. The size and effect of this particular gender gap appears to be diminishing in most PISA countries. As Marks (2008) and Guiso et al (2008) point out, the largest difference in performance lies in reading, a gap that is exacerbated as boys grow into men.

*Inequality in socio-economic background.* The extant analyses confirm prior research results, indicating that students from disadvantaged backgrounds score more poorly than their peers with more access to resources. These analyses reaffirm that not only family income but cultural capital, social mobility and national welfare policies all impact student performance. These studies often took student-level effects into consideration nested within schools or countries. Given the emphasis on student and family characteristics as a primary variable of interest, even when aggregated to a school mean, these articles were collectively categorized under a general student-level umbrella by the author for the sake of clarity. Drawing upon a large body of interdisciplinary literature, the constructs of the inequality studies frequently were grounded in cultural capital theory, contrasted or supplemented by social capital, human capital or rational choice theory. Taken together, these articles provide a robust synthesis of major sociological, economic, psychological and, at times, pedagogical theories. Through these articles it becomes evident that one of the benefits of the PISA data set is the extensive resource of data supplied by multiple supplemental background questionnaires, relatively clean of data error and easily accessible. The same ease of access proves to be a detriment to some of these analyses: clarity and focus of purpose is blurred in some comprehensive models, which sacrifice parsimony for the sake of unnecessary comprehensiveness.

That being said, several articles are notable for not only the depth of analysis, but also the parsimony and relevance of the reported results. Turmo (2004) takes advantage of PISA sub-scores, which identify test items by competency. Turmo separates out those test items that assess the process of learning as compared with test items designed to assess final knowledge, or product. Through this distinction, his analysis suggests that cultural capital effects are more strongly correlated with *process* than with *product*. That is to say, a student's background may influence the way she thinks about science (*process*) more than her ability to produce a final correct answer (*product*). While Turmo drills down to a pedagogical level, others yet relate inequality to macro socio-political indicators. Peter et al (2010) argue that educational policy corresponds with social policy, modeling student performance within a typology of welfare states: liberal, conservative and social-democratic. The typology of welfare states defines liberal as Anglo-Saxon nations, conservative as continental European nations and social-democratic as Scandinavian.

Their results find that educational inequality is less in social-democratic states than in conservative ones. The authors unexpectedly found that conservative states also exhibit more educational inequality than liberal states. These results are confirmed in part by Schlicht et al (2010), who find that inequality in student socio-economic background tends to be mitigated in European nations with high educational expenditures.

While these three articles contribute well-structured results to the literature, Barone (2006) and Nonoyama-Tarumi (2008) present theoretical and methodological contributions for consideration. Barone gathers PISA data from 32 countries in order to test cultural capital theory, anticipating that the effects of class ethos proposed by Bandura may be mitigated through modern mechanisms of social mobility: ambition and economic resource. Nonoyama- Tarumi employs various constructs of socio-economic status (SES), concluding that the addition of cultural resources to traditional parental education and occupation provides more robust results. Furthermore, she suggests that the omission of parental occupation (as was the case in Baker et al, 2002) diminishes the predictive strength of the SES variable.

*Immigration.* Given the breadth of international participation in the PISA surveys, researchers have taken advantage of the opportunity to empirically investigate a long-standing inquiry of interest: the effects of immigrant status on academic performance. Overall, authors concurred in demonstrating a consistent relationship between student background characteristics, such as family occupation or language spoken at home, and achievement. Generally speaking, non-native students perform more poorly in reading, with mixed results in math and science. However, when researchers focus on the context within which these students study and live, results among analyses differed. Focusing on students whose families immigrated to Germany, Ammermueller (2007) establishes that immigrants experienced an academic disadvantage equivalent to approximately one school year; however, poor performance is put down to characteristics attributed by the author to the student such as late enrolments and grade repetition. Ammermueller states that any school effect is small.

By contrast, Pásztor (2008) follows Turkish students to several European destination countries. Controlling for student factors, she demonstrates that certain school effects – namely, grade repetition and tracking – bear significant negative consequences. In Canada, Ma (2003) also identifies certain school characteristics which positively affect student performance – namely, a small student–teacher ratio. In an attempt to parse out destination country effects from country of origin, Levels and Dronkers (2008) and Levels et al (2008) highlight that the political stability or national economic attributes of origin countries carry more weight than destination-country political status. Levels et al also identify a strong immigrant community effect; in other words, immigrant students who are surrounded by similar students tend to perform better. Konan et al (2010) support these results by suggesting that as the percentage of immigrants in a nation increases, not only does the performance of non-natives increase, that of native students does too. Weiss (2009) provides a table that relates immigrant to native student achievement, showing that in Ireland, New Zealand, Australia and Canada immigrant scores add to national performance, while in other countries their scores are consistently lower. From these studies it is clear that not all immigrants perform equally in all countries. Especially because of national variation, identifying the main effects appears to require additional research.

*Student motivation and technology use.* Taken as a group, student gender, immigrant status and socio-economic status address student characteristics over which the student (or school) has little direct control. Consequently, most of these reports base the research question on classic social science theories. By contrast, motivation and technology tend to be mutable; teachers and schools can impact student access to computers or influence attitudes. Studies that focus on motivation and digital skills more frequently draw upon pedagogical theory to frame their analysis and, not surprisingly, offer more suggestions for school or classroom interventions. Using a cluster analysis, Linnakylä and Malin (2008) group Finnish students into six groups according to self-efficacy. Controlling for gender and SES, those students with better relationships with their teachers or higher self-image outperformed others. McConney and Perry (2010a) corroborate these findings in part, proposing that students with higher self-efficacy perform better. However, taking national patterns into consideration, these authors find that Australian school SES magnifies self-efficacy; in other words, students with strong motivation who attend a wealthier school perform better.

Drechsel et al (2011) move in the opposite direction, disaggregating student interest data to determine what exactly about science motivates students. The authors discover a differentiation by gender: girls are more interested in living systems, while boys are more interested in physical/technological systems. Most importantly, the authors did not find a relationship between student interest and national performance. With regard to technology, researchers determine that after books, access to computers enhances academic performance more than television (Notten & Kraaykamp, 2009). Luu and Freeman (2011) suggest not only that students in Canada and Australia benefit from experience with computers, but that perceived ability to use information and communication technology (ICT) also positively impacts academic performance. Several studies concur that computers are most effective when used for targeted purposes (Kubiatko & Vlckova, 2010; Luu & Freeman, 2011). Taken together, two cross-national articles complement each other: Notten et al (2009) investigate the 'digital divide' between students who have access to computers and those who don't.

The authors determine that access is related to family background, not to country characteristics like national wealth. In a final summary, the authors speculate that perhaps rather than national wealth, ICT penetration rates are predictive of digital access – in other words, they predict which students have access to computers. Zhong (2011) tests a similar hypothesis in 16 countries; the results of his multilevel analysis move beyond access to skills. National ICT penetration (or any other national characteristic, for that matter) is not related to digital skills. These studies confirm that students benefit from daily access to computers at home and at school.

### School-level Analyses

*School management, teachers and the classroom.* School-based management, decentralization and school autonomy have been core topics of educational reform over the past decade or two in OECD countries. PISA addresses this theme through the school administrator questionnaire by asking principals to report the responsible party for several decisions. Ho (2005), Maslowski et al (2007) and Alacacı and Erbaş (2010) all concur that the degree of decentralization or school autonomy has no discernible effect on student academic achievement. In Hong Kong, Ho notes that high levels of teacher participation in decision-making do have an effect on performance; however, this effect is explained by stronger relationships to school climate and student attitudes once student characteristics are taken into consideration. Alacacı and Erbaş find that in Turkey differences in school management are not related to student performance. Rather, high school selectivity and high SES composition effects are more strongly related to achievement. Masklowski et al provide a robust literature review to contextualize their cross-national analysis. The authors combine data from 25 OECD countries to confirm that any management effects are reduced once controls for school composition are included.

Tackling an alternative aspect of school management, White and Smith (2005) investigate the teacher labor market in OCED countries. The authors determine that while school administrators are concerned about a shortage of quality teachers, this shortage cannot be related to the school-level variables provided by PISA data. Taken together, these four studies indicate that either PISA data or the methods of analysis employed by these researchers may not be adequately suited to investigations of school management/ autonomy. Despite this, several researchers were able to successfully investigate classroom behavior through the school background questionnaires. Dettmers et al (2009) peel back several layers of analysis to look at a hotly contested issue: the effect of homework on achievement. Applying the amount of time reported by students across 40 countries, mixed results suggest that while in 11 countries homework bears a positive relationship to student performance, in 12 countries more time spent on homework is an indicator of poor performance. It appears that homework may be used as a mechanism of remediation in some countries, while in others homework time is an indicator of a pedagogical method and school policy. However, Dettmers et al note that any country-level effects are reduced once student characteristics are taken into consideration.

Liang (2010) switches her focus to assessments, asking whether high mathematics scores in Canada and Finland could be attributed to the role of assessments as pedagogical tools rather than to benchmark standards. According to Liang's analysis, teacher-developed tests contribute positively to student achievement in Canada and the USA. In contrast, assessments used to improve instruction and curriculum in the USA appear to have a negative effect on student performance. Neither type of assessment contributes significantly to Finnish student performance, a finding that Liang attributes to the coherence between schools in Finland. This article, grounded in a contextual framework and strong methodology, provides a well-informed contribution to contemporary assessment practices.

*School entry age, retention and tracking.* Cross-national system analyses highlight the importance of how the researcher identifies, defines and models the research question. Suggate (2009) and Sprietsma (2010) both target school entry age (SEA) in their analyses, addressing a question of central import to education specialists: does the age at which a student begins studying affect later performance? Using reading scores from PISA 2006 in 55 countries, Suggate determines that SEA is not related to reading scores. However, Sprietsma uses reading and math scores from 16 countries that participated in PISA 2003. Her results suggest that in fact SEA improves performance in about half of the countries, in line with reading and literacy literature. Since PISA does not provide a standard operational definition for SEA, these researchers varied in the method by which they calculated school entry age. Suggate imputed data from UNESCO, while Sprietsma derived her indicator from student background information and country-level cut-off dates for enrolling in primary school.

With regard to student retention, Dupriez et al (2008) and Conboy (2011) provided relatively consistent results: retained students perform more poorly than others. However, Conboy focuses on Portugal, magnifying systematic differences in which students are selected for retention (boys, immigrants, rural students, and students who attend poor schools), while Dupriez et al identify variation in national approaches to retention and tracking of low-achieving students. Based on an academic differentiation typology developed by Mons, the latter study suggests that countries with more uniform systems show more educational inequity than those countries with individualized or specialized academic routes. These results coincide with Marks (2005, p. 501), in which an analysis of 30 countries proposes that tracking 'can but need not necessarily' exacerbate inequality; the relationship between tracking and inequality hinges upon the type of academic differentiation, providing Austria and the Netherlands as examples where early differentiation does not appear to exacerbate socio-economic background inequalities. In 2006, Marks returns to the topic to reveal that although at the country level inequality, tracking and performance are related, this is not the case at the level of individual performance. Articles by Hanushek and Wößmann (2006) and Horn (2009) independently confirm the effect of tracking on inequity, especially noting early selection as a factor that widens the gap between students. Horn extends the research question to system standardization (centralization and accountability). While he finds that centralization reduces inequality, accountability shows no relationship. While Horn's work appears to contradict Dupriez et al, Dupriez et al focus specifically on mathematics performance of the lowest-achieving students, while Horn analyzes overall mathematics and reading literacy. The results of these two articles highlight the critical role that operational definitions play when compiling statistical research.

### System-level Analyses

*School choice, accountability and efficiency.* The consistency and availability of international assessments has enabled some researchers to use multiple assessments as benchmarks for comparison within their analyses. Wößmann (2005) combined data from TIMSS, TIMSS-R and PISA to look at the effects of centralized examinations on student performance. He summarizes that standardized tests appear to increase parental information, while affecting most students equitably. Furthermore, this article suggests a relationship between accountability and school autonomy: the effect of testing is higher in those schools that have increased responsibilities in critical decision-making.

A central question to researchers has been that of school choice: how do students from similar backgrounds perform in different school settings? Corten and Dronkers (2006) apply PISA data to 19 countries in order to differentiate student performance in public schools, private schools that receive public subsidy, and independent private schools. By narrowing the focus to poor students, Corten and Dronkers confirm results from previous studies, showing that these students perform better when they attend government-funded private schools. However, in this study poor students who attend independent private schools fare worse than their counterparts at public schools. Dronkers and Robert (2007) confirm these results: controlling for socio-economic background, the school climate at government-dependent private schools shows a stronger effect on student achievement.

Escardíbul and Villarroya (2009) take the question of school choice into a single-country context in order to estimate what characteristics influence parent choice. These researchers suggest that in Spain students who attend a private school, be it government-dependent or independent, tend to come from a family background with more resources. Family choice is related to geographical distribution; in other words, school proximity is a relevant factor, as is the number of immigrants in a community, and preference. This preference is known as family fidelity, wherein parents who enroll their children in private schools from preschool tend to prefer to stay in private schools. The authors question the efficiency of publicly funded private schools, which in Spain seem to mirror independent schools. Afonso and St. Aubyn (2006) modeled system efficiency by assessing student performance against traditional inputs, especially how much time students spend in school. Even given the expected cross-national variation, the authors estimate that on average, systems could reduce inputs by 11% while obtaining similar results.

*Longitudinal studies.* A standard criticism of any educational cross-sectional survey is that cross-sectional studies do not allow for the over-time modeling of changes, which is essential to establishing causal relations. In order to address these concerns, at least six countries (Australia, Canada, the Czech Republic, Denmark, Switzerland and Uruguay) have constructed longitudinal surveys linked to a PISA survey. In Switzerland, the Transitions from Education to Employment Survey (TREE) consortium follows PISA 2000 participants up to the age of 22, thereby capturing educational and occupational outcomes. Bertschy et al (2009) track students who enter into 3-year vocational training, using reading scores as the predictive variable instead of the outcome. By narrowing the analyses to vocational education choices, results indicate that while reading scores influence employment, literacy is subsumed by a more rigorous apprenticeship type. However, this study does infer that students with higher reading scores are more likely to attend a more demanding vocational school.

The Equivalent National Tertiary Entrance Rank (ENTER) study, linked to PISA 2003 Australian students, records scores on the national college entrance examination. The outcome score largely determines what level of postsecondary education a student will complete, if any. Controlling for student background characteristics, Marks (2010) focuses on school-level factors. The analysis indicates that two academic factors, academic context and academic press (pressure), are related to high entrance examination scores. In other words, the more emphasis a school puts on academics, the more likely students are to attend college.

In Canada, government officials have created the Canadian Youths in Transition Survey (YITS) to follow PISA 2000 students through higher education experiences, collecting data on access and graduation. Murdoch et al (2011) report YITS initial results, estimating that reading scores can predict initial college enrollment, but not persistence to graduation. Taking into consideration the fact that 40% of university students have not yet completed their studies, graduation data are still incomplete. Allowing for a more technical approach to longitudinal studies, Schubert and Becker (2010) employ pair-wise matching to create 'synthetic twins' from the PISA 2000 and PIRLS 2001 surveys in Germany. This study addresses questions relevant to socio-economic inequalities, suggesting that in Germany students from lower social classes are at a systematic comparative disadvantage to their wealthier counterparts. The authors specifically cite early educational differentiation at the end of primary school as a contributing factor to inequality. Although their article produces a technical longitudinal analysis, Schubert and Becker remind the reader that results from cross-sectional assessments cannot imply cause-and-effect correlations.

*Innovative use of PISA survey data.* Although the great majority of these analyses constructed models of inquiry using student-, school- and system-level variables to predict academic achievement, several researchers have discovered innovative ways to apply PISA data to empirical studies. The raw survey data include individual test items classified by cognitive domain, identifying the particular aspect of 'literacy' that the item assesses. In Turkey, Erbaş and Okur (2010) re-administer ten PISA 2003 mathematics test items to five high school freshmen in order to investigate student problem-solving and metacognitive strategies. By distinguishing process from product, these researchers discern that students could reach a correct answer by incorrect means, noting in their conclusion several pedagogical strategies to overcome this discrepancy.

Similarly, Pinto and El Boudamoussi (2009) deconstruct the PISA 2006 science assessment. In this study, 30 experienced Spanish teachers identify the specific scientific competency tested and describe how they apply that sort of knowledge and competency in their classroom. Teachers correctly identify the more elemental aspects of the scientific process (describe, explain, predict); however, these teachers score less well on the more complex test items (understand scientific investigation, interpret conclusions and evidence).

In Flanders, Coertjens et al (2010) construct an attitudinal analysis to evaluate school effects on environmental awareness. After controlling for student characteristics, constructivist teaching methods appear to be positively related to student awareness. Interestingly, in contrast, school climate effects, such as programs stressing the relevance of science to society, are not found to correlate to environmental awareness in this study. Also in Flanders, van Petegem and Vanhoof (2007) test the feedback function attributed to large-scale international assessments. Surveying five Flemish school administrators, the researchers identify essential characteristics of an effective feedback report by which to evaluate the PISA and TIMSS-R school reports. Both reports are deemed insufficient, with a dearth of useful information from which administrators can make decisions.

## Discussion

Taken together, these secondary analyses represent a substantive contribution to contemporary discussion of educational policy and practice. These researchers have confirmed results of smaller-scale studies, highlighted topics which need more investigation, and challenged conventional wisdom. Of particular interest are the discussions regarding academic performance and gender parity (where boys seem to be at a disadvantage through the course of a lifetime), immigrants (where results suggest that the cohesion of an immigrant community can influence student success), and decentralization or school autonomy (which, despite recent popular support, seems ultimately to have minimal effect on performance). Researchers have demonstrated that PISA data can be used effectively to investigate the intersection of our classrooms and communities, heeding Torrance's (2006) call to put these surveys to good use.

### *Limitations and Directions for Development*

Several limitations of the PISA data set do become apparent through this review. First, the voice or behaviors of teachers are conspicuously absent. The background questionnaires rely on school administrators to supply some information about teachers; however, investigating links between the student and the system suffers from the absence of this critical participant. While one article sought to address this absence (Pinto & El Boudamoussi, 2009) through an innovative application of the assessment, research would be well served by direct teacher representation in some aspect of this survey. A technical limitation in the survey design also has implications for research results. Currently, PISA data are nationally representative, but not school-based. This national sample design limits the ability of researchers to fully investigate the school as an influential organizational unit within national systems. Finally, while national participation in PISA appears to be increasing over the years, caution must be heeded when interpreting these 'international' or 'global' results. Foshay called for comparative analyses to suggest what may be educationally possible. In as much as PISA participation continues to demonstrate a non-random omission of participating regions and nations, policymakers, practitioners and parents must tread lightly when inferring generalizations of what is possible.

## Conclusion

Howie and Plomp (2005) have described the function of international assessments as points on a scale: description, benchmarking, monitoring, enlightenment. While the summary league table results often serve to benchmark national performance, thoughtful academic cross-national research can serve to enlighten by clarifying assumptions, highlighting similarities and exploring differences. Increasingly, the researcher has been called upon to move assessment results beyond superficial relationships into the realm of conceptual and theoretical knowledge (Torrance, 2006; Bray, 2007). To that end, PISA has made a wealth of data freely available to scholars around the world, with the hopes that researchers will in turn complement initial survey results with a rich evidence base, analyses that can be utilized by policy makers as they steer the course of national education systems (OECD, 1999).

Through this review of 74 secondary analyses, the reader can surmise several pertinent thoughts. First, the empirical methods of analysis employed by many researchers apply complex multi-level relationships to variables, allowing current research to isolate more (and less) relevant findings than the initially reported summary comparisons. The duty of the researcher is to further clarify the practical significance of these findings, plainly separating important information from less in a way that lends itself to easy interpretation by other comparativists (parents, practitioners, policy makers). Second, as researchers across the globe have applied PISA data to a variety of investigative scenarios, discrepancies in results have appeared. Rather than settle for mixed results, the challenge of the researcher is to continue prying ever more deeply into the mechanisms of these discrepancies, by addressing previous research and identifying differences in methodological approach. Finally, to the extent that researchers employ rigorous conceptual frameworks, PISA secondary analyses can make genuine contributions to the theoretical progress of core social science disciplines. The PISA data set provides a rich resource for the theoretical exploration of far more than national student performance, moving beyond league tables into fine-grained inquiry.

## References

Baker, David, Goesling, B. & LeTendre, G. (2002) Socioeconomic Status, School Quality, and National Economic Development: a cross-national analysis of the 'Heyneman-Loxley Effect' on mathematics and science achievement, *Comparative Education Review*, 46(3), 291-312.

Bray, Mark (2007) Actors and Purposes in Comparative Education, in Mark Bray, Bob Adamson & Mark Mason (Eds) *Comparative Education Research: approaches and methods*. Hong Kong: Comparative Education Research Center.

Foshay, Arthur W. (1962) The Background and the Procedures of the Twelve-Country Study, in Arthur W. Foshay, Robert L. Thorndike, Fernand Hotyaat, Douglas A. Pidgeon & David A. Walker (Eds) *Educational Achievements of Thirteen-year-olds in Twelve Countries*. Hamburg: UNESCO Institute For Education.

Howie, Sarah & Plomp, Tjeerd (2005) International Comparative Studies of Education and Large-scale Change, in Nina Bascia, Alister Cumming, Amanda Datnow, Kenneth Leithwood & David Livingstone (Eds) *International Handbook of Educational Policy*, vol. 1. Dordrecht: Springer.

Kousha, Kayvan & Thelwall, Mike (2007) Google Scholar Citations and Google Web/URL Citations: a multi-discipline exploratory analysis, *Journal of the American Society for Information Science and Technology*, 58(7), 1055-1065.

Organisation for Economic Co-operation and Development (OECD) (1999) *Measuring Student Knowledge and Skills: a new framework for assessment.* Paris: OECD.

Schagen, Ian & Hutchison, Dougal (2007) Comparisons between PISA and TIMSS: we could be the man with two watches, *Education Journal*, 101 (March), 34-35.

Torrance, Harry (2006) Globalizing Empiricism: what, if anything, can be learned from international comparisons of educational achievement? In H. Lauder, P. Brown, J.A. Dillabough & A.H. Halsey (Eds) *Education, Globalization & Social Change*. New York: Oxford University Press.

Wu, Margaret (2009) A Comparison of PISA and TIMSS 2003 Achievement Results in Mathematics, *Prospects*, 39(1), 33-46.

## APPENDIX
## Peer-reviewed Secondary Analyses

Afonso, António & St. Aubyn, Miguel (2006) Cross-country Efficiency of Secondary Education Provision: a semi-parametric analysis with non-discretionary inputs, *Economic Modelling*, 23(3), 476-491.

Alacacı, Cengiz & Erbaş, Ayhan Kürşat (2010) Unpacking the Inequality among Turkish Schools: findings from PISA 2006, *International Journal of Educational Development*, 30(2), 182-192.

Ammermueller, Andreas (2007) Poor Background or Low Returns? Why Immigrant Students in Germany Perform so Poorly in the Programme for International Student Assessment, *Education Economics*, 15(2), 215-230.

Bailey, Mark & Vani K. Borooah (2010) What Enhances Mathematical Ability? A Cross-country Analysis Based on Test Scores of 15-year-olds, *Applied Economics*, 42(29), 3723-3733.

Barone, Carlo (2006) Cultural Capital, Ambition and the Explanation of Inequalities in Learning Outcomes: a comparative analysis, *Sociology*, 40(6), 1039-1058.

Bertschy, Kathrin, Cattaneo, M. Alejandra & Wolter, Stefan C. (2009) PISA and the Transition into the Labour Market, *Labour* 23 (Special Issue), 111-137.

Chen, Shiu-Sheng & Luoh, Ming-Ching (2009) Are Mathematics and Science Test Scores Good Indicators of Labor-force Quality? *Social Indicators Research*, 96(1), 133-143.

Coertjens, Liesje, Boeve-de Pauw, Jelle, de Maeyer, Sven & Van Petegem, Peter (2010) Do Schools Make a Difference in Their Students' Environmental Attitudes and Awareness? Evidence from PISA 2006, *International Journal of Science and Mathematics Education*, 8(3), 497-522.

Conboy, Joseph (2011) Retention and Science Performance in Portugal as Evidenced by PISA, *Procedia– Social and Behavioral Sciences*, 12, 311-321.

Condron, D.J. (2011) Egalitarianism and Educational Excellence: compatible goals for affluent societies? *Educational Researcher*, 40(2), 47-55.

Corten, Rense & Dronkers, Jaap (2006) School Achievement of Pupils from the Lower Strata in Public, Private Government-Dependent and Private Government-Independent Schools: a cross-national test of the Coleman-Hoffer Thesis 1, *Educational Research and Evaluation*, 12(2), 179-208.

Cromley, Jennifer G. (2009) Reading Achievement and Science Proficiency: international comparisons from the Programme on International Student Assessment, *Reading Psychology*, 30(2), 89-118.

Dettmers, Swantje, Trautwein, Ulrich & Lüdtke, Oliver (2009) The Relationship between Homework Time and Achievement is Not Universal: evidence from multilevel analyses in 40 countries, *School Effectiveness and School Improvement*, 20(4), 375-405.

Drechsel, Barbara, Carstensen, Claus & Prenzel, Manfred (2011) The Role of Content and Context in PISA Interest Scales: a study of the embedded interest items in the PISA 2006 Science Assessment, *International Journal of Science Education*, 33(1), 73-95.

Dronkers, Jaap & Robert, Peter (2007) Differences in Scholastic Achievement of Public, Private Government-dependent, and Private Independent Schools: a cross-national analysis, *Educational Policy*, 22(4), 541-577.

Dupriez, Vincent, Dumay, Xavier & Vause, Anne (2008) How Do School Systems Manage Pupils' Heterogeneity? *Comparative Education Review*, 52(2), 245-273.

Edgerton, Jason D., Peter, Tracey & Roberts, Lance W. (2008) Back to the Basics: socio-economic, gender, and regional disparities in Canada's educational system, *Canadian Journal of Education/Revue Canadienne de l'Éducation*, 31(4), 861-888.

Else-Quest, Nicole M., Hyde, Janet Shibley & Linn, Marcia C. (2010) Cross-national Patterns of Gender Differences in Mathematics: a meta-analysis, *Psychological Bulletin*, 136(1), 103-127.

Erbaş, Ayhan Kürşat & Okur, Serkan (2010) Researching Students' Strategies, Episodes, and Metacognitions in Mathematical Problem Solving, *Quality & Quantity*, 46(1), 89-102.

Escardíbul, Josep-Oriol & Villarroya, Anna (2009) The Inequalities in School Choice in Spain in Accordance to PISA Data, *Journal of Education Policy*, 24(6), 673-696.

Fonseca, Jesuina, Valente, Maria Odete & Conboy, Joseph (2011) Student Characteristics and PISA Science Performance: Portugal in cross national comparison, *Procedia – Social and Behavioral Sciences*, 12, 322-329.

Gorard, Stephen & Smith, Emma (2004) An International Comparison of Equity in Education Systems, *Comparative Education*, 40(1), 15-28.

Guiso, Luigi, Monte, Ferdinando, Sapienza, Paola & Zingales, Luigi (2008) Culture, Gender, and Math, *Science*, 320(5880), 1164-1165.

Güzel, Çiğdem Iş & Berberoğlu, Giray (2005) An Analysis of the Programme for International Student Assessment 2000 (PISA 2000) Mathematical Literacy Data for Brazilian, Japanese and Norwegian Students, *Studies in Educational Evaluation*, 31(4), 283-314.

Hanushek, Eric & Wößmann, Ludger (2006) Does Educational Tracking Affect Performance and Inequality? Differences-in-Differences Evidence across Countries, *Economic Journal*, 116 (March), C63–C76.

Ho, Esther Sui Chu (2005) Effect of School Decentralization and School Climate on Student Mathematics Performance: the case of Hong Kong, *Educational Research for Policy and Practice*, 4(1), 47-64.

Horn, Daniel (2009) Age of Selection Counts: a cross-country analysis of educational institutions, *Educational Research and Evaluation*, 15(4), 343-366.

Hvistendahl, Rita & Roe, Astrid (2004) The Literacy Achievement of Norwegian Minority Students, *Scandinavian Journal of Educational Research*, 48(3), 307-324.

Kjærnsli, Marit & Lie, Svein (2004) PISA and Scientific Literacy: similarities and differences between the Nordic countries, *Scandinavian Journal of Educational Research*, 48(3), 271-286.

Konan, Paul N'Dri, Chatard, Armand, Selimbegovi, Leila, & Mugny, Gabriel (2010) Cultural Diversity in the Classroom and its Effects on Academic Performance, *Social Psychology*, 41(4), 230-237.

Kubiatko, Milan & Vlckova, Katerina (2010) The Relationship between ICT Use and Science Knowledge for Czech Students: a secondary analysis of PISA 2006, *International Journal of Science and Mathematics Education*, 8(3), 523-543.

Leino, Kaisa, Linnakylä, Pirjo& Malin, Antero (2004) Finnish Students' Multiliteracy Profiles, *Scandinavian Journal of Educational Research*, 48(3), 251-270.

Levels, Mark & Dronkers, Jaap (2008) Educational Performance of Native and Immigrant Children from Various Countries of Origin, *Ethnic and Racial Studies*, 31(8), 1404-1425.

Levels, Mark, Dronkers, Jaap & Kraaykamp, Gerbert (2008) Immigrant Children's Educational Achievement in Western Countries: origin, destination, and community effects on mathematical performance, *American Sociological Review*, 73(5), 835-853.

Liang, Xin (2010) Assessment Use, Self-efficacy and Mathematics Achievement: comparative analysis of PISA 2003 data of Finland, Canada and the USA, *Evaluation & Research in Education*, 23(3), 213-229.

Linnakylä, Pirjo & Malin, Antero (2008) Finnish Students' School Engagement Profiles in the Light of PISA 2003, *Scandinavian Journal of Educational Research*, 52(6), 583-602.

Linnakylä, Pirjo, Malin, Antero & Taube, Karin (2004) Factors Behind Low Reading Literacy Achievement, *Scandinavian Journal of Educational Research*, 48(3), 231-249.

Liu, Ou Lydia & Wilson, Mark (2009a) Gender Differences and Similarities in PISA 2003 Mathematics: a comparison between the United States and Hong Kong, *International Journal of Testing*, 9(1), 20-40.

Liu, Ou Lydia & Wilson, Mark (2009b) Gender Differences in Large-scale Math Assessments: PISA Trend 2000 and 2003, *Applied Measurement in Education*, 22(2), 164-184.

Luu, King & Freeman, John G. (2011) An Analysis of the Relationship between Information and Communication Technology (ICT) and Scientific Literacy in Canada and Australia, *Computers & Education*, 56, 1072-1082.

Ma, Xin (2003) Measuring Up: academic performance of Canadian immigrant children in reading, mathematics, and science, *Journal of International Migration and Integration*, 4(4), 541-576.

Marks, Gary N. (2005) Cross-national Differences and Accounting for Social Class Inequalities in Education, *International Sociology*, 20(4), 483-505.

Marks, Gary N. (2006) Are Between- and Within-school Differences in Student Performance Largely Due to Socio-economic Background? Evidence from 30 Countries, *Educational Research*, 48(1), 21-40.

Marks, Gary N. (2008) Accounting for the Gender Gaps in Student Performance in Reading and Mathematics: evidence from 31 countries, *Oxford Review of Education*, 34(1), 89-109.

Marks, Gary N. (2010) What Aspects of Schooling are Important? School Effects on Tertiary Entrance Performance, *School Effectiveness and School Improvement*, 21(3), 267-287.

Martins, L. & P. Veiga (2010) Do Inequalities in Parents' Education Play an Important Role in PISA Students' Mathematics Achievement Test Score Disparities? *Economics of Education Review*, 29(6), 1016-1033.

Maslowski, Ralf, Scheerens, Jaap & Luyten, Hans (2007) The Effect of School Autonomy and School Internal Decentralization on Students' Reading Literacy, *School Effectiveness and School Improvement*, 18(3), 303-334.

McConney, Andrew & Perry, Laura B. (2010a) Socioeconomic Status, Self-efficacy, and Mathematics Achievement in Australia: a secondary analysis, *Educational Research for Policy and Practice*, 9(2), 77-91.

McConney, Andrew & Perry, Laura B. (2010b) Science and Mathematics Achievement in Australia: the role of school socioeconomic composition in educational equity and effectiveness, *International Journal of Science and Mathematics Education*, 8(3), 429-452.

Milford, T., Ross, Shelley P. & Anderson, John O. (2010) An Opportunity to Better Understand Schooling: the growing presence of PISA in the Americas, *International Journal of Science and Mathematics Education*, 8(3), 453-473.

Montt, G. (2010) Cross-national Differences in Educational Achievement Inequality, *Sociology of Education*, 84(1), 49-68.

Murdoch, Jake, Kamanzi, Pierre Canisius & Doray, Pierre (2011) The Influence of PISA Scores, Schooling and Social Factors on Pathways to and within Higher Education in Canada, *Irish Educational Studies*, 30(2), 215-235.

Nash, Roy (2003) Is the School Composition Effect Real? A Discussion with Evidence from the UK PISA Data, *School Effectiveness and School Improvement*, 14(4), 441-457.

Nonoyama-Tarumi, Yuko (2008) Cross-national Estimates of the Effects of Family Background on Student Achievement: a sensitivity analysis, *International Review of Education*, 54(1), 57-82.

Notten, Natascha, Peter, Jochen, Kraaykamp, Gerbert & Valkenburg, Patti M. (2009) Research Note: digital divide across borders – a cross-national study of adolescents' use of digital technologies, *European Sociological Review*, 25(5), 551-560.

Notten, Natascha & Kraaykamp, Gerbert (2009) Home Media and Science Performance: a cross national study, *Educational Research and Evaluation*, 15(4), 367-384.

Pásztor, Adél (2008) The Children of Guest Workers: comparative analysis of scholastic achievement of pupils of Turkish origin throughout Europe, *Intercultural Education*, 19(5), 407-419.

Peter, Tracey, Edgerton, Jason D. & Roberts, Lance W. (2010) Welfare Regimes and Educational Inequality: a cross-national exploration, *International Studies in Sociology of Education*, 20(3), 241-264.

Pinto, Roser & El Boudamoussi, Samira (2009) Scientific Processes in PISA Tests Observed for Science Teachers, *International Journal of Science Education*, 31(16), 2137-2159.

Sáenz, Cesar (2009) The Role of Contextual, Conceptual and Procedural Knowledge in Activating Mathematical Competencies (PISA), *Educational Studies in Mathematics*, 71(2), 123-143.

Schlicht, Raphaela, Stadelmann-Steffen, Isabelle & Freitag, Markus (2010) Educational Inequality in the EU: the effectiveness of the national education policy, *European Union Politics*, 11(1), 29-59.

Schubert, Frank & Becker, Rolf (2010) Social Inequality of Reading Literacy: a longitudinal analysis with cross-sectional data of PIRLS 2001 and PISA 2000 utilizing the pair wise matching procedure, *Research in Social Stratification and Mobility*, 28(1), 109-133.

Sikora, Joanna & Saha, Lawrence (2009) Gender and Professional Career Plans of High School Students in Comparative Perspective, *Educational Research and Evaluation*, 15(4), 385-403.

Sprietsma, Maresa (2010) Effect of Relative Age in the First Grade of Primary School on Long-term Scholastic Results: international comparative evidence using PISA 2003, *Education Economics*, 18(1), 1-32.

Suggate, Sebastian P. (2009) School Entry Age and Reading Achievement in the 2006 Programme for International Student Assessment (PISA), *International Journal of Educational Research*, 48(3), 151-161.

Täht, Karin & Must, Olev (2010) Are the Links between Academic Achievement and Learning Motivation Similar in Five Neighbouring Countries? *Trames: A Journal of the Humanities and Social Sciences*, 14(3), 271-281.

Tuksino, Prakittiya, Kanjanawasee, Sirichai & Pasiphol, Shotiga (2010) A Quality Assessment of Science Instructional Management in Basic Education Schools: an application of a value-added model and differential item functioning, *International Journal of Learning*, 17(5), 81-94.

Turmo, Are (2004) Scientific Literacy and Socio-economic Background among 15-year-olds: a Nordic perspective, *Scandinavian Journal of Educational Research*, 48(3), 287-305.

van Petegem, Peter & Vanhoof, Jan (2007) Towards a Model of Effective School Feedback: school heads' points of view, *Educational Research and Evaluation*, 13(4), 311-325.

Weiss, Volkmar (2009) National IQ Means Transformed from Programme for International Student Assessment (PISA) Scores, and their Underlying Gene Frequencies, *Journal of Social, Political and Economic Studies*, 34(1), 71-94.

White, Patrick & Smith, Emma (2005) What Can PISA Tell Us about Teacher Shortages? *European Journal Of Education*, 40(1), 93-112.

Williams, Trevor, Williams, Kitty, Kastberg, David & Jocelyn, Leslie (2005) Achievement and Affect in OECD Nations, *Oxford Review of Education*, 31(4), 517-545.

Wößmann, Ludger (2005) The Effect Heterogeneity of Central Examinations: evidence from TIMSS, TIMSS-Repeat and PISA, *Education Economics*, 13(2), 143-169.

Zhong, Zhi-Jin (2011) From Access to Usage: the divide of self-reported digital skills among adolescents, *Computers & Education*, 56(3), 736-746.

CHAPTER 2

# Finland's PISA Results: an analysis of dynamics in education politics

## JANNE VARJO, HANNU SIMOLA & RISTO RINNE

ABSTRACT In this chapter the authors experiment with the idea of combining path dependency, convergence and contingency in explaining Finnish particularity in education policy and politics since the early 1990s, with special reference to Finland's status as renowned Programme for International Student Assessment (PISA) high-flyer. The focus of this chapter is especially on quality assurance and evaluation (QAE) in comprehensive schooling. The authors elaborate on and contextualize the Finnish QAE model by analyzing the ambiguous ways in which global QAE practices have – or have not – been received and mediated in Finland. Applying the theoretical concept of dynamics, they aim to subject a specific social field of education to scrutiny through the analysis of relations between the main actors and institutions, and the essential discursive formations and practices. The research material consists of documents concerning the provision of compulsory education at national level: laws and legislative drafts, memorandums and reports by various actors. It appears that the global education reform discourse has achieved a hegemonic position in the national educational rhetoric, whereas in the processes of implementation at the local level there remains a certain antipathy –against previous normative control mechanisms and equally against the present idea of ranking lists.

## Introduction

Global rankings – their media visibility and political prominence in particular – have highlighted the topicality and significance of comparative studies in education. This recognition has not entailed the development of theoretical instruments in the field, however. On the contrary, ahistorical and decontextualized concepts like *efficiency*, *accountability* and *quality* are colonizing the educational world, self-explanatory and uncontested, largely due to the fact that they have been advocated by transnational organizations such as the World Bank, the Organisation for Economic Co-operation and Development (OECD) and the European Union (EU).

Thus far, the whole paradigm of comparative education has been rather mechanistic, still suffering from certain methodological deficits and under-theorization (Simola et al, 2011a, b; Kauko et al, 2012). Commonly the term 'comparative' has been taken as a synonym for 'international', which refers to a descriptive collection of educational issues from different nations. In this respect, comparison has become a tool for identifying differences and similarities; methodologically this approach is trivial (Simola & Rinne, 2010; Simola et al, 2013).

Nevertheless, it is evident that greater global interconnectedness and a nascent global educational community, mediated, translated and conceptualized within national and local education structures, is creating a certain resemblance among educational policies across nations (Simola et al, 2013). Global policy reforms ('traveling policies') have a tendency to diffuse around the globe and socially and politically reshape different societies with dissimilar histories. It is noteworthy that these transnational trends and tendencies do not shape the regional, national or local policies in any predictable or straightforward way. Rather, they intertwine with 'embedded policies' to be found in 'local' spaces (national, provincial or local) where global policy agendas come up against existing practices and priorities (Ozga & Jones, 2006).

According to Kauko et al (2012, p. 213), international comparisons like Programme for International Student Assessment (PISA) studies have highlighted essential questions: What do those rankings actually measure? How do the results and rankings relate to schooling realities and practices? Is PISA achievement a consistent sign of a successful education system? (see Riley & Torrance, 2003; Goldstein, 2004; Prais, 2004; Bracey, 2005; Bautier & Rayou, 2007; Dohn, 2007). Tools for improving quality, equity and efficiency are highly context-sensitive; as such, separate elements of a complex system – like education – rarely function adequately in isolation in a new environment. The quality in education strongly depends on contextualized cultural and political factors, among others. Therefore, comparing more or less artificial common criteria identified from a global perspective does not necessarily make much sense.

Nóvoa and Yariv-Mashal (2003) have shown that 'facts' and 'realities' are incomparable by definition. One can *contrast* them in order to highlight the differences and similarities, but it is difficult to go beyond that. It is possible to presume wishfully that a substantial number of indicators included in complicated negotiations may gradually give a more solid and detailed picture of diverse education systems. It is argued that these collections of performance indicators will construct mainly parallels and juxtapositions (Kauko et al, 2012).

It has been also noted by Kauko et al (2012, p. 214), that the key to a comparative understanding of a national educational politics lies in the analysis of *dynamics* – namely, in the complexities of interaction between actors. The starting point of any meaningful research in comparative historical sociology and politics must be based on 'the unique nature of a variety of situations in time and space and the cultural resources available in these situations' (Hedström & Wittrock 2009, p. 8). For instance, despite being the PISA high-flyer, Finland is a nation state whose educational policies and practices are running in many respects counter to the dominating doctrines of 'GERM' (the global education reform movement; Sahlberg, 2011) or 'EEP' (the epidemic of education policy; Levin, 1998), which emphasize accountability, quality assurance and replacement of monopolistic forms of generic state provision of education with competitive individual ones.

The aim of this chapter is twofold. First and explicitly, we interpret Finnish policies and practices concerning quality assurance and evaluation (QAE) in basic education by capitalizing on three conceptualizations: *convergence, path dependence* and *contingency*. Second, and indirectly perhaps, we reflect on traditional functionalist and rationalist explanations of comparative research in education. We elaborate how it has been possible for the Finnish comprehensive school (*peruskoulu*) to go against the dominating supra-national doctrines and – in spite of or because of it – become renowned for global educational spectacles such as PISA. The 'Finnish Lesson' has demonstrated two things: on the one hand, it is possible to combine quality and equity of education at a reasonable financial cost; on the other hand, this has been possible to achieve without school inspection, standardized curriculum and high-stakes student assessments, test-based accountability, or a race-to-the-top mentality in terms of educational change (Sahlberg, 2011; Simola et al, 2013).

**Introducing a Dynamics Perspective**

Analysis of dynamics investigates the relationship between structure, agency and coincidence (Joas, 2008; Simola et al, 2010, 2011a, b). This approach emphasizes the insecurity and openness of the horizon of expectations and the freedom of actors. One of the most interesting questions referred to in recent discussions concerns the relationship between convergence, path dependence and contingency. The former two are conventional conceptualizations of transnational and national policy relations, while the latter arrives from a more recent social theorization. In comparative studies, convergence and path dependence have commonly been understood as simplistic dualism: the former refers to international tendencies, and the latter covers major national historical specificities (Simola et al, 2011a, b).

Despite increasing international interdependence, which seems to generate pressures toward *convergence*, advanced industrial societies continue to exhibit differences in their institutional practices concerning education. As Green (1999, p. 56) points out:

> As regards education, there is very little evidence across the globe that nation states are losing control over their education systems or ceasing to press them into service for national economic and social ends, whatever the recent accretions of internationalism. In fact the opposite may be true. As governments lose control over various levers on their national economies and cede absolute sovereignty in foreign affairs and defence, they frequently turn to education and training as two areas where they do still maintain control. The argument in relation to educational convergence is, however, more complex, for whilst education systems remain essentially national they may nevertheless be experiencing a degree of convergence under the impact of international forces.

According to Green (1999, p. 69), there is evidence of policy convergence within Europe around a range of broad policy themes, including decentralization in regulation and governance and increasing use of quality assurance and evaluation mechanisms. However, this does not appear to have led to convergence in structures and processes.

There is no single definition of *path dependence*. Sewell (1996, pp. 262-263) refers to the causal relevance of preceding stages in a temporal sequence, suggesting in a very broad sense that path dependence means 'that what happened at an earlier point in time will affect the possible outcomes of a sequence of events at a later point in time'. Levi's (1997, p. 28) definition is narrower, and highlights the difficulty of exiting from a path once it has been chosen:

> [O]nce a country or a region has started down a track, the costs of reversal are very high. There will be other choice points, but the entrenchments of certain institutional arrangements obstruct an easy reversal of the initial choice. Perhaps the better metaphor is a tree, rather than a path. From the same trunk, there are many different branches and smaller branches.

According to Pierson (2000, p. 251), the whole notion of path dependence is generally used to support a few key claims: (1) specific patterns of timing and sequence do matter; (2) starting from similar conditions, a wide range of social outcomes may be possible; (3) 'large' consequences may result from relatively 'small' or contingent events; (4) particular courses of action, once introduced, can be most difficult to reverse; and (5) consequently, political development is often punctuated by critical moments (*junctures*) that shape the basic contours of social life. These features stand in contrast to modes of argument and explanation which attribute 'large' outcomes to 'large' causes, emphasizing the prevalence of unique and predictable outcomes, the irrelevance of timing and sequence, and the capacity of rational actors to design and implement optimal solutions (that take into account their resources and constraints) to the problems that confront them (Pierson, 2000, p. 251).

It is noteworthy that convergence and path-dependence approaches do not recognize the insecurity and openness of the horizon of expectations and the relative freedom of the more or less conscious and informed actors (Simola et al, 2013). Joas (2008) has characterized our time as an 'Age of Contingency'. It seems plausible that the concept of contingency is able to capture something essential in our social order, in that it carries attributes such as post-traditional (Giddens), postmodern (Bauman) and risk society (Beck).

According to Joas (2004, p. 394), '[a] fact is contingent if it is neither necessary nor impossible – something that is but does not have to be'. As such, the concept of contingency carries a double meaning: on the one hand it signifies *coincidence* or *conjunction*, and on the other, it is *free will* or *volition* (Joas, 2008, p. 209). In the former sense, it refers to the uncertainty and ambivalence, and in the latter sense to possibilities and the *Spielraum* of the actor. This dimension (contingency as uncertainty) emphasizes the fact that our existence and history are essentially haphazard and random: things often happen by mere accident. In latter sense (contingency as freedom), contingency could be seen as the ability of an actor to face and handle the sudden and surprising characteristics of reality.

| Dimension | Level of analysis | Questions |
|---|---|---|
| (1) The political situation | Macro | What is possible in a specific socio-historical and trans-national situation? Dimension of structural opportunity and chance. |
| (2) The political possibilities | Intermediate | What is possible due to the excising discursive formations? What is politicized and what is not? Dimension of discursive conditions and resources; problématiques. |
| (3) The political Spielraum | Micro | How can the relevant actors act and react? How do they capitalize on the existing situations and possibilities? Space for 'politicking'. |

Table I. Framework for analysis of dynamics in politics.
Sources: Palonen, 2006; Kauko, 2011; Kauko et al, 2012.

Kettunen (2008, p. 21) proposes that while crossing these two dimensions – path dependence and contingency on the one hand, and path dependence and convergence on the other – we might find histories and comparisons as forms of reflexivity in social practices. In order to link path dependence, convergence and contingency – and to develop a new analytical conception – Kauko et al (2012; see also Palonen, 2006; Kauko, 2011) have distinguished three dimensions of dynamics in politics: *the political situation, the political possibilities* and *the Spielraum* (see Table I).

### The Political Situation

According to Kauko (2011; see also Palonen, 2006; Kauko et al, 2012), politics as a situation bears the idea of a distinguished moment when politics can be changed. Politics as a situation illustrates the moment of *Kairos* where a historical rupture is visible. In analyzing the political situation, we turn to the socio-historical analysis of complexity in education and, even more, political history. By understanding the socio-historical situation, the aim is to break through the 'unbearable narrowness of the national view' (Kettunen, 2008) in order to comprehend how the national is constituted by its interconnections, meetings and crossings with the trans-national (e.g. Strange, 1997; Werner & Zimmermann, 2006).

### The Political Possibilities

Political possibilities owe a lot to what is up to be seized in a certain frame of a political situation. Actors in politics evaluate their chances and develop an understanding of their possibilities to maneuver. There are always possibilities for acting 'otherwise', but the most vital question is finding these options (Palonen, 2006; Kauko, 2011). This dimension focuses on the formulation of politico-administrative problems. In a comparative sense, it has been argued that 'facts' and 'realities' are, by definition, incomparable, whereas *problématiques* or what constitutes the problems may facilitate complex and strong comparison. There is thus a need to trace genealogies of problems that are specific to a certain discursive field in order to expose their dynamics (e.g. Ball, 2001, 2003; Dean, 2002, 2007; Simola, 2006, 2009; Popkewitz, 2008, 2009; Ozga et al, 2011).

### The Political Spielraum

Finally, framed by the political situation and possibilities, an essential element for the dynamics in politics is the *Spielraum* for 'politicking'. This refers to the potential of actors to capitalize on existing situations and possibilities, compared with opponents less ready to tolerate or make use of the presence of contingency. This relates to the question of agency, as *Spielraum* refers to individual clearance and leeway of actors in politics – how they 'play with contingency' (Palonen, 2006; Kauko, 2011; Kauko et al, 2012).

Crucially, the interplay between these three dimensions, which may vary considerably across different contexts, formulates the feasible paths or trajectories that education politics may take, and therefore introduces path-dependencies. By implication, the feasibility and likelihood of trans-national convergence in education politics depends significantly on the constellation of the given dimensions (Kauko et al, 2012.)

## The Short History of Finnish QAE Policy

Of noteworthy importance is the fact that Finland was among the last countries in Europe to establish a compulsory education system. Additionally, as the expansion of the folk school was slow, compulsory education was not fully implemented until the 1930s. These facts are essential while seeking to make sense of the dynamics within the Finnish trajectory of QAE in basic education: in contrast to other European nations, both compulsory education and its evaluation are relatively new social practices.

During the 1990s, as a result of many interrelated social, political and administrative reforms and changes, the discourse of quality assurance and evaluation ascended within the field of Finnish educational policy and governance. The growing interest in quality assurance and evaluation in education found its juncture in the context of the changing political atmosphere and the deep economic recession of 1991-93. The changes in Finnish education policies enacted by Prime Minister Harri Holkeri's right-left coalition cabinet (1987-1991) were only a part of a general wave of decentralization and deregulation. In general, the municipal practices of budgeting, accounting and auditing the administration and finances were changed in accordance with the New Public Management (NPM) doctrine. For instance, the new state subsidy system granted funding according to annual calculations per pupil, lesson or other unit, and liberated the municipalities from the former detailed 'earmarked' budgeting in exchange for the allocation of block grants, which could be freely used by the municipalities according to their preferences and priorities.

The grand idea of moving towards QAE-based steering mechanisms was expressed by the late Secretary General of the Ministry of Education: evaluation is a pivotal element of the new steering system, since it 'replaces the tasks of the old normative steering, control and inspection system' (Hirvi, 1996, p. 93). The 1995 Framework for Evaluating Educational Outcomes, published by National Board of Education (NBE), was a rather loose model for a national evaluation system. While analyzing the selected 'evaluation objects', the Framework introduced concepts of *economy, efficiency* and *effectiveness* (NBE, 1995). The change in regime of the 1990s is tangibly present in the Framework's rhetoric: the three Es are the cornerstones of the NPM doctrine (Lähdesmäki, 2003, pp. 65-69).

The emphasis on decentralization and NPM has connections to the recession of 1991-1993, which marked the deepest crisis of Finland's economy during peacetime. The common retrospective insight is that without shifting decision-making to the local level, municipalities would not have been able to decrease their spending as much as they did during the recession. Thus, the new decentralized and deregulated mode of governance was molded into the economic principles of savings and cutbacks (Simola et al, 2009, p. 167).

The field of Finnish QAE in comprehensive education took its current form in the late 1990s. The 1995 Local Government Act introduced a new organ, a municipal auditing committee, in order to prepare matters related to the administrative and financial audits for council decision and assess whether the operational and financial targets have been achieved (Law 365/1995, 1995). The essential role of evaluation in education was legalized in the Basic Education Act of 1999 (Law 628/1998, 1998). According to the law, the municipality (as a major education provider in Finland) shall evaluate the education it provides and its impact, and take part in external evaluations of its operations conducted by the Education Evaluation Council. Thus, the obligation to evaluate comprehensive education is twofold: on the one hand, it is one of the municipal auditing committee's duties as set out in the Local Government Act; and on the other, the Basic Education Act requires that education providers both self-evaluate and submit themselves to the required external evaluation. The dual form of norms steering the field of evaluation has also grouped the actors.

The NBE has so far mainly executed the external evaluations authorized by the Ministry of Education and Culture (MEC), and has given instruction on self-evaluation. Also, the Association of Finnish Local and Regional Authorities (AFLRA) has produced educational indicators in the form of evaluation guidelines (AFLRA, 2001). A new actor arrived in the field of quality assurance and the evaluation of comprehensive education in 2003 when the Basic Education Act was amended. The mandate of the NBE was replaced with a loose 'network of evaluation experts':

> For the purpose of external evaluation, there shall be a separate
> Education Evaluation Council attached to the Ministry of
> Education to organise activities in a network with universities, the
> National Board of Education and other evaluation experts. (Law
> 32/2003, 2003)

The NBE has conducted two surveys (Rajanen, 2000; Löfström et al, 2005) of QAE implementation at the local level. According to the 2000 survey, only one third of the providers of basic education said they had some system of evaluation to underpin their work (Rajanen, 2000, p. 31). This can be seen as indicative of the low priority given to QAE. The Committee for Education and Culture (CEC) of the Finnish Parliament concluded in 2002:

> The evaluation work done has had very small effects at the level of
> municipalities and schools. Nation-level evaluations have been
> implemented to a creditable extent, but there is no follow-up on
> how these evaluations affect the actions of the evaluated and the
> development of the schools ... Only evaluation of the biggest
> providers of schooling seem to be systematic enough and based on

a system provided by the present model of administration. Many municipalities are at the very beginning in the evaluation of education. (CEC, 2002)

According to Hannus et al (2010, p. 252), the whole field of quality assurance and evaluation in comprehensive education is confused and the authority is unclear. The most distinctive features of the network formation seem to be the internecine struggle for legitimacy with regard to individual evaluations, the non-existent coordination and the equally lacking authority to set binding norms. Very recently, there have been signals that the dynamics within the loose 'network of evaluation experts' will alter in favor of a single powerful agency. According to Prime Minister Jyrki Katainen's government (2011, p. 57):

> The official evaluation activity concerning education carried out by the National Board of Education, the Finnish Education Evaluation Council and the Finnish Higher Education Evaluation Council will be concentrated into an independent Education Evaluation Centre.

### Four 'Truths' in the Finnish QAE Model

Next we will introduce four standpoints taken by comprehensive education regarding QAE, which are essential while elaborating Finnish national special characteristics concerning the policy outlines once made, the unarticulated common beliefs, and things that might have happened otherwise.[1]

1.  QAE data and information is, in the first instance and above all, addressed for administration and decision-making at national and local levels – and only secondarily for other interest groups – that is, pupils and their parents.
2.  The purpose of QAE in education is to develop – not to control, sanction or allocate resources.
3.  Sample-based learning-result assessments are favored instead of mandatory national testing of the whole age cohort.
4.  There is no basis or need to publish school-based ranking lists.

These standpoints are 'truths' (see Simola et al, 1998) that are formed by the interaction between various actors. They are widely accepted and shared as the constituent parts of the national self-understanding in terms of QAE in basic education. In terms of Pierson (2000, p. 251), they can be seen as significant *junctures* – curious combinations of path dependence, convergence and contingency, which are constituted by numerous crossing trajectories and interactions by various actors.

## Data and Information for Administration Only

While drafting the new education legislation in 1993-1996, a parliamentary committee headed by Director General Vilho Hirvi articulated a seminal definition of policy: the purpose of evaluation is to produce information addressed *primarily* for the educational authorities. Families and their need for evaluation information in order to make parental school choices are referred to only incidentally.

> The purpose of the evaluation system is to produce the information needed in local, regional and national development work and educational decision-making. Besides this, the evaluations should produce information on which students and their families can base their choices. (Ministry of Education [ME], 1996, p. 85)

The definition of policy had an apparent lock-in effect. Neither the Basic Education Act (Law 628/1998, 1998) nor the Decree on Evaluation of Education (Decree 150/2003) made reference to families or parents – or citizens or customers – among those interested in the evaluation of education beyond the school achievements of their own children. According to the decree, the aims for evaluation of education are:

1. to provide and analyze information to support national decision-making and developmental activities;
2. to provide and analyze information to support local developmental activities and decision-making; and
3. to promote pupils' learning, teachers' work and developmental activities at schools (Decree 150/2003, 2 §).

All sorts of statements concerning the value of evaluation results while pupils and their families make personal decisions on educational issues are absent from the legislation. It appears that, as a target group for the information production, legislators value citizens less than administration. This interpretation of path dependence is strengthened while reading the memorandum on the future development of Finnish national evaluation system. As expected, it first recapitulates the aims of evaluation as articulated in the Decree, and only then notes: 'It has considered important, that evaluations are also producing information for students and their guardians to base their educational choices on' (ME, 2007a, pp. 12-13).

Nevertheless, these dynamics have changed as the *Spielraum* has been (moderately) opened up for new actors. Contrary to previous legislation, the new Basic Education Act (Law 628/1998, 1998) noted parental choice –even though choice can only occur after children have been placed by the municipal education authorities. In the Committee for Education and Culture in Finland's Parliament, this right was formulated as the right to attend one's *neighborhood school*, which means that the schools are able to enroll pupils only if there is room left after the intake of allocated 'neighborhood school students'. Of importance is the fact that the convergent trend is an option only in major cities, whereas in most of the smaller towns and all rural municipalities there is no real school choice – and presumably due to this, no actual push for school-based QAE information (Seppänen, 2006).

## The Use of QAE for Developmental Purposes Only

The second 'truth' concerns 'soft', non-sanctioned features of Finnish QAE policies. The Ministry of Education Working Party, while deliberating the framework for evaluating educational outcomes in Finland in 1990, strongly emphasized *developmental* characteristics of evaluation. The aim of evaluation was to 'set a solid foundation for intentional and open development of education' (ME, 1990, p. 30), as a categorical counterpoint for administrative surveillance. Since the middle of the 1990s, official memorandums and reports have repeatedly stated that the evaluation is 'for developing educational services and not an instrument of administrative control' (e.g. ME, 1996, p. 85).

Nevertheless, during the 1990s and 2000s the developmental emphasis on QAE has been criticized by Regional State Administrative Agencies (ME, 1996, p. 98) and the Ministry of Finance (e.g. AFLRA & MF, 1998, p. 13). Besides a number of state agencies, AFLRA has also challenged the common interpretation by claiming that QAE had been misleadingly promoted to schools and teachers primarily as an instrument for development. According to AFLRA, all evaluation implemented in municipal organizations is part of municipal evaluation, which means at the same time that it is a tool of municipal management and administrative control (e.g. AFLRA, 2001; Granö-Suomalainen & Lovio, 2002).

Furthermore, the emphasis on this developmental function has required that the interpretation of evaluation results and the allocation of resources – or any other administrative sanctions – are divorced from one another. For instance, the national Evaluation Strategy (ME, 1997) outlined the options to bind evaluation results and resource allocation by distinguishing additional *profitability grants* (based on evaluation reports) from the statutory Central Government Transfer System.

> [T]he financing of education is based on the Central Government Transfer System, which takes into account the municipal special features, and as the funds are not earmarked, the education providers can use them at their discretion. Due to the structure of the system, the results of evaluations do not have an effect on the primary financing of education. In order to exhort the education providers, municipalities and schools can be rewarded based on current evaluation criteria. Due to the small quantity of rewards, they will not be linked to the Central Government Transfer

System, and they will not influence the principles concerning the allocation resources. (ME, 1997, p. 9)

Additionally, since its formation in 2003, the Finnish Educational Evaluation Council (FEEC) has highlighted the developmental characters of evaluation. Notably, in order to preserve developmental features, a certain autonomy of evaluation has been demanded. In practice this has meant that evaluations and administrative decisions are assumed to be conducted by entirely separate authorities:

> A key point in safeguarding independence is that administration
> and decision-makers have no authority over the evaluation
> organisation and its resources, programmes or evaluation
> processes. Independence is better secured when the parties and
> experts involved in educational development have no active role in
> external evaluation. (FEEC, 2005, p. 16)

The principle of evaluation autonomy became politicized when new education legislation was enacted at the latter half of the 1990s. The NBE's double role as both a central agency in charge of various executive duties and an evaluator of learning outcomes – and education in general – had already been criticized in 1996. Since then, the autonomy of evaluation has been a salient and recurrent argument, while the distribution of work and mandates between different evaluation actors were outlined in the 2000s.

## No National Testing

There has been a consensus among education politicians and officials at state and local levels that thematic, sample-based evaluation would be enough for quality assurance. The execution of a national test for an entire age cohort was unanimously seen as too expensive, besides bringing negative side effects, well known from the Anglo-American research literature (Simola et al, 2009). The central organization of employers, the Confederation of Finnish Industries and Employers (CIE), found a new gear for its education policy activities at the beginning of 1980s. A pamphlet titled 'The Productivity of Education' (CIE, 1990) questioned the cost-effectiveness of different types of educational establishments. According to this document, schools should be regularly and extensively measured for their productivity. The pamphlet advocated the measurability of learning outcomes, optimal resource allocation and consumer satisfaction. The general – and at the same time very convergent – idea was that the productivity of comprehensive education would improve through measurement. Significantly, while challenging the locked-in path dependence, the CIE has also supported final national examinations, such as the Matriculation Examination in the upper-secondary school (Purhonen, 2005, p. 63).

The idea of national achievement tests was introduced into the Finnish comprehensive education policy agenda at the beginning of the 1990s. While working with the first draft of the 1999 education legislation, the Ministry of Education Working Party brought up the idea of national achievement tests in compulsory education:

> It has been considered that there would be uniform nation-wide achievement tests conducted annually at various subjects. Based on the results of these exams, the level of teaching and the accomplishment of educational aims at municipalities and schools would be evaluated. (Numminen, 1994, pp. 105-106)

However, it is apparent that thus far, the political situation in Finland has not been favorable to 'GERM' and 'EEP', advocating that schools and teachers become more accountable for learning results. Traditionally, the evaluation of student outcomes has been the task of each teacher and school in Finland. The only standardized high-stakes assessment is the matriculation examination at the end of upper-secondary school before students enroll in tertiary education. Prior to this, no external national tests or exams were required (Aho et al, 2006, p. 12).

The Framework for Evaluating Educational Outcomes in Finland by the NBE (1995, p. 36) outlined a policy that proved to be consistent. The NBE's Framework defines sample-based *national exams* as the Finnish equivalent to general *achievement tests*. National examinations were understood as a categorical counterpoint to *final exams*, which were considered ... 'problematic in many ways, so they won't be used in the common comprehensive school' (NBE, 1995, p. 37). The NBE's Framework does not take into account final exams as a method to produce data about the whole age cohort or all schools, and thus open the opportunity for school-specific evaluation results and league tables. It is noteworthy that sample-based national exams are taken for granted, and no explicit reason for the viewpoint against final exams is given. Instead of stating reasons for existing policy outlines in terms of given aims, the Framework is based on antipathy rather than on any conscious and articulated principles.

There have also been discussions within the body of civil servants about the possibility of more extensive testing practices. Recently, the path dependence of national sample-based learning-result assessment has proved to be not as stable as previously assumed. Timo Lankinen stated in his one-man disquisition report just six months before he was appointed to the post of the Director General of the NBE:

> The follow-up of learning results will be carried out as web-based examinations in all schools. These exams would assess what learning goals have been attained and give an overall diagnosis of the state of education. The aim is to give up the sample-based learning result assessments and produce evaluation information and feedback for the whole age cohort and all appropriate teachers. (ME, 2007b, p. 194)

### No School Ranking Lists

Thus far, very few education official or politician has publicly supported the provision of ranking lists or making schools transparent in competition by comparing them in terms of average performance indicators. Paradoxically, what has been considered to strengthen the path dependence concerning antipathy to rankings is the Finnish bureaucratic tradition (e.g. Tiihonen 2004; Pekonen 2005), according to which administrative innovations are basically considered to support the system and its developments rather than to open it or inform citizens about it. The Parliament of Finland's Committee for Education and Culture stated the following, first in 1998 and then again in 2004:

> The publicity concerns only the main results of evaluations. The purpose of the new Basic Education Act is not to publish information directly linked to an individual school or teacher. Publishing the evaluation results cannot in any case lead to the ranking of schools or the categorization of schools, teachers or pupils as weak or good on unfair grounds. (CEC, 1998)

Also the Finnish Education Evaluation Council highlighted the developmental features of evaluation and the anonymity of schools in its evaluation strategy:

> In publicizing evaluation results schools will not be ranked, nor will schools or teachers be labeled as of high or low standard on the basis of one-sided evidence. When reporting upon an analysis based on a nationwide sample, no data identifying individual schools will be given, but in cases concerning only a small group of schools, a national evaluation report may also include information on a single school. A prerequisite for so doing is that the evaluation takes place in co-operation with the school and is made for expressly developmental purposes. (FEEC, 2005, p. 36)

Furthermore, education officials and politicians, principals and teachers are openly against ranking lists. The informal consensus at the municipal level not to study schools in a way that would enable the results to be used to produce ranking lists provides a good example (Simola et al, 2009; Rinne et al, 2011). Before the early 2000s, the CIE remained virtually the only body to openly be in favor of national testing and ranking lists (CIE, 1990). The publication of evaluation reports was tested in court in two separate appeals in 2000 and 2003, which were made to regional administrative courts against municipal education authorities' decisions not to publish school-specific information. In both cases, the focus of the appeals was on school-specific school performance indicators that were considered essential information for parental school choice. Both cases were located in large Finnish cities (Turku and Vantaa); behind the appealing party in both cases were major media corporations (Simola, 2006).

In the first case, the Turku Administrative Court took the side of municipal education authorities, refusing to require them to hand over the evaluation results of individual schools for publication. In the second case, the Helsinki Administrative Court provided an opposite ruling. It ordered Vantaa educational authorities to deliver the school-specific evaluation results to the appealing party. The municipality of Vantaa took the case to the Supreme Administrative Court, requesting that the appeal be dismissed. The Supreme Administrative Court ordered Vantaa to hand over the school-specific evaluation results to the appealing party (Simola, 2006). The path dependence remains locked; only a couple of provincial newspapers have published school-specific evaluation results or taken any actions in that direction thus far.

## The Dynamics between Convergence and Path Dependence

We may emphasize that since the early 1990s the dynamics between *convergence* and *path dependence* in Finnish education policy have shifted. After the decades of *Finlandisierung* there was a strong push for convergence: to be accepted as a genuine western advanced liberal society. Simultaneously, there remains strong path dependence in social and educational policies and practices, based on traditional social democratic and agrarian values of equality. Finland's position between east and west framed most of the international cooperation – and somehow averted convergence – until the fall of the Berlin Wall and the collapse of 'Real Socialism' in Europe in the 1990s. Influence from OECD and other supra-national organizations came considerably late. In the 1990s the political context in Finland was changing rapidly. The conservative governments allied with the employers in promoting the market-liberal values of effectiveness, marketization, parental choice and management by results. Simultaneously, more emphasis was laid on international comparisons and cooperation as well as on the recommendations of supranational organizations.

Various commentators have noted the receptive stance of the Finnish education policy elite toward the OECD. Finland has been perceived as the OECD's 'model pupil' in applying neoliberal innovations in education – but through technical and incremental policy rather than through making strong neoliberal declarations (Rinne et al, 2001; Kauko & Varjo, 2008). According to the OECD's own account,

> Finland has a record of heeding the advice of past OECD
> education reviews. The review seems likely to continue that
> pattern, helping to shape the future of a dynamic education sector.
> (OECD, 2003)

Among other things, PISA has taught Finnish education politicians and officials the 'market value' of international comparisons. The OECD is appreciated as a transcendent carrier of reason (Niukko, 2006, p. 112), which may be seen as creating a consensual community (Weber), a discourse of truth (Foucault), and a style of reasoning (Hacking). The OECD is referred as 'the instrument, catalyst and certain framework for comparison', operating 'as a neutral tool of the national education policy' (Niukko, 2006, p. 130). Nevertheless, some actors have also criticized the OECD as 'the judge', and others have characterized it as 'the doctor' or 'the psychiatrist' (Rinne et al, 2004; Grek et al, 2009, pp. 15-16).

In terms of path dependence, Finland has been strongly bound to traditional social democratic and agrarian values of equality: it is hard to over-emphasize the fact that Finland was among the last countries in Europe to establish compulsory education. Because of the late historical formation and massification of the educational system, the educational gaps between older and younger generations in their educational levels are still considerably wide (Simola & Rinne, 2010). Outside of the Finnish success story in education, the modernization of the occupational structure represents a recent historical phenomenon. Finland belongs to the group of European nations that have most recently left behind their agrarian society and way of life. Therefore, Finnish culture strongly emphasizes a traditional understanding of egalitarianism. Compared with Central European and other Nordic countries, the processes of industrialization and urbanization were slow and gradual until the Second World War. As an indication of the symbolic power of traditional social democratic-agrarian *equality* in Finnish educational discourse, there is no analogous concept for *equity*. The concept of equality is used in two contrasting ways, which were connected in a seminal definition of policy published by the Finnish Educational Evaluation Council:

> The economic and social welfare of Finnish society is based on an egalitarian public system of schooling. Its mission is to guarantee for every citizen *both* educational opportunities of good quality regardless of his/her sex, dwelling place, age, mother tongue and economic position and the right to tuition accordant with his/her capabilities and special needs and his/her self-development.
> (FEEC, 2005, p. 15, emphasis added)

The above-outlined Finnish QAE policies and practices do not formulate any systematic or intentional agenda; despite few national definitions of policy, it is difficult to see the trajectory as a functional entity, coordinated and directed normatively. Rather, the path-dependent 'truths' we have elaborated above represent a silent or mute consensus, based on antipathy and resistance – instead of convergence – against something characterized as 'GERM' or 'EEP'. Appreciably, only the national sample-based learning-result assessment (as an alternative to national testing) and developmental evaluation (as compared with tasks of control and resource allocation) are based on conscious and articulated decisions. Two others (no school ranking lists and data and information for administrative use only) just oppose a given phenomenon without real explicit policy alternatives. Hence, the Finnish trajectory of QAE in basic education manifests itself as a combination of unarticulated consensus on the direction of advancement, endogenous origins of the reform, and passive but persistent resistance to global models of education restructuring.

## The Contingent Factors in Finnish QAE Trajectory

Something unexpected and dramatic – in our analytical conception: contingent – happened in Finland in the early 1990s. The recession in 1991-93 was the deepest peacetime crisis in Finland's economy. It is widely accepted among the political and economic elite that without radical decentralization, municipalities could not have been able to cut spending as much as they did during the recession (Rinne et al, 2002; Simola et al, 2009). The 1990s recession extended municipal autonomy, to a degree where the decentralization level of the educational administration became one of the most extreme in Europe:

> One of the most serious institutional issues in our educational system is the unsatisfactory relation between the state and the municipalities. ... The decentralization level of the educational administration in Finland is one of the highest in Europe, according to the information of the OECD. (Temmes et al, 2002, p. 129)

The trajectory of decentralization opened *Spielraum* for the AFLRA to take its place as a distinguished actor in restructuring the Finnish nation–municipality relationship in general, and in the field of education policy in particular. While cooperating with governmental agencies, AFLRA is contributing both as a lobbyist and an expert in major decision-making processes concerning education. At the local level, the AFLRA produces indicators, reference values and best practices for municipal councils and officials. According to AFLRA (2001), municipalities are no longer mere education providers executing top-down, national-level decisions, but rather are true political actors possessing an intent of their own – and thus a vast amount of *Spielraum* can be perceived in this peculiar twofold system, where the nation-state *and* the municipalities are the main actors in education policy (see Kauko & Varjo, 2008).

The radical decentralization and deregulation have produced two coalitions in the national QAE field of basic education, neither of which has exact normative authority over the municipalities and schools. On the one hand, the Ministry of Education and Culture and the National Board of Education approach QAE from the perspective of the education system; on the other hand, the Association of Finnish Local and Regional Authorities and the Ministry of the Interior – often accompanied by the Ministry of Finance – conduct QAE in terms of municipal service production. Both of these coalitions have attempted to assume the leading role in determining the discourse of evaluation in the context of education (Simola et al, 2009).

The 1990s recession also somehow revitalized the Nordic egalitarian ethos. For example, Ahonen (2003) argues that the recession altered the political atmosphere in favor of market liberalism back to traditional Nordic welfare values, thus defending the common comprehensive school. Ahonen's argument is plausible when contextualized to national plans at the time to restructure the education system. In the late 1990s, almost any political actor was willing to question the rhetoric of the equality-in-education discourse (Grek et al, 2009, p. 12). Curiously, it can be pondered how PISA's success in general, and low variation between schools in particular, have later reaffirmed this egalitarian effect.

Another totally unexpected event was the Finnish success in PISA studies. Finland used to do reasonably well in school performance assessments, such as IEA studies, but it never came up as a top performer. It has been noted that the spectacle of PISA international comparisons used to be more a matter of academic rather than administrative interest in Finland (Simola, 2009, p. 165). It seems that this success, on the one hand, has suppressed pressures for change in municipal autonomy, and on the other, buffered market-liberalist policies in Finnish comprehensive schooling.

The Finnish comprehensive QAE model balances the dominating doctrines of 'GERM' and 'EEP' and the embedded egalitarianism. To comprehend the dynamics involved this confrontation, the concept of contingency appears useful. Inevitably, contingent events – such as radical municipal autonomy, recession and revitalization of the idea of comprehensive education – have thus far favored the path-dependent egalitarianism rather than convergent market-liberalism.

### Concluding Remarks

Our analysis has revealed that a contradiction has emerged between converging pursuits of, on the one hand, international acceptance as a consenting adult in the western advanced liberal family, and, on the other, a deep-rooted path dependence on traditional social democratic and agrarian egalitarianism. This contradiction makes Finnish QAE policy remarkably double-layered. In official rhetoric, the NPM-reform discourse has been more present, whereas at the local level a silent consensus based on antipathy and resistance against national tests and ranking lists exists. Second, bringing the concepts of path dependence and contingency together does assist, at least in part, in understanding the persistence of this poorly articulated, silent consensus that has shown its stubborn power where the municipalities have restrained themselves from implementing studies that could be used to create public school-specific ranking lists. This analysis does not, of course, completely explain the Finnish case, and without suggesting that we offer an exhaustive explanation, we have outlined some other historical factors elsewhere (Rinne et al, 2002; Simola et al, 2002; Simola & Rinne, 2010).

As may be expected, our analysis can open up new conversations and analyses on the dynamics of education politics in the field of comparative education. Two theoretical issues must be taken account in particular. The first, as noted by Kauko et al (2012), relates to economics, political science and history; it could be characterized as the 'unbearable narrowness of the national view' (Strange, 1997; Kettunen, 2008). To be able to overcome this theoretical deficit we have to emphasize the socio-historical analysis of complexity (Schriewer, 2009) and the history of the 'transnational' and the 'inter-crossing' (Werner & Zimmermann, 2006).

Another issue – as noted in Kauko et al (2012) again – references sociology and the philosophy of science and methodology. This issue concerns the *relationship between structure, contingency and agency*. Theoretical perspectives on the age of contingency (Joas & Knöbl, 2009), the cultural turn in the sociology of modern society (Wagner, 2008) and neostructuralism (Frank, 1989; Heiskala, 2001) are significant approaches that emphasize the insecurity and openness of the horizon of expectations and the freedom of actors. The basic assumption here is that the world is complex and it cannot be comprehend adequately through rational implementation of policy and its possible failings.

Our conceptualizations aim to build a theoretical tool for understanding and explaining the dynamics in complexity with special emphasis on the actor, the meaning and the historicity. First, they will adjust our focus from international to cross-national. The *cross-national* dimension elaborates the development of trans-national, national and local *interplay*. The national and local must be analyzed in this interplay where the dynamics of the policymakers, the schools and the families will meet, confront and collide (see Kauko et al, 2012). Second, they emphasize dynamics rather than taxonomies. Many national models advocate the use of taxonomies in different contexts, but for comparison purposes they have little to offer and such approaches have been criticized: These taxonomies include the stages heuristics [2] in political science (Jenkins-Smith & Sabatier, 1993), the interest approach in sociology (Emirbayer, 1997), and periodizations in social history (Sewell, 1996). Furthermore, from our point of view, institutions, legislation and periods in history are not as interesting as the changes in the interplay between actors in different fields of education – that is, as the dynamics (see Kauko et al, 2012). Finally, and drawing on the two previous conclusions, our conceptualizations take seriously the complexity of the world and the contingency emphasizing the insecurity, the openness of the horizon of expectations and the relative freedom of more or less conscious and informed actors. Contemporary complexivist perspectives on the politics of education share our perspective where 'it is actually the emergence of order and predictability that requires explanation' (Biesta & Osberg, 2010, p. 2). This ultimately means a better understanding of the contexts in which different actors of education function, rather than focusing on the differences in systems.

## Notes

[1] This construction draws on our earlier elaborations (e.g. Simola et al, 2010, 2011a, b; Simola et al, 2013).

[2] According to this theory the policy is divided and analyzed in several stages. The most common ones are: problem formation, selection of policy, implementation, and evaluation.

## References

Aho, E., Pitkänen, K. & Sahlberg, P. (2006) *Policy Development and Reform Principles of Basic and Secondary Education in Finland since 1968.* The World Bank Education: Working paper series no. 2. Washington, DC: World Bank.

Ahonen, S. (2003) *Yhteinen koulu: tasa-arvoa vai tasapäisyyttä?* [Common school: equality or leveling off?] Tampere: Vastapaino.

Association of Finnish Local and Regional Authorities (AFLRA) (2001) *Sivistystoimen arviointi on osa valtuustotason arviointia* [The evaluation of education and culture is the Municipal Council's duty]. Yleiskirje 13/80/2001. Helsinki: Suomen Kuntaliitto.

Association of Finnish Local and Regional Authorities (AFLRA) & Ministry of Finance MF (1998) *Julkisten palveluiden laatustrategia* [The quality strategy for public services]. Helsinki: Suomen Kuntaliitto. Valtiovarainministeriö.

Ball, S.J. (2001) Global Policies and Vernacular Politics in Education, *Curriculo Sem Fronteiras*, 1(2), xxvii–xliii.

Ball, S.J. (2003) The Teacher's Soul and the Terrors of Performativity, *Journal of Education Policy*, 18(2), 215-228.

Bautier, E. & Rayou, P. (2007) What PISA Really Evaluates: literacy or students' universes of reference? *Journal of Educational Change*, 8(4), 349-357.

Biesta, G. & Osberg, D. (2010) Complexity, Education and Politics from the Inside-out and the Outside-in: an introduction, in D. Osberg & G. Biesta (Eds) *Complexity Theory and the Politics of Education.* Rotterdam: Sense.

Bracey, G. (2005) Research: put out over PISA, *Phi Delta Kappan*, 86(10), 797-798.

Committee for Education and Culture (CEC) (1998) Sivistysvaliokunnan mietintö SiVM 3/1998 [Memorandum from Committee for Education and Culture]. Helsinki: Parliament of Finland.

Committee for Education and Culture (CEC) (2002) Sivistysvaliokunnan mietintö SiVM 11/2002 [Memorandum from Committee for Education and Culture]. Helsinki: Parliament of Finland.

CIE (1990) *Koulutuksen tuottavuus* [The productivity of education]. Helsinki: Suomen Työnantajain Keskusliitto.

Dean, M. (2002) Liberal Government and Authoritarianism, *Economy and Society*, 31(1), 37-61.

Dean, M. (2007) *Governing Societies: political perspectives on domestic and international rule*. Maidenhead: Open University Press.

Decree 150/2003 (2003) *Asetus koulutuksen arvioinnista* [Decree on Evaluation of Education]. Helsinki: Parliament of Finland.

Dohn, N.B. (2007) Knowledge and Skills for PISA: assessing the assessment, *Journal of Philosophy of Education*, 41(1), 1-16.

Emirbayer, M. (1997) Manifesto for a Relational Sociology, *American Journal of Sociology*, 103(2), 281-317.

Finnish Education Evaluation Council (FEEC) (2005) *New Directions in Educational Evaluation. Evaluation Programme 2004-2007*. Publications of the Finnish Education Evaluation Council 3. Jyväskylä: Finnish Education Evaluation Council.

Frank, M. (1989) *What is Neostructuralism?* Minneapolis: University of Minnesota Press.

Goldstein, H. (2004) Education for All: the globalization of learning targets, *Comparative Education*, 40(1), 7-15.

Granö-Suomalainen, V. & Lovio, M. (Eds) (2002) *Mihin me pyrimme? Miksi arvioida kunnan koulutus- ja kirjastopalveluja* [Where are we aiming to? Why evaluate municipal educational services]. Helsinki: Suomen Kuntaliitto.

Green, A. (1999) Education and Globalization in Europe and East Asia: convergent and divergent trends, *Journal of Education Policy*, 14(1), 55-71.

Grek, S., Lawn, M., Lingard, B., Ozga, J., Rinne, R., Segerholm. C. & Simola, H. (2009) National Policy Brokering and the Construction of the European Education Space in England, Sweden, Finland and Scotland, *Comparative Education*, 45(1), 5-21.

Hannus, S., Kauko, J., Kynkäänniemi, H., Pitkänen, H. Simola, M, Varjo J. & Väätäinen, E. (2010) A Dream Well Planned: discursive space and social positions in Finnish comprehensive education quality assurance, in J. Kauko, R. Rinne & H. Kynkäänniemi (Eds) *Restructuring the Truth of Schooling: essays on discursive practices in the sociology and politics of education. A Festschrift for Hannu Simola*. Research in Educational Sciences 48. Turku: Finnish Educational Research Association.

Hedström, P. & Wittrock, B. (2009) Introduction: frontiers of sociology, in P. Hedström & B. Wittrock (Eds) *Frontiers of Sociology*. Leiden: Koninklijke Brill.

Heiskala, R. (2001) Theorizing Power: Weber, Parsons, Foucault and neostructuralism, *Social Science Information*, 40(2), 241-264.

Hirvi, V. (1996) *Koulutuksen rytminvaihdos* [Changing rhythm of education]. Helsinki: WSOY.

Jenkins-Smith, H.C. & Sabatier, P.A. (1993) The Study of Public Policy Processes, in P.A. Sabatier & H.C. Jenkins-Smith (Eds) *Policy Change and Learning: an advocacy coalition approach*. Boulder, CO: Westview Press.

Joas, H. (2004) Morality in an Age of Contingency, *Acta Sociologica*, 47, 392-399.

Joas, H. (2008) Kontingenssin aikakausi [The era of contingency], *Sosiologia*, 45(3), 203-212.

Joas, H. & Knöbl, W. (2009) *Social Theory: twenty introductory lectures.* Cambridge: Cambridge University Press.

Kauko, J. (2011) *Korkeakoulupolitiikan dynamiikat Suomessa* [Dynamics in Finnish higher education politics]. Helsinki: University of Helsinki, Department of Behavioural Sciences.

Kauko, J., Simola, H., Varjo, J. & Kalalahti, M. (2012) What Could a Dynamics Perspective Contribute to Comparative Research? In J. Kivirauma, A. Jauhiainen, P. Seppänen & T. Kaunisto (Eds) *Koulutuksen yhteiskunnallinen ymmärrys* [Social perspectives on education]. Research in Educational Sciences 59. Turku: Finnish Educational Research Association.

Kauko, J. & Varjo, J. (2008) Age of Indicators – Changes in the Finnish Education Policy Agenda, *European Educational Research Journal,* 7(2), 219-231.

Kettunen, P. (2008) *Globalisaatio ja kansallinen me: kansallisen katseen historiallinen kritiikki* [Globalisation and us: a historical critique of the national gaze]. Tampere: Vastapaino.

Lähdesmäki, K. (2003) *New Public Management ja julkisen sektorin uudistaminen* [New Public Management and reforms of public sector], *Acta Wasaensia,* 113. Vaasa: University of Vaasa.

Law 365/1995 (1995) *Kuntalaki* [The Local Government Act]. Helsinki: Parliament of Finland.

Law 628/1998 (1998) *Perusopetuslaki* [The Basic Education Act]. Helsinki: Parliament of Finland.

Law 32/2003 (2003) *Laki perusopetuslain 21 §:n muuttamisesta* [Amendment to The Basic Education Act]. Helsinki: Parliament of Finland.

Levi, M. (1997) A Model, a Method and a Map: rational choice and historical analysis, in M. Lichbach & A. Zuckerman (Eds) *Comparative Politics: rationality, culture and structure.* Cambridge: Cambridge University Press.

Levin, B. (1998) An Epidemic of Education Policy: (what) can we learn from each other? *Comparative Education,* 34(2), 131-141.

Löfström, E., Metsämuuronen, J., Niemi, E., Salmio, K. & Stenvall, K. (2005) *Koulutuksen paikallinen arviointi vuonna 2004* [The local evaluation of education in 2004]. Arviointi 2/2005. Helsinki: Opetushallitus.

Ministry of Education (ME) (1990) Koulutuksen tuloksellisuuden arvioinnista. Arviointimenettelyä selvittäneen työryhmän Muistio [On evaluation of educational outcomes]. *Opetusministeriön työryhmien muistioita,* 23. Helsinki: Opetusministeriö.

Ministry of Education (ME) (1996) Koulutuksen lainsäädännön kokonaisuudistus [The reform of education legislation]. *Komiteamietintö,* 4. Helsinki: Opetusministeriö.

Ministry of Education (1997) Koulutuksen arviointistrategia [Evaluation strategy for education]. Helsinki: Opetusministeriö.

Ministry of Education (ME) (2007a) Koulutuksen arviointijärjestelmän kehittämistyöryhmän muistio [Memorandum from working group developing national system of educational evaluation]. *Opetusministeriön työryhmämuistioita ja selvityksiä,* 27. Helsinki: Opetusministeriö.

Ministry of Education (ME) (2007b) Opetushallituksen asema, rooli ja tehtävät sekä koulutustoimialan ohjaus muuttuvassa toimintaympäristössä [The position, role and tasks of Finnish National Board of Education and the steering of the educational branch in a changing operating environment]. *Opetusministeriön työryhmämuistioita ja selvityksiä*, 46. Helsinki: Opetusministeriö.

National Board of Education (NBE) (1995) Koulutuksen tuloksellisuuden arviointimalli [A framework for evaluating educational outcomes in Finland], *Arviointi*, 9/1995. Helsinki: Opetushallitus.

Niukko, S. (2006) 'Yhteistyötä ilman riskejä?' OECD: n rooli Suomen koulutuspolitiikassa ['Co-operation without risks?' The role of OECD in Finnish education policy], *Annales Universitatis Turkuensis*, C: 251. Turku: University of Turku.

Nóvoa, A. & Yariv-Mashal, T. (2003) Comparative Research in Education: a mode of governance or a historical journey? *Comparative Education*, 39(4), 423-439.

Numminen, J. (1994) *Koulutuspolitiikan vaihtoehdot* [The alternatives of education policy]. Helsinki: Otava.

Organisation for Economic Co-operation and Development (OECD) (2003) *Polytechnic Education in Finland. Reviews of National Policies for Education*. Paris: OECD.

Ozga, J., Dahler-larsen, P., Segerholm C. & Simola, H. (2011) (Eds) *Fabricating Quality in Education. Data and Governance in Europe*. London: Routledge.

Ozga, J. & Jones, R. (2006) Travelling and Embedded Policy: the case of knowledge transfer, *Journal of Education Policy*, 21(1), 1-17.

Palonen, K. (2006) *The Struggle with Time. A Conceptual History of 'Politics' as an Activity*. Hamburg: Verlag Münster.

Pekonen, K. (2005) *Suomalaisen hallitsemiskäsitteistön historiaa* [On the history of Finnish administrative concepts]. Helsinki: Yliopistopaino.

Pierson, P. (2000) Increasing Returns, Path Dependence and the Study of Politics, *American Political Science Review*, 94(2), 251-267.

Popkewitz, T.S. (2008) *Cosmopolitanism and the Age of School Reform: science, education, and making society*. New York: Routledge.

Popkewitz, T.S. (2009) National Imaginaries, the Indigenous Foreigner, and Power: comparative educational research, in J. Schriewer (Ed.) *Discourse Formation in Comparative Education*, 3rd rev. edn. Frankfurt am Main: Peter Lang.

Prais, S.J. (2004) Cautions on OECD's Recent Educational Survey (PISA): rejoinder to OECD's response, *Oxford Review of Education*, 30(4), 569-573.

Prime Minister Jyrki Katainen's Government (2011) Government Programme. Helsinki: Finnish Government.

Purhonen, K. (2005) Eteläranta peruskoulun ja yksityiskoulujen puolesta [Confederation of Finnish Industries support comprehensive and private schools], in K. Hämäläinen, A. Lindström & J. Puhakka (Eds) *Yhtenäisen peruskoulun menestystarina* [The success story of common comprehensive school]. Helsinki: Yliopistopaino kustannus.

Rajanen, J. (2000) Selvitys koulutuksen paikallisen tason arvioinnin tilasta [The state of local level evaluation], *Arviointi*, 11/2000. Helsinki: Opetushallitus.

Riley, K. & Torrance, H. (2003) Big Change Question: as national policy-makers seek to find solutions to national education issues, do international comparisons such as TIMSS and PISA create a wider understanding, or do they serve to promote the orthodoxies of international agencies? *Journal of Educational Change*, 4(4), 419-425.

Rinne, R., Kallo, J. & Hokka, S. (2004) Too Eager to Comply? OECD Education Policies and the Finnish Response, *European Educational Research Journal*, 3(2), 454-485.

Rinne, R., Kivirauma, J. & Hirvenoja, P. (2001) Nordic Educational Policy under Siege: educational politicians tell their stories, in S. Lindblad, & T.S. Popkewitz (Eds) *Listening to Education Actors on Governance and Social Integration and Exclusion*. Uppsala Reports on Education 37. Uppsala: University of Uppsala, Department of Education.

Rinne, R., Kivirauma, J. & Simola, H. (2002) Shoots of Revisionist Education Policy or Just Slow Readjustment? The Finnish Case of Educational Reconstruction, *Journal of Education Policy*, 17(6), 643-658.

Rinne, R., Simola, H., Mäkinen-Streng, M., Silmäri-Salo, S. & Varjo, J. (2011) *Arvioinnin arvo. Suomalaisen perusopetuksen laadunarviointi rehtoreiden ja opettajien kokemana* [The value of evaluation. Principals' and teachers' perceptions of Finnish quality assurance and evaluation in basic education]. Research in Educational Sciences 56. Turku: Finnish Educational Research Association.

Sahlberg, P. (2011) *Finnish Lessons: what can the world learn from educational change in Finland?* New York: Teachers College, Columbia University.

Schriewer, J. (2009) Coping with Complexity in Comparative Methodology: issues of social causation and processes of macro-historical globalisation, in R. Alexander, P. Broadfoot & D. Phillips (Eds) *Learning from Comparing: new directions in comparative education research, vol. 1. Contexts, Classrooms and Outcomes*. Oxford: Symposium Books.

Seppänen, P. (2006) *Koulunvalintapolitiikka perusopetuksessa. Suomalaiskaupunkien koulumarkkinat kansainvälisessä valossa.* [School-choice policy in comprehensive schooling – school markets of Finnish cities in the international perspective]. Research in Educational Sciences 26, Turku: Finnish Educational Research Association.

Sewell, W. (1996) Three Temporalities: toward an eventful sociology, in T. McDonald (Ed.) *The Historic Turn in the Human Sciences*. Ann Arbor: University of Michigan Press.

Simola, H. (2006) Globalisation of Finnish Educational Governance – School Performance Indicators and their Publication as a Case in Point, in J. Kallo & R. Rinne (Eds) *Supranational Regimes and National Education Policies. Encountering Challenge*, pp. 337-352. Turku: Finnish Educational Research Association.

Simola, H. (2009) Trans-national Technologies, National Techniques and Local Mechanisms in Finnish University Governance. A Journey through the Layers, *Nordic Educational Research*, 29(1), 6-17.

Simola, H., Heikkinen, S. & Silvonen, J. (1998) A Catalog of Possibilities: Foucaultian history of truth and education research, in T.S. Popkewitz & M. Brennan (Eds) *Foucault's Challenge*. New York: Teachers College Press.

Simola, H. & Rinne, R. (2010) Education Politics and Contingency: belief, status and trust behind the Finnish PISA miracle, in Miguel Pereyra (Ed.) *PISA under Examination: changing knowledge, changing tests, and changing schools*. Rotterdam: Sense.

Simola, H., Rinne, R. & Kivirauma, J. (2002) Abdication of the Education State or Just Shifting Responsibilities? The Appearance of a New System of Reason in Constructing Educational Governance and Social Exclusion/Inclusion in Finland, *Scandinavian Journal of Educational Research*, 46(3), s. 247-264.

Simola, H., Rinne, R., Varjo, J. & Kauko, J. (2013) The Paradox of Educational Race: How to win the rankings by sailing to headwind, *Journal of Education Policy*.

Simola, H., Rinne, R., Varjo, J., Kauko, J. & Pitkänen, H. (2009) Quality Assurance and Evaluation (QAE) in Finnish Compulsory Schooling: a national model or just unintended effects of radical decentralisation? *Journal of Education Policy*, 24(2), 163-178.

Simola, H., Varjo, J. & Rinne, R. (2010) Vasten valtavirtaa – kontingenssi, polkuriippuvuus ja konvergenssi suomalaisen perusopetuksen laadunarviointimallin kehityskuluissa [Against the mainstream – contingency, path dependence and convergence of quality evaluation models in the Finnish basic education system], *Hallinnon tutkimus*, 29(4), 285-302.

Simola, H., Varjo, J. & Rinne, R. (2011a) Contra la corriente: dependencia del camino, convergencia y contingencia en la comprensión del modelo finlandés de la garantía de la calidad en educación (QAE) [Against the mainstream – contingency, path dependence and convergence of quality evaluation models in the Finnish basic education system], *Profesorado – Revista de currículum y formación del profesorado*, 15(1), 211-227.

Simola, H., Varjo, J. & Rinne, R. (2011b) À Contre-courant: dépendance au sentier, convergence et contingence. Vers une meilleure compréhension du modèle finlandais d'assurance-qualité et d'évaluation [Against the mainstream – contingency, path dependence and convergence of quality evaluation models in the Finnish basic education system], *Éducation et Sociétés: Revue internationale de sociologie de l'éducation*, 28(2), 35-51.

Strange, S. (1997) The Future of Global Capitalism – Or, Will Divergence Persist Forever? In C. Crouch & W. Streek (Eds) *Political Economy of Modern Capitalism. Mapping Convergence and Diversity*. London: Sage.

Temmes, M., Ahonen, P. & Ojala, T. (2002) *Suomen koulutusjärjestelmän hallinnon arviointi* [Evaluation of the Finnish Education Administration]. Helsinki: Opetusministeriö.

Tiihonen, S. (2004) *From Governing to Governance: a process of change*. Tampere: Tampere University Press.

Wagner, P. (2008) *Modernity as Experience and Interpretation: a new sociology of modernity*. Cambridge: Polity Press.

Werner, M. & Zimmermann, B. (2006) Beyond Comparison: histoire croisée and the challenge of reflexivity, *History and Theory*, 45(1), 30-50.

CHAPTER 3

# The Theory and Practice of Building Pedagogical Skill in Finnish Teacher Education

## TIINA SILANDER & JOUNI VÄLIJÄRVI

ABSTRACT Education has been an essential part of the development of the Finnish nation and economy. Teachers have always played an important and respected role in society. Prior to the comprehensive school reform of the 1970s, the issue of teacher training was the subject of many major controversies. The process resulted in the final transfer of training for all comprehensive and upper-secondary school teachers to the university level. In order to maintain the high status and respect of teachers and strengthen the academic basis of teachers' work, a master's degree was established as the basic level of teacher qualification. Familiarising teacher students with the latest research and training them to conduct research became integral components of that degree. Today the status of a teacher is largely comparable to that of a lawyer or a doctor. The teaching profession has also remained a popular choice among young people. As a result, only 10-15% of the large number of applicants are selected for the primary teacher programmes. This chapter also explores the impact on learning outcomes of the high academic standards of teacher education and the popularity of the profession. It also analyses the present structures, the contents and the future orientations of teacher education at Finnish universities.

## Introduction

The high quality of teachers and teacher education is often considered to be the main reason for the success of Finnish students in the Programme for International Student Assessment (PISA). The teaching profession is highly valued in Finland compared with most other developed countries. Finnish parents regard education still as the best policy to ensure a positive future for their children. Moreover, in Finland, parents' trust in education and teachers is less dependent on their social status than in many older industrialised countries. The teaching profession has also remained a popular choice among young people (Linnakylä et al, 2011; Sahlberg, 2011).

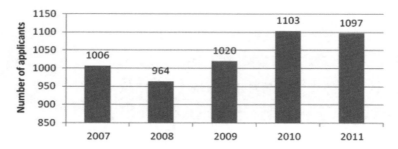

Figure 1. Applicants for primary teacher programme at Jyväskylä University.

One indicator of the appreciation of the teaching profession is the popularity of teacher education as a study line. To date, Finnish teacher education has not faced any serious problems in attracting applicants, with the exception of mathematics and some foreign languages. In the University of Jyväskylä, for example, for the 80 student places offered in primary teacher education, there are annually about 1000 applicants (Figure 1). The situation is similar in most other Finnish universities. This enables universities to select the best students for these programmes with respect to their suitability to work as teachers, their study motivation and their previous academic achievement.

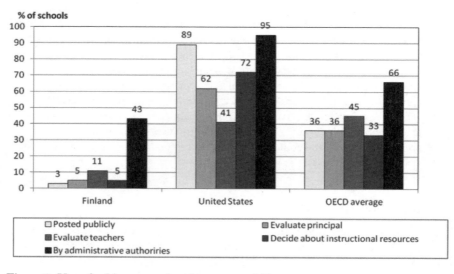

Figure 2. Use of achievement data for accountability purposes.

In the Finnish education system, schools and their teachers have a large amount of autonomy to develop school curricula and the learning environment, choose materials and decide on their instructional and assessment methods. This culture of trust presumes that teachers, principals, parents and their communities know how to provide their children and youth with the best possible education (Aho et al, 2006).

Finland has not followed the Anglo-Saxon accountability movement in basic education, which believes in making schools and teachers accountable for learning outcomes. There are consequently no inspection systems or centrally organised examinations or nationwide tests in basic education. Only in very few cases are teachers evaluated – for example, by the principal or school authorities for accountability purposes (Figure 2). Finns have never been enthusiastic about making schools compete with each other, although parents can now freely choose the school their child goes to.

**From Bisection towards Unification**

Teacher training in Finland has taken shape gradually and separately for each school type and even for each individual type of teaching assignment. The bisection of the education system into folk school and academic secondary school created in the nineteenth century also determined that teacher training was divided into two main streams: teachers for folk schools graduated from teacher training colleges ('seminaries'), whereas secondary school teachers were trained at universities.

Prior to the comprehensive school reform of the 1970s, the issue of teacher training was the subject of many major controversies. The issues to be solved included the unification of teacher training and transferring the training of primary school teachers (class teachers) from teacher training colleges to universities.

The new Teacher Education Act was ratified in December 1971. The main purpose of the act was to unify primary and secondary school teacher education and to develop programmes of an academically high standard for training all new teachers (Niemi, 2002; Linnakylä, 2004). The new decree in 1978 led to the creation of degree programmes for class teachers, comprehensive and upper-secondary school subject teachers and educational planners, as well as programmes for special needs teachers and student counsellors, which could be characterised as postgraduate studies (see Figure 3).

The latest reform at the beginning of this millennium aimed to further reinforce the academic basis of the teaching profession. The new curriculum of teacher education emphasises teachers' readiness to apply research knowledge in their daily work. Research-based teacher education leans on the idea that teachers' professional development should be supported as a process that continues throughout their career. Student teachers' personal involvement in research activities provides a basis for this process. Success in this, however, requires that teacher education integrates research with the everyday problems encountered in teachers' work (Jakku-Sihvonen & Niemi, 2006).

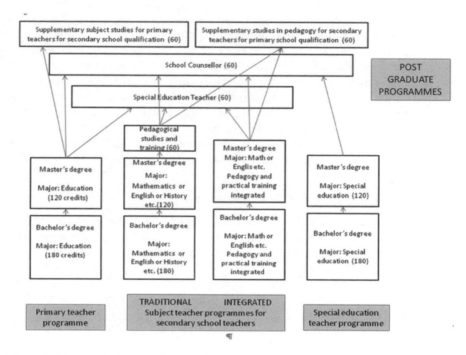

Figure 3. Most typical programmes in Finnish teacher education.

## Structure of Teacher Education at Universities

The teacher education system in Finland is twofold: part of the responsibility for training lies with the faculties of education, while another part is carried out in co-operation with the faculties of education and the faculties of different teaching subjects. Studies conforming to the decrees governing teacher education and degrees in education can be completed at eight universities in Finland. In addition, three art universities have their own systems for teacher education (Hökkä et al, 2010).

The *primary school teacher* programmes are organised by the faculties of education. The main subject for prospective primary school teachers is education. During their studies for the bachelor's degree (180 credits) [1], the students become acquainted with the philosophy, history, psychology and sociology of education, as well as with the foundations of the guidance of learning. Students are introduced to the school subjects taught in grades 1-6 and the didactics of the subjects. The aim of the master's studies (120 credits) is to provide a theoretical and practical foundation for taking charge of teaching duties. Students learn to examine learning, studying and their own teaching from various theoretical perspectives. The scope of the master's degree in education is in total 300 credits and students with the degree are eligible for postgraduate studies in education (Linnakylä, 2004).

In *subject teacher* programmes, the traditional model includes bachelor's and master's degrees in the teaching subjects. After completing these, the student can apply for pedagogical studies, including practical training (60 credits). In integrated programmes, the subject studies, pedagogical studies and teaching practice are integrated from the outset. In this model the student applies for the subject teacher programme already when entering the university.

Subject teachers are still typically teaching grades 7-9, while grades 1-6 are taught by primary school teachers. However, a subject teacher can nevertheless get a qualification to teach also at the primary level if he/she takes multi-disciplinary school subject studies (60 credits) organised by the Faculty of Education. The aim of these studies is that students attain professional skills in the multidisciplinary teaching of the subjects in grades 1-6. The studies also introduce students to participative education and multiculturalism. By the same token, a primary school teacher can obtain a qualification to teach the lower-secondary grades by taking supplementary studies in the teaching subject concerned (60 credits). It is also possible to integrate these studies in the ordinary primary school teacher programme.

There are two ways to become a *special education teacher*. Many universities provide a standard 300-credit special education teacher programme. The other option for gaining this qualification is taking a 60-credit post-graduate programme, which requires a prior primary or secondary school teacher qualification. At some universities it is possible to include 60-credit special education studies as part of the primary teacher education programme.

Similarly, *school counsellor* programmes (60 credits) are usually intended for postgraduates – that is, for qualified primary and secondary school teachers. However, one university also offers a master's programme in guidance and counselling.

### Student Selection

In Finland the university-based teacher qualification is comprehensive. It gives eligibility for teaching at any school of the particular type in the country and is valid permanently throughout the teacher's career. For this reason, it is very important to have already tested applicants for their suitability for the teaching profession before admitting them into the teacher education programmes. Such a test is a mandatory prerequisite for admission. Even when there is a shortage of applicants, the suitability tests are intended to screen out unsuitable candidates.

Each programme and university may arrange the suitability tests in their own way. However, often different universities and/or subject teacher programmes organise joint admission tests or entrance examinations. Below is a description of how students are selected for primary school teacher programmes at different universities.

At present, seven Finnish universities providing primary teacher education administer joint admission tests. An applicant only submits one application, but can identify at most three universities in order of preference. In the first phase of student selection all applicants (usually about 6000) are invited to complete a paper-and-pencil test, which is the same at every university. For this examination, the applicants are expected to read a number of academic articles and other literature. The list of this reading material is published on the Internet about three months before the exam. The purpose of this examination is to assess how well the applicants can use and apply knowledge so as to resolve different problems encountered in educational contexts.

The second phase of student selection is organised by each university independently and using its own procedures. Based on the paper-and-pencil test, at the University of Jyväskylä approximately the top 10% of the first-phase applicants are invited to the second round. The aim of this second phase is to assess the applicants' suitability for the teaching profession. In Jyväskylä this test includes two parts. In the first part, two separate personality questionnaires are used to survey applicants' relationship skills, psychological adjustment, and ability to develop skills and gain knowledge relevant in the teaching profession. The second phase of selection ends with a personal interview designed to assess, among other things, the applicant's motivation and engagement in teachers' work (Hökkä et al, 2010).

## The Latest Reform of Teacher Education Curricula

The Finnish universities have been revising their curricula on teacher education following the guidelines of the European-wide Bologna process (Jakku-Sihvonen & Niemi, 2006; Välijärvi, 2011). The teacher education programme of each faculty of education has its own emphasis within the common frames that determine the general scope of the programme, as well as the contents that are necessary to fulfil the requirements defined by the national educational system. All universities accentuate the importance of a teacher's pedagogic thinking, their readiness to make use of research, their reflection on the theory and practice of teaching and learning, as well as their continuing professional development throughout their teaching career. Table I illustrates how primary school teacher studies are organised at the University of Jyväskylä (300 credits, roughly 4 to 5 years). Students may choose their secondary subject studies fairly freely. For example, a student may concentrate on some comprehensive school subject. Alternatively, the secondary subject studies may include modules of philosophy, social sciences, humanities, or any other faculty in the student's own or another university. Each student is required to produce a master's thesis as part of their advanced studies in education.

| | Example of the courses |
|---|---|
| 1. Communication and orientating studies (25 credits) | *Information and communication technology and acquiring information 1* (3 credits)<br>Students become acquainted with information and communication technology and learn to use it in studying and teaching. Students examine the development of their own work and innovative teaching methods with the help of information literacy, pedagogic and ICT competence and information retrieval skills.<br>Mode of study: lectures, tutorials, exercises |
| 2. Basic studies in education (25 credits) | *Guidance of growth and learning* (6 credits)<br>Students examine the school's teaching and learning concepts, as well as human and information concepts from the pupils' and teacher's perspectives. Relationship between these concepts and teacher's and pupils' actions are discussed. Students learn to analyse pedagogical interaction.<br>Mode of study: lectures, home groups, book exam. |
| 3. Intermediate studies in education (35 credits) | *Interaction skills in a group and networks* (4 credits)<br>Students learn to recognise and evaluate group processes and the individual's activity as a member of a group from the learner's and teacher's perspectives. Students develop their interaction skills by working with students, their parents and other interest groups. The importance of the group for the learning community's well-being is discussed.<br>Mode of study: lectures, tutorials, written assignment |
| 4. Advanced studies in education (80 credits) | *Teacher's ethics and educational philosophy* (3 credits)<br>Students become aware of the ethical aspect of teaching and differentiate their own education and teaching philosophy. Students evaluate their own personal qualities as a teacher on the basis of their own teaching practice experiences. The aim is that students understand the limits and responsibilities of professionalism. The course also deals with the feelings aroused in students by the experience of entering working life and becoming a responsible adult.<br>Mode of study: lectures, tutorials |

| | |
|---|---|
| 5. Studies in subjects and theme areas taught in the comprehensive school (60 credits) | *History* (3 credits)<br>The three central themes in the history studies are: (1) the nature of historical knowledge, (2) the significance of history for the individual and the community, and (3) human knowledge. The complexity and relativity of knowledge is critically examined from different perspectives. Special attention is paid to source-critical reading. The significance of history is approached through individual and collective identities.<br>Mode of study: lectures, tutorials, exercises |
| 6. Studies in a secondary subject (60 credits) | e.g. Preschool and initial teaching (25 cr), Visual arts (25 cr), Physical education (25 cr), Textile craft education (25 cr) |
| 7. Free-choice studies (15 credits) | |

Table I. The contents of primary teacher programme at the University of Jyväskylä.

*Subject teacher education* consists of three major elements. First, prospective teachers have to master the subject matter they are going to teach. Their education aims at the acquisition of expert knowledge in these subjects, so that the teachers are able to guide their students in solving also more difficult problems. Second, teachers also need competencies for research and ability to engage in theoretical thinking. These are essential in planning and providing instruction, as well as in student assessment and in guiding the students' learning. Teachers should also be able to contribute to curricular planning at their school. Third, subject teachers need to be able to integrate the subject matter and pedagogic research knowledge into their personal pedagogical theory.

Subject teacher programmes are organised co-operatively between the department of the teaching subject concerned and the Faculty of Education. Programmes includes studies in one, two or three teaching subjects and the teacher's pedagogical studies as part of the master's degree. Teaching subject studies consist of advanced studies in one subject, with a minimum scope of 80-90 credits, and intermediate studies in a second and possibly third subject, with a minimum scope of 50-60 credits in each. Subject teacher qualification calls for 60 credits of pedagogical studies organised by the Faculty of Education. These pedagogical studies are divided into two components. *Basic studies in education* deal with the fundamentals of growth and learning (15 credits) and also comprise practical training under a supervisor's guidance (10 credits). *Intermediate pedagogical studies* extend subject teachers' competencies especially for communication, educational ethics and the methodologies of educational research (20 credits). Nearly as great a share of the pedagogic studies (15 credits) is allocated for practice teaching in classrooms, as practical training in the classroom and consequent reflection of this experience play a central role in teacher education (Lavonen et al, 2007).

## Merging Theory and Practice

The three pillars of Finnish teacher education are research-based teaching and learning, integrating theory and practice in a dialogical process and producing reflective teachers who are life-long learners with readiness for professional development throughout their careers.

*Research-based learning* is, nowadays, a central theoretical and organising theme of teacher education from the very beginning. All parts of the teacher education programme are justified by a systematic totality and focus on a teacher's thinking process, which may be characterised by criteria used in research work (Kansanen, 1999b; Kansanen et al, 2000).

Teacher education has an active and intensive relationship with research work in different disciplines needed in teachers' work. Research results should also provide a knowledge base for teachers' work and professional development at the school level. It means that teachers are familiar with recent research in their subject matter and in pedagogy, and their competencies include critical scientific literacy. They should also be able to integrate academic research-based knowledge with their own professional behaviour in a reflective way. Research-based teacher education means also that teachers' professionalism is founded on sound scientific knowledge and that they have capacity to broaden and deepen their competence through their own exploration and critical reflection on their professional practices (Niemi, 2009).

Making use of research knowledge and familiarisation with research methods are included in most study requirements. Research orientation means, above all, testing and extending one's knowledge and understanding by means of empirical observation and critical reflection. Research-based learning places emphasis on the use of personal experiences and feelings as empirical material for learning about and from various educational phenomena. The closest observation data on a student consist of the mental and social processes of his or her learning (Jyrhämä et al, 2008).

The research-based approach culminates in a master's thesis, which is obligatory for every student.

This process provides students with an opportunity to complete an authentic project, in which they have to formulate a problem of a particular educational field, independently collect information and data relative to the problem, elaborate on them in the context of recent research in the area, and synthesise the results in the form of a written thesis.

Work on the master's thesis formally begins in the third year of study when the teacher education department introduces its ongoing research projects to students in a 'mini-conference'. Students can either join one of the ongoing projects or choose a theme of their own and proceed independently with the help of their supervisor. Independent topics are typically related to the issues faced during the teaching practice. The topics chosen independently vary greatly across different themes, including practical aspects of teachers' work, pedagogy, learning environments, special education, and family and community partnerships. The following are examples of topics in these areas: 'Coping with Teaching Nervousness', 'Teachers' Sense of Efficacy and Its Connection to Well-Being at Work', 'The Association of Teachers' Pedagogical Strategies with the Motivational Climate of a Group', 'Functional Geometry', 'Sixth-grade Students Using Social Media', 'Attention-deficit Disorder Co-occurring with Learning Disabilities in Reading', and 'Class Teachers' Emotional Responses in Building Trusting Parent-Teacher Relationships'. After choosing the topic, students are divided into seminar groups based on their research topics and/or methodology.

Thesis seminar 1 (5 credits) concentrates on planning the research and collecting data. Students deepen their understanding of the purpose of research and the stages of a research process. They become acquainted with data-collection methods and acquire skills in research communication – for example, in information literacy and argumentation. Students compile their research plans and collect data. Thesis seminar 2 (5 credits) focuses on analysing the data and writing the research report. Students become acquainted with the analysis methods and apply them in the data collected for the thesis. They also apply research-methodological skills: reporting about research and writing a research report. Students present a sketch of their thesis while other students act as opponents.

Each seminar lasts for one semester and includes 24 hours of guided instruction and independent work by students. Parallel with the project seminars, the students are involved in methodological studies. In addition to the support given in seminars and in methodological courses, each student has one or two supervisors for the master's thesis (30 credits). In the course of the writing process, students get feedback about their work from their supervisors in writing, and they also have regular tutoring meetings. When the thesis is nearly ready, the supervisors review the work and suggest possible improvements. After the revision, the supervisors and an independent examiner give their evaluation about the theme of the research, the theoretical background and references, the research problem, the methods, data collection and analysis, the reporting of the results, the conclusions and discussion, the reliability, the language and the coherence of the text. Although the process is instructed, the aim is also to support the independent work of students.

### Reflective Thinking

The central purpose of all teacher education programmes is to integrate the various aspects of teachers' work through research-based thinking and argumentation. The aim is that students internalise a research-oriented attitude towards their work and professional development. Important aspects of professional literacy include an ability to choose and critically evaluate research for one's own use. Everyday intuitive thinking, with justifications from one's own experiences and discussions with colleagues, attracts rational arguments. Although pedagogical thinking is mainly mixed with intuitional and rational arguments, a research-based attitude makes it possible to steer this thinking systematically towards a rational educational understanding. Students learn to reflect scientific knowledge, combining it with their own conclusions based on their observations and experiences. Reflection is a way to gain knowledge about the interaction in the teaching-studying-learning process. Kansanen (1999a) points out that reflection calls for a certain distance in order to focus properly on one's own decisions and their role in practice. In this process, the teacher may use his/her knowledge about research-based thinking skills. Research orientation means extending his/her own understanding by using empirical observations and critical reflection gained by using scientific literature.

### Pedagogical Studies and Teaching Practice

The practical aspects and theoretical basis of teachers' work are seen as complementary to each other. Pedagogical studies including teaching practice combine theory and practice. During these studies students develop their own teaching philosophy through reflective, dialogic and practical activities.

The pedagogical studies are obligatory for teacher qualification and are approximately the same for both primary and secondary teachers. These studies give a formal pedagogical qualification to teachers at all levels in the Finnish educational system regardless of the programme in which they are provided. According to legislation, pedagogical studies must be studies in the science of education with an emphasis on didactics. These studies are in essence intermediate studies in education, which emphasise teachers' pedagogical thinking as well as pedagogical research, and include teaching practice. The pedagogical studies build on a scientific analysis of teachers' work and the knowledge to be mediated in the work. When describing this starting point, different researchers use different terms, such as 'research-based teacher education' (Kansanen, 1999b), 'evidence-based teacher education' (Niemi, 2000, 2008), or 'teacher as a researcher' (Korpinen, 1999). What is common to all these definitions is that they emphasise research knowledge as a basis for all teacher education. In other words, approaches and methods typical of research should be present in all education.

Pedagogical studies comprise the basic studies and the subject studies (60 credits in total). In teacher's pedagogical basic studies (25 credits), students orient themselves to the work and functional environments in the field of education, and different educational perspectives are examined. In pedagogical subject studies (35 credits), the focus is on learning and its guidance, which is approached from various perspectives. The aim is to acquire a versatile understanding of the different forms of learning and guidance as a multi-layered phenomenon.

---

TEACHING PRACTICE 1. From self-understanding to interaction (4 credits)
Students observe the activity, learning environment and pupil diversity of a class community from the perspective of both teaching and learning. Students identify their own modes of observation and action, identify and question the established and self-evident practices of school culture and their relationship to learning. Students plan and implement short learning situations and set themselves realistic goals for development as educators and teachers.

TEACHING PRACTICE 2. Planning as the basis of teaching and learning (6 credits)
Students plan, implement and evaluate teaching modules that are more extensive than single learning situations. Students learn to understand the planning of teaching as a process where the goals set in the curriculum are examined and interpreted from various viewpoints. In planning and implementing their teaching, students are able to take into account pupils' learning prerequisites, experiences and interests. Students learn to envisage different alternative goals and implementations for their teaching and make justified choices from among the alternatives.

TEACHING PRACTICE 3 Supervising and evaluating learning (8 credits)
Students plan, implement and evaluate extensive teaching modules and learn to justify their pedagogical choices in terms of the school's educational and didactic goals. Students learn to manage different learning processes and support different learners and evaluate learning using appropriate means.

TEACHING PRACTICE 4 School community and society (8 credits)
Students learn to understand the freedoms and obligations of the teaching profession in relation to the school community and society. Students are able to act professionally in the work community, in home–school relationships and in multi-professional collaboration. Students learn the skills to work in accordance with the professional ethics of teachers. Students learn to justify their actions as teachers in terms of theoretical knowledge relevant to education and teaching.

---

Table II. Teaching practice modules at the University of Jyväskylä.

Teaching practice is an integral part of pedagogical studies. Every practice teaching period is combined with detailed theoretical studies that relate to the topic in question, and thus teaching practice periods are closely interlinked with other teacher studies. The idea is that theoretical studies will provide a basis for each practical period. In order to obtain more knowledge to facilitate their teaching practice, the students may read relevant research literature and discuss the subject with each other and with the teacher educators.

In the research-based model, practice teaching is started as early as possible and interaction between practice and educational theory studies is emphasised at all stages. Each study period has aims and characteristics of its own (Table II). An integrated whole comprising educational theory, pedagogical content knowledge and practice constitutes the ideal goal in this respect.

In the beginning teaching practice is strictly supervised, but later on the student teacher will gain more responsibility and autonomy. During their teaching practice, students work in a small groups sharing and reflecting experiences. They also form a small learning community within which they learn from each other and give and receive mutual support. During the practice period each group has two supervisors – an educator from the Department of Teacher Education and a teacher from the school – working closely together. Both supervisors comment on, for example, lesson plans, the aims of teaching-learning sessions and pedagogical choices made by students. Supervisors encourage students to explore new ways of teaching so that the student is able to find his/her personal teaching style. After each teaching session the student gets feedback from the teacher, and the university lecturer organises group discussion in which more theoretical aspects are talked about. The supervisor accompanies the student in an essential role through the different phases, although the nature of guidance changes gradually from strict supervision to feedback on an equal basis. At best, this kind of supervisory relationship can develop into a productive partnership in which the experienced teacher and the teacher student reflect on their teaching experiences as equal colleagues. The encounter between the long experience of the supervisor and latest research knowledge mediated by the student helps both of them in gaining a deeper understanding of the essence of teachers' work.

Teaching practice also provides a good opportunity to gain experiences and research data for the master's thesis. School reality typically involves the intertwining of a diversity of individual, communal, cultural and social processes. Looking into one phenomenon, such as a learning difficulty, leads the student teacher inevitably on to other learning-related phenomena. These include, for instance, the effects on learning of a student's social background and motivation, or the school community's strategies for dealing with individual differences (Kansanen, 1999a).

Teaching practice at university training schools and ordinary community schools is organised in rotation. Every university that organises teacher education has a teacher training school. The training school functions basically as any other comprehensive school and follows the same curriculum. However, the teachers have special qualification requirements and are experienced supervisors. Then again, the ordinary field schools represent the everyday practice of schools in general (Kansanen, 1999a; Jyrhämä et al, 2008; Kontoniemi & Salo, 2011).

The present curriculum for teacher education emphasises dialogue as a learning method. A teacher should be able to critically evaluate different ways of working with children as well as to continuously question his or her own thinking patterns. Teachers need to be ready to listen to other people and also to be able to argue for their own views. This applies to teacher students as well as to their educators. When reflecting together on educational and pedagogical issues, the educators and the students may ideally make up a genuine learning community.

At the University of Jyväskylä long-term study groups are used as a method to support dialogue and reflective discussion. Students begin their studies in a home group ($n=16$) with an assigned teacher in charge. Most of the first-year studies are done in this home group. A similar idea of a close relationship among students and between students and educators is maintained throughout the programme. The curricula accordingly emphasise the dynamic and collaborative nature of scientific knowledge and learning. In this line of thinking, teacher educators and teacher students are researchers of teachers' work and are searching for new information. Educators are learners, as well. In this way teacher education seeks to concretise the student's mental representations of what teachers' continuing professional development throughout their career actually means.

The Finnish teacher education curricula place emphasis on process goals rather than on the contents to be learnt or on objectives related to students' post-training behaviour. In the end, teacher education should yield autonomous teachers who are able to think and act independently and justify their own educational decisions. Teachers are experts in pedagogical practice who are willing to develop their own professional skills in a continuing process throughout their careers, and who are capable of doing so. During the programme students learn to understand that developing as a teacher is a lifelong process. They also learn to see how social changes are reflected in the school and in the teaching work.

### In-service Training

When teachers' professional development is defined as a process continuing throughout the career, integration between pre-service and in-service education becomes a crucial issue. Today, the responsibility for teachers' pre-service education rests with the universities, whereas their role regarding in-service training is but a small one. In-service training for teachers is provided by many private as well as publicly funded organisations. In general, the provision for in-service training is poorly coordinated and the quality of services varies to a great extent.

In Finland teaching staff are obliged to participate in in-service training with a minimum scope of three workdays outside school hours per school year. This type of continuing education is free of charge for teachers. The responsibility for funding such education rests with the teachers' employers – that is, mainly with the municipalities. The contents and implementation practices are decided by individual employers. In addition, many teachers participate in voluntary in-service training either during the school year or when they are on vacation. This is usually funded by the local authorities and/or the teachers themselves. Teachers may also apply for some grants for these purposes.

One of the key questions for Finnish teacher education in the future is how to integrate pre-service and in-service training more effectively so as to support teachers' professional development throughout their careers (Figure 4). Another important point relates to support for newly graduated teachers entering the working life.

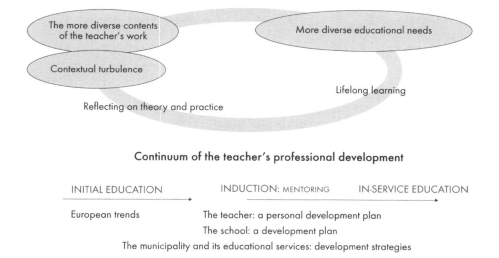

**Continuum of the teacher's professional development**

INITIAL EDUCATION                INDUCTION: MENTORING          IN-SERVICE EDUCATION

European trends            The teacher: a personal development plan
                           The school: a development plan
           The municipality and its educational services: development strategies

Figure 4. Teachers' professional development.

In the future, universities will quite likely take greater responsibility for teachers' in-service training as well. In-service training should advance the development process commenced in the university. To be effective, in-service training should be based on longer-term planning than it is today. A teacher's personal study plan should fit together the needs of the individual teacher, the school and the education provider (the municipality). In practice, these needs are partly different and sometimes even contradictory (Jokinen & Välijärvi, 2004; Välijärvi, 2011).

In recent years teachers' in-service training has become an important policy issue. Since 2010 the Finnish Ministry of Education and Culture has allocated annually €8 million for projects to develop new innovative models for teachers' in-service training (the OSAAVA programme). This means around a 60% increase in the yearly investments in teachers' career development. The Ministry has especially supported such new forms of training that promote longer-term programmes, educational effectiveness and linking with teachers' pre-service training. Other key areas for this new funding include both mutual collaboration between schools and networking with the local community.

The following groups have been seen as the most important target groups for the OSAAVA programme:

- newly qualified teachers who have just entered the teaching profession;
- school leaders (rectors, potential rectors, heads of municipal education administration);
- teaching staff, over 55 years of age; and
- persons who have not participated in professional development at all or who have done so only infrequently in recent years (Hämäläinen et al, 2011).

At the University of Jyväskylä the OSAAVA programme has made it possible to develop new forms of support for newly qualified teachers. The university is coordinating the activities in the network of seven other universities and five vocational teacher education units so as to develop mentor training for the field of education. In this type of training, experienced teachers are introduced into mentoring, familiarising them with recent research knowledge and preparing them for various forms of mentoring. Each mentor trainee should have a group of mentees, with whom they can test things they have learnt in training and develop their own personal practices. Collecting new research knowledge and applying it in the development of training makes up an integral part of the network's activities. The network also produces materials to support mentors' work (Heikkinen et al, 2012).

## Teachers' Professional Development

Teachers' work today accentuates readiness to apply knowledge of different scientific fields and draw on research knowledge for the purpose of continuous professional development. In their daily work teachers need, increasingly, to be able to interact and exchange experiences with the learners and other stakeholders. Professionalism also includes an ability to recognise one's own ways of acting and reacting in daily work settings. Teachers' professionalism is understood as shared expertise among teachers qualified in different areas. Indeed, a characteristic of a well-functioning school is how well its different experts of teaching are working together (Luukkainen, 2000; Välijärvi, 2000).

The national curriculum for the Finnish comprehensive school underlines that the most important thing in teachers' work is guiding the learning and growth of children and youth. This guidance should prepare the students for life-long and life-wide learning after school. Students are also seen as citizens who need to be equipped to participate, as full members, in social activities and reforms. As for reaching these goals, what the teachers teach is not the decisive factor; rather, it is how learning and studying are organised in the school that is important. The way the school operates and organises its work serves as a model for the students of how society works. Hence, a teacher also has extensive social authority and responsibility. Teachers need competencies for interaction and guidance also with regard to co-operation with other teachers, parents and other stakeholders.

The purpose of continuing education throughout a teacher's career is to enable the teacher to continuously develop his or her educational views and pedagogical competencies. A central challenge after pre-service education relates to the utilisation of teachers' work experience so that the theoretical views adopted in university would gain depth and diversity. For the development of pedagogical expertise, it is necessary that the teacher is capable of continuous critical analysis of his or her own actions.

Niemi (2009) stresses that teachers play a crucial role in supporting the learning experience of young people and adult learners. Teachers should, therefore, be able to reflect on the processes of learning and teaching through an ongoing engagement with subject knowledge, curriculum content, pedagogy, innovation, research, and the social and cultural dimensions of education. Niemi refers to the evolving common European principles for teacher education within the European Union (see Commission of the European Communities, 2007), according to which every teacher should have the opportunity to continue post-graduate studies to the highest level in order to develop their teaching competencies and to increase their opportunities for progression within the profession. The objective is for teachers to be recognised as key agents for promoting the values of inclusion at the level of individuals and more broadly in society in general. They should be highly educated and continuously developing and reflecting on their competencies. That is why teachers should graduate from a higher education institution or equivalent. Furthermore, teacher education programmes should be delivered in all three cycles of higher education. Also, the contribution of research and evidence-based practice to the development of new knowledge about education should be promoted.

To meet these European objectives in the reality of the educational institutions it is important that teacher students' involvement in the expert community on an equal basis is an integral part of their studies. In Finland, students' involvement has been promoted, for example, by applying problem-based learning in teacher education (Nummenmaa & Virtanen, 2002). Communality and taking responsibility for the whole work community have become essential requirements in today's school. To be successful in their work, teachers now need to be more ready to engage in open and equal co-operation with students with various skills and needs, with other staff, and with parents and other stakeholders possibly coming from different cultures (Figure 5).

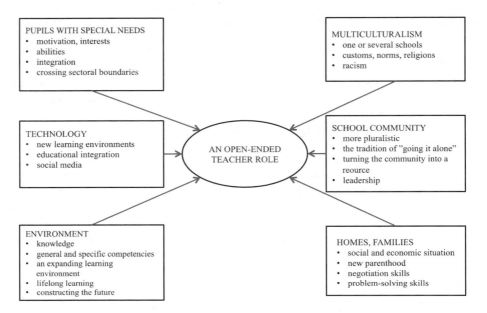

Figure 5. New roles for teachers.

In teacher education, students' involvement in the community means working together and equity between the educators and the students. To achieve this, teacher educators have to be ready to share problems and include students in joint problem-solving discussions. Ideally, teacher educators should serve as a good example of a collaborative-learning model. Through these learning situations the students also get an idea of how research knowledge can be applied in solving different pedagogical problems (Välijärvi, 2000; Linnakylä, 2004).

## Conclusions

An evident strength of the Finnish basic education system is attributable to teachers' high professional competence and their strong ethical commitment to their work. Research has shown that the work of Finnish teachers is also characterised by emphatic autonomy and independence: teachers are highly educated pedagogical experts who have the necessary competence for any demands of schoolwork. Independence is stressed even to the extent that a teacher may often feel he/she has to struggle alone in the classroom, without adequate support from the school community (Luukkainen, 2000).

For a teacher, independence is at the same time an opportunity, a challenge, and a requirement. In the context of students' increasing social problems and learning difficulties, the high social respect for and accentuated autonomy of Finnish teachers may turn into a threat to teachers' general and professional well-being (Välijärvi, 2000; Luukkainen, 2000). This raises the question of how the high personal competencies could be used effectively as a resource for the whole school community. The strong teacher autonomy has not actually been ideal for the development of co-operation models between school and external expert organisations. An obvious challenge to Finnish schools and teachers is how to open classrooms, more than they are today, for co-operation with colleagues, parents, and other experts involved in students' lives. Nevertheless, teachers' high expertise acquired through their education, the high social status of the profession, and teachers' strong influence in school-based decision-making provides a good basis for the development of the teaching profession towards more collaborative approaches.

In the future, one of the key strengths of effective schools comprises advanced leadership and a sophisticated management system. The management culture of educational institutions in Finland has, however, stayed much the same for decades. The management culture and structures of educational institutions are often characterised by the fact that educational institutions are not highly organised internally and they do not favour shared management responsibilities. Consequently, management culture is in need of strong development, where distributed leadership and rotating responsibilities would involve all members of the working community both in development activities and in decision-making processes. Establishment of the role of a managing teacher and expansion of the duties of vice-principals may be development trends worth considering. These would create opportunities for career advancement at school, on the one hand, and ease the overwhelming workload of principals, on the other.

Trust and openness are cornerstones of the development of the teaching profession. Society in general and parents in particular need to be able to trust in schools and teachers, in that there should be confidence that the children are provided with equal high-level learning opportunities irrespective of their place of residence or their family's social background. Teachers, for their part, need to be able to trust that they are allowed to work like other highly educated experts, as autonomous pedagogical professionals, in a way that takes full advantage of their potential. This Finnish model of the teacher's role, which is based on trust, seems to be yielding excellent results in international comparison. Maintaining and further increasing the respect for the teaching profession and the trust in teachers' professional competence are therefore cornerstones for the development of teacher education, as well. Trust is easy to lose, but much harder to regain.

## Notes

[1] A credit corresponds to about 25-30 hours of students' work.

## References

Aho, E., Pitkänen, K. & Sahlberg, P. (2006) *Policy Development and Reform Principles of Basic and Secondary Education in Finland since 1968.* Washington, DC: World Bank.

Commission of the European Communities (2007) Improving the Quality of Teacher Education. Communication from the Commission to the Council and the European Parliament, 3 August. Brussels.

Hämäläinen, K., Kangasniemi, J. & Hämäläinen, K. (2011) Finnish State-funded Continuing Professional Development System for Education Personnel. Paper presented at the Annual Conference of the Association for Teacher Education in Europe, 24-28 August, in Riga, Latvia.

Heikkinen, H., Jokinen, H. & Tynjälä, P. (Eds) (2012) *Peer-group Mentoring for Teacher Development.* New York: Routledge.

Hökkä, P., Eteläpelto, A. & Rasku-Puttonen, H. (2010) Recent Tensions and Challenges in Teacher Education as Manifested in Curriculum Discourse, *Teaching and Teacher Education,* 26, 845-853.

Jakku-Sihvonen, R. & Niemi, H. (Eds.) (2006) Research-based Teacher Education in Finland. Reflections by Finnish Teacher Educators, *Research in Education Sciences,* 25. Tyrku: Finnish Educational Research Association.

Jokinen, H. & Välijärvi, J. (2004) Experiences from the Mentoring Process during Induction in Supporting Novice Teachers' Professional Development. Paper presented at the ECER 2004 conference, in Rethymnon, Crete.

Jyrhämä, R., Kynäslahti, H., Krokfors, L., Byman, R., Maaranen, K., Toom, A. & Kansanen, P. (2008) The Appreciation and Realisation of Research-based Teacher Education: Finnish students' experiences of teacher education, *European Journal of Teacher Education,* 31(1), 1-16.

Kansanen, P. (1999a) Teaching and Teaching-Studying-Learning Interaction, *Scandinavian Journal of Educational Research,* 43(1), 81-89.

Kansanen, P. (1999b) Research-based Teacher Education, in J. Hytönen, C. Razdevšek-Pučko & G. Smith (Eds) *Teacher Education for Changing School,* pp. 135-141. Ljubljana: University of Ljubljana, Faculty of Education.

Kansanen, P., Tirri, K., Meri, M., Krokfors, L., Husu, J. & Jyrhämä, R. (2000) *Teachers' Pedagogical Thinking: theoretical landscapes, practical challenges.* New York: P. Lang.

Kontoniemi, M. & Salo, O.-P. (Eds.) (2011) *Educating Teachers in the PISA Paradise: perspectives on teacher education at a Finnish university.* Jyväskylä: Jyväskylä University Training School.

Korpinen, E. (1999) Kohti tutkivaa opettajuutta.[Towards teachers' new professionalism], in H. Heikkinen, P. Moilanen & P. Räihä (Eds) *Opettajuutta rakentamassa* [Building teachers' professionalism for the future], *Opettajankoulutuslaitos. Opetuksen perusteita ja käytänteitä,* 34, 135-147.

Lavonen, J., Krzywacki-Vainio, H., Aksela, M., Krokfors, L., Oikkonen, J. & Saarikko, H. (2007) Pre-service Teacher Education in Chemistry, Mathematics and Physics, in E. Pehkonen, M. Ahtee & J. Lavonen (Eds) *How Finns Learn Mathematics and Science.* Rotterdam: Sense Publishers.

Linnakylä, P. (2004) Finland, in H. Döbert, E. Klieme & W. Stroka (Eds) *Conditions of School Performance in Seven Countries: a quest for understanding the international variation of PISA results*, pp. 150-218. Munster: Waxmann.

Linnakylä, P., Välijärvi, J. & Arffman, I. (2011) Finnish Basic Education: when equity and excellence meet, in K. Branden, P. Avermaet & M. Houtte (Eds) *Equity and Excellence in Education: towards maximal learning opportunities for all students*, pp. 190-214, *Routledge Research in Education*, 50. New York: Routledge.

Luukkainen, O. (2000) Teachers in 2010. Final Report. Anticipatory Project to Investigate Teachers' Initial and Continuing Training Needs (OPEPRO), Report 15. Helsinki: National Board of Education.

Niemi, H. (2000) Teacher Education in Finland: current trends and future scenarios, *Proceedings of the Conference on Teacher Education Policies in the European Union and Quality of Lifelong Learning*, 22-23 May, Loulé, Portugal. European Network on Teacher Education Policies.

Niemi, H. (2002) Active Learning – A Cultural Change Needed in Teacher Education and School, *Teaching and Teacher Education*, 18, pp. 763-780.

Niemi, H. (2008) Research-based Teacher Education for Teachers' Lifelong Learning, *Lifelong Learning in Europe*, 13(1), 61-69.

Niemi, H. (2009) Why from Teaching to Learning? *European Educational Research Journal*, 8(1), 1-17.

Nummenmaa, A.R. & Virtanen, J. (2002) Ongelmaperustainen opetussuunnitelma muutosstrategiana.[Problem-based learning as a strategy for change], in E. Poikela (Ed.) *Ongelmaperustainen oppiminen – teoriaa ja käytäntöä* [Problem-based curriculum – theory and practice], 165-182. Tampere: Tampere University Press.

Sahlberg, P. (2011) *Finnish Lessons: what can the world learn from educational change in Finland?* New York: Teachers College Press.

Välijärvi J. (Ed.) (2000) Koulu maailmassa – maailma koulussa [School in the world – world in the school]. Future challenges for general education and teacher training. Anticipatory project to investigate teachers' initial and continuing training needs (OPEPRO), Report 9. Helsinki: National Board of Education.

Välijärvi, J. (2011) Teachers' Professional Skills and Research-based Teacher Education for the Future, *Korean Journal of Teacher Education*, 27(3), 289-315.

CHAPTER 4

# What Does PISA Performance Tell Us about Mathematics Teaching Quality? Case Studies from Finland and Flanders

## PAUL ANDREWS

ABSTRACT Over the last decade Finnish students' performance on the mathematical literacy components of PISA has created much international interest. However, with respect to the two times Finland has participated in the Trends in International Mathematics and Science Study (TIMSS), Finnish students' mathematical performance has painted a very different picture, particularly at grade 8. What is less well known is that Flanders, whose Programme for International Student Assessment (PISA) achievements have been masked by those of Belgium as a whole, has performed as well as Finland with respect to mathematical literacy and, on the three TIMSS in which it has participated, it has been the most successful European system at grade 8. Thus, while Finnish performance on tests of technical competence, despite success on tests of mathematical applicability, has been moderate, Flemish students have led the Europeans on both. In this chapter, the author examines two sequences of videotaped lessons taught on percentages, a topic resonant with ambitions of both technical competence and mathematical applicability, by case-study teachers considered against local criteria to be effective. The evidence suggests that Finnish mathematics didactics are more likely to explain Finnish TIMSS failure than PISA success. Flemish didactics may have greater explanatory potential for both PISA and TIMSS success. Such findings suggest that performance on international tests of achievement may be unrelated to didactical quality as other, typically hidden, cultural factors intercede.

### Introduction

In this chapter I compare the two most successful European educational systems – Finland and Flanders – from the perspective of the mathematics achievement of their students and the evidence available with regard to how the two systems construe and, through the practices of their teachers, present mathematics to their students. In so doing, I demonstrate that Programme for International Student Assessment (PISA) success is neither a guarantee nor a consequence of pedagogic quality. I show, also, that it is not necessarily a predictor of mathematics achievement against other forms of assessment like the Trends in International Mathematics and Science Study (TIMSS) but, in some cases, is a consequence of cultural factors that extend substantially beyond the classroom.

But first, by way of background, I summarize the recent histories of the two systems. Both are economically strong, have similar populations and are relatively recent additions to the map of European nations. Finland achieved independence from her successive Swedish and Russian masters in 1919, following a short but violent civil war between, essentially, conservative Swedish-speaking middle classes and the landed agrarian population on the one hand and Finnish-speaking urban workers and the landless agrarian population on the other. Belgium, as a French-speaking Catholic nation, achieved full independence from the Dutch-speaking protestant Netherlands after the treaty of London in 1839. However, the formal recognition of the sovereign region of Flanders began in the second quarter of the twentieth century when its provinces were granted the right to conduct their business in their dialect of Dutch, and continued until the end of the twentieth century when Belgium became federated in 1993. In other words, both systems are relatively modern and have been subjected to considerable foreign, typically imperialist, influences in their development.

**Finnish and Flemish Performance on PISA and TIMSS**

Over the last two decades two series of large-scale international tests of mathematical competence have dominated much of the mathematics education discourse and provided the basis, whether warranted or not, for much research and political decision making. These have been the five published manifestations (1995, 1999, 2003, 2007 and 2011) of the Third International Mathematics and Science Study (TIMSS) and four published cycles (2000, 2003, 2006 and 2009) of the Programme for International Student Assessment (PISA). The emphasis of each PISA has varied, with the first focusing on literacy, the second on mathematical literacy and problem solving, the third on scientific literacy, and the fourth on literacy again. That said, each assessment has included substantial assessments of students' ability to apply their mathematical knowledge and skills in authentic settings, both within mathematics itself and in the wider world (Adams, 2003). The five TIMSS assessments have typically retained the same focus – an examination of mathematics and science curricula at three levels (the intended, the implemented and the attained curricula; Howie & Plomp,

2005) – although most published material has focused on the achievement of students at grades 4 and 8.

| | PISA (age 15) | | | | TIMSS (age 14) | | | | | PISA problem solving |
|---|---|---|---|---|---|---|---|---|---|---|
| | 2000 | 2003 | 2006 | 2009 | 1995 | 1999 | 2003 | 2007 | 2011 | 2003 |
| Finland | 536 | 544 | 546 | 541 | *** | 520 | *** | *** | 514 | 548 |
| Flanders | 543 | 553 | 541 | 537 | 565 | 558 | 537 | *** | *** | 547 |

Table I. Finnish and Flemish mathematics performance on all PISA and TIMSS assessments.

Finnish PISA success (Table I) has prompted 'more than 100 delegations from all over the world ... to find out how the Finnish system works' (Crace, 2003). What is less well known has been the performance of Flanders, mainly because its achievements have been masked by the OECD's reporting of Belgian performance as a whole. However, internal reports (de Meyer et al, 2002; de Meyer et al, 2005; de Meyer, 2008; de Meyer & Warlop, 2010) have shown that Flemish mathematics-related PISA achievement has been consistently comparable to Finnish achievement.

The two countries' TIMSS scores present very different pictures. Flanders was consistently the highest-performing European nation on the three cycles on which it participated. Finland participated in TIMSS 1999 and 2011 only and its scores were, by European standards, unexceptional. Significantly, its 1999 performance on algebra and geometry (Table II) was poor and elicited negative reactions from the Finnish mathematics community, who argued that current procedural emphases had not only marginalized logical thinking, elegance, structure and proof (Malaty, 2010) but were incompatible with the preparation of students for higher mathematics (Astala et al, 2006; Tarvainen & Kivelä, 2006).

| TIMSS 1999 (age 14) (international mean 487) | | | | |
|---|---|---|---|---|
| | Fractions and number sense | Measurement | Data representation analysis and probability | Geometry | Algebra |
| Finland | 531 | 521 | 525 | 498 | 494 |
| Flanders | 557 | 549 | 544 | 535 | 540 |

Table II. Finnish and Flemish performance on the five mathematics domains of TIMSS 1999.

## Perspectives on Finnish PISA Success

While the literature with regard to Flanders is scant, that concerning Finland is extensive and attributes PISA success to, *inter alia*, the comprehensive school system, high expectations of all participants, a well-qualified and committed teaching force that enjoys the trust of society in general and parents in particular (Välijärvi, 2004; Tuovinen, 2008) and the systemic investment in the language acquisition and competence of special educational needs students (Kivirauma & Ruoho, 2007). Less bullish commentators have suggested that an understanding of Finnish educational success requires a 'social and cultural analysis of the place and meaning of education in contemporary Finnish society' (Antikainen, 2005, p. 6), not least because Finnish history has brought about a collective mindset closer to that of the Pacific Rim than that of Europe (Simola, 2005), as well as a strong cultural homogeneity conducive to educational achievement (Välijärvi, 2004).

Other evidence presents a different perspective on Finnish PISA success. First, while Finnish teachers may be well qualified and enjoy high status, neither is a guarantee of teaching quality. Indeed, research has found a tradition of teacher-dominated practice that had changed little in fifty years (Carlgren et al, 2006), prompting a commission of enquiry to advocate a 'diversification of teaching methods' and a shift of emphasis from 'routine skills onto development of thinking' (Kupari, 2004, p. 11). The outcomes included curricular decentralization but, it seemed, little change to teachers' practices (Savola, 2010), as a conservative workforce, uncertain how to adapt to expected changes, continued to teach as it always had (Norris et al, 1996). Today, Finnish teachers continue to subordinate the teaching of mathematical concepts to procedures (Desimone et al, 2005) and rarely, despite decades of systemic encouragement, incorporate mathematical problem solving into their repertoires (Pehkonen, 2009).

| Finnish-speaking Finns | Swedish-speaking Finns | Swedish-speaking Swedes |
|---|---|---|
| 541 | 527 | 494 |

Table III. PISA 2009 mathematics literacy scores for three cultural groups.

Second, claims about Finnish cultural homogeneity mask a significant issue for the Finnish authorities. The largest minority in Finland is the Swedish-speaking community living mainly in the south and west of the country and comprising around 6% of the population. It comprises a disproportionate 24% of the board members of the 50 largest companies listed on the Helsinki stock exchange (Wallgren, 2011) and invests, per capita, three times as much in shares as the majority Finnish-speaking community (Karhunen & Keloharju, 2001). In such circumstances, it would seem reasonable to expect this economically powerful group to perform at least as well as the Finnish-speaking community, particularly as the systemic investment in schools is independent of the language group to which a school belongs (Kupiainen et al, 2009). But this is certainly not the case, as shown in the figures of Table III.

In sum, Finnish mathematics-related PISA success appears to defy simple explanation and to be a consequence of a range of socio-cultural factors possibly unrelated to classroom practice. However, relatively little is known about Flanders, not least because it has failed to attract the attention given to Finland. In this chapter, therefore, I present analyses of two pairs of lessons, one Finnish and one Flemish, each taught on percentages to students in grade 5. In so doing, I aim to examine the extent to which the achievement of Finnish and Flemish students may be explained by the mathematics teaching they experience. The analyses are framed against notions of adaptive expertise, a widely accepted objective of the international reform movement in mathematics education resonant with PISA's mathematics-related objectives and stemming from an awareness that the procedural emphases of traditional mathematics teaching offered inadequate preparation for both further study and a changing labor market (Hiebert, 1999). Traditional mathematics teaching, focused on routine expertise (Hatano & Inagaki, 1986), emphasized facts and skills, which are learned with little understanding and then applied to familiar problems (Lloyd, 1999). Routine experts lack the resources to solve non-routine problems different from the familiar (Martin et al, 2005). In contrast, reform mathematics emphasizes deep conceptual knowledge and connections between concepts as the means by which procedural skills are made sensible (Hiebert, 1999). Learners are encouraged to solve non-routine problems both individually and cooperatively (Lloyd, 1999). Reform mathematics, which encourages students to make links within mathematics itself and between mathematics and the real world (Cady et al, 2007), valorizes adaptive expertise, whereby learners have sufficient and connected underlying understanding to solve non-familiar problems (Heinze et al, 2009). Adaptive experts understand why the procedures they use work, and can modify them or even invent new ones (Hatano & Inagaki, 1986).

## The Project

The data presented in this chapter draw from those collected by the European Union-funded Mathematics Education Traditions of Europe (METE) project, whose broad aim was to examine how teachers conceptualize and present mathematics to students in the age range 10-14 in Flanders, England, Finland, Hungary and Spain. These countries reflect well not only the cultural diversity of Europe but also variation in achievement on both TIMSS and PISA. Project data were video recordings of four or five successive lessons on topics agreed as representative of their countries' curricula. The teachers involved, four per country, were selected against local criteria of effectiveness, thus not only minimizing selection bias but offering the opportunity to understand how a system construes effectiveness. The Finnish teacher, Jari, was one of several engaged in teacher education with the project university who would have had 'to prove they are competent to work with trainee teachers' (Sahlberg, 2011, p. 36). Moreover, the same teacher education department had been nominated by the Finnish authorities as a Centre of Excellence in Mathematics Teacher Education. The Flemish teacher, Emke, was also engaged in teacher education activities at the project university and, having been identified as exemplary, had been videotaped over several successive lessons as part of a government-funded project to create teacher training materials for use by student teachers as part of both cooperative and independent learning. In other words, at least as far as teacher education expectations were concerned, both were viewed as models of good practice.

In all cases, a tripod-mounted camera was placed near the rear of the room, guided by the objective of capturing all utterances made by the teacher and as much board work as possible. Teachers wore radio microphones, while strategically placed telescopic microphones captured as much student-talk as possible. After filming, tapes were digitally compressed and transferred to CD for coding, copying and distribution, with the first two lessons of each sequence being transcribed and translated into English to create subtitled recordings. With respect to analysis, each subtitled video was viewed several times to get a feel for how the lesson played out. Next, an annotated transcript was produced. This meant that with each viewing, notes were inserted into the transcript to document emergent understandings of the discourse being enacted. Thus, the annotated transcript was refined with each viewing of the video. For reasons outlined above, this chapter draws on Finnish and Flemish data and for reasons of space, focuses on a single topic – percentages. However, this is a topic located in the application of mathematics to a world beyond school and is appropriate, therefore, for analyzing the relationship between didactics and PISA success.

## The Teaching of Percentages

The two teachers introduced the topic in very different ways. Jari began by asking, *what do we mean by per cent?* A student volunteered *one hundredth* and Jari wrote this on the board. Students were then invited to write, in equation form, three ways of denoting this, after which a girl, Salla, wrote on the board, with no hesitation, $1/100 = 1\% = 0.01$. Next, Jari asked for examples of one hundredth from everyday life. Several examples were offered, both correct and incorrect, that evoked the single-word response, *yes*, before he announced that percentages could be seen in the labels on alcoholic drinks. Jari then modeled several equations connecting fractions, percentages and decimals. Typically, he sketched a cake and shaded one fifth, which a volunteer declared to be equal to 20%. In response to Jari's questioning, another volunteer asserted that this was equal to *zero point two*. Finally Jari asserted that in order to retain a logical connection between decimals and percentages, it would be better to write decimals as hundredths, and rewrote 0.2 as 0.20.

Jari's introduction is interesting for a number of reasons. First, although he had been informed that this class had not met percentages before, Salla's confidently presented equation implied that students must have experienced a range of informal opportunities to make such links. That said, linking the three forms of representation in this manner appeared to be a clear attempt to make explicit conceptual relationships. Second, during students' offering of real-world examples, Jari responded, irrespective of the relevance of the suggestion, by saying *yes* and nothing else, leaving observers to infer whatever sense they could. Third, emphasizing alcoholic drinks with no reference to issues of health seemed incongruous in the education of 11-year-olds. Fourth, this was the only explicit link to a world beyond the classroom in the sequence of five lessons. Fifth, in instructing students to retain a logical connection by writing 0.2 as 0.20, he indicated an expectation that students would learn rules without understanding. This sense of rote permeated other aspects of the introduction, with Jari generally asking procedural questions demanding numerical answers that went without comment or clarification. Students, it seemed, were left to infer whatever meaning they could from the opportunities they received.

Emke began by asking her students to show the percentage-related artifacts they had brought from home before asking questions to elicit their understanding of the relationships embedded in them. For example, in relation to a yoghurt pot containing 9% fruit, Emke asked, *does this mean there are nine pieces of fruit in the yoghurt? Nine grams? Would it make a difference if the pot were larger or smaller?* A volunteer said it would stay the same. The same process was repeated with various other artifacts such as advertisements cut from newspapers and magazines pertaining to, say, sales in furniture shops or bank loans.

Emke's introduction located the teaching of percentages explicitly in the real world and invited students to think about percentages as representing proportions. It could be argued that embedded in her approach was an allusion to the Dutch realistic mathematics education (RME) tradition, based on problems or tasks that are imaginably real (van den Heuvel-Panhuizen, 2003). Students' artifacts highlighted well the variety of contexts in which percentages are located and made them real, it is argued, for her students. The episode was conceptually focused with no obvious attempt to introduce any procedural matters.

The episodes following the introductions were also very different. Jari posed and solved publicly several questions, based on shading parts of a hundred square, to elicit, for example, the equivalence of five percent, five hundredths and zero point zero five. This was followed by several minutes of individual working before invited students read out answers in equation form. Finally, Jari posed the question, *if you take 40% from a cake, what percentage is left?* He sketched a cake and asked *if 40% has been eaten, how much of the cake should be shaded?* A volunteer suggested splitting it into ten and taking four of the pieces. Jari replied *what if they have too little patience to do that?* Another suggested dividing the cake into five and taking two of the pieces. When prompted, another suggested that two fifths expanded by two would yield four tenths and, if the process is repeated by ten, would give forty hundredths or 40%. Jari agreed and sketched the five portions. *Now, we want to know what is left, how do we do that?* A child volunteered 100 minus 40, after which Jari wrote 100%-40%=60%. A second example was completed similarly before students were invited to continue individually.

Jari's first exercise, based on the hundred square, was an opportunity for students to rehearse the earlier equation, a process supported by his modeling of the first few examples. For example, the dialogue with respect to the first example went as follows:

Jari: How much of the square is red? ... Give it first as a fraction. Aku?
Aku: Five hundredths.
Jari: Yes. What about as a percentage? ... In percentages, Eemeli?
Eemeli: Five percent.
Jari: And as a decimal? ... Noora?
Noora: Zero point fifteen
Jari: Yes.

Throughout this exchange Jari neither offered nor sought explanation. Answers, not solutions, seemed to be the expected norm, although the manner in which the process was undertaken allowed all students to infer a straightforward rule – the number of shaded unit squares provided the answer to each component of the equation – that would provide an unambiguous procedure for getting the correct answer. However, this absence of ambiguity was undermined when Jari introduced the cake problem. In this case, students were taken on a protracted and seemingly irrelevant journey to the conclusion that 60% remained. Admittedly, there was some important work undertaken with respect to equivalences and related procedures, but this seemed unrelated to the goal of determining how much cake remained and left one to ponder what the students were expected to infer from the intervention.

Emke's next phase exploited base ten number blocks. She invited students to take four hundreds and place five cubes in front of each hundred. A short discussion highlighted the arbitrary nature of prepositions and led to the discussion of equivalent expressions like *five for each 100 of four hundred* or *five at each 100 of four hundred*. That is, she alerted her students to the fact, at least as far as their dialect of Dutch was concerned, that sentences beginning *five for each*, *five at each* and *five on each* were mathematically equivalent and logically consistent statements. At this stage, Emke wrote what she called the formulation, '(5 for each 100) of 400', on the board. Several related tasks were completed similarly, including, for example, '(8 on each hundred) of 450', before Emke shifted attention in various ways. First, she asked students to construct concrete models for different formulations. Second, she asked them to stack their blocks rather than lay them side by side. That is, she continued to offer formulations like '(3 per 100) of 400', but expected students to work with a stack rather than with separately placed hundred squares. Third, she showed various concrete representations from which students had to write formulations. Fourth, she drew representations – for example, three squares with two in front of each – and invited students to write the formulation. Finally, she offered, orally, examples like *two for every hundred of three hundred* and asked students to write both diagrams and the formulations. The first lesson closed with her asking students to work in pairs and use the blocks to write formulations for their artifacts.

Throughout this phase of the lesson, which lasted around forty minutes, Emke's attention was on the conceptual basis of percentages. Each task, involving the use of number blocks, was solved individually before being discussed collectively. The various shifts of attention reinforced this conceptual objective alongside Emke's repeated emphases on linguistic matters and the arbitrariness of the preposition. Interestingly, her formulations, all of which were written on the board, trailed the procedure she would introduce in the following lesson. Thus, procedures were beneath the surface of the lesson but subordinated to a deep conceptual knowledge.

Jari's second lesson, after volunteers had read the equations yielded by their homework, began with his drawing three columns on the board, headed *fraction*, *decimal* and *percentage*. He then wrote 1/6 under the fraction heading and asked how it could be converted to a decimal. After Aku had volunteered *one divided by six*, Jari began the division, which he said should be to an accuracy of one hundredth. Students were invited to call out each step, which Jari undertook with no seeking or offering of clarification. Having got as far as 0.166, Jari reminded the class of the desired accuracy and wrote 0.17 under the decimal column. Next, reminding the class that when decimals are written to an accuracy of a hundredth, percentages can be read directly, Jari wrote 17% under the final column. Other examples were managed similarly before he shifted attention by asking how percentages could be changed into fractions. A brief discussion led to the conclusion that 20% was equivalent to 20/100 and, by a process of simplification, 1/5, before the process was repeated by collectively reducing 45% to 9/20. The lesson ended with an exercise based on these procedures.

As with his earlier lesson, Jari's work seemed focused strongly on procedures. The conversion of the fraction to a decimal by division, following a student's suggestion, was managed without reference to the meaning of any of the actions involved. For example, Jari asserted that 0.166 was equivalent to 0.17 to an accuracy of one hundredth. In a similar vein, when converting percentages to fractions, Jari drew on student responses to closed questions to derive the desired answers, but never was any clarification as to the conceptual basis of the procedures or rationales for them sought or offered.

Emke's second lesson began with a discussion, involving several students, focused on summarizing the previous lesson. This was followed by her inviting her students *to imagine that one thousand and three hundred was placed in front of them* and to think about the result of placing two at each hundred. In response to an invitation to formulate, a girl offered '(2 for every 100) of 1300'. Next, Emke asked, *so how many unit cubes are there?* A short discussion led to the conclusion that there were 26, as a consequence of 13 lots of two. Several further examples were resolved similarly before she showed the class *four for every hundred of five hundred* and asked students to write not only the formulation but also the calculation. A volunteer said that 4 for every 100 of 500 equals 20 because 4 times 5 is 20. This was followed by similar examples, including four at every hundred of two hundred and fifty. Finally, she invited her students to complete a worksheet-based exercise before initiating a discussion that led to the conclusion that they had been calculating percentages.

In this phase of her sequence Emke revised explicitly what had occurred during the previous lesson. Although she continued to allow the use of blocks, This was followed by her encouraging her students to imagine them where possible. However, the main thrust of the lesson was her making explicit the calculation implicit in the formulation she had encouraged her students to develop. In so doing, she drew explicit links between the dominant concepts and the subordinated procedure.

### Discussion

It is difficult conveying the complexity of lessons in a short chapter. However, I hope the above offers enough to help the reader see some substantial differences, despite superficial similarities, between the two teachers' practice. In terms of similarities, both teachers seemed prepared to take whatever time was necessary to complete the tasks they had initiated. Both ensured, implicitly at least, that students had time to think and make notes in their books. Also, assuming that 'a mathematical problem presents an objective with no immediate or obvious solution process' (Xenofontos & Andrews, 2012) and, importantly, is not 'a property inherent in a mathematical task' but a 'a particular relationship between the individual and the task' (Schoenfeld, 1985, p. 74), neither teacher encouraged their students to solve problems, but worked in teacher-managed ways that circumvented student decision making. That is, while both Jari and Emke modeled the tasks on which their students worked, neither offered anything that could be construed as non-routine.

Despite such similarities, the data indicate that Jari's practice tends toward routine expertise while Emke's tends toward adaptive (Hatano & Inagaki, 1986). Jari's constant privileging of procedures at the expense of conceptual knowledge – highlighted by implicit allusions to conceptual links between number representations – and the rarity with which he sought or offered clarification during public exchanges point towards rote-learned skills focused on problems amenable to simple and mechanically learned procedures. Emke privileged conceptual knowledge above procedural; the various ways in which she shifted the focus of attention onto the structural relationships between the concrete, the iconic and the symbolic representations of the various formulations were clearly focused on establishing the conceptual knowledge necessary for student acquisition of meaningful procedures. This perspective found resonance in subsequent lessons, in which she introduced a conceptually based procedure whereby students were encouraged to calculate 1% of an amount before multiplying the outcome by the required percentage. Emke did not teach rote procedures but focused on instilling a secure conceptual understanding from which students would always be able to reconstruct, if necessary, procedures from first principles.

In a related vein, the ways in which the two teachers managed public discourse supported these differing learning outcomes. On the one hand, Jari drew extensively on closed questions rarely requiring more than a numerical response. He also drew extensively on students, as with Salla's equation connecting three representations of number with the mathematical competence to provide the intended model from which less competent learners might learn. Moreover, there was no evidence of his construing incorrect student offerings as opportunities for exposing and rectifying underlying misconceptions for the benefit of both individual and collective. Such practices confirm the findings of earlier studies that Finnish mathematics teaching has changed little for decades (Norris et al, 1996; Desimone et al, 2005; Carlgren et al, 2006; Savola, 2010). In short, Jari's practice appeared largely incommensurate with the attainment of adaptive expertise and, by implication, PISA mathematics-related expectations. Therefore, it is not unreasonable to infer that if the practice of effective teachers is unsympathetic to such goals, then the practice of typical teachers would not be sympathetic either. This prompts the following question: if teachers' practice presents an unlikely explanation for Finland's PISA success, then, particularly in the light of relatively poor Finnish attainment with regard to the technical competence expectations of TIMSS, what does explain it?

Explanations found in the literature tend to take one of two forms: those that are located in policy and, essentially, replicable; and those that are located in culture and beyond replication. In terms of replicable explanations, there is evidence that the Finnish curriculum is closely aligned with PISA expectations (Uljens, 2007), particularly when compared with countries like France (Bodin, 2007) and Ireland (Shiel et al, 2007). Also, there is increasing evidence that equitable systems produced not only equitable outcomes but higher overall achievement than inequitable systems

(Wilkinson & Pickett, 2009). Thus, the well-established comprehensive school system (Välijärvi, 2004; Tuovinen, 2008) and the systematic support of special educational needs students (Kivirauma & Ruoho, 2007), both of which reflect commitments to equity, are likely contributors to repeated PISA success. However, significant though these are likely to be, they would not explain the achievement disparity between the Finnish-speaking and Swedish-speaking communities.

Non-replicable factors can be found in the influence of the centuries-old Lutheran expectation that Finns were permitted to marry only if they were able to demonstrate publicly their reading competence (Linnakylä, 2002), a tradition creating a community with a strong appreciation for education (Halinen & Järvinen, 2008; Simola & Rinne, 2011; Niemi, 2012). It is not surprising, therefore, that Finnish students, who are invariably born of literate parents, have a higher engagement with and greater interest in reading than students elsewhere, as evidenced in their borrowing more library books than anyone else (Linnakylä, 2002; Sahlberg, 2007). Such traditions are significant in the light of research showing a strong correlation between Finnish students' reading competence and mathematical word problems (Vilenius-Tuohimaa et al, 2008). Acknowledging Finland's very high PISA reading performance, as well as evidence that when students struggle with reading they tend to struggle with mathematics (Light & DeFries, 1995), and the greater-than-average correlations between Finnish PISA literacy scores and the other PISA content domains (Kjaernsli & Molander, 2003), one can, in sum, construe Finnish PISA success not as a function of didactic excellence but as a complex juxtaposition of replicable systemic policies and non-replicable factors pertaining to the nature of being Finnish in general and the deeply embedded cultural emphasis on reading in particular.

Emke, on the other hand, engaged in authentic bouts of questioning focused on student understanding not only of the conceptual issues under scrutiny but of how they underpinned the procedures being introduced. This was particularly so in the second lesson, when students were expected to explain publicly the reasoning underpinning their answers. Such practice, with its lack of problem solving but strong emphasis on conceptual knowledge, mathematical structures and subordinated procedural skills, is resonant with earlier analyses of Flemish mathematics teaching (Andrews 2009a,b) and is entirely commensurate with the development of adaptive expertise. Thus, if all Flemish teachers privilege such goals, then there may be PISA-related explanations to be found in Flemish classrooms. Fortunately, this speculation finds support in the Flemish mathematics curriculum, which presents the objectives for each content area in three sections – concept formation, procedures, and cohesion between concepts – indicative of a structure conducive to adaptive expertise. However, this prompts the following question: if Flemish didactics are better aligned with PISA expectations than Finnish, why do Flemish students not outperform Finnish students?

As with Finland, it is possible to interpret Flemish PISA success against policy- and culture-related characteristics of Flemish education. For example, Flanders operates a diverse school system with three quarters being government-funded independent and one quarter consisting of public schools (Corten & Dronkers, 2006). The former, typically Catholic, allow parental choice, work within similar curricular frameworks and receive equal state funding (Dronkers & Robert, 2008). Within all secondary schools, although the mathematics curriculum remains similar, students elect to follow one of three tracks – vocational, humanities or classical – which are informally construed as an intellectual hierarchy (Op 't Eynde et al, 2006). Government-funded independent schools produce more proficient readers than public schools (Pustjens et al, 2007; Dronkers & Robert, 2008). Despite this, Flanders produces, in relation to PISA, very competent readers, being consistently the second-ranked European nation behind Finland. However, there is no deep-seated reading tradition, although it is not unlikely that curricular emphases on 'effective cognitive and metacognitive strategies that facilitate text comprehension' (de Corte et al, 2001, p. 532) will have influenced student achievement. Importantly, both school type and student track have been shown to impact on mathematics achievement (Opdenakker et al, 2002; Pustjens et al, 2007). Thus, in negotiating an ethnic heterogeneity not found in Finland, and a school system more likely to perpetuate rather than ameliorate inequity, Flemish teachers, who are viewed positively by Flemings (Verhoeven et al, 2006), appear able to create competent learners in circumstances less conducive than those found in Finland.

Thus, and acknowledging the somewhat speculative nature of the previous paragraphs, the successes of Finland and Flanders seem attributable to a variety of replicable and non-replicable characteristics of their respective cultures. Finnish PISA success appears to be a consequence of non-replicable cultural factors associated with what it is to be a Finn and replicable policies linked to the maintenance of social equity. Flemish PISA success, located in policies unlikely to foster equity, seems based on something missing in Finnish classrooms – a didactic tradition conducive to the acquisition of adaptive expertise.

## Acknowledgements

The METE project team acknowledges the generous support of the European Union, Socrates Action 6.1 Programme Code 2002-5048.

## References

Adams, Raymond (2003) Response to 'Cautions on OECD's Recent Educational Survey (PISA)', *Oxford Review of Education*, 29(3), 377-389.

Andrews, Paul (2009a) Comparative Studies of Mathematics Teachers' Observable Learning Objectives: validating low inference codes, *Educational Studies in Mathematics*, 71(2), 97-122.

Andrews, Paul (2009b) Mathematics Teachers' Didactic Strategies: examining the comparative potential of low inference generic descriptors, *Comparative Education Review*, 53(4), 559-581.

Antikainen, Ari (2005) Introduction: the construction of a learning society, in Ari Antikainen (Ed.) *Transforming a Learning Society: the case of Finland*, pp. 5-21. Berne: Peter Lang.

Astala, Kari, Kivelä, Simo, Koskela, Pekka, Martio, Olli, Näätänen, Marjatta & Tarvainen, Kyösti (2006) The PISA Survey Tells Only a Partial Truth of Finnish Children's Mathematical Skills, *Matilde*, 29, 9.

Bodin, Antoine (2007) 'What Does PISA Really Assess? What Does it Not? A French View', in Stefan Hopmann, Gertrude Brinek & Martin Retzl (Eds) *PISA According to PISA: does PISA keep what it promises?*, pp. 21-55. Vienna: LIT Verlag.

Cady, JoAnn, Meier, Sherry & Lubinski, Cheryl (2007) The Mathematical Tale of Two Teachers: a longitudinal study relating mathematics instructional practices to level of intellectual development, *Mathematics Education Research Journal*, 18(1), 3-26.

Carlgren, Ingrid, Klette, Kirsti, Mýrdal, Sigurjón, Schnack, Karsten & Simola, Hannu (2006) Changes in Nordic Teaching Practices: from individualised teaching to the teaching of individuals, *Scandinavian Journal of Educational Research*, 50(3), 301-326.

Corten, Rense & Dronkers, Jaap (2006) School Achievement of Pupils from the Lower Strata in Public, Private Government-dependent and Private Government-independent Schools: a cross-national test of the Coleman-Hoffer thesis, *Educational Research and Evaluation*, 12(2), 179-208.

Crace, John (2003) Heaven and Helsinki, *Guardian*, 16 September.

de Corte, Erik, Verschaffel, Lieven & van de Ven, An (2001) Improving Text Comprehension Strategies in Upper Primary School Children: a design experiment, *British Journal of Educational Psychology*, 71(4), 531-559.

de Meyer, Inge (2008) *Science Competencies for the Future in Flanders: the first results from PISA 2006*. Ghent: University of Ghent.

de Meyer, Inge, de Vos, Hilde & van de Poele, Luc (2002) *Worldwide Learning at Age 15: first results from PISA 2000*. Ghent: University of Ghent.

de Meyer, Inge, Pauly, Jan & van de Poele, Luc (2005) *Learning for Tomorrow's Problems: first results from PISA 2003*. Ghent: University of Ghent.

de Meyer, Inge, & Warlop, Nele (2010) *Leesvaardigheid van 15-jarigen in Vlaanderen: De eerste resultaten van PISA 2009*. Ghent: University of Ghent.

Desimone, Laura, Smith, Thomas, Baker, David & Ueno, Koji (2005) Assessing Barriers to the Reform of US Mathematics Instruction from an International Perspective, *American Educational Research Journal*, 42(3), 501-535.

Dronkers, Jaap & Robert, Peter (2008) Differences in Scholastic Achievement of Public, Private Government-dependent, and Private Independent Schools, *Educational Policy*, 22(4), 541-577.

Halinen, Irmeli & Järvinen, Ritva (2008) Towards Inclusive Education: the case of Finland, *Prospects*, 38(1), 77-97.

Hatano, Giyoo & Inagaki, Kayoko (1986) Two Courses of Expertise, in Harold Stevenson, Hiroshi Azuma & Kenji Hakuta (Eds) *Child Development and Education in Japan*, pp. 262-272. New York: Freeman.

Heinze, Aiso, Star, Jon & Verschaffel, Lieven (2009) Flexible and Adaptive Use of Strategies and Representations in Mathematics Education, *ZDM*, 41(5), 535-540.

Hiebert, James (1999) Relationships Between Research and the NCTM Standards, *Journal for Research in Mathematics Education*, 30(1), 3-19.

Howie, Sarah & Plomp, Tjeerd (2005) TIMSS – Mathematics Findings from National and International Perspectives: in search of explanations, *Educational Research and Evaluation*, 11(2), 101-106.

Karhunen, Jussi & Keloharju, Matti (2001) Shareownership in Finland 2000, *Liiketaloudellinen Aikakauskirja* [Finnish Journal of Business Economics], 2, 188-226.

Kivirauma, Joel & Ruoho, Kari (2007) Excellence through Special Education? Lessons from the Finnish School Reform, *International Review of Education*, 53(3), 283-302.

Kjaernsli, Marit & Molander, Bengt-Olov (2003) Scientific Literacy: content knowledge and process skills, in Svein Lie, Pirjo Linnakylä and Astrid Roe (Eds) *Northern Lights on PISA. Unity and Diversity in the Nordic Countries in PISA 2000*, pp. 63-70. Oslo: University of Oslo, Department of Teacher Education and School Development.

Kupari, Pekka (2004) Recent Developments in Finnish Mathematics Education, *Nordic Studies in Mathematics Education*, 9(2), 7-20.

Kupiainen, Sirkku, Hautamäki, Jarkko & Karjalainen, Tommi (2009) *The Finnish Education System and PISA*. Helsinki: Helsinki University and Ministry of Education, Finland.

Light, Jacquelyn Gillis & DeFries, John (1995) Comorbidity of Reading and Mathematics Disabilities, *Journal of Learning Disabilities*, 28(2), 96-106.

Linnakylä, Pirjo (2002) Reading in Finland, in Constantinos Papanastasiou and Victor Froese (Eds) *Reading Literacy in 14 Countries*. Lefkosia: University of Cyprus Press.

Lloyd, Gwendolyn (1999) Two Teachers' Conceptions of a Reform-oriented Curriculum: implications for mathematics teacher development, *Journal of Mathematics Teacher Education*, 2(3), 227-252.

Malaty, George (2010) Mathematics and Mathematics Education Development in Finland: the impact of curriculum changes on IEA, IMO and PISA results. Paper presented at the 10th International Conference of the Mathematics Education into the 21st Century Project, 11-17 September, at Dresden University of Applied Sciences, Dresden, Germany.

Martin, Taylor, Rayne, Karen, Kemp, Nate, Hart, Jack & Diller, Kenneth (2005) Teaching for Adaptive Expertise in Biomedical Engineering Ethics, *Science and Engineering Ethics*, 11(2), 257-276.

Niemi, Hannele (2012) The Societal Factors Contributing to Education and Schooling in Finland, in Hannele Niemi, Auli Toom and Arto Kallioniemi (Eds) *Miracle of Education: the principles and practices of teaching and learning in Finnish schools*, pp. 19-38. Rotterdam: Sense.

Norris, Nigel, Asplund, Rita, MacDonald, Barry, Schostak, John & Zamorski, Barbara (1996) *An Independent Evaluation of Comprehensive Curriculum Reform in Finland*. Helsinki: National Board of Education.

Opdenakker, Marie-Christine, van Damme, Jan, de Fraine, Bieke, van Landeghem, Georges & Onghena, Patrick (2002) The Effect of Schools and Classes on Mathematics Achievement, *School Effectiveness and School Improvement*, 13(4), 399-427.

Op 't Eynde, Peter, de Corte, Erik & Verschaffel, Lieven (2006) Beliefs and Metacognition: an analysis of junior-high students' mathematics-related beliefs, in Annemie Desoete & Marcel Veenman (Eds) *Metacognition in Mathematics Education*, pp. 83-101. New York: Nova Science.

Pehkonen, Erkki (2009) How Finns Learn Mathematics: what is the influence of 25 years of research in mathematics education?' In , Madik Lepis (Ed.) *Teaching Mathematics: retrospectives and perspectives*, pp. 71-101. Tallinn, Estonia: Tallinn University, Institute of Mathematics and Natural Sciences.

Pustjens, Heidi, van de Gaer, Eva, van Damme, Jan, Onghena, Patrick & van Landeghem, Georges (2007) The Short-term and the Long-term Effect of Primary Schools and Classes on Mathematics and Language Achievement Scores, *British Educational Research Journal*, 33(3), 419-440.

Sahlberg, Pasi (2007) Education Policies for Raising Student Learning: the Finnish approach, *Journal of Education Policy*, 22(2), 147-171.

Sahlberg, Pasi (2011) The Fourth Way of Finland, *Journal of Educational Change*, 12(2), 173-185.

Savola, Lasse (2010) Comparison of the Classroom Practices of Finnish and Icelandic Mathematics Teachers, *Journal of Mathematics Education at Teachers College*, 1 (Fall-Winter), 7-13.

Schoenfeld, Alan (1985) *Mathematical Problem Solving*. Orlando, FL: Academic Press.

Shiel, Gerry, Perkins, Rachel, Close, Seán & Oldham, Elizabeth (2007) *PISA Mathematics: a teacher's guide*. Dublin: Department of Education and Science.

Simola, Hannu (2005) The Finnish Miracle of PISA: historical and sociological remarks on teaching and teacher education, *Comparative Education*, 41(4), 455-470.

Simola, Hannu & Rinne, Risto (2011) Education Policies and Contingency: belief, status and trust behind the Finnish PISA miracle, in Miguel A. Pereyra, Hans-Georg Kotthoff & Robert Cowen (Eds) *PISA Under Examination*, pp. 225-244. Rotterdam: Sense.

Tarvainen, Kyösti & Kivelä, Simo (2006) Severe Shortcomings in Finnish Mathematics Skills, *Matilde*, 29, 10.

Tuovinen, Juhani E. (2008) Learning the Craft of Teaching and Learning from World's Best Practice: the case of Finland, in Dennis McInerney & Gregory Liem, *Teaching and Learning: international best practice*, pp. 51-77. Charlotte, NC: Information Age Publishing.

Uljens, Michael (2007) The Hidden Curriculum of PISA: the promotion of neo-liberal policy by educational assessment, in Stefan Thomas Hopmann, Gertrude Brinek & Martin Retzl (Eds) *PISA According to PISA: does PISA keep what it promises?*, pp. 295-303. Vienna: LIT Verlag.

Välijärvi, Jouni (2004) The System and How Does it Work some curricular and pedagogical characteristics of the Finnish comprehensive school, *Education Journal*, 32(1), 31-55.

van den Heuvel-Panhuizen, Marja (2003) The Didactical Use of Models in Realistic Mathematics Education: an example from a longitudinal trajectory on percentage, *Educational Studies in Mathematics*, 54(1), 9-35.

Verhoeven, Jef, Aelterman, Antonia, Rots, Isabel & Buvens, Ina (2006) Public Perceptions of Teachers' Status in Flanders, *Teachers and Teaching: theory and practice*, 12(4), 479-500.

Vilenius-Tuohimaa, Maria, Piia, Aunola, Kaisa & Nurmi, Jari-Erik (2008) The Association Between Mathematical Word Problems and Reading Comprehension, *Educational Psychology: an international journal of experimental educational psychology*, 28(4), 409-426.

Wallgren, Dag (2011) Swedish-speaking Finns have Strong Presence in Major Corporations, *Helsingin Sanomat International Edition*, 28 August.

Wilkinson, Richard & Pickett, Kate (2009) *The Spirit Level*. London: Allen Lane.

Xenofontos, Constantinos & Andrews, Paul (2012) Prospective Teachers' Beliefs about Problem-solving: Cypriot and English cultural constructions, *Research in Mathematics Education*, 14(1), 69-85.

CHAPTER 5

# Globalization and the Emergence of an Audit Culture: PISA and the search for 'best practices' and magic bullets

## DAVID H. KAMENS

ABSTRACT This chapter argues that national societies are increasingly perceived as open systems as globalization has intensified. As a result, educational systems are losing their national distinctiveness as bounded systems and products of unique national histories. Instead they are viewed as being comparable on many important dimensions. As a result, educators are no longer accused of trying to compare apples with oranges when they announce the recent results of PISA or TIMSS achievement tests. On many dimensions they thus become comparable in the minds of politicians and educators. And furthermore, in the face of global economic, political and cultural competition they are expected to produce outcomes that give their nations a competitive advantage (e.g. high levels of literacy and numeracy). This emerging 'horse race' mentality about educational progress and success has the effect of creating standardized outcomes that all systems are supposed to aspire to. This increases the sense that they can and should be comparable on important goals. While narrowing the goals of education, such competitive processes have given rise to an international audit culture in which comparing national education systems is now a legitimate enterprise in many parts of the world.

We should be looking beyond our shores to learn the lessons from others who have faced similar problems. (Prime Minister David Cameron of the UK, discussing the London riots and policing efforts in the House of Commons, *The New Yorker*, 9 January 2012, p. 20)

*David H. Kamens*

## Introduction

The purpose of this chapter is to argue that world society has spawned an assessment culture that is spreading across nation-states and regions. As more countries become part of the network of global society, this culture spreads rapidly. Thus assessments of all kinds are becoming common in education across the world as schools and universities become defined as organizational actors responsible for achieving specific goals and purposes (see Krucken & Meier, 2006). This change is a relatively new phenomenon but it is becoming increasingly hard to resist. As schools are linked by this global rationalizing drive to set national development goals, they are under heavy pressure to become open systems rather than communities with distinctive 'sagas' and missions (see Clark, 1972). Innovation and accountability become the organizational mantras. It is not surprising, then, that an 'audit culture' emerged in the latter part of the twentieth century, and that it is diffusing quickly. No sector is immune, particularly those that are viewed as critical for national success. And education is seen as one of the most important in the high-stakes international competition for economic and political power (see Baker & LeTendre, 2006, pp. 154ff.).

This phenomenon engulfs all kinds of social units from individuals to families, organizations and nation-states. As all these entities become defined as rational actors with broad responsibilities for national development, assessing their success and failure becomes a compelling, and irresistible, feature of world culture. World league tables are now a thriving enterprise as the frenzy of evaluation spreads. Val Rust (2011) has found 13 different league tables for ranking world-class universities; the *Economist* publishes a yearly international ranking of the top business schools; Mo Ibrahim's Foundation rates 53 African governments on their relative effectiveness and success; and Transparency International ranks 150 countries on their relative level of corruption.

In education, testing and transparency is no longer a luxury, reserved for the rich OECD countries. Evaluation is a requirement for all, rich and poor. In this new environment, accountability and transparency are believed to be the routes to progress and social development. This fact is brought home by the data in Tables I and II. They show the growing use of different kinds of assessments by *low-income* countries from 1960 to 2009. Table I shows the growth over time of all kinds of assessment, with national assessments showing the most spectacular growth among these countries. The marginals tell us that even high-stakes international testing is growing among these countries. There is more international achievement testing, and more low-income countries are participating. In the 1960-1989 decades the *only* assessments available were high-stakes international achievement tests; but this changes in later ones. By 2009 countries had a variety of choices. Thus, in 2009 only 29% of the countries were involved in international testing. However, 61.95% were doing national assessments. Low-income countries opted overwhelmingly for *national assessments* of their own students as the vehicle for making school systems and teachers more accountable (see Kamens & Benavot, 2011).

| Period | International | Regional | National |
|--------|-------------|----------|----------|
| 1960-1989 | 100% (43) | 0 (0) | 0 (0) |
| 1990-1999 | 20.6% (66) | 15% (49) | 64% (205) |
| 2000-2009 | 29% (152) | 8.9% (47) | 61.9% (324) |

Total *n* of tests = 886.

Table I. Percentage of total tests during each period
that are international, regional or national assessments.

Table II shows the regional distribution of the use of various kinds of assessments. The data suggest three points about the distribution of evaluation technologies. First, the relatively richer countries use the OECD as a reference group and are more likely to use high-stakes international achievement tests like PISA and TIMSS as vehicles for national assessment. The Arab countries, for example, are much more likely to participate in international testing than sub-Saharan Africa (47.6% vs. 13%). Second, countries that belong to regional associations in Africa and Latin America are more likely to use *regional* assessment and comparison as an assessment technique. Third, the poorest countries that are not attached to regional associations of nations overwhelmingly opt to use *national* assessments. This spares them the embarrassment and political humiliation of comparing themselves with richer countries with more educated populations. It may also give them more national sovereignty and control over their own educational systems. And such assessments are cheaper and easier to administer, since they may be tied to the end of particular schooling cycles.

| Region | International % | Regional % | National % |
|--------|---------------|-----------|-----------|
| Sub-Saharan Africa (45) | 13.0 | 60.0 | 51.0 |
| Arab States (21) | 47.6 | 9.5 | 57.0 |
| East Asia & Pacific (30) | 30.0 | 0 | 60.0 |
| South and West Asia (10) | 20.0 | 0 | 40.0 |
| Latin America and Caribbean (34) | 47.0 | 53.0 | 73.5 |
| Central & Eastern Europe & Central Asia (9) | 77.7 | 0 | 33.0 |

*n* of countries = 151.
Total number of tests (50) (47) (85).

Table II. Percentage of developing countries in each world
region conducting at least one of three types of learning assessment.

The overwhelming point of these data is to show that testing and evaluation are growing – even among the poorest countries in the world. While low-income countries use national and regional assessments rather than international high-stakes testing to assess performance, this movement indicates that low-income countries, like others, are under the gun to establish some kind of accountability of their educational systems. Their creditors, their elites, and parents are all demanding some measure of transparency.

These data raise the question of how this culture of assessment emerged so quickly and spread so fast. This is a question I turn to in the next section.

## Changing Intellectual Models in the Post-1970s World

A major change in international discourse is the growing concern about governance, transparency and accountability that intensified globalization has produced (see Drori et al, 2006, pp. 91ff.). This trend has political and cultural as well as economic sources. As democratization has spread, these concerns now have an urgency that was previously lacking. And they center around two issues: (1) economic efficiency and social development; and (2) democratic responsiveness and accountability. In both these scenarios corruption and lack of transparency are seen as major obstacles to development. Given the critical importance of education in modern discourses on social development, the accountability and comparative effectiveness of national educational systems have taken on an urgency that they did not have in the early days of national achievement testing in the 1960s.

In the early years of the International Association for the Evaluation of Educational Achievement (IEA, founded in 1958), Torsten Husén and his colleagues viewed national education systems as distinctive, historic systems. In their view they were like apples and oranges: non-comparable. Thus the early math and science testing regimes were *not* conducted with the idea of locating 'best practice' models that produced high achievement. They were designed with more pragmatic policy considerations at the fore. In its memoriam for Torsten Husén, the IEA secretariat notes:

> One of the prime motivations for conducting the First International Mathematics Study was to produce empirical evidence relative to the question of whether newly implemented comprehensive schools systems in various European countries were having a negative effect on educational achievement, when compared with more traditional and selective systems of secondary education. Issues specific to mathematics education were of secondary interest to the leaders of this first study. (IEA Secretariat, 2009; see also Postlethwaite, 2000)

With the pressure for expanded enrollments in democratizing societies, this was one model that was being considered in Europe. Husen himself thought that such a system might undermine achievement. While Europe took a different direction in expanding its secondary educational system, this was one of the concerns that underlay the first IEA studies (see Kamens et al, 1997).

The initial IEA research did accept the premise that comparison between different educational systems was possible. But it was aimed at macro questions such as the effects of comprehensive education in Sweden, Germany and England, and the effects of tracking on the utilization of talent for society (see Postlethwaite, 2000, pp. 3, 4). Postlethwaite (2000, p. 5) observes that in the late 1950s Husen became convinced that research in education was relevant to policy but that it was only useful for elucidating *macro* problems – for example, the effects of early testing on social bias in selection for advanced schooling. It was, he believed, of little use in solving *micro* problems, such as how the teacher should optimally go about his or her tasks in the classroom. This sophisticated view of policy suggests that imitating other countries' educational policies at the system level might be useful – for example, comprehensive vs. tracked secondary school systems or early vs. late selection for advanced education. But it cast doubt on the utility of trying to copy specific kinds of micro educational practices – for example, classroom practices. While the distinction is not entirely clear-cut in all cases, it is clear that Husen and the IEA did not imagine that they could pick and choose 'best practices' at the meso and micro level to affect particular outcomes that policy makers wanted to alter.

This model of discourse lasted up through the 1970s. A dominant intellectual image of national education systems continued to be one of tightly bounded systems, filled with status groups and organizational precedents that produced inertia and resistance to planned innovation and organizational design. Similar perspectives prevailed in other disciplines like organizational theory (see Scott, 2001). From this viewpoint the idea of copying 'best practices' elsewhere makes no sense. The only reasonable innovation is that produced by slow evolutionary change within a given educational community. In this perspective schools are 'natural systems' with an organic structure. They are also viewed as relatively closed systems. Much research in education still retains this flavor (see Goodson, 2004). In this older scenario, characteristic of the early IEA, searching for models of 'best practices' makes little sense. If the structures of departments, schools, universities and national educational systems are largely unique historical products, what could possibly be gained by comparative assessment? Or even organizational assessments?

As Heinz Meyer (personal communication) has pointed out, this view was rooted in a 'deep belief in and respect for national sovereignty and the plurality of excellences represented by the various national educational systems. All were seen as having unique historical trajectories and cultural commitments.' In this world view the student outcomes of these systems were also seen as distinctive. France produced students who had been immersed in Cartesian logic and philosophy. This education corresponded to the ideal of the 'rational citizen' of the Republic, detached from religion and other bonds. It was also seen as the necessary education for those who were to become part of the French state, whose job was to guide society on a rational path of enlightenment. In England students were versed in conservative political philosophy, economics and history. This was the education that corresponded to the 'British gentlemanly ideal'. In this world view curricula represented national values as well as political compromises based on political demands for loyalty and economic demands. Schooling was a cultural project of the *nation*, aimed at reproducing cultural cohesion and community. And the concept of 'student' was also linked to national traditions of what such students were to become in adult life.

Globalization and the rise of the EU changed this perspective in the post-1970s (see Pizmony-Levy, 2012). In the new model, schooling is a cultural project of *world* society, built around the values of international capitalism, human rights and political democratization. Thus these values are political compromises between the universal values of world capitalism and democratization that are themselves in conflict, and political expediency flowing from the demands of nation-states and factions within them. States still want to retain the loyalty of citizens and to remain cohesive political communities in the midst of a global economy and an international political system.

In the new models based on 'human capital' theory, human rights theories and new models of nationhood, and new social science models of 'rational organizations', the old assumptions about the uniqueness of national traditions and even the value of national sovereignty are discarded. In this view, 'a school is a school is a school', to paraphrase Gertrude Stein. In some cases uniqueness may even be defined as 'backwardness' – for example, the lack of foreign language instruction in much of the American curriculum. Global capitalism, democratization and world culture have undermined the notion of nation-states as key actors. In much social science thinking they are now part of an inter-dependent global world. There are of course power differences, but no one nation-state is able to control either international capital or the cultural flows of ideas, innovations and models of appropriate behavior of states. In this world smaller countries often become international models. Finland, for example, is one of the current world models of an effective educational system. New Zealand is the model for transparent government. And Eastern Europe became the model for the peaceful use of social movements to democratize autocratic states.

These models of society rest for their plausibility on the spread of capitalism, science, bureaucracy and democracy across the globe (Collins, 1999). These institutions are now prevalent throughout the globe, whereas in the nineteenth century they were present primarily in the West. The spread of these formerly western institutions across world society have undermined the idea that schools, national educational systems and nation-states are bounded entities that are highly inert and path dependent. Instead, in new intellectual models, all such systems are imagined to be open ones, unified around collective, universal goals and capable of developing rational organization to achieve desired purposes (see Krucken & Meier, 2006, on universities). Both the goals and the institutional recipes for achieving them have become highly codified in world culture. The idea of highly unique, organizational 'sagas', missions and historically distinctive systems fades under this onslaught (see Clark, 1972). Nationalism itself becomes 'tamed', and the language of national 'exceptionalisms' becomes muted. National sovereignty and international mutual inter-dependence now co-exist.

The end result of these changes is that education in these views is no longer seen as a *national* cultural project. Correspondingly, the role of history, as actor and cause, declines in more recent discourse. The uniqueness of national educational systems is now a possible source of new models, not an artifact of national sovereignty to be celebrated and reified. In this vein, Torsten Husén is reported to have asked: 'Why don't we test for academic achievement internationally? The *world* could be our laboratory' (Heyneman & Lee, 2012, p. 1). From this perspective, rational planning and international borrowing of 'best practices' become favored activities. International benchmarking also becomes significant as a way to improve organizational functioning.

### Methodological Implications

In the post-1970s world the idea that educational systems are unique like apples vs. oranges also breaks down. Under the onslaught of social science models the idea has gained traction that comparison is not only possible, but also imperative. That in fact became the World Bank's motto in the post-1980s: 'examine, assess, and compare' (see Kamens & McNeely, 2010). Anyone who has seen the film of Andreas Schleicher evangelically describing the virtues of PISA's program of comparative assessment can see how far this change in discourse has come (see http://www.OECD/PISA). The search for 'best practices' is now an international mantra with extraordinary legitimacy and funding. The OECD secretariat is leading and funding the search, so much so that with biting irony Heinz Meyer described the OECD as an un-elected 'world ministry of education' (PISA Conference, 3 September 2011).

One immediate result of this new way of thinking is that there has been a shift from small samples to the use of large samples. Similarly, the mode of analysis has changed from a case-study methodology to statistical analyses at a number of analytical levels: analysis of country differences; community and school variation; the effects of peer groups and classroom dynamics; and the effects of individual student differences. To illustrate, the first IEA study of mathematics in 1964 had 12 cases. Starting in the 1990s, these numbers balloon upwards. The 1990 reading study had a sample of 32 and the third TMSS study of science and mathematics in 1994-95 had 45 countries in its sample (Heyneman & Lee, 2012, pp. 33ff.). And the number keeps getting bigger, even though Andreas Schleicher of the OECD claims that they do not have an interest in adding more Third World countries to the samples.

In the new world ushered in by globalization, facilitated by the spread of social science theorizing and statistical models, comparison is viewed as not only possible but required for advancing knowledge. In this line of thinking apples and oranges can, of course, be compared. Their comparative levels of acidity can be measured, for instance. Similarly, school systems can be compared in a variety of ways, which PISA and others have done – for example, the level of pre-school preparation of students; the administrative autonomy of schools; the level of training and selectivity of faculty and students, etc. And one can combine these characteristics to develop typologies of the 'best' and 'worst' school systems. PISA is in fact a leading practitioner of this kind of comparison. In addition, its studies create an equivalent of world league tables of the relative ranking of national school systems.

If one can compare school systems in terms of their characteristics and outcomes, the idea of borrowing features from the 'best' systems is a natural corollary. This has become the major discourse of post-1980s world society. Thus the march is on for comparative assessment and is joined by the search for the best models and practices that ensure high achievement and other desired outcomes.

### The European Union as a Mirror

This process has been facilitated by the rise of the EU as an exclusive club and as a major reference group for many aspiring countries, particularly in Eastern Europe, Central Asia and the Arab World in North Africa and the Middle East. It became an important mirror and benchmark for countries across the world. This is one reason that so many of these countries were eager to join in the international achievement tests of the 1980s and 1990s. They wanted the prestige of competing and benchmarking themselves against the exclusive club of rich countries represented by the OECD (Stephen Heyneman, personal communication). This change has led PISA and TIMSS, the successors to the IEA studies, to shift from a Eurocentric focus to an international one. Until recently, the 'best' models have in fact come from Asia in these studies. Only recently has a European 'white knight' been discovered: Finland. And visitors are flocking to see it first-hand.

Rosenmund's (2006, p. 175) cross-sectional analysis of national education reports documents this latest shift in tone. Countries now emphasize the role of education in helping them to adapt to external change. The old focus on personnel training for a presumed static occupational structure or on five-year industrial plans is gone. In addition, the reports also describe the importance of producing cosmopolitan individuals who can help nations adjust to the rapid pace of change ushered in by economic and political globalization. Thus the comparative search is on for those systems that can produce the following kinds of students: good patriots of the nation; global citizens attuned to the larger world; those with cognitive flexibility to adapt to changing economies and to political democracy; and those who are open to diversity at home and abroad.

As a result of this change in discourse, international benchmarking has become a highly legitimate activity. Once an 'audit culture' is established, it legitimates all kinds of assessment activity. Thus one would expect all varieties of assessment to flourish. And empirically we see some evidence of this happening.

## The Rising Importance of the OECD as a Mirror for Outsiders

Network theory has long noted the importance of ties between social units as conduits for the flow of innovation and cultural invention. As Meyer (2009, pp. 36-67) has noted, the very weakness of contemporary world society structure makes the system a very effective channel for the flow of information and cultural innovation. This is a macro-level instance of the idea in network theory of the strength of weak ties. Innovation can spread quickly through world society because there is no central authority that can control either the flow of borrowing or the pace of invention.

In addition, globalization has also altered the international landscape. It has been a stimulus for nations to organize with others into blocks that offer various forms of self-protection and competitive advantage in a variety of domains. This process has lent increased prominence and visibility to members of the OECD, the rich nations club. As other nations have emerged as global economic-political successes, they too get added to the list of world models of economic and political success. As such, these nations are now important role models for other countries in the minds of their educated elite. Their institutions become the mirrors that less successful societies use to judge their own progress in a wide variety of domains – for example, education, economic success, human rights achievements, successful democratization, the institutionalization of the rule of law, health standards, etc.

In the process, the old 'developing country ghetto' of the 1960s and 1970s broke down. Russia, Indonesia, India, China, Brazil, South Africa and many more joined the ranks of the OECD admirers' club. This new group included the 27 countries of Europe and Central Asia, not just Russia. These 'developing' countries began to measure their success in national development against the OECD countries. Hence the demand for participation in OECD comparisons rose.

The transformations in Eastern Europe and the former Soviet Union also played a role in this process. Similarly, emerging middle-income countries (South Africa, India, Brazil, China and Indonesia) began to focus their eyes on the OECD. One instance of this change is the fact that the participation of the OECD countries in educational testing lured many of these other countries in to participating. Being able to compete against the OECD block of countries was a sufficient incentive to get many of these countries to participate, regardless of any material rewards they might get out of it (personal communication, Stephen Heyneman). The prestige of being included among the 'great' powers was incentive enough.

This competition between the OECD countries and emerging ones helped transform assessment and benchmarking into a badge of good citizenship. It became a signal to others that the given country and its elite were ready to participate in standard rituals of nationhood in an international community in which assessment had become a major ritual of rationality. To assess in this new international climate became an activity that defined a nation-state as a responsible member of world society.

### Funding Assessment

Groups like the OECD and the EU also acted as funders of international organizations and of assessment studies. In the early days of testing, the IEA and UNESCO played important roles in getting funding for the early science, math, language and civics studies. But these were relatively small-scale, low-budget enterprises compared with the later ones of TIMSS and PISA. This changed in the 1990s. Then the World Bank became interested in assessment (see Lockheed & Verspoor, 1990). It sponsored the World Education Indictor project and helped the international benchmarking project along. The World Education Indicator project started in 1997 with 12 initial countries. This project (WEI) financed UNESCO and the countries that had expressed an interest in being included in the OECD indictors. This opened the door considerably for international participation. Then when the Program for International Student Assessment (PISA, formed in 1997) was first initiated, the OECD invited 'co-operating' (non-OECD) countries to participate, on the advice of the Board of International and Comparative Studies in Education of the National Science Foundation. All the WEI countries, and many others, expressed an interest and, following precedent, the World Bank as well as other aid agencies helped make financing possible (Stephen Heyneman, personal communication). At the present time the OECD countries finance PISA with lavish budgets for each round of assessment.

In addition, the OECD countries provide networks of professionals and support a variety of NGOs involved in comparative education and assessment. These are important consultant groups for developing countries that wish to do assessment. They also provide training for local professionals in the developing world. For example, the SACMEQ (the Southern and Eastern Africa Consortium for Monitoring Educational Quality) website lists 11 non-member countries that partner with them. Table III lists the countries and external professionals who work alongside local professionals to monitor education in the member countries.

| Country | External professionals |
|---------|------------------------|
| Argentina | David Andrich |
| Australia | Dhurumbeer Kulpoo |
| France | Frank van Cappelle |
| Japan | Joseph Chimombo |
| Kenya | Juliana Nzomo |
| Malawi | Kenneth Ross |
| Mauritius | Laura Paviot |
| Netherlands | Linda Zuze |
| South Africa | Mioko Saito |
| United Kingdom | Neville Postlethwaite |
| Zimbabwe | Patrick Griffin |
| | Saul Murimba |
| | Servaas van der Berg |
| | Stéphanie Dolata |

Table III. Non-member and member partner countries: external professionals: 'Friends of SACMEQ'.

The SACMEQ consortium was founded in 1995 with the help of financial support from the government of the Netherlands. It includes 15 member countries. The non-member countries give support by making available the professionals listed in column 2 of Table III, who are officially described as the 'friends' of SACMEQ. Their biographies are also listed on the website to show their expertise and experience regarding the issues of concern to the consortium and its members. Those on the list are all experts in various fields relevant to education, and advise SACMEQ professionals on the design and methodology of studies the group decides to pursue. Such regional associations represent the likely future. They too will become promoters and carriers of the audit culture.

### The Rising Supply of Scholars and Professionals and New Social Science Models

In the early days of assessment one of the problems was the lack of trained personnel capable of designing and carrying out large-scale testing. This is still a problem in many parts of the world. In Latin America, for example, there is an absolute dearth of trained statisticians, psychometricians and methodologists (Gilbert Valverde, personal communication). But the growth of universities and enrollments worldwide since the 1980s has helped remedy this problem. It produced a huge corps of scholars that were not available in the 1970s (see Schofer & Meyer, 2005; Heyneman, personal communication). Since in-country experts are paid at locally prevailing salaries, this development also makes it cheaper for countries to do evaluation studies.

In addition, this growth curve in tertiary education has also created a large corps of external experts who are available to help local ministries of education. They are both experts and carriers of the culture of assessment. While they are expensive because of their developed-world economies, their salaries are often paid by partnering countries or international organizations. This further reduces the costs of evaluation.

The existence of these networks of experts has several additional consequences that further the likelihood of assessment. In his study of national efforts at assessment, Pizmony-Levy (2012) has found in interviews with officials that local experts 'push' their countries to establish assessment studies. Like scholars elsewhere, once trained, they offer a stream of solutions that are waiting for an appropriate stream of problems. Not surprisingly, they discover them. There are also benefits from methodological transfers that encourage more testing. After the 1970s the presence of trained professionals has become an incentive to do assessments. Competent scholars who have had experience participating in one or another of these efforts can now be found in far-flung places where they did not exist 20 years ago.

Pizmony-Levy's (2012) interview data also suggest that professionals develop rationales that create incentives for more testing. International and local professionals perceive that one benefit of participating in international assessments is 'capacity building'. His interview data show that actors at global and local levels make strong efforts to justify short cycles of assessments (every 3 to 4 to 5 years rather than once a decade) and try to get such shorter cycles built into national policy regimes. The point they make is that short cycles keep the organizational structure of evaluation experts and personnel stable and save on training costs and start-up expenses. Thus the professional perspective of local scholars and experts leads them to establish economic and logistic rationales for an institutionalized system of evaluation.

The same process is likely to harness the professional interests of external experts in alliance with local professionals. Both have professional perspectives that make a persuasive case for instituting more assessment and evaluation. Ministries of education may be held hostage to these demands, given external or local funding. Furthermore, such activities make ministers and ministries look good at international conferences and events. They and their countries get good reputations for actively pursuing modern values. This activity may also have important material benefits. International agencies may find it convincing proof that national elites are credible partners for loans or aid.

In addition, ministers and officials know that they may not have to actually implement the proposals that come out of this research. They have some control over how the results of research are actually used. Ministries and politicians can thus support such research where it is convenient to do so, and de-couple the activity from actually altering the structure of schools or pedagogical practices where such efforts would cause political problems. I am not suggesting that this is done with malice or cynicism, though it may be in some cases. The point is to draw attention to the fact that the political imperatives of evaluation may not always coincide with the imperatives of running a national educational system and a country. As a result, one should expect some disconnection between assessment and implementation of recommended reforms.

The production of scholars and the rise of universities and professional training programs has also led to the institution of new *models* of research. The hegemony of North American social sciences after the 1960s increased the spread of quantitative models and training throughout the world. And the rising status of disciplines like economics and sociology has helped legitimate the intellectual models of these disciplines and the quantitative methodology attached to them as *the* way to evaluate their plausibility (see Fourcade, 2006, on economics). This development has had two important consequences. First, it has strengthened the intellectual support for comparative research and evaluation by demonstrating how it can be done. It becomes harder for nations to resist comparison across countries or schools when reputable professionals tell you that it can be done in ways that meet the stringent demands of science. Second, since these disciplines pioneered the use of statistical models and have trained legions of followers in these methods in both developed and developing countries, statistical methods and models of research now have the prestige of 'science' attached to them. Their use is also very widespread, particularly in Asia. Furthermore, many of the elites of developing countries have been trained in these disciplines themselves, or know about them, so they too are less likely to resist the use of these kinds of studies. Fourcade (2006), for example, shows that many central bankers and officials at ministries of planning worldwide have been trained in modern economics.

This widespread distribution of training among elites may explain the declining resistance to quantitative research that was once characteristic of places like Latin America. Stephen Heyneman suggests that there was a shift (particularly in Latin America) from an overt hostility to quantitative methods to acceptance of these methodologies in the field of education. In the 1970s, such methods were taken to be due to the influence of northern, Anglo-Saxon countries. They were viewed as another facet of northern hegemony over the emerging south. Qualitative, historical research was dominant locally and was associated with leftist forms of social analysis. It was also compatible with an intense sense of nationalism and national pride that insisted on the uniqueness of national traditions and histories. And it was in tune with the models that the IEA itself was using.

Globalization may have had regional effects by lowering the plausibility of local and national models of education. These countries are looking to modernize quickly and, like elsewhere, education is seen as the key institution. Thus they are looking around for effective models, and comparing themselves with other countries in Latin America now seems reasonable. There are now local, regional models, and most countries in this area are members of a regional association that sponsors such assessments. Furthermore, the political and economic geography has shifted in this region. New countries have become models and competitors. In Latin America the new power to be admired and feared is Brazil. In Asia it is India or China. The rising significance of these formerly poor countries has produced a new multi-polar world and with it an increasing cosmopolitanism. This change may have paved the way for quantitative methodologies of assessment to prevail by lowering the ideological barriers. Social science models and quantitative methods are now international. The main problem now may be the shortage of people in local areas who are trained in these disciplines and competent to carry out such studies.

### National Variation: limitations of the search for magic bullets

It should be clear that the search for 'best practices' is now an international one. With it come high expectations that there are easily borrowed protocols that can vastly improve local educational systems. This is perhaps to be expected because of the very nature of education. In organizational theory, education has features which lead people to believe in magical solutions. It is an enterprise with broad and diffuse goals as opposed to precise operational goals. And it is an activity in which the means to achieve these purposes are not well understood or easily replicable. James March (1988) has argued that under these circumstances, the solutions that emerge often involve a good deal of magical thinking or inspirational faith. This seems to be true of education as an institution, as opposed to, say, engineering.

One should view the search for 'best practices' through this lens. It is built on an optimistic faith that 'a school is a school is a school'. And it assumes that a practice that works in, say, Finland will work as well in the United States or Germany. In March's terms, it assumes that education is like engineering. But this is clearly not the case. One of the problems with the current search for 'best practices' is that it often overlooks important features of the contexts in which these practices are embedded. That was a virtue of older forms of research. They paid a good deal of attention to these environments (e.g. Goodson, 2004).

What we do know about academic achievement suggests that we should be cautious about the idea that one can pick and choose educational reforms without being concerned about the larger context of which they are a part. This idea may be one of the pernicious outcomes of international testing. Based on the PISA results, Finland, Flanders and Shanghai have become the poster children for educational excellence. But the larger contexts which play an important part in determining high achievement in these countries may be hard to replicate in other places. That is a message no one wants to hear.

And it is one that PISA officials and other experts spend a good deal of time denying. Thus shamanism and magical thinking thrive in education.

Looking at these poster children it becomes clear that education 'works' in these countries because it is supported by many other features of the society that may be hard to replicate elsewhere. Part of the larger context of Finland is the extensive level of pre-school training all children get, the high levels of social equality and low levels of poverty in the population, and a declining birth rate that lowers the number of children per school and per teacher. In this sense it is similar to Cuba. As Martin Carnoy (2007, pp. 145ff.) shows, the success of Cuba is linked to the prevailing level of social equality among families and the fact that almost all children are full-time students and do not work. These features of Cuba help explain part of its success in boosting achievement, which is the highest in Latin America. In addition, central control of the educational system and its salary structure distributes highly trained teachers more equitably across schools. Cuba and Finland both appear to have a management system that monitors younger teachers to ensure competent teaching for *all* students, unlike the United States. They both also keep teachers with the same pupils over multi-year periods. This means that pupils of all social class levels are surrounded by literate adults who matter and who know them. Coleman made the same case for the success of American Catholic schools.

Another less well-known poster child is Flanders, whose PISA record is even better than Finland's, as Paul Andrews (2011) documents. In the case of Flanders, a powerful Lutheran religious effect on family literacy, the motivation to learn and achievement has persisted. Family literacy is high in Flanders. Almost all families have in-home libraries. Literacy was valued because it was linked historically to membership of the Lutheran religious community. Illiteracy meant condemnation to a life of celibacy. Sex is a very powerful incentive to learn. In Flanders illiterates were not admitted to membership of the Lutheran community, which included religious communion and the sacraments. As non-members, they could *never* marry within the religious community. The tradition of family literacy, once started and enforced further by the religious community, continues and influences both parental education levels and students' motivation to learn. This is another source of educational motivation that is hard to transfer between countries.

In Shanghai, China, a new poster child of excellence, the penalty for failure or low performance on national college exams is a life of poverty outside the middle class, and a lifetime of knowing that one has disappointed one's parents, as their only child. Not only will parents be hurt, but the failed child will also never be able to repay them for the economic and other sacrifices they made to help their child's educational career. The one-child-per-family policy means that each child is his or her parents' only hope for educational and later economic success. Many parents sacrifice to send their children to 'cram schools' that help prepare them for the exams (see Baker & LeTendre, 2006, on 'shadow education').

Furthermore, the level of discipline and seriousness in the Shanghai educational system parallels that of Finland. The teaching methods may be different, but the level of discipline is similar. Aspirations are also similar – and high – among *all* students. Eighty percent of Shanghai students go on to post-secondary education (see http://www.AsiaSociety.edu/Shanghai). In Shanghai schools, children are geared to an exam-oriented culture and a teaching system that emphasizes memorization and rote learning. They drill a lot and learn basic facts and structures of logic from these repetitive exercises. Competition on the national college exam is fierce in the compulsory subjects (English, math and Chinese). To add to this pressure, the national college exam is the exclusive determinant of the quality of college/university one will be able to enter – or of whether one will be able to enter at all. So success on it is critical for one's post-high school career. This system prepares students for high-stakes tests and contributes to their motivation in taking them.

These are all examples of contexts which produce high family literacy, high student abilities, high motivation to learn, and high student achievement on PISA tests. The point is that these larger contexts matter. Educational systems are embedded in them and draw their strengths – and weaknesses – from them. They are part of the reason that particular curricular or teaching practices are successful. The point that needs emphasizing is that borrowing these specific educational practices and policies may not produce the same effects when these larger contexts are absent. This does not mean that we should cease looking internationally for better models of successful schools and teacher training. But it does suggest that we should temper our expectations about the results such borrowing will bring.

Another lesson from comparative studies of education is that we should also expect that borrowed practices will often be de-coupled from the actual structures within schools when they conflict with local expectations and well-understood rules and practices. This happened with the 1995 educational reforms in China, designed to produce more creative and imaginative students. These were in conflict with the exam-centric culture and teachers' practices of emphasizing rote learning that prepared students for the national college tests. Thus, while they remained a part of the intended curriculum of the 1995 reforms, they were effectively scrapped as part of the actual implemented curriculum in the classroom. This has happened with many other well-intended reforms, like the new math in the United States. Teachers and parents didn't understand it, so it was never fully implemented.

The case of Argentina is also instructive. Argentina as a *country* cares a lot about international testing, but its *students* have little interest or motivation. Whole classrooms have turned in their PISA test booklets blank! In this case the resistance to benchmarking is direct and comes from the supposed beneficiaries of such efforts. Teachers and parents may indirectly collude in such acts of passive withdrawal by downplaying the importance of such tests. While this reaction may also cloak the fact that students are unprepared for such international exercises, and teachers know it, it also suggests that the tests are at odds with much of local educational practice and parental culture. Argentina has a history of evaluating teaching and curricular practices, but this has taken other forms than student testing (see Gvirtz, 2006).

Thus, the political message of such case studies is a com___ ne. There are no magic panaceas for low national educational ___t, as measured by results on international tests like PISA and ___ccess in education depends on some of the same practices tha___ success in sports: love of the game; learning the fundamen___ through good coaching; lots of drill, practice and repetition; tea___th others under the eyes of watchful coaches and other adults who ___the game; and high levels of personal and team discipline. The case s of Finland, Flanders and Shanghai suggest that there may be lots of family and school organizational structures that can produce these conditions under local circumstances. The job of the good practitioner or policy analyst is to find the ones that work under local conditions. This requires an experimental mind set and familiarity with local practices and expectations. It also requires patience, persistence and the willingness to perceive failure when it occurs and change course.

These may not be characteristics that are encouraged by the emerging international 'faith' that there are short-term fixes that can be borrowed from other societies and that will magically cure the ills of any national school system. Instead, what we are likely to be left with is the 'horse race' mentality that surrounds the three-year cycles of PISA and the inevitable sense of 'crisis' among the countries that perceive themselves as 'losers'. The result will be yet another wave of international educational fads and fashions designed to cure these ills and bolster national morale (see Alex Wiseman's chapter in this volume).

### Future Scenarios

In a recent unpublished paper, Stephen Heyneman and Bommi Lee (2012, pp. 11ff.) observe that 21 countries have instituted educational reforms in response to their students' achievement levels on the 1990s TMSS and PISA tests. Thus, these tests have propelled almost 50% of the countries in the PISA and TMSS samples ($N= 40, 45$) to pursue educational reforms. The reforms range from instituting standardized assessments for assessing student achievement (Russia) to major reforms such as the introduction of National Education Standards in Germany. Thus such tests are having quite pronounced short-term effects on national educational policy.

This fact raises an important question: what is the likely future for educational systems dominated by testing and assessment? Baker and

LeTendre (2005) have articulated one scenario for the future based on past experiences with testing and assessment. We will suggest a second possibility.

Baker and LeTendre (2005) observe that the spread of international testing has produced its own dynamic in shaping educational systems. In general, the modern obsession with education also produces intense interest in testing, which inevitably leads to cycles of reform. These in turn intensify the demand for more testing, and more assessment, to determine the merits of such reforms (Baker & LeTendre, 2005; Stevenson and Stigler, 1992; McKnight et al, 1987). This is one of the paradoxes of the institutionalization of education and its 'transcendental' character (Baker & LeTendre, 2005, p. 178). No matter how well their students perform on international tests, educators and political elites are constantly looking for ways to improve their educational systems. In the context of a globalizing economy, every country is looking for an edge that makes it more competitive. Accordingly, all countries have the urge to compare and compete.

In this atmosphere, countries that perceive their youth to be 'failing' science and mathematics testing have a sense of 'doom' about them (Baker & LeTendre, 2005, p. 154). Thus, books and reports about 'crises' in education tend to come in waves, and regularly appear right after any given test results are made public (e.g. Mullis & Jenkins, 1988; National Center for Education Statistics, 1992). This international sensitivity adds to the urgency with which the impulse to reform is communicated and felt.

The paradox here is that the institutionalization of education leads to continuous and intensified efforts to improve it. High volumes of education reform are thus characteristic of the modern world system. In this environment a good deal of *standardization* occurs across countries, as they scan the horizon for reforms that will improve their own educational systems. National variation occurs, but it increasingly is subject to pressures to bring local practices in line with international standards and models of 'best practice' (Baker & LeTendre, 2005). Baker and LeTendre argue that the testing process intensifies the development of standardization because it increases the transparency (and accountability) of national educational systems. The testing process itself helps to construct definitions of 'failure' and 'success' and makes such assessments public.

In this context tilted in favor of benchmarking, various structural factors act to accelerate the diffusion of successful models. Adopting common models identified as successful in different settings is a typical process that organizational theorists have pointed to as speeding diffusion (Powell & DiMaggio, 1991). Furthermore, as benchmarking becomes the normative means for assessing national and world educational progress, adoption of like policies and approaches becomes more likely (Strang & Meyer, 1993). Copying and imitating 'leaders' is also likely to be taken as a positive sign internationally that a country takes very seriously its obligations to improve society by managing educational outcomes. Thus, compliance may confer international legitimacy on a country's educational and political authorities.

In this scenario, test scores become symbols of a nation's viability in the modern world, and thus impact national self-perceptions and comparisons. The result is that testing produces cycles of reform within countries and across groups of countries whose school children have not done well on particular kinds of international tests. Furthermore, perceived 'failure' is much more visible than 'success'. The fact, for example, that the United States has scored relatively well in reading tests has been dwarfed by outcries about the failure of US students in math and science (McKnight, 1987; Elley, 1992).

These arguments imply that international testing, and perhaps assessment, will produce waves of reform movements internationally and efforts to emulate the countries whose students score well on tests. From a world-system perspective this is one more source of pressure toward standardizing educational systems.

An alternative scenario emphasizes the limits on this process of standardization. It suggests that the institutionalization of testing and assessment will produce a 'learning curve' among political and educational elites that may help institutionalize testing and assessment but dampen the sense of crisis that these cycles often produce. Thus more national variation may survive testing and assessment cycles than the Baker/LeTendre scenario predicts. This may occur for several reasons. First, educational research may play a role in this process by de-limiting the claims of educational ideology and subjecting them to empirical analysis. This is already happening in the case of the empirical effects of test scores on economic development (Hanushek & Kimko, 2000; Ramirez et al, 2006). It will become clear that the links between education and social goals like economic growth are complex and multi-dimensional (see Rubinson & Fuller, 1992). Furthermore, research has also uncovered anomalies that suggest that there are trade-offs surrounding different kinds of educational systems. US students, for example, score well in reading tests but do badly on math and science (Elley, 1992).

Second, this knowledge, along with the steady institutionalization of testing and assessment, may help educational and political elites clarify the trade-offs of different national educational systems. It is apparent, for example, that the US educational system is not good at producing students who score well on international tests in math and science. But it does produce students and adults who are good at working in lateral relationships. They are opportunistic and good at 'hustling'. And American students are highly self-motivated and organized around personal goals (see Labaree, 2009). Recognition of these differences between systems may produce more informed debate and realization of what the trade-offs are among different ways of organizing education. This process might in fact reduce the drive toward standardization and imitation.

In this scenario, the robust institutionalization of testing and education itself could result in more nuanced movements of reform within countries. The end result might turn out to be considerable national variation within a world frame of purposes and conforming structures. The political arrangements of given countries and within world regions would determine the kinds of trade-offs elites would find acceptable. Pressures for change from above and below will also open options for limited reforms. Reform in this scenario would itself become institutionalized, and testing and assessment will become routine aspects of this process.

## Conclusion

I have offered an explanation in this chapter for the institutionalization of an international audit culture that has occurred. The result, as we have seen, is that even very poor countries are driven to produce assessments of some kind. And it leads to the prediction that these rates of evaluation will continue to increase. While I have focused on student assessment, it is likely that the urge to assess will spill over into many other areas. Assessment of university training is already the next item on the international testing agenda. But why stop there? In the drive to rationalize education and make it more productive (to use an economic metaphor that has become increasingly popular), teachers, faculty, administrators, hiring practices, enrollment and many other areas of education are all grist for the mill of assessment (see Krucken & Meier, 2006).

With the spread of globalization it seems very likely that these future evaluation practices will also become international. They will be copied by those countries that can afford to do so. And there will be efforts to help even the poorest countries carry out these examinations. But it is not at all clear that they will benefit education, students, parents or communities – especially poor ones. First of all, many of the recommended reforms will *not* be implemented. Thus a good deal of de-coupling can be anticipated, as proffered reforms run up against established and agreed-upon procedures, local custom and political obstacles.

Second, as the case studies I alluded to suggest, many of the purported reforms and 'best practices' work because of the larger context in which they are embedded. The most important parts of these contexts are often hard to manipulate or engineer through policy. It may be hard, for example, to emulate the practice of Finland and Cuba of equalizing the distribution of highly qualified teachers across the student population. This may require either more social equality in society or the ability to assign teachers to geographical areas to which they may not wish to go. In its early years, the Catholic Church in America appears to have been successful in achieving this effect, but its ability to do this now is fading, as the supply of church personnel dwindles and teachers' salaries and opportunities elsewhere increase. Similarly, the 'Lutheranism' of Flanders, and its historical effects, may also be hard to replicate in other places by normal policy processes.

We can also expect that as comparative evaluation expands, more and more attention will be paid to what are deemed 'best practices' of countries that score high on some measure of interest. But we do not know what the effect will be. A major question that Noel McGinn (2004) has raised is whether the focus on international 'best practices' will drive attention away from more relevant local policy alternatives. The answer to this question may depend on the quality of the evaluations and the quality of the theorizing that is used in analyzing these comparisons. These are important considerations because they may deter thoughtful people from believing that they can import particular practices and expect to get the same result that other countries do despite their differences in other respects. Thus one effect of good educational research may be to temper expectations and to foster a more experimental, as opposed to magical, mind set in thinking about the utility of particular educational practices.

But such considerations may not deter officials, politicians, parents and communities from enacting their favorite reform, gleaned from international comparisons, and believing that it is a magic bullet. This follows from the fact that schooling is such a high-stakes activity for all involved. 'Failure' in this endeavor is unthinkable. And PISA and TIMSS are helping to institutionalize an international definition of educational success. Under these conditions, schooling is highly open to fads and fashions of the moment. The charter school movement in the United States is a case in point. Charter schools are no more successful than public schools on average, unless they are able to 'cherry pick' the most promising students. But the belief persists despite the facts. In an area like education where uncertainty about how to create desired outcomes is high, a major policy question is: how does one get supposed adults, and particularly policy makers, to stop believing in magic?

The manic search for 'best practices' may in fact ensure that adult populations continue to search for solutions that are rooted in inspiration and magical thinking. A 'shamanic culture' is thus likely to persist in education, precisely because it is such an important institution in modern society but one whose structure does not make it amenable to engineering-type solutions. This outcome is the downside of the cult of assessment. The question of how to overcome this dangerous side effect should be a major policy issue.

### References

Andrews, Paul (2011) Curriculum Models and PISA Outcomes: mathematics instruction in Flanders and Finland. Paper presented at the Conference on PISA, 3 December, at SUNY Albany.

Baker, David P. & LeTendre, G. (2005) *Global Similarities and National Differences.* Stanford, CA: Stanford University Press.

Carnoy, Martin (2007) *Cuba's Advantage: why students in Cuba do better in school.* Stanford, CA: Stanford University Press.

Clark, Burton (1972) The Organizational Saga in Higher Education, *Administrative Science Quarterly*, 17, 178-183.

Collins, Randall (1999) The European Sociological Tradition and 21st Century World Sociology, in Janet Abu- Lugod (Ed.) *Sociology for the 21st Century*, pp. 26-42. Chicago: University of Chicago Press.

Drori, Gili S., Meyer, John W. & Hwang, Hokyu (2006) *Globalization and Organization: world society and organizational change.* Oxford: Oxford University Press.

Elley, Warwick (1992) *How in the World do Students Read?* Grindeldruck: International Association for the Evaluation of Educational Achievement.

Fourcade, Marion (2006) The Construction of a Global Profession: the transnationalization of economics, *American Journal of Sociology*, 112(1) (July), 145-194.

Fuller, Bruce & Rubinson, Richard (1992) *The Political Construction of Education: the state, school expansion, and economic change.* New York: Praeger.

Goodson, Ivor (2004) *Ideology and Curriculum.* London: Liffey Press.

Gvirtz, Silvina (2006) Micro-politics and the Examination of Curricular Practices: the case of school notebooks, in A. Benavot & C. Braslavsky (Eds) *School Knowledge in Comparative and Historical Perspective*, pp. 155-173. Hong Kong: Springer.

Hanushek, Erik & Kimko, Dennis (2000) Schooling, Labor Force Quality and the Growth of Nations, *American Economic Review*, 90, 1184-1208.

Heyneman, Stephen & Lee, Bommi (2012) The Impact of International Studies of Achievement on Policy and Research. Unpublished paper, April.

International Association for the Evaluation of Educational Achievement (IEA) Secretariat (2009) Torsten Husén, 1916-2009. IEA website.

Kamens, David H. & Benavot, Aaron (2011) Trends in Assessment, *Globalization, Societies and Education*, 9(2) (June), 285-300.

Kamens, David H. & McNeely, Connie (2010) Globalization and the Growth of International Educational Testing and National Assessment, *Comparative Education Review*, 54(1), 5-27.

Kamens, David H., Meyer, John W. & Benavot, Aaron (1997) Worldwide Patterns in Academic Secondary Education Curricula, 1920-1990, *Comparative Education Review*, 40(2) (May), 116-139.

Krucken, Georg & Meier, Frank (2006) Turning the University into an Organizational Actor, in G. Drori, J.W. Meyer & H. Hwang (Eds) *Globalization and Organization*, pp. 241-257. Oxford: Oxford University Press.

Labaree, David (2009) 2 Million Minutes. Moderated Discussion, *Comparative Education Review*, 5(1), 126-129.

Lockheed, Marlaine & Verspoor, Adrian (1990) *Improving Primary Education in Developing Countries.* Washington, DC: World Bank.

March, James (1988) *Decisions and Organizations*. Oxford: Basil Blackwell.

McGinn, Noel F. (2004) An Argument for Dialogue in Definition of National Policies for Education, *Journal of International Cooperation in Education*, 7(1), 15-25. CICE Hiroshima University.

McKnight, Curtis, Crosswhite, F. Joe, Dossey, John A., et al (1987) *The Underachieving Curriculum: assessing U.S. mathematics from an international perspective*. Champaign, IL: Stipes Publishing Co.

Meyer, John W. (2009) *World Society: the writings of John W. Meyer*, ed. Gili Drori & Georg Krucken. Oxford: Oxford University Press.

Mullis, Ina & Jenkins, Lyn (1988) *The Science Report Card: elements of risk and recovery*. Princeton, NJ: Educational Testing Service.

National Center for Education Statistics (1992) *International Mathematics and Science Assessments: what have we learned?* Washington, DC: US Department of Education.

Pizmony-Levy, Oren (2012) Testing for All. PhD dissertation, Stanford University.

Postlethwaite, T. Neville (2000) Torsten Husén (1916-), *Prospects: the quarterly review of comparative education*, XXIII(3/4), 677-686. Paris: UNESCO, International Bureau of Education,

Powell, Walter & DiMaggio, Paul (1991) *Neo-Institutionalism in Organizational Analysis*, revised edn. Chicago: University of Chicago Press.

Ramirez, F.O., Luo, Xiaowei, Shofer, Evan & Meyer, John W. (2006) Student Achievement and National Economic Growth, *American Journal of Education*, 113(1), 1-31.

Rosenmund, Moritz (2006) The Current Discourse on Curriculum Change: a comparative analysis of national education reports on education, in A. Benavot & C. Braslavsky (Eds) *School Knowledge in Comparative and Historical Perspective*, pp. 173-195. Hong Kong: Springer.

Rust, Val (2011) New Developments in University Ranking Systems. Paper presented at the annual meeting of the Comparative and International Education Society, 2 May, Montreal, Canada.

Schofer, Evan & Meyer, John (2005) Worldwide Expansion of Higher Education, *American Sociological Review*, 70(6) (December), 898-920.

Scott, Richard (2001) *Institutions and Organizations*. Thousand Oaks, CA: Sage.

Stevenson, H. & Stigler, J. (1992) Why our Schools are Failing and What We Can Learn from Japanese and Chinese Education. New York: Summit Books.

Strang, David & Meyer, John W. 1(993) Institutional Conditions for Diffusion, *Theory and Society*, 22(4), 487-511.

CHAPTER 6

# The OECD and Cold War Culture: thinking historically about PISA

## DANIEL TRÖHLER

ABSTRACT The Cold War is understood as an encompassing cultural agenda according to which an enduring global peace and welfare under the leadership either of the United States or the Soviet Union was being promised. In the West the notion of 'One World' had become popular; it indicated the idea of a safe and united world based on the security and well-being of common people throughout the world, provided by US world leadership. However, when one of the former allies, the Soviet Union, started to express similar ambitions on its own agenda it became an increasingly distracting factor for the global vision of 'One World' under the leadership of the United States. As much as the *Weltanschauungen* and the political legitimation rhetoric between the two competitors for world peace differed, many of its means and measures – especially in the field of education – were surprisingly similar. This chapter demonstrates this thesis, taking the example of the genealogy of PISA, understanding it as a tool whose roots have been developed ideologically and methodologically in the course of the Cold War.

Between April and November 1989 the European world changed dramatically. The Polish labor union 'Solidarity' was legalized and captured an overwhelming majority in the Parliament, East Germans attending the 'Pan-European Picnic' in Hungary broke through the Iron Curtain and fled into Austria, the Hungarian Parliament held multi-party parliamentary elections, and in November 1989 tens of thousands of East Berliners flooded checkpoints along the Berlin Wall and crossed into West Berlin: the Iron Curtain – separating an eastern from a western part of Europe – fell, and with this it symbolized the beginning of the end of the global Cold War.

These events triggered many contradictory interpretations. The most-discussed thesis came from a sociologist, Francis Fukuyama, at the RAND corporation, a Cold War institution that was set up in 1946 by the United

States Air Force (and largely supported by the Ford Foundation and the US government) to define US military strategy. The famous sentence in Fukuyama's analysis is this:

> What we may be witnessing is not just the end of the Cold War, or the passing of a particular period of post-war history, but the end of history as such: that is, the end point of mankind's ideological evolution and the universalization of Western liberal democracy as the final form of human government. (Fukuyama, 1989, p. 3)

The end of the Cold War is seen as not a singular event *in* history; it symbolizes the end *of* history, history understood as process resulting from ideological tensions. The end of the Cold War is not being interpreted as a double-sided event, but as a one-sided event: the surrender of the Marxist ideology, or the triumph of the 'western liberal democracy'. It is seen as opening two different locks in both directions – a physical one and an idealistic one: Whereas *people* from Eastern Europe came physically to visit the West, western *ideas* overflowed the East. The eastern oppression and totalitarianism had come to an end, and the western ideals – not ideologies – of individualism, freedom and true democracy had finally found a new sphere to spread out und fulfill their mission.

A quarter of a century later, the situation is no longer so clear, and not only because of the tensions with radical Muslims in different parts of the world. We have heard very little of individualism and freedom these last years, but increasingly of 'standardization', 'benchmarks', 'corporate identity', 'corporate behavior', 'monitoring', and of four- or five-year plans in private enterprises or in universities. Self-determination, a key element of freedom and democracy at both the individual and the national level, does not seem to be very highly rated any more, for global players such as the World Bank and the Organisation for Economic Co-operation and Development (OECD) have taken over the agenda and now exert pressure on national governments and therefore also on individuals in the educational institutions. More than twenty years after the fall of the Iron Curtain it no longer seems so clear whether in 1989 it was only people that traveled from the East to the West and only ideas from the West to the East. One might gain the impression, rather, that history – if history were a goddess like Fortuna – would have a little superior laugh on her face as she watched humans struggling to give themselves meaning with overarching and misdirected interpretations of contemporary history. Was the story entirely different from what we had thought? Did the East not collapse *in toto*? Was it the East that won in the end in 1989, transferring and disseminating central parts of its anti-individualistic ideology to the West?

The idea that the West was free of ideology – and, respectively, that only the East was characterized by ideology – is not Fukuyama's invention. It was formulated at the time when Fukuyama was still a child: in 1960 the sociologist and journalist Daniel Bell published his extremely successful *The*

*End of Ideology* (Bell, 1960). In the book, Bell acknowledged the eclipse of class ideology in western countries and the emergence of a welfare system in which people would solve their problems pragmatically with the help of new scientific and technological tools. In contrast, Bell accused the eastern countries such as Russia and China of being committed to the ideology of economic growth at any cost, accepting even oppression of its people for the overall aim:

> The fascination these countries [Russia and China] exert is no longer the old idea of the free society, but the new one of economic growth. And if this involves the wholesale coercion of the population and the rise of new elites to drive the people, the new repressions are justified on the ground that without such coercions economic advance cannot take place rapidly enough. (Bell, 1960, p. 373)

Aren't we today at least a little bit in a situation in which Bell in 1960 thought the East would be? And if so, was it only in 1989 that these ideas began to dominate the West, originally characterized by freedom, individualism, true democracy? The following deliberations are assembled around the overall thesis that the vision of the western 'free-of-ideology' world around 1960 was itself an ideology in which, beyond propaganda about the true advantages and dignities of the West, differing policy strategies were developed that really became tangible after the end of the Cold War: many of the characteristics attributed exclusively to the East – centralization, standardization, uniformity, training (instead of free education), corporate identity, technocratic elitism – were also part of the West and were perceived publicly only after the end of the Cold War. By the notion of the Cold War, I do not restrict myself to the arms race or the striving for military supremacy. Rather, it indicates an encompassing cultural agenda according to which an enduring global peace and welfare under the leadership of the United States was lying ahead. In this context, the notion of 'One World' had become popular; it indicated the idea of a safe and united world based on the security and well-being of common people throughout the world, provided by US world leadership (Fousek, 2000, p. 79). However, when one of the former allies, the Soviet Union, started to express similar ambitions in its own agenda, it became an increasingly distracting factor for the global vision of 'One World' under the leadership of the United States. As much as the *Weltanschauungen* and the political legitimation rhetorics between the two competitors for world peace differed, many of their means and measures – especially in the field of education – were surprisingly similar. I will demonstrate this thesis by taking the example of the Programme for International Student Assessment (PISA), understanding it as a tool whose roots have been developed ideologically and methodologically in the course of the Cold War.[1]

In the first section, I focus on how Sputnik educationalized the Cold War in the West, foremost in the United States. Then I look at different psychologies relevant for education, behaviorism and cognitive psychology, and at the dream of teaching machines, which promised easy and perfect learning. However, since these measures did not seem to produce enough success, the stakeholders in the United States switched their traditional input paradigm to an output-steering model in education; I then discuss this. Following that, I analyze how the same shift took place in the OECD with the challenge of developing instruments for statistical comparisons, in order to reconstruct PISA as the ultimate instrument of this ideology. Finally, in the outlook, I make a plea for a research agenda that is not culturally indifferent but that considers cultural differences as irreducible cultural conditions of education and learning.

## Sputnik or the Educationalization of the Cold War

Before the Soviet Union launched a satellite called Sputnik – a 23-inch metal ball – as the first human-made object to orbit the earth, the US authorities were completely certain that the United States had taken the global lead in education, science and technology. In a five-part series of booklets, *100 Things You Should Know About Communism*, published in 1949 by the US House of Representatives Committee on Un-American Activities led by Richard Nixon, the Soviet Union was said to have 'wrecked' the school system in Russia and replaced higher institutions with 'cheap diploma mills', whereas the lower schools had been 'turned into nothing more than revolutionary clubs, where students were fed godless Communist slogans rather than knowledge' (House Committee on Un-American Activities, 1949, p. 56). According to the booklets, the whole Soviet system was set up to give loyal teachers 'new and extreme authority over their pupils, who in turn have become cowed, uniformed puppets' (House Committee on Un-American Activities 1949, p. 57). Whereas the United States is depicted as having developed science and technology as result of a good education system and free individualism, the Soviets are accused of having relevant knowledge only from espionage:

> They have never been able to do enough original planning,
> development, or expansion on their own, to bring off a real
> industrial expansion equal to their needs ... Since World War II
> the Soviets have been copying United States patents, spying in
> United States factories, and grabbing scientists and engineers
> from all over Europe to put real brains into their program.
> (House Committee on Un-American Activities 1949, p. 63)

According to the Committee, individual freedom is the condition of progress, and where it is missing, no progress can be made:

The trouble starts with the basic Communist theory that a man should be a cog in a machine, not an independent thinker on his own. That theory, applied in schools dominated by Communism, turns out people who are trained but *not* educated. (House Committee on Un-American Activities 1949, p. 63, original emphasis)

The difference mentioned between training and education is fundamental, a 'difference between freedom and jail'. 'Education' aims at independent thinkers, and 'training' at fulfilling a given task: 'A monkey can be "trained" but only a human being can be "educated"' (House Committee on Un-American Activities 1949, p. 54). The consequences of training instead of education are sobering in terms of politics: 'Result: They can't run their country on their own, as we run ours' (House Committee on Un-American Activities 1949, p. 63).

Against this interpretative background, the launch of Sputnik eight years later had to be a shock, and it triggered several reactions. One involved the founding of the National Aeronautics and Space Administration (NASA) in 1958, and another aimed to rearm education. After Sputnik, former President Herbert Hoover explained:

The trouble is that we are turning out annually from our institutions of higher education perhaps fewer than half as many scientists and engineers as we did seven years ago. The greatest enemy of all mankind, the Communists, are turning out twice or possibly three times as many as we do ... The harsh fact is that the high schools are not preparing youngsters for the entrance requirements which must be maintained by our institutions training scientists and engineers. (*Time* Magazine, 1957)

After Sputnik in 1957, the assessment of the Soviet education system had changed dramatically, and it triggered an educational offensive designed to serve both the military and the economic development. In accordance with the then developed human capital theory foremost in Chicago, education became increasingly understood as a predictable 'investment' (Weisbrod, 1962; Schultz, 1963; Becker, 1964).

In this context, Vice-Admiral Hyman G. Rickover (the 'father of the Nuclear Navy' [Wallace, 1958]) made a plea for – for the first time, if I am not mistaken – incentives, national standards, and monitoring experts to improve American education, and we find more or less exactly the same ideas in today's dominant educational policy:

In some fashion we must devise a way to introduce uniform standards into American education. It would be best to set up a private agency, a Council of Scholars, financed by our colleges and universities as a joint undertaking – or perhaps by Foundations. This council would set a national standard for the high school diploma, as well as for the scholastic competence of teachers. High schools accepting this standard would receive official accreditation, somewhat in the order of the accreditation given medical schools and hospitals. (*Time* Magazine, 1957)

How severe the situation was is shown by Dwight Eisenhower, who was President of the United States at the time. In January 1958 Eisenhower spoke to Congress, making some 'Recommendations Relative to Our Educational System' (Eisenhower, 1958). These recommendations were necessary, Eisenhower said, as 'American education faces new responsibilities in the cause of freedom' and therefore has to 'place principal emphasis on our national security requirements', aiming 'to continue to strengthen our Armed Forces and improve the weapons at their command' (Eisenhower, 1958, p. 103). Eisenhower had an easy job of convincing Congress to pass the very first national law in education – the National Defense Education Act of 1958 (NDEA, 1958). The rational for the NDEA was as follows: 'The Congress hereby finds and declares that the security of the Nation requires the fullest development of the mental resources and technical skills of its young men and women' (NDEA, 1958, Sec. 101). As the 'defense of this Nation depends upon the mastery of modern techniques developed from complex scientific principles', the act continued, more young people should be educated in three core subjects – namely, in 'science, mathematics and modern foreign languages and trained in technology' (NDEA, 1958, Sec. 101). We see here, for the first time, the prioritization of three school subjects – science, mathematics and modern foreign languages – that much later would be at the center of PISA, too, with the only difference that the NDEA fosters foreign languages rather than native language.

### Technocracy, Behaviorism, Cognitive Psychology and Teaching Machines

The educationalization of the Cold War after Sputnik was not designed to extend the educational ideals and practices that were dominant at the time in the United States – quite the contrary. Admiral Hyman G. Rickover attacked those doctrines, which had been subsumed under the notion of 'life adjustment':

If the local school continued to teach such pleasant subjects as 'Life Adjustment' and 'How to know when you are really in love,' instead of French and physics, its diploma would be, for all the world to see, inferior. Taxpayers will begin to wonder whether they are getting their money's worth. (*Time* Magazine, 1957)

If Rickover's dictum was right – namely, that 'Education is our first line of defense' (Rickover, 1959, p. 15) – then curriculum and educational practice had to be reformed fundamentally.

146

In the end, this reform was based on a fundamental cultural shift in which the way of looking at education and its organization changed. The education system – basically a cultural system – was seen through an engineer's perspective and in that way became a technological system that could be steered as a machine. This engineer's perspective at the end of the 1950s was no *deus ex machina* but had been developed successfully during the Second World War as an effective and efficient model of problem solving by collaborating military, scientific and political experts at Massachusetts Institute of Technology (MIT) or in the context of the Manhattan Project at Los Alamos (see Hughes & Hughes, 2000). One of the most popular experts concerning the shift from problem-solving processes of the Second World War to the post-war period was Vannevar Bush, a trained engineer and initiator of the Manhattan Project, who in 1944 had been asked by President Roosevelt to prepare a report on the following question, among others: 'What can be done, consistent with military security, and with the prior approval of the military authorities, to make known to the world as soon as possible the contributions which have been made during our war effort to scientific knowledge?' (Bush, 1945). Why should strategies that had proven to be successful in wartime not be promising in peace?

Bush's report, titled *Science, The Endless Frontier*, and delivered on 25 July 1945 to President Harry S. Truman, related the future fight against diseases, defense against aggressors, and establishment of a welfare state closely to 'new knowledge' that 'can be obtained only through basic scientific research' (Bush, 1945, Summary), and doing science meant a teamwork of experts, exactly as it had been practiced during the Second World War:

> Science can be effective in the national welfare only as a member
> of a team, whether the conditions be peace or war. But without
> scientific progress no amount of achievement in other directions
> can insure our health, prosperity, and security as a nation in the
> modern world. (Bush, 1945, Summary)

Evidently, science education as a program for the 'renewal of our scientific talent' (Bush, 1945, Chapter 4) was of the highest importance for the future.

Against this military-technocratic background, after Sputnik the political stakeholders began to reform the school system. One of the major events in these reform attempts was the Woods Hole Conference held in 1959. By invitation of the Education Committee of the National Academy of Sciences – a society serving as 'advisers to the nation on science, engineering, and medicine' – a group of 34 scientists and scholars assembled for a 10-day conference at Woods Hole, Massachusetts. Financially supported by the Air Force, the RAND cooperation mentioned above where Fukuyama worked when he was proclaiming the end of history, and the National Academy of Sciences (Bruner, 1960, p. ix), the conference aimed at 'creating curricula and ways of teaching science' (Bruner, 1960, p. vii). Heading the conference was Jerome Bruner, a cognitive psychologist at Harvard University, who did not consider himself an expert in education. In his autobiography, Bruner (1983) reported:

> About a quarter of a century ago, I was plunged into the midst of an educational debate then raging. It was sparked by Sputnik. For a decade I was deep into it, sometimes after hours and on weekends, for a short period of eighty hours a week. ... I have never been a proper member of an education faculty or (save in an honorary capacity) a member of a professional society of education. ... I even took a year's leave from Harvard to build a curriculum, and spent a term of it teaching ten-year-olds part time in a Brookline school. I doubt I am a particularly odd duck in all this. (Bruner, 1983, p. 64)

In his notes taken during the conference at Woods Hole, Bruner explicitly advocated an engineering perspective on questions of education, and this perspective focused 'not just on the optimum performance of a given human/technological system' but on 'the entire array of possible alternatives that might be created by using existing or newly developed technologies ... from scratch' (Bruner, cited in Rudolph, 2002a, p. 94) – 'from scratch' indicating the idea of a culturally undetermined approach in organizing education. The experts at the conference had agreed that 'the goals of education ... expressed in terms of the human functions and tasks to be performed ... can be as exactly and objectively specified as can the human functions and tasks in the Atlas Weapon System' (Bruner, cited in Rudolph 2002a, p. 99). Steering this kind of system disengages the experts from cultural constraints; they focus less on understanding the way in which a system is a cultural construction or how the system works as a historically evolved system – and later on, this would prove exactly to be the ideological basis of PISA.

Needless to say, education techniques were to be changed, too. Whereas traditionally the teacher had been at the center of teaching and learning, the stakeholders began to advocate radio, television and teaching machines (and later computers) (see Cuban, 1986). 'Programmed instruction' became magic words, and connected to it were the hopes in the teaching machine that had been developed – based on forerunners – by behavioral psychologist B.F. Skinner in the mid-1950s. Skinner described the teaching machine as 'a device which creates vastly improved conditions for effective studying' (Skinner, c.1954, film narration). The general idea behind programmed instruction and teaching machines was that knowledge can be split in many easy-to-learn, small and consecutive steps to be learned individually. These isolated steps are presented to the students in a small window of a teaching machine. There,

> [the] student sees a bit of text ... This may be a sentence or two, or an equation in arithmetic. Some small part is missing, and the student must supply it by writing on an exposed strip of paper.

This response may be an answer to a question or the solution of a problem, but generally it is simply a symbol or word, which completes the material he has just read. As soon as the student has written his response, he operates the machine and learns immediately whether he is right or wrong. (Skinner *c.*1954, film narration)

This immediacy was one of the central advantages of the teaching machine, Skinner emphasized, for the student did not have to wait for the teacher to find time to correct tests. Another advantage was individuality, for the teaching machine allows each individual to learn according to his or her own pace. A third advantage was its inherent perfectibility, for it builds a whole step by step (Skinner *c.*1954, film narration). This educational trinity seemed to be the infallible pedagogical solution in the technocratic turn around 1960, and Skinner profited enormously from funding provided by the programs set up in the context of the National Defense Education Act in 1958. However, the programs proved to be rather unsuccessful, despite the organized propaganda financed by different foundations – among others, the Ford Foundation mentioned above. A few years later the Ford Foundation would also finance the OECD Centre for Educational Research and Innovation (CERI), the later womb of PISA after the end of the Cold War.

### Reform Failures in the United States and the Shift to Output Steering

Basically, in the years around 1960, today's globally dominant way of thinking about education and schooling became dominant in the United States. It included:

- a general technocratic view of the school (created from scratch, see above);
- a preference for math and sciences and foreign languages (today: native language);
- confidence in experts and skepticism towards lay democracy; and
- skepticism towards traditional educational theory in the universities and institutions of teacher education.

However, the ideology was still input steered, as we would say today. In the realm of the ideas then dominant, new curricular programs needed to be prepared and implemented, teachers better educated, and teaching tools and machines developed. Under President Lyndon Johnson's administration and his vision for a 'Great Society', Congress passed a second National Educational Act, the Elementary and Secondary Education Act of 1965 (Public Law 89-10). This act shows precisely the fundamental legal dilemma of educational administration in the United States, a dilemma that would eventually generate the idea of output steering. The Elementary and Secondary Education Act aimed at central power in decision making but in a constitutional, legal and cultural context that was and is still today highly local. The act dealt with this dilemma by committing to non-interference with provisions against a national curriculum and by allocating federal funding for professional development, instructional materials and educational programs in desired school subjects. In accordance with their constitutions, the local schools should not be forced to accept curriculum and teaching reforms, but they were to be motivated by tempting incentives (funding).

However, to invest billions of dollars and not be sure about the effects was understandably unsatisfying for the capital providers in their educational mission of the Cold War, for the constitutional sovereign right of the local authorities in education prevented the federal government from seeing what kind of results their money effectively had in the schools. It is precisely here that the idea of comprehensive and comparative testing arose. If the federal government could not govern directly, it at least wanted to see what effects its incentives had, and for this purpose a test instrument had to be developed. This instrument was the National Assessment of Educational Progress (NAEP) in 1964, which developed tools of comparative testing that were used 35 years later at a global level in the PISA. However, this comparative testing initiative was anything but undisputed.

The cultural tension between this expert-driven centralized governance and the local culture of schooling became immediately evident, for defenders of the local sovereign right in education denied Washington's right to collect data from their schools. Despite that, the central authorities prevailed at least to some degree. It is no coincidence that the most prominent supporter of national assessment was the United States Commissioner of Education and father of the Elementary and Secondary Education Act in 1965, Francis Keppel, who was basically the person making the decisions on the funds to be invested in the school system on the basis of the act. Keppel (1966) argued in favor of this kind of testing:

> American education today is woefully short of the basic
> information needed to carry forward our many educational
> purposes, to set sound goals, and to work together to reach them.
> The US Office of Education, for example, can report on all sorts
> of things about education: how many teachers we have, how any
> school children, how many school buildings, and possibly whether
> the buildings are painted or not. But as yet we do not know how
> much our children really know, the subjects in which they are
> strong or weak, the relation between income level and learning, or
> a host of other matters. (Keppel, 1966, p. 5)

It took five years to develop a testing instrument from the initial ideas in 1964 to the first NAEP assessment in 1969 – which was conducted on a voluntary basis. However, parallel to this half-successful implementation, the civil rights movement led to new expectations of the school: anti-discrimination became a dominant issue in the education policy, and for a short period the Cold War seemed to retreat into the background, at least in the United States. However, the stakeholder's educational agenda was in any case not limited to the United States but encompassed (at least) all western countries, and the primary vehicle for its dissemination was the OECD. The OECD had been founded in 1961 by including the United States and Canada in the Organisation for European Economic Co-operation (OEEC) (1948-1961), itself a child of the anti-communist Marshall Plan for Europe.

It is no coincidence that one of the first OECD conferences, held in October 1961 in Washington, DC, was dedicated to educational issues. In his keynote address to the plenary session of the conference, Walter H. Heller, economic advisor to the President of the United States, said that educational issues were of superior importance and therefore not to be left to the educational field: 'May I say that, in this context, the fight for education is too important to be left solely to the educators' (OECD, 1961, p. 35). Heller was an economist by training, as was also another keynote speaker at the OECD conference in 1961, Philipp H. Coombs, who then became the head of the UNESCO International Institute for Educational Planning in 1963, a position he held until 1968, the year he published his bestseller, *The World Educational Crisis* (Coombs, 1968). In the same year, the OECD founded the CERI, where PISA was developed later on.

### The OECD and the Dissemination of Educational Governance Ideas in the West

At the beginning of the OECD, the important educational questions were discussed in the Committee for Scientific and Technical Personnel (CSTP), a committee that had been set up in 1958 as reaction to Sputnik in the realm of the Marshall Plan initiative OEEC, the precursor to the OECD. The British chemist Alexander King, later co-founder of the Club of Rome, was secretary, and James Ronald Gass, a British social scientist who did 'not know much about education' (Eide, 1990, p. 9), was deputy. This committee was 'responsible for the work of the Organization relating to the expansion and rational utilization of the scientific and technical training necessary for meeting the needs arising from economic growth' (as cited in OECD, 1965, p. 8).

It is interesting to see how the OECD, in contrast to policies in the United States, never even mentioned the possibility of the use of military power as the aim of science and technology; instead its purpose was – in accordance with human capital theory – to serve economic growth, general welfare and progress. Defining the outline of the general program of the Committee for Scientific and Technical Personnel (CSTP) in the newly founded OECD, the Council declared: 'We are deeply convinced that science and technology, and the advanced education on which they must be based, are the pillars on which future social and economic progress must be built' (OECD Archives, C(61)70, 1). In the rhetoric of the early OECD, the purpose of education reform – economic growth – serves a nobler aim: 'social development'. In the OECD papers, statements such as the following are repeated like a mantra: 'The O.E.C.D. policy approach ... may be simply expressed as the recognition that education must be looked upon as an investment which is intimately related to the future of economic and social progress of the individual nations, and of the O.E.C.D. area as a whole' (OECD Archives, STP (63)5, 1) (OECD, n.d.).

In some sense, the CSTP faced similar problems as those challenging policy makers in the United States: how to get a grip on the individual school systems. National reports were produced and broadly discussed at the three annual meetings of the CTSP and recommendations formulated.

As a matter of fact, the national reports came to sobering conclusions. Michel Debeauvais, a French administrative scientist who took an international comparative approach and who was a former collaborator with the ministry of foreign affairs (1947-59), politely labeled the data 'of great interest' but assessed the data succinctly as 'not suitable for international comparison for lack of common methodology' (Debeauvais, 1962, p. 85). Debeauvais traced the problems identified in part back to ideological differences between educationalists and economists, for educators were identified as 'used to talking in terms of teaching and social objectives but are chary of the terminology and concerns of economists and manpower experts' (Debeauvais, 1962, p. 86). However, the major problem was lack of an appropriate methodology. Comparative statistics had to be developed, for only comparative data were considered to be helpful to the mission of the OECD: 'The qualitative aspects of educational programs are of course most important, but are specific to each country and do not lend themselves to generalization. Here, again, a number of parameters should be considered' (Debeauvais, 1962, p. 95).

A few years later, Frederick H. Harbison, Professor of Economics at Princeton University, explained to the OECD that precisely because the different countries were 'at different stages of modernization', comparative analysis of comparable data was essential: 'From the standpoint of practical politics, the consideration that really influences policy-makers, and even the people as well, is comparison with other countries. In this respect, nations resemble individuals – they want to keep up with the Joneses.[2] And this is true of all countries, including the United States' (Harbison, 1966, p. 54). This opinion reflected the general view of the OECD since 1964. In a confidential revision of the CSTP by the Deputy General-Secretary of the OECD, Michael Harris had favored for the future of the CSTP only those quantitative projects that allowed for comparative data, and he proposed to turn down all experiments that were not paid for by the member countries and all qualitatively oriented projects such as curriculum reform or the development of teaching aids (OECD Archives, CES(64)22) (OECD, n.d.).

In 1966, the participating member countries of the OECD had willingly accepted the new educational ideology. Running out of money, the OECD stopped its financial assistance to all countries, which triggered a heated discussion in the CSTP (OECD Archives, STP/M(64)3, 4-24) (OECD, n.d.). Indeed, this suspension of funding turned out to be a real test for the pertinent activities of the OECD. Most of the Western European countries – having participated in the 'Investment Planning in Educational Development' (IPE) – were willing to continue and to bear the costs themselves. They had already adopted the educational planning ideology and had therefore set up administrative organizations in their respective countries. Of all the countries, Germany had been the first, by establishing the *Institut für Bildungsforschung* [Institute for Educational Research] in the realm of the Max-Planck-Society in 1963-64. The United Kingdom founded the Schools Council for the Curriculum and Examinations in 1964, Greece established a National Pedagogical Institute in 1964, and the Netherlands founded a Foundation for Educational Research in 1965.

In 1966, two years before the CERI was founded and at a time when tools for comparative quantitative research and statistical methods were developed on both sides of the Atlantic, the new Cold War ideology was firmly established, if not in universities or circles of teacher education, then in circles of education policies. The national delegates of the member countries had forgiven the OECD for the fact that the OECD had not really involved them in the planning and execution of the different activities or in the selection of the external experts and consultants. They had complained about this strongly in 1963 and had then been told by the secretary of the CSTP, Alexander King, that they – the delegates – were not familiar enough with the issues at stake to evaluate the Committee's work (OECD Archives, STP/M(63)2, 9f) (OECD, n.d.). The Cold War was an encompassing cultural agenda and one of the organizations emerging from this agenda, the OECD, had given them an important place in the reformed educational bureaucracies of their respective countries, and conversely, they implemented the new logic of educational planning with reports and popular publications published in their countries and not with OECD publications from Paris.

### The Making of PISA

The collective endeavors involved in establishing comparative statistics created a magic word, 'indicators' – indicators allegedly providing empirical evidence on the state of the art of the different schools to be compared. On a global level, the initiative was from the United States, which had just published *A Nation at Risk* – an expert report on the failures of the education system in view of the economy going through a huge crisis. The United States brought perspectives of social equity to an end, helped the notion of 'excellence' to become prominent, and was determined to implement the US strategy in the OECD. However, when, following *A Nation at Risk* in the 1980s, the United States relaunched the idea of collecting international comparative data, most of the OECD members were hardly amused, for many of them seemed to doubt the feasibility and the usefulness of international comparisons and favored the more 'individual' development of the single education systems. Not until the United States threatened to withdraw its money from the CERI was the idea to restart the collection of comparable indicators in education accepted. Stephen P. Heyneman reported from the CERI board of directors' meeting in 1983:

> The US delegate was said to have put a great deal of pressure and in very direct language for OECD to engage itself in a project collecting and analyzing statistical education 'inputs and outcomes' – information on curricular standards, costs and trends and the like. The reaction among the staff of CERI was one of shock, and deep suspicion. Those whom I interviewed believed it was unprofessional to try and quantify such indicators, and that it would oversimplify and misrepresent OECD systems, and that it would be rejected by the twenty-four member states whose common interests they were charged to serve. (Heyneman, 1993, p. 375)

Despite skepticism among the CERI staff, the United States' concern was accepted and the path to the first OECD report paved.

Because in the individual countries the policy makers had founded bridging institutions between the OECD (and other transnational organizations) and the national policy stakeholders, usually bypassing research in universities, people to collect these desired data were available. Independent of education research at the universities, these organizations became the national partners in the new programs of the CERI. It took a few years until the first report was actually published in 1992, three years after the end of the Cold War. Titled 'Education at a Glance', the publication was a highly attractive instrument for policy makers (Weymann & Martens 2005, p. 79). A new edition of 'Education at a Glance' is still published each year. This project of analyzing indicators was the cradle of PISA, which started only a couple of years later.

What output steering is meant to be becomes evident in the OECD report. The indicators had been pre-defined and collected in the individual countries. In 1993, 38 indicators had been defined and clustered into three groups. Twenty-one of these indicators were grouped in the cluster 'costs, resources and school processes', seven in the cluster 'contexts of education', and 10 in the cluster 'results of education'. A highly complex analysis scheme was to relate the third cluster, 'results of education', to the two other clusters (see Figure 1).

'Education at a Glance' is a most remarkable witness of cultural transfer and dissemination from one nation to (at least one part of) the world. It is an export and at the same time a generalization of a historically grown governance model that was owing to three particular circumstances of the United States: the Cold War phobia of a nation heading for world leadership;

the favoring of expertocratic and technocratic governance; and the culturally and constitutionally anchored localism in education that was meant to be overcome. It is within this particular set of cultural and political framework conditions of the United States in the Cold War that the model of output steering started to make sense – at least to the technocratic policy makers in the United States.

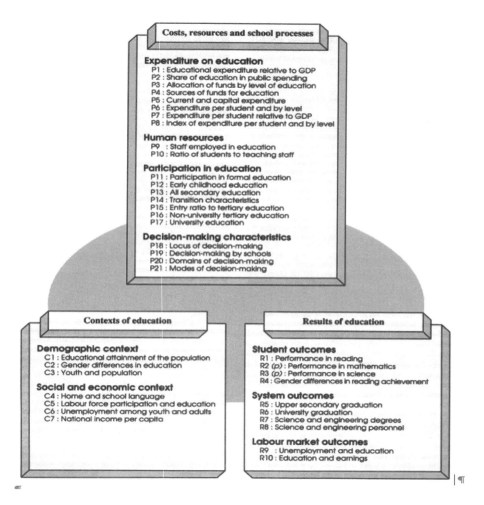

Figure 1. OECD education indicators (source: OECD, 1993, p. 12).

With the OECD and the CERI, or, more precisely, with the initiative for 'Education at a Glance', this particular steering model was implemented in countries that had very different cultural and political framework conditions. Nowhere in the world is the principle of localism as radical as it is in the

United States, not even in Switzerland, where locally elected school board members are laymen, too – and not to mention France or England. In other words, the solution that the US elites found for dealing with the constitutionally prohibited direct interfering in school affairs – output steering with the tool of incentives – was being applied to countries where there was no need for this solution, for these countries have effectively had manifold opportunities to interfere actively in regional and local educational policies.

Indeed, 'Education at a Glance' and its indicators suggest cultural indifference. The cluster 'contexts of education' is clearly not meant to be a cultural context, where social meanings are constructed by human interaction. 'Contexts of education' are reduced to figures and statistics that are correlated with other figures and statistics. Hence, comparative research within this program was not intended to analyze the different cultural and historical implementation of school systems and to understand the different historically grown performances of what is called schooling. Quite the contrary, comparative research was reduced to measuring outcomes in the background of this one generalized model of governance. Therefore, ignoring cultural peculiarities is in fact not cultural indifference but the expression of one dominant cultural mode of governance. With only slight alterations compared with the National Defense Education Act of 1958, the important school subjects were reading, mathematics and science.

The dissemination of this governance model has had thorough and very costly consequences. To obtain more comparable data about the systems, curricular contents had to be standardized, the individual schools made more autonomous, and monitoring systems established. Backed by the authority of the meanwhile powerful OECD, the educational governances defined to a large degree the education research agenda. Education, curriculum theory, and history and philosophy of education conducted at the universities were successfully excluded from this agenda, whereas representatives of the subject disciplines (languages, mathematics, sciences) formulated standards, and cognitive psychologists collected the data.

PISA was the tapering of this new model, for it disregarded not only cultural factors but also the actual curriculum. The idea of competencies to be used in later life rather than knowledge to be learned at school indicates the global sphere of this Cold War ideology (OECD, 2001, p. 14). Because PISA aims to look at 'young people's ability to use their knowledge and skills in order to meet real-life challenges' (OECD, 2001, p. 16), the focus is not on what students learn at school on the basis of their curriculum and textbooks: 'Assessments that test only mastery of the school curriculum can offer a measure of the internal efficiency of school systems. They do not reveal how effectively schools prepare students for life after they have completed their formal education' (OECD, 2001, p. 27). In the intellectual horizon of the OECD, this 'life' is not culturally and empirically framed but universal: 'PISA offers a new approach to considering school outcomes, using as its evidence base the experiences of students across the world rather than in the specific cultural context of a single country' (OECD, 2001, p. 27).

## Outlook

Concerned people in the West considered the East a 'totalitarian dictatorship' (Sager, 1959, p. 2) in which – and after Sputnik this became very clear – the sciences and science education in the schools had a considerable amount of freedom (Sager, 1959, p. 2). Whereas before Sputnik there had been agreement that political totalitarianism and academic progress were incompatible and that to obtain useful knowledge, the East depended on espionage (see the relevant comments of the House Committee on Un-American Activities [1949] mentioned above), after Sputnik the question arose as to how political totalitarianism and freedom of the sciences could work. The answer of the western Cold Warriors was that the Russians were in total control of the human and social sciences and would punish all public questioning of the dominant ideologies; one of the dear exhibits was of course the poet Boris Leonidowitsch Pasternak (Sager, 1959, p. 3), who had been awarded the Nobel Prize for Literature in 1958 for his 1957 novel *Doctor Zhivago* but who was forced by the Russian authorities to decline the prize.

In the West the reason for the relative freedom of the Soviet scientists was seen in the nature of science and technology itself. As the explanation goes, 'Technicians are used to working with the causal law of the hard sciences, but the politicians may not rely on these simple forms of relation' (Sager, 1959, p. 20, freely translated here). Therefore, the two spheres could be treated in different ways, and the politician had to control anything political, social and philosophical, whereas the scientist could be provided with freedom (Sager, 1959, p. 20). This freedom has provided the Soviet scientists and technicians with all the possible benefits, foremost a 'central institute' with 2300 employees collecting information from over 90 countries in over 10,000 journals, with 20,000 part-time translators and 13,000 scientists evaluating the international developments and making the results available to the scientists, so that a Soviet scholar is usually better informed about the American developments than an American scholar is (Sager, 1959, pp. 18-21).

The centralized promotion of the sciences and technology has been pretty much the same in both of the blocks of the Cold War, the West and the East. Its expertocratic ideology thus did not come across the border from the East to the West in 1989. Both blocks were equally designed to help fulfill the global mission that the leaders had been promising: progress, freedom, welfare. In consequence, in both parts of the world the social and human sciences were rather neglected, although to a different degree and with very different consequences. Whereas the social and human scientists in the East had to conform to the dominant ideology of Marxism – often only in the introductions of their books – the neglected western social and human scientists, at least in education, had a hard time emancipating themselves from their national origins. In turn, their reaction to the new doctrines in education, once they became tangible after the end of the Cold War, was to focus a fortiori on their past heroes – Democrat and Congregationalist John Dewey in the United States, for instance (Tröhler, 2011b), or in Germany the grand, undemocratic Lutheran heroes of *Bildung*: Humboldt, Flitner or Spranger (Tröhler, 2011a).

With the specific concern of the Cold War, education in the 40 years since Sputnik has become a technocratic affair that is dominated by experts and operates largely outside the traditional research institutions, and that means outside the traditional control mechanisms of academia (peer review). It is no coincidence that the OECD has itself published its own results in countless series and publications, foremost in journals dedicated to cognitive psychology.[3] Cognitive psychology, with its fundamental idea that the cognitive processes are uniform in principle, regardless of a person's age or situation, and 'that intellectual activity anywhere is the same, whether at the frontier of knowledge or in a third-grade classroom' (Bruner, 1960, p. 14), was the perfect mode to serve the technocratic visions of the Cold Warriors at the end of the 1950s (see Rudolph, 2002b), and it is still the most important academic reference of PISA today, as the stakeholders themselves admit (Klieme et al, 2003, pp. 23-26; Deutsches PISA-Konsortium, 2001, p. 22).

Experts in policy were to advise politicians at national and international levels, research was often conducted outside the traditional places, with the lead discipline becoming cognitive psychology, and empiricism was sacrificed to the ideology of a culturally indifferent world of education. When PISA pretends to look at 'young people's ability to use their knowledge and skills in order to meet real-life challenges' (OECD, 2001, p. 16), the focus is obviously not on what students learn at school on the basis of their curricula and textbooks. In an irritating way, these 'real-life challenges' are anything but the students' school life, nor are they outside school – as if a 15-year-old is not exposed to particularly many of these 'real-life challenges'. No, as a matter of fact, PISA is not interested in learning experiences in which 'real-life situations' are mastered successfully, for this interest would have demanded the acceptance of differences and plurality in the settings of learning. Rather than commit to the empirical given plurality, PISA follows the vision of a uniform world in the future and believes that it can test how students will master the culturally indifferent 'real-life challenges' some 10, 20 or 30 years ahead of them. The overall vision of the 'One World', so often preached in the early Cold War, has become operationalized at the expense of the empirical dimension of education, of all things by a research approach defining itself as empirical. A quarter of a century after the end of the Cold War it might be appropriate to realize that the Cold War is gone and that the ideology that technocratic research is free of ideology was itself an ideology of the Cold War.

## Notes

[1] Some of the following ideas were developed in other publications (Tröhler, 2010, 2011a, b).

[2] Meaning that they strive to match their neighbors in spending and social standing. This is an American expression from the twentieth century. It originated with Arthur (Pop) Momand's comic strip in the *New York Globe* called *Keep Up With The Joneses*. Jones was a very common name, and 'the Joneses' was merely a generic name for 'neighbors' (http://www.phrases.org.uk/meanings/216400.html, accessed 19 August 2011).

[3] It is only recently that those scientists profiting most by the new governance – often in the footsteps of Jerome Bruner as cognitive scientists – have become strong and self-confident enough to publish in journals. The journal *Cognitive Psychology* was founded as early as in 1970, but it was not until the very end of the Cold War that cognitive psychology became a broad movement; the International Association for Cognitive Education and Psychology was founded in 1988, the *Journal of Cognitive Psychology* started as the *European Journal of Cognitive Psychology* exactly at the end of the Cold War (in 1989); the *Journal of Cognitive Psychotherapy* came into being two years earlier in 1987, as did also the journal *Applied Cognitive Psychology*, and *Advances in Cognitive Psychology* and the *Journal of Cognitive Education and Psychology* appeared in 2005.

## References

Becker, Gary S. (1964) *Human Capital: a theoretical and empirical analysis, with special reference to education.* New York: National Bureau of Economic Research.

Bell, Daniel (1960) *The End of Ideology: on the exhaustion of political ideas in the fifties.* Glencoe, IL: Free Press.

Bruner, Jerome (1960) *The Process of Education.* New York: Random.

Bruner, Jerome (1983) *In Search of Mind: essays in autobiography.* New York: Harper & Row.

Bush, Vannevar (1945) *Science, The Endless Frontier: a report to the President by Vannevar Bush, Director of the Office of Scientific Research and Development, July 1945.* Washington, DC: United States Government Printing Office. http://www.nsf.gov/od/lpa/nsf50/vbush1945.htm

Coombs, Philip H. (1968) *The World Educational Crisis.* New York: Oxford University Press.

Cuban, Larry (1986) *Teachers and Machines: the classroom use of technology since 1920.* New York: Teachers College Press.

Debeauvais, Michel (1962) Methods of Forecasting Long-term Manpower Needs, in OECD & H.S. Parnes (Eds) *The Mediterranean Regional Project. Planning Education for Economic and Social Development.* Paris: OECD Publishing.

Deutsches PISA-Konsortium (Eds) (2001) *PISA 2000. Basiskompetenzen von Schülerinnen und Schülern im internationalen Vergleich.* Opladen: Leske+Budrich.

Eide, Kjell (1990) *30 Years of Educational Collaboration in the OECD*. Oslo: Royal Ministry of Education and Research.

Eisenhower, Dwight D. (1958) Recommendations Relative to Our Educational System, *Science Education*, 42(2), 103-106.

Fousek, John (2000) *To Lead the World. American Nationalism & the Cultural Roots of the Cold War*. Chapel Hill: University of North Carolina Press.

Fukuyama, Francis (1989) The End of History? *National Interest*, 16 (Summer), 3-18.

Harbison, Frederick H. (1966) Strategies for Human Resources Development (1), in *Human Resources Development Training Course. Lectures and Methodological Essays on Educational Planning*, ed. OECD, pp. 39-54. Bergneustadt, 6-24 July 1964. Paris: OECD Publishing.

Heyneman, Stephen P. (1993) Quantity, Quality, and Source, *Comparative Education Review*, 37(4), 372-388.

House Committee on Un-American Activities (1949) *100 Things You Should Know About Communism*. Washington, DC: US Government Printing Office.

Hughes, Agatha C. & Hughes, Thomas P. (Eds) (2000) *Systems, Experts, and Computers: the systems approach in management and engineering, World War II and after*. Cambridge, MA: MIT Press.

Keppel, Francis (1966) National Educational Assessment: we badly need it, in eds. American Association of School Administrators & National Education Association of the United States (Eds) *National Educational Assessment: pro and con*. Washington, DC: American Association of School Administrators and Organization Relations Division and Publications Division of the National Education Association.

Klieme, E., Avenarius, H., Blum, W., et al (2003) *Zur Entwicklung nationaler Bildungsstandards*. Berlin: Bundesministerium für Bildung und Forschung.

NDEA (1958) National Defense Education Act of 1958. United States Public Law 85-864. (P.L. 85-864; 72 Stat. 1580). http://www.scribd.com/doc/57012400/National-Defense-Education-Act-of-1958

Organisation for Economic Co-operation and Development (OECD) (1961) *Policy Conference on Economic Growth and Investment in Education. Washington 16th-20th October 1961*. Paris: OECD Publishing.

Organisation for Economic Co-operation and Development (OECD) (1965) *The Mediterranean Regional Project: an experiment in planning by six countries*. Paris: OECD Publishing.

Organisation for Economic Co-operation and Development (OECD) (1993) *Education at a Glance: OECD indicators*. Paris: OECD Publishing.

Organisation for Economic Co-operation and Development (OECD) (2001) *Knowledge and Skills for Life: first results from PISA 2000*. Paris: OECD Publishing.

Organisation for Economic Co-operation and Development (OECD) (n.d.) OECD Archives, Paris (unpublished).

Rickover, Hyman G. (1959) *Education and Freedom*. New York: E.P. Dutton.

Rudolph, John (2002a) *Scientists in the Classroom: the cold war reconstruction of American science education*. New York: Palgrave Macmillan.

Rudolph, John (2002b) From World War to Woods Hole: the use of wartime research models for curriculum reform, *Teachers College Record*, 104(2), 212-241.

Sager, Peter (1959) *Wissenschaft und Politik in der Sowjetunion, vol. 4*. Bern: Schriftenreihe des Schweizerischen Ost-Instituts.

Schultz, Theodore W. (1963) *The Economic Value of Education*. New York: Columbia University Press.

Skinner, B.F. (*c*.1954) Teaching Machines and Programmed Learning [Film]. http://www.youtube.com/watch?v=jTH3ob1IRFo&feature=related

*Time* Magazine (1957) Education: what price life adjustment? *Time Magazine*, LXX(23), 2 December.

Tröhler, Daniel (2010) Harmonizing the Educational Globe: world polity, cultural features, and the challenges to educational research, *Studies in Philosophy and Education*, 29, 7-29.

Tröhler, Daniel (2011a) Concepts, Cultures, and Comparisons: PISA and the double German discontentment, in M.A. Pereyra, H.-G. Kotthoff & R. Cowen (Eds) *PISA under Examination: changing knowledge, changing tests and changing schools*, pp. 245-257. Rotterdam: Sense Publishers. Printed also in D. Tröhler (2011) *Languages of Education: protestant legacies, national identities, and global aspirations*. New York: Routledge.

Tröhler, Daniel (2011b) The Global Language on Education Policy and Prospects of Education Research, in D. Tröhler and R. Barbu (Eds) *The Future of Education Research: education systems in historical, cultural, and sociological perspectives*. Rotterdam: Sense Publishers.

Wallace, Robert (1958) A Deluge of Honors for an Exasperating Admiral, *Time Magazine*, 8 September, 104-106, 109-116, 118.

Weisbrod, Burton A. (1962) Education and Investment in Human Capital, *Journal of Political Economy*, 70(5), 106-123.

Weymann, Ansgar & Martens, Kerstin (2005) Bildungspolitik durch internationale Organisationen – Entwicklung, Strategien und Bedeutung der OECD, *ÖsterreichischeZeitschrift für Soziologie*, 30(4), 68-86.

CHAPTER 7

# Causes and Consequences of International Assessments in Developing Countries

## MARLAINE LOCKHEED[1]

ABSTRACT The increase in the number of developing countries that participate in international assessments is incontrovertible, with much participation enabled through the financial and technical support of international donor agencies, particularly the World Bank, the Organisation for Economic Co-operation and Development (OECD), the United Nations Development Programme (UNDP) and the United Nations Educational, Scientific and Cultural Organization (UNESCO). This chapter argues that the analytic and policy questions of economists as well as an increasing demand for evidence of 'aid effectiveness' have fuelled a demand for more countries, particularly developing countries, to participate in international assessments. In the context of this 'globalization' of assessment, the chapter draws attention to the remarkable rise in visibility of the Programme for International Student Assessment (PISA) as compared with the formerly dominant International Association for the Evaluation of Educational Achievement (IEA) assessments; this rise is attributed in part to the positioning of PISA results in publications read by economists. The chapter argues that participation in all types of international assessments has benefited developing countries both indirectly and directly. Indirectly, participation has influenced norms for curriculum and teaching practice, leading to curricular reform and increased attention to teacher professional development. Directly, participation has strengthened the assessment capacity of their national testing agencies, through assessment-related training and hands-on experience in the process of developing and implementing large-scale assessments.

### Introduction

The rise of international large-scale assessments over the past five decades has been widely documented and has been the subject of considerable debate regarding content coverage, methodological issues in design and secondary analysis, and possible impact on education policy and practice (Porter & Gamoran, 2002; Kamens & McNeely, 2009; von Davier & Hastedt, 2009; Rutkowski et al, 2010). But little research has explored the reasons for developing-country participation in international large-scale assessments or provided evidence regarding the impact of such participation on education policy or practice in developing countries.[2] This chapter seeks to fill this gap. The first section reviews how multi-lateral and bi-lateral donors contributed to the rise of international large-scale assessments in developing countries; the next section suggests reasons why one 'latecomer' assessment (the Programme for International Student Assessment [PISA] of the Organisation for Economic Co-operation and Development [OECD]) has come to dominate policy discussions; the section following that summarizes the evidence regarding the impact of international large-scale assessments on education policy, education practice and assessment capacity in developing countries.

## The Rise of International Large-scale Assessments in Developing Countries

Developing countries – particularly low- and lower-middle-income countries – are recent participants in international large-scale assessments (Lockheed, 2011). No developing countries participated in the first-ever 1959-60 international large-scale assessment, carried out in 12 developed countries to test whether such a study was possible, or in the second study that followed in 1964. Three developing countries (Chile, India and Iran) participated in a third study in 1970-71, and eight developing countries (China [3], Ghana, Nigeria, Papua New Guinea, Philippines, Poland, Thailand, and Zimbabwe) participated in several studies in the early 1980s. Still, fewer than 5% of developing countries were represented in these early studies, as compared with nearly half of the larger developed countries.

Not until the 1990s did a significant number of developing countries begin to participate in international large-scale assessments (Figure 1). Their participation was often encouraged and enabled through external technical and financial support from donor agencies. What motivated international donor agencies to support the participation of developing countries in international large-scale assessments? It is useful to compare developed countries' rationale for participation with that of developing countries.[4]

*Motivation for Developed Countries*

Developed countries such as the United States participated in international assessments as a way to improve their own education systems through the study of other education systems; the earliest assessments were called 'studies' rather than 'assessments'. As articulated in the *Framework Principles for International Comparative Studies of Education,* 'the most important reason for United States participation in international studies of education is to improve understanding of our own education system' (Bradburn & Gilford, 1990, p. 1). Participation in 'international comparative studies' would provide educators and education policy makers in developed countries with information about: (a) how their countries measured up relative to other developed countries with respect to student performance in such areas as mathematics, science and reading; and (b) the educational inputs, processes and institutions that were associated with higher student achievement, as well as those that had no relationship to higher achievement. In the United States, this led to increased financing for, as well as methodological scrutiny of, the assessments.

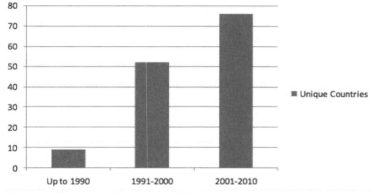

Figure 1. The rise of low- and middle-income countries participating in international large-scale assessments, pre-1990 to 2010.

Financial support for international large-scale assessments in developed countries began in 1988, when the US National Center for Education Statistics (NCES) funded the University of Illinois to create an international database on student learning achievement and teaching practices from the International Association for the Evaluation of Educational Achievement's (IEA's) Second International Mathematics Study (Suter, 2011). This database supplemented existing international databases on education indicators – mainly student enrollments, staffing and expenditures – compiled for their member countries by the OECD and the United Nations Educational, Scientific and Cultural Organization (UNESCO). Then, to ensure that international studies met professional standards for measurement, data collection and analysis, the NCES and the National Science Foundation (NSF) created and financed, from 1988 to 2003, an appointed board of nationally known statisticians and education researchers - the Board on International Comparative Studies in Education (BICSE) - to oversee educational research and statistical activities conducted in the United States in conjunction with other countries. During these 15 years, BICSE advised on the design and analysis of 15 international comparative studies sponsored by the IEA, two studies sponsored by the Educational Testing Service and two studies sponsored by the OECD (see Annex 1).

## Motivation for Developing Countries

Developing countries generally joined international large-scale assessments with the encouragement of, and when supported by, international donor agencies. Although BICSE's remit was to provide advice to the United States, among its appointed members was a volunteer representative of the World Bank [5], who articulated the need to include developing countries in the international assessments and provide capacity building and financial support that would enable these countries to participate. The World Bank's interest was driven by its own information and accountability needs as well as by the needs of its researchers, typically economists and sociologists, for data that could justify the bank's investment in the education sector.

As early as 1990, the lack of adequate measures of student learning achievement in developing countries – both national and cross-national – had been pointed out in major World Bank publications. This lack compromised the ability of both developing countries and their bi-lateral and multi-lateral donors to monitor improvement and to measure the results of investments and reform programs in the sector. World Bank policy papers in the 1990s (*Primary Education* in 1990; *Priorities and Strategies for Education* in 1995) emphasized the need for monitoring indicators based on measures of learning achievement, an emphasis recently reclaimed in the 2011 World Bank education strategy *Learning for All: investing in people's knowledge and skills to promote development*. While many developing countries had examination bodies that regulated access to increasingly higher levels of education, the measures were often inconsistent over time and – in line with their selection purpose – did not measure achievement across the full range of learning. Examination systems could not provide the information needed for accountability.

In part, participating in international assessments was a quid pro quo for international donor support for a country's education sector, driven by growing donor concerns for results and accountability. Monitoring and accountability for results were key dimensions of declarations from the four high-level fora on aid effectiveness, beginning with the Paris Declaration of 2005 and continuing through the Busan Declaration of 2011 (OECD, 2005, 2011). Although one donor-supported study examined aid effectiveness vis-à-vis learning in primary education (IEG, 2006), much of the evidence for aid effectiveness in education relied on data regarding the quantity of education, rather than its quality (e.g. Michaelova & Weber, 2007).

Data needs for research, monitoring and evaluation arose concurrently with the increasing power of statistical packages to manage multi-level and longitudinal data. As development economists and sociologists analyzed larger and larger data sets, to explore questions of sector efficiency and the determinants and consequences of human capital formation, the small number of countries reporting valid and reliable cross-nationally comparable measures of human capital (that is, cognitive skills as indicated by standardized test scores) became a handicap (Hanushek & Kimko, 2000; Woessmann, 2000). Such measures were necessary to examine such topics as the comparative efficiency of education systems of developing countries; the relationship between national and international investments in the education sector and human capital formation in developing countries; cross-national differences in determinants of human capital growth, with particular attention to such input determinants as books, teachers and class size and such institutional determinants as incentive systems, accountability and school autonomy; and the effect of human capital growth (improvements in cognitive skills) on economic growth.

Cross-country studies require data on many countries. By 2000 most of the larger higher-income countries were already participating in large-scale international assessments, so the only way to expand the number of countries in the data set was to add the low- and middle-income developing countries. And the main way to increase the participation of developing countries was to finance and otherwise support their participation in international assessments.

*Donor Support*

Donor support for developing-country participation became essential, and included both capacity development and financial support. Efforts to develop a country's *capacity for assessment* moved along three tracks. The first track was training related to national assessment. In the 1990s, the World Bank Institute, then called the Economic Development Institute, offered short courses on testing and assessment for education ministry officials from developing countries (Murphy et al, 1996). During the same period, the World Bank issued various 'how to' books on national assessments and examinations (Kellaghan & Greaney, 1992; Greaney & Kellaghan, 1996).[6] Also in the 1990s, UNESCO prepared a handbook on national assessments (Chinapah, 1997) and the International Institute for Educational Planning (IIEP) held a series of workshops on improving data on education quality (Ross & Mählck, 1990).

A second track was the inclusion of 'testing sub-components' in World Bank education projects, largely motivated by the general lack of any evidence regarding the effectiveness or efficiency of education systems in developing countries, as measured by improvements in student achievement. This support would 'help countries make informed decisions about interventions to improve educational quality' and 'monitor trends in the nature and quality of student learning over time' (Lockheed & Murphy, 1996, p. 3), in order to reduce poverty (World Bank, 2006). Most testing sub-components of projects were designed to establish or improve national testing systems as a step toward providing this evidence. The share of education projects with testing components increased from virtually no projects prior to 1990 to 42 percent of education projects funded in FY91 and FY92, and to nearly 70% of education projects funded in 2004 (Larach & Lockheed, 1992; World Bank, 2006).

The third track for capacity development was the hands-on experience obtained from a country's participation in an international large-scale assessment, which required additional financial assistance to cover the participation fees and other direct costs associated with attending meetings and training.

Several donors provided financial support that helped offset these costs for low- and middle-income countries, boosting the number of countries participating in the Trends in International Mathematics and Science Study (TIMSS), Progress in International Reading Literacy Study (PIRLS), the Southern and Eastern African Consortium for Monitoring Education Quality (SACMEQ, an African cross-national assessment) and the Regional Comparative and Explanatory Study (ERCE, a Latin American cross-national assessment), as well as PISA. The amount and regularity of donor contributions have varied enormously from assessment to assessment and from donor to donor.

World Bank education projects with 'testing sub-components' often included funding intended to cover the local costs for data collection for an international large-scale assessment. In addition, the World Bank supported the participation of dozens of low- and middle-income countries in TIMSS and PIRLS, largely through a series of matching grants to the IEA to cover the costs of annual fees and travel costs for national study directors to attend coordination and training meetings. The first grant of approximately $3 million supported the participation of 18 low- and middle-income countries in the Third International Mathematics and Science Study of 1999. A second grant of approximately $5.8 million supported the participation of 24 low- and middle-income countries in one or both of PIRLS 2001 and TIMSS 2003. The final grant of approximately $7.5 million supported the participation of 20 countries in PIRLS 2006 or TIMSS 2007 or both; this grant also provided support to SACMEQ and the Program of Analysis of the Education Systems of the Conference of Ministers of National Education (PASEC, in francophone West Africa).

Other donors also provided financial support. The United Nations Development Program/Regional Bureau of Arab States (UNDP/RBAS) assisted the participation of five Arab States in TIMSS 2003. UNESCO's International Institute for Educational Planning (IIEP) supported administrative overhead costs for SACMEQ I in 1995-97 and for SACMEQ II in 2000-02, and UNESCO, through its Latin American Laboratory for Assessment of Educational Quality (LLECE), supported the 1998 First Regional Comparative and Explanatory Study (PERCE) and the 2005/6

Second Regional Comparative and Explanatory Study (SERCE). Finally, the OECD encouraged central bankers in developing countries to support their country's participation in PISA beginning in 2001. Most recently, a Russian trust fund has provided $9 million to support nine developing countries to improve their assessment systems, including support for participation in international assessments (World Bank, 2013).

This short history highlights an essential difference between developed and developing countries in what motivated their participation in large-scale international assessments. While developed countries were motivated by *their own* interest in improving their own educational quality, developing countries were being encouraged *by others* to participate in international assessments, ostensibly so that the developing countries might improve their own national assessments, use assessments for monitoring and accountability purposes as their education systems became more decentralized, and place the results of their education systems on a common, international scale.

As a result of all these actions and motivations, the number of low- and middle-income countries participating in international assessments grew dramatically between the early 1990s and 2010. Although the various tests used in these international assessments provided human capital measures for different ages, grades and content, development economists placed the results on a common scale, and they as well as development sociologists began answering questions regarding education-sector efficiency, as well as human capital formation and its determinants and consequences, but, remarkably, not to assess aid effectiveness (e.g. Ramirez et al, 2006, Hanushek & Woessmann, 2009). And the scale they used became based on PISA.

### PISA's Growing Influence

Although PISA is the 'last in line' of the 50 years of international assessments, its influence has begun to outstrip that of the other international assessments. For example, PISA is overtaking TIMSS, the dominant international assessment of the 1980s and 1990s, as evidenced by *n*-grams, articles and citations. *N*-grams record the frequency of occurrence of a phrase or word in millions of documents, over time; *n*-grams for TIMSS and PISA [7] show many more instances of TIMSS than PISA prior to 2000, but a sharp decline in references to TIMSS around 2002, when PISA begins to take off (Figure 2).

Scholarly articles and references also show a TIMSS publication advantage that diminishes over time. The ratio of scholarly articles mentioning TIMSS to the number of such articles mentioning PISA is about 4:1 prior to 2007, but only about 2:1 since then (Table I). In terms of actual content, PISA differs little from other international assessments in that it tests reading, mathematics and science knowledge, comprehension and application (Neidorf et al, 2006; Hutchinson & Schagen, 2007), but in terms of context, there are two differences that help explain PISA's rising influence.

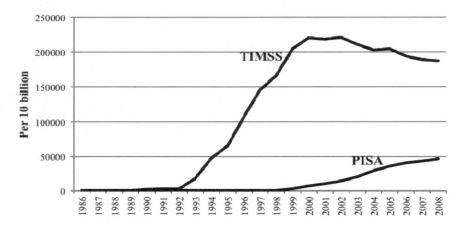

Figure 2. *N*-grams – TIMSS rising, PISA rising, TIMSS falling, 1985-2008.
Source: Google Books Ngram Viewer. http://books.google.com/ngrams

| | Ratio of TIMSS to PISA journal articles | | Share of TIMSS and PISA articles in business and economics journals | |
| --- | --- | --- | --- | --- |
| | Articles in all journals | Articles in business and economics journals | TIMSS | PISA |
| Pre-2007 | 4:1 | 1.5:1 | 8.5 | 14.6 |
| 2007-2011 | 2:1 | 1:1 | 7.4 | 14.1 |

Table I. Comparison of journal articles based on TIMSS and PISA, pre-2007 and 2007-2011. Source: Data downloaded from Google Scholar, 2012.

First of all, PISA is positioned to be more visible to economists. In part this is because PISA is sponsored by the OECD, an organization staffed largely with economists. But it is also because other non-OECD economists conduct secondary analyses based on PISA. The growing PISA publication advantage shows up in two ways. First, as compared with the TIMSS publication advantage in all journals, its publication advantage is much smaller for articles published in economics or business journals: 1.5:1 prior to 2007 and about 1:1 since then. Second, a higher share of all PISA articles appear in business and economics journals, as compared with the share of all TIMSS articles that appear in these journals (Table I). Thus PISA has a greater likelihood of influencing education policy, since policy-makers are often readers of these journals.

Second, since PISA is a budget-line item of the OECD, its resources are higher and more secure than those of other international assessments. For example, in 2009, the OECD reported that the expenditure budget for PISA was around $17 million, which was nearly three times the IEA expenditure budget for TIMSS and PIRLS in the same year. This suggests that the OECD secretariat for PISA has more resources to disseminate the results of PISA as compared with the representatives of other international assessments.

The combination of targeted visibility to economists and association with the OECD (an economics organization) for a strong resource base has meant that the results of PISA are often cited in education policy discussions. PISA is cited more often for these reasons, and not because it is a better test than, for example, TIMSS or PIRLS, or because it covers more countries than these assessments.

## The Impact of International Assessments on Knowledge and Education Policy

The findings from international assessments such as TIMSS and PISA have benefited developing countries through providing knowledge and influencing education policy, but only to a limited degree.

### Knowledge

International assessments have provided countries with knowledge about the quality of their human capital, in an international context. Unfortunately, this knowledge is often not used. The dismally poor performance of low- and middle-income countries on these assessments has often motivated these countries to distance themselves from their results, completely eliminating the possibility for the assessment to influence policy. Countries have declined to publicize or discuss the poor achievement of their students, or have decided to drop out from future assessments, possibly to avoid embarrassment. For example, none of the three developing countries that participated, and ranked lowest, in the first international reading literacy study in 1971 participated in the second study of 1991. Some other examples: in Africa, Botswana participated in the 1991 reading literacy study but did not participate again until PIRLS 2011, and South Africa participated in TIMSS 1995, 1999 and 2003, but not in TIMSS 2007 due to 'outrage in different circles starting with the Department of Education, which had difficulty accepting the very low performance of South African learners' (Howie, 2011, p. 301). In Central Asia, the Kyrgyz Republic participated in PISA in 2006 and 2009, performed the least well of all 65 participating education systems, and decided not to participate in 2012, despite significant encouragement from the international community to participate. In part these decisions may be sensible, since the tests themselves may be somewhat inappropriate for developing countries. For example, they may not be designed to measure improvements in performance that take place towards the lower end of the continuum, in the range of achievement for many students in developing countries – such as the nearly 82% of students tested in Peru whose PISA scores fell below 400 points and were considered 'illiterate'.

## Policy

International assessments have also influenced some types of education policy. Education policy covers myriad policy activities, from lowering class size to implementing voucher programs to establishing accountability systems, but these policy activities can be classified into five types (Wyckoff, 2009):

- redistribution activities (moving money from one group to another, as in the case of education vouchers);
- investment activities (directing money into human or physical capital, as in the case of school buildings);
- service activities (providing goods or services, as in the case of education);
- regulatory (establishing rules for social and economic activity, as in the case of secondary school graduation requirements); and
- behavioral (trying to change the behavior of groups of individuals, as in the case of teaching practice).

The results and analyses from international assessments *could* motivate all five types of policy activity, but so also could the results and analyses from national assessments. But international assessments could be particularly effective vis-à-vis investment, regulatory and behavioral policies. With respect to investment policies, *only* international assessments can document the poor performance of a country relative to other countries at similar levels of economic development, which could – under the right circumstances – motivate a country to alter its investments in human capital development through education. With respect to regulatory policies, *only* a detailed analysis of the strengths and weaknesses of a nation's curriculum as compared with that of other higher-performing countries could motivate regulatory reform regarding the content and methods of instruction. With respect to behavioral policies, *only* the documentation of cross-country differences in teaching strategies between high-achieving and low-achieving countries could lead to efforts to change the behavior of teachers through programs of pre-service and in-service professional development. Recent increased attention to Cuba's education system (Carnoy, 2007), Singapore's mathematics curriculum and Finland's teacher policies (Sahlberg, 2011) suggests these policy effects from the results and analyses of ERCE, TIMSS and PISA, respectively.

Concrete evidence that international assessments have led to any policy changes specifically in developing countries is relatively slim, however. Admittedly, normative statements regarding the share of gross domestic product (GDP) that should be invested in education abound, and development agencies such as the World Bank often encourage countries to invest a higher share of their budgets in education when the observed share is lower than some target number. But government investments are largely determined by factors outside the education sector itself. With respect to inputs and institutional determinants of human capital formation, many analyses have failed to examine the interaction effects between inputs and level of development or between institutions and level of development, and hence do not provide guidance for developing countries. Two recent studies are exceptions. Lavy (2010) finds that additional instructional time is more effective in promoting learning achievement in developed countries, as compared with developing countries. Hanushek et al (2011) find that while greater school autonomy boosts student achievement in developed countries, it is associated with declining student achievement in developing countries.

The evidence regarding the effects of international assessments on certain regulatory and behavioral policies in developing countries is more abundant. Several studies – relying on surveys and interviews with government officials within and across the more than 40 developing countries that have participated in TIMSS, PIRLS or SACMEQ – are very consistent in concluding that international assessments have influenced regulatory policy activities related to curriculum content and performance standards and behavioral policy activities related to classroom instruction and teacher professional development.

An evaluation of IEA's Third International Math and Science Study Repeat (TIMSS-R) of 1999 found that education officials in low- and middle-income countries 'were able to point to reforms in mathematics and science curricula [and] in teaching style' directly attributable to TIMSS-R (Elley, 2002). Elley observed that '[i]n many cases, it is unlikely that such reforms would have occurred without the galvanizing effect of the results of the survey', with reforms in Macedonia, Malaysia and Romania highlighted.

A second evaluation, of IEA's 2003 Progress in Reading Literacy Study and the 2003 TIMSS, noted that the results of these studies 'provide the impetus for reforms and changes in the reading, mathematics and science curricula [and] approaches to teaching' in 20 developing countries (Gilmore, 2005).

Another evaluation of the effects of TIMSS 2003 on policies in five Arab states observed that this international assessment had 'already led to meaningful educational reforms in curriculum', 'heightened awareness of the need for reforms in such areas as teaching methodologies, teacher training and licensing' and 'recognition of the urgent need for shifting the emphasis from rote learning to application of knowledge', particularly in Egypt and Palestine (Aggarwala, 2004).

Interviews with 26 education officials from developing countries that participated in TIMSS 2007 or PIRLS 2006, conducted as part of an evaluation of a World Bank-funded program of support to a consortium of assessment institutions, underscored the positive effects of earlier assessment results on the same two aspects of education policy: reforms in curriculum and teacher education (Lockheed, 2010).

A new study of the effect of TIMSS on education policy finds that changes in test scores over time in Jordan are related to policy changes vis-à-vis curriculum content and teacher professional development (Abdul-Hamid et al, 2011).

Going beyond the IEA studies, another set of examples come from the impact of SACMEQ on education policy in southern African countries. Unlike the IEA studies, SACMEQ's large-scale assessments are designed to address specific policy questions identified by the ministers of education of participating countries, and results from SACMEQ II have informed education policy in these countries. For example, Murimba notes that 'the greatest impact SACMEQ has had on ministries of education is on policy-related, system development processes' (2005, p. 98). He notes how SACMEQ's results influenced ministry of education officials' understanding of the discrepancies between (a) official norms for schools inputs and the actuality of these inputs in Zimbabwe, Kenya, Malawi, and the Seychelles and (b) actual practice and 'policy rhetoric' regarding school fees and repetition in all participating countries. Whether or not this increased understanding led to policy activities is not mentioned, but a recent evaluation of SACMEQ undertaken for UNESCO mentions policy suggestions informed by the results of the assessment in Malawi, Namibia, Seychelles and Botswana (Ercikan et al, 2008). Another study concludes that SACMEQ results affected policies regarding curricula, standards and teacher development in Kenya and Namibia (Nzomo & Makuwa, 2006).

## Impact of International Assessments on Capacity for Assessment

Building capacity for assessment was one of the intended objectives of donor support for assessment in developing countries. Assessment capacity is variously defined, but typically includes: (a) technical capacity for developing the assessment instrument and accompanying survey questionnaires; (b) administrative capacity regarding the physical (or electronic) preparation of tests and related materials, including any necessary translation, test administration, professional scoring of answers to test questions, and data entry, including quality control; (c) analytic capacity regarding sampling, test reliability, scale score construction, analysis; and (d) communication capacity for dissemination of results. In addition, institutional capacity for assessment, which Galiani and Corrales (2006) identify as stability, coherence and coordination and quality of implementation, is important.

International assessments expose assessment specialists in developing countries to international quality standards in testing and measurement, build participants' management capacity for undertaking large research endeavors and help education officials prepare reports for policy makers. Capacity building is a long-term process, and the short-term impacts of international assessments may elude measurement, but they are suggested by self-reports of study participants, as well as by the regularity of a country's participation in international assessments, the regularity and quality of its own national assessments and the association between participating in international large-scale assessments and conducting large-scale national assessments.

*Self-reports of Impact*

Interviews with developing-country officials and national research coordinators for TIMSS 2007 were consistently positive about how participation in this IEA study, and the numerous training activities associated with it, had strengthened and enhanced their technical knowledge and skills for assessment (Lockheed, 2010). Over 70% of the respondents gave high ratings to practical training in data quality control, data collection and field work, test scoring of constructed responses, questionnaire development, test development and sampling. For example, in response to the question 'What specific skills or knowledge have you learned or expanded through your participation in TIMSS', national research coordinators noted:

- 'We had never done this type of test before. Every aspect of testing I've learned in TIMSS. All logistics, training teachers and test administrators, scoring open questions, all computer-related questions, use of secure plastic bags to distribute tests.'
- 'Main thing was principles of sampling; I got familiar with different types of procedures for sampling. In questionnaire development, in translating and revising. In data quality control and the use of programs to ensure quality.'
- 'Research methods, including everything!'
- 'Learned a lot: management as a NRC, to manage the whole process. How to build a national data base, enter data, control quality, administer tests, how to score items, how to write manuals, how to work in a team. If I had read tens of books I would not have learned what I learned from participation in TIMSS.'
- 'Learned a lot on project management – how to manage a large research project. The tasks and deadlines were well defined, which was different from our normal situation, in which we end up doing things at the last minute.'
- 'How to use data management software (WIN W35, WINDEM), how to organize "such a huge assessment" (contacting schools and principals

through phone, email, letters with stamp of Ministry of Education), adapting questionnaires to national needs, many things.'

- 'Analysis – how to use data and make reports for policy makers.'
- 'Policy report writing based on empirical evidence; we used to write reports based on expert opinion only.'

Moreover, in some countries, the capacity building had spill-over effects on national assessments:

- 'Our national assessment learned from the international assessment.'
- 'Helped in writing national assessment items, how to interpret data, using IEA software for data entry of national assessment, disseminated IEA items to teachers to improve their question-writing skills, became aware of Item Response Theory.'

Cariola et al (2011) note that, in Chile, participation in international assessments contributed strongly to improvements in evaluation techniques as well as statistical analyses, which were applied to the national assessment, SIMCE. Similar results were found in studies regarding the impacts of PISA and SERCE (Solano-Flores & Bonk 2008; Murphy, 2010).

Hands-on experience appears more effective than technical assistance. When asked to assess their country's current capacity for carrying out student assessments, respondents attributed higher technical capacity in the areas in which they had hands-on experience through the in-country activities of TIMSS (sampling, test development, questionnaire development, data collection, and data entry and quality control) and in-country communication about the assessment. They attributed lower capacity to technical areas for which the IEA provided software and technical support: scoring, scaling, technical report writing and policy report writing.

In part, international large-scale assessments build technical skills *because* they are international, and require cross-country cooperation. With support from donors, researchers from developing countries meet regularly with those from developed countries and 'learn by doing' as part of country teams and international teams. Outside of meetings, the Internet enables technical experts in one country to assist others, in real time. This type of learning is a powerful tool for enhancing performance, and builds capacity for participating in subsequent assessment, whether international or national.

### Capacity for International Assessments

A country's participation in one international large-scale assessment is strongly related to its participation in a subsequent international large-scale assessment. Table II summarizes the results of 10 analyses measuring the association between a country's participation in either an international assessment (blocks A and B) or national assessment (blocks C and D) at one period of time and the same country's participation in a subsequent international or national assessment. For international assessments (block A), all three measures of association are .42 or more, with high levels of statistical significance. For example, 76% of the 17 developing countries participating in the first PISA 2000 and 68% of the 25 developing countries participating in PISA 2006 had previously participated in at least one prior IEA study. This suggests that the capacity that has been built is enduring.

| Large-scale assessment base period | Subsequent large-scale assessment period | | | | |
|---|---|---|---|---|---|
| | 1996-2000 | 2001-2005 | 2006-2010 | 1996-2000 | 2001-2005 |
| *International* | *International (Block A)* | | | *National (Block B)* | |
| 1991-1995 | 44.83*** (41.75***) | – | – | 2.45 n.s. (1.68) | – |
| 1996-2000 | – | 41.53*** (38.99***) | – | – | 12.74 *** (11.41**) |
| 2001-2005 | – | – | 49.90*** (47.34***) | – | – |
| *National* | *International (Block C)* | | | *National (Block D)* | |
| 1991-1995 | 10.45** (8.35**) | – | – | 48.43*** (43.11***) | – |
| 1996-2000 | – | 8.03** (6.78**) | – | – | 27.88*** (25.60***) |
| 2001-2006 | – | – | 11.01** (9.88**) | – | – |

*** $p < .001$, ** $p < .01$.

Table II. Summary of cross-tabulations of countries, Pearson chi-square statistics with continuity correction in parentheses ($n = 158$ low- and middle-income countries; $df = 1$). Source: author's analysis.

### Capacity for National Assessments

Countries with the capacity to undertake a national assessment also appear to retain that capacity and continue to conduct such assessments; for both time periods for which data are available, the associations are strong and statistically significant (Table II, block D). Indicators of the quality of these national assessments are generally unavailable. Two comprehensive studies in Latin America reviewed institutional capacity for assessment, but included little information about the quality of the assessment instruments themselves (Ferrer, 2006; Galiani & Corrales, 2006). For example, Ferrer (2006, p. 28) notes: 'Technical validation of test items or questions is a critical element in developing assessment instruments; unfortunately, national technical reporting on this subject is not particularly detailed, so it is difficult to provide much information about technical validation experiences in Latin America.' Lockheed (2008, p. 6) observes that 'little public information is available about the technical characteristics of national learning assessments' in developing countries.

*Diffusion of Capacity*

Whether participating in international large-scale assessments actually increases a country's probability of undertaking a national large-scale assessment (or vice versa) is moot; it appears that the two move hand in hand. The total number of countries that have carried out at least one 'national assessment' grew from 65 countries in 1995-1999 to 111 countries in 2000-2006, including 80 developing countries (Benevot & Tanner, 2007). Of these 80 developing countries, 41% have participated in at least one international assessment. However, the empirical association between participating in an international assessment and conducting a subsequent national assessment – or the converse – is weak (Table II, block B for international assessments and subsequent national assessments, and block C for national assessments and subsequent international assessments). The lack of a strong spill-over effect may be due to the fact that different agencies have responsibility for these two types of assessments in some countries.

## Conclusion

The increase in the number of developing countries that participate in international assessments is incontrovertible, with much participation enabled through the financial and technical support of international donor agencies, particularly the World Bank, OECD, UNDP and UNESCO. This chapter argues that the analytic and policy questions of economists as well as an increasing demand for evidence of 'aid effectiveness' fuelled a demand for more countries, particularly developing countries, to participate in international assessments. In the context of this 'globalization' of assessment, the chapter draws attention to the remarkable rise in visibility of PISA as compared with the formerly dominant IEA assessments, a rise that is attributed in part to the positioning of PISA results in publications read by economists.

Participation in all types of international assessments has benefited developing countries indirectly, through influencing norms for curriculum and teaching practice, leading to curricular reform and increased attention to teacher professional development.

Participation in international assessments also has benefited these countries directly, by strengthening the assessment capacity of their national testing agencies, through assessment-related training and hands-on experience in the process developing and implementing large-scale assessments.

## Notes

[1] From 1985 to 2004 the author was a member of the World Bank's staff, holding research and sectoral management positions in the Human

Development Network, the Middle East and North Africa Region, and the World Bank Institute.

[2] Porter & Gamoran, 2002; von Davier & Hastedt, 2009; Rutkowski et al, 2010.

[3] China was represented by students in four cities only.

[4] It is worth noting that the rise in the number of countries participating in international assessments occurred concurrently with the rise in education reforms related to decentralization of education systems.

[5] World Bank staff who served on BICSE were Stephen Heyneman, from 1989 to 1994, and Marlaine Lockheed, from 1995 to 2001.

[6] The World Bank is currently issuing an expanded set of resources for countries, including the following books: Anderson & Morgan, 2008; Greaney & Kellaghan, 2008, 2012; Kellaghan et al, 2009.

[7] PISA was entered into the *n*-gram search as 'Programme for International Student Assessment' to avoid confusion with the Italian city of the same name.

## References

Abdul-Hamid, H., Abu-Lebdeh, K. & Patrinos, H. (2011) *Assessment Testing Can Be Used to Inform Policy Decisions*. WPS5849, December. Washington, DC: World Bank.

Aggarwala, N. (2004) *Quality Assessment of Primary and Middle Education in Mathematics and Science (TIMSS)*. Takoma Park, MD: Eaton-Batson International.

Anderson, P. & Morgan, G. (2008) *Developing Tests and Questionnaires for a National Assessment of Educational Achievement*. Washington, DC: World Bank.

Benevot, A. & Tanner, E. (2007) The Growth of National Learning Assessments in the World, 1996-2006. Background paper prepared for the Education for All Global Monitoring Report, 2008. Paris: UNESCO.

Bradburn, N. & Gilford, D. (Eds) (1990) *A Framework and Principles for International Comparative Studies in Education*. Washington, DC: National Academy Press.

Cariola, L., Covacevich, C., Gubler, J., Lagos, E. & Ortiz, M. (2011) Chilean Participation in IEA Studies, in C. Papanastasiou, T. Plomp & E. Papanastasiou (Eds) *IEA 1958-2008: 50 years of experiences and memories*. Nicosia, Cyprus: Cultural Center of the Kykkos Monastery.

Carnoy, M. (2007) *Cuba's Academic Advantage: why students in Cuba do better in school*. Stanford, CA: Stanford University Press.

Chinapah, V. (1997) *Handbook on Monitoring Learning Achievement: towards capacity building*. Paris: UNESCO.

Elley, W. (2002) Evaluating the Impact of TIMSS-R (1999) in Low- and Middle-income Countries: an independent report on the value of World Bank support for an international survey of achievement in mathematics and science. Amsterdam: International Association for the Evaluation of Educational Achievement.

Ercikan, K., Arim, R., Oliveri, M. & Sandilands, D. (2008) Evaluation of Dimensions of the Work of the Southern and Eastern Africa Consortium for Monitoring Educational Quality (SACMEQ) and of its Programme of Cooperation with the International Institute for Educational Planning (IIEP). Document IOS/EVS/PI/93, August. Paris: UNESCO Internal Oversight Service Evaluation Section.

Ferrer, G. (2006) *Educational Assessment Systems in Latin America: current practice and future challenges.* Washington, DC: PREAL.

Galiani, S. & Corrales, J. (2006) *Academic Evaluation Offices in Latin America: an index of institutional capacity.* Background paper prepared for the World Bank. Washington DC: World Bank.

Gilmore, A. (2005) The Impact of PIRLS (2001) and TIMSS (2003) in Low- and Middle-income Countries: an evaluation of the value of World Bank support for international surveys of reading literacy (PIRLS) and mathematics and science (TIMSS). Amsterdam: International Association for the Evaluation of Educational Achievement.

Greaney, V. & Kellaghan, T. (1996) *Monitoring the Learning Outcomes of Education Systems.* Washington DC: World Bank.

Greaney, V. & Kellaghan, T. (2008) *Assessing National Achievement Levels in Education.* Washington, DC: World Bank.

Hanushek, E. & Kimko, D. (2000) Schooling, Labor-force Quality and the Growth of Nations, *American Economic Review,* 90(5), 1184-1208.

Hanushek, E., Link, S. & Woessmann, L. (2011) Does School Autonomy Make Sense Everywhere? Panel Estimates from PISA. NBER Working Paper 17591. Cambridge, MA: National Bureau of Economic Research.

Hanushek, E. & Woessmann, L. (2009) Do Better Schools Lead to More Growth? Cognitive Skills, Economic Outcomes and Causation. NBER Working Paper 14633. Cambridge, MA: National Bureau of Economics Research.

Howie, S. (2011) The Involvement of African Countries in the IEA Studies Over 50 Years, in C. Papanastasiou, T. Plomp & E. Papanastasiou (Eds) *IEA 1958-2008: 50 years of experiences and memories.* Nicosia, Cyprus: Cultural Center of the Kykkos Monastery.

Hutchinson, D. & Schagen, I. (2007) Comparisons between PISA and TIMSS – Are We the Man with Two Watches? In T. Loveless (Ed.) *Lessons Learned: what international assessments tell us about math achievement.* Washington, DC: Brookings.

Independent Evaluation Group (IEG) (2006) *From Schooling Access to Learning Outcomes: an unfinished agenda.* Washington, DC: World Bank.

Kamens, D. & McNeely, C. (2009) Globalization and the Growth of International Educational Testing and National Assessment, *Comparative Education Review,* 54(1), 5-25.

Kellaghan, T. & Greaney, V. (1992) *Using Examinations to Improve Education: a study in fourteen African countries.* Washington, DC: World Bank.

Kellaghan, T., Greaney, V. & Murray, T.S. (2009) *Using the Results of a National Assessment of Educational Achievement.* Washington, DC: World Bank.

Larach, L. & Lockheed, M. (1992) *World Bank Lending for Educational Testing: a general operational review.* Washington, DC: World Bank.

Lavy, V. (2010) Do Differences in Schools' Instruction Time Explain International Achievement Gaps in Math, Science and Reading? Evidence from Developed and Developing Countries. NBER Working Paper 16227. Cambridge. MA: National Bureau of Economic Research.

Lockheed, M. (2008) Measuring Progress with Tests of Learning: pros and cons for progress-based aid in education. CGD Working Paper 147. Washington, DC: Center for Global Development.

Lockheed, M. (2010) *The Craft of Education Assessment: does participating in international and regional assessments build assessment capacity in developing countries?* Amsterdam: International Association for the Evaluation of Educational Achievement.

Lockheed, M. (2011) Policies, Performance and Panaceas: what international assessments are good for (and not good for) in developing countries. Paper presented at the Annual Meeting of the Comparative and International Education Society, 1-5 May, in Montreal, Canada.

Lockheed, M. & Murphy, P. (1996) Introduction, in P. Murphy, V. Greaney, M. Lockheed & C. Rojas (Eds) *National Assessments: testing the system.* Washington, DC: World Bank.

Michaelova, K. & Weber, A. (2007) Aid Effectiveness in Primary, Secondary and Tertiary Education. Background paper commissioned for the EFA Global Monitoring Report 2008, 'Education for All by 2015: will we make it?' Paris: UNESCO.

Murimba, S. (2005) The Impact of the Southern and Eastern Africa Consortium for Monitoring Educational Quality (SACMEQ), *Prospects*, 35(1), 91-108.

Murphy, P., Greaney, V., Lockheed, M. & Rojas, C. (Eds) (1996) *National Assessments: testing the system.* Washington, DC: World Bank.

Murphy, S. (2010) The Pull of PISA: uncertainty, influence and ignorance, *Inter-American Journal of Education for Democracy*, 3(1), 28-44.

Neidorf, T., Binkley, M., Gattis, K. & Nohara, D. (2006) *Comparing Mathematics Content in the National Assessment of Educational Progress (NAEP), Trends in International Mathematics and Science Study (TIMSS), and Program for International Student Assessment (PISA) 2003 Assessments.* Washington, DC: National Center for Education Statistics.

Nzomo, J. & Makuwa, D. (2006) How Can Countries Move from Cross-national Research Results to Dissemination, and Then to Policy Reform? In K.N. Ross & I. Jurgens-Genevois (Eds) *Cross-national Studies of the Quality of Education: planning their design and managing their impact.* Paris: IIEP (UNESCO).

Organisation for Economic Co-operation and Development (OECD) (2005) *2005 Paris Declaration on Aid Effectiveness.* Paris: OECD.

Organisation for Economic Co-operation and Development (OECD) (2011). *2011 Busan High Level Forum on Aid Effectiveness.* Paris: OECD.

Porter, A. & Gamoran, A. (2002) *Methodological Advances in Cross-national Surveys of Educational Achievement.* Washington, DC: National Academy Press.

Ramirez, F., Luo, X., Schofer, E. & Meyer, J. (2006) Student Achievement and National Economic Growth, *American Journal of Education*, 113 (November), 1-31.

Ross, K. & Mählck, L. (Eds) (1990) *Planning the Quality of Education: the collection and use of data for informed decision-making.* Paris: UNESCO/IIEP.

Rutkowski, L., Gonzalez, E., Joncas, M. & von Davier, M. (2010) International Large-scale Assessment Data: issues in secondary analysis and reporting, *Educational Researcher*, 39(2), 142-151.

Sahlberg, P. (2011) *Finnish Lessons: what can the world learn from educational change in Finland?* New York: Columbia University Teachers College Press.

Solano-Flores, G. & Bonk, W. (2008) Evaluation of the Latin American Laboratory for the Evaluation of Education Quality (LLECE). Document IOS/EVS/PI/91, August. Paris: UNESCO Internal Oversight Service Evaluation Section.

Suter, L. (2011) Guiding International Comparative Studies (1981-2009): reflections of a US program director, In C. Papanastasiou, T. Plomp & E. Papanastasiou (Eds) *IEA 1958-2008: 50 years of experiences and memories.* Nicosia, Cyprus: Cultural Center of the Kykkos Monastery.

von Davier, M. & Hastedt, D. (2009) *IERI Monograph Series: issues and methodologies in large-scale assessments*, vol. 1. Princeton: IEA-ETS Research Institute.

Woessmann, L. (2000) Schooling Resources, Educational Institutions and Student Performance: the international evidence. Kiel Working Paper 983. Kiel, Germany: Kiel Institute of World Economics.

World Bank (2006) *From Schooling Access to Learning Outcomes: an unfinished agenda.* Washington, DC: World Bank.

World Bank (2011) *Learning for All: investing in people's knowledge and skills to promote development.* Washington, DC: World Bank.

World Bank (2013) Russian Aid to Education for Development (READ) Trust Fund. http://web.worldbank.org/WBSITE/EXTERNAL/TOPICS/EXTEDUCATION/ EXTREAD/0,,menuPK:7526437~pagePK:64168427~piPK:64168435~theSiteP K:7526432,00.html

Wyckoff, P. (2009) *Policy and Evidence in a Partisan Age: the great disconnect.* Washington, DC: Urban Institute Press.

## ANNEX A.
## International Comparative Studies in
## Education Advised by BICSE, 1988-2003

| Study year | Study |
|---|---|
| 1980-1982 | IEA's Second International Science Study (analysis only) |
| 1986-1994 | IEA's Pre-primary Study (Phase 1) |
| 1988 | ETS's International Assessment of Educational Progress (IAEP) |
| 1989-2003 | IEA's Pre-primary Study (Phase 2) |
| 1990-1991 | IEA's Reading Literacy Study |
| 1991 | ETS's IAEP II |
| 1989-1992 | IEA's Computers in Education Study |
| 1993-2003 | IEA's Pre-primary Study (Phase 3) |
| 1995 | IEA's Third International Mathematics and Science Study (TIMSS) |
| 1995 | IEA's TIMSS Video Study, |
| 1998-1999 | IEA's Second Information Technology in Education Study (Module 1) |
| 1999 | IEA's TIMSS Repeat |
| 1999 | IEA's Second TIMSS Video Study |
| 1999 | IEA's Second International Civic Education Study |
| 2000 | OECD's Programme on International Student Achievement |
| 2000-2001 | IEA's SITES (Module 2) |
| 2001 | IEA's Progress in International Reading Literacy Study |
| 2003 | IEA's Trends in International Mathematics and Science Study |
| 2003 | OECD's Programme on International Student Achievement |

CHAPTER 8

# PISA and the Expanding Role of the OECD in Global Educational Governance[1]

## SAM SELLAR & BOB LINGARD

ABSTRACT This chapter examines the success and expansion of the Programme for International Student Assessment (PISA) and its role both in strengthening the position of the Education Directorate within the Organisation for Economic Co-operation and Development (OECD) and in enhancing the significance of the OECD's education work globally. The authors provide a brief contextualization of the changing role of the OECD in response to economic globalization. This is followed by an account of the changing place of the Education Directorate within the OECD's organizational structure since the 1990s, related to the rise of PISA and the recent development of a cross-directorate Skills Strategy. They then analyse the expansion of PISA in three domains: the broadening scope of PISA (what is measured); its increasing scale (the extent of coverage); and efforts to enhance its explanatory power (to inform policy makers of what works). Data collected through more than thirty interviews with policy actors located at the OECD and within national education systems (Australia and England), as well as OECD documents, provide an empirical basis for the analysis. Overall, the authors argue that the OECD and PISA have contributed to the creation of new modes of global governance in education.

### Introduction

In this chapter we are concerned to document and understand the enhanced significance of the education work of the Organisation for Economic Co-operation and Development (OECD) globally, particularly the expansion of the Programme for International Student Assessment (PISA) and its role in strengthening the position of the Education Directorate within the overall economic policy work of the OECD. These two developments, as we will demonstrate, are intimately connected and are linked particularly to the priorities of the OECD's work in relation to skills (and to a lesser extent, social cohesion) and the context of globalization. The recent publication of the cross-directorate OECD *Skills Strategy* (OECD, 2012) demonstrates the work being done on skills across the Organization. We argue that a skills focus as one meta-framing of the OECD's work across all directorates and within economic policy considerations has contributed to the enhanced internal significance of the Education Directorate and of PISA specifically. Other national education policy developments and demands in the wake of the end of the Cold War and the rise of globalization, including the press for international comparative performance data of schooling systems, have also enhanced the global significance of PISA, as we will show.

Our specific focus then in this chapter is the role and significance of PISA, but we are also concerned with the enhanced role of the OECD, through PISA, in global governance in education (Martens & Jakobi, 2010). Additionally, we will argue that the global success and national policy influence of PISA have provided a policy prototype for the OECD to expand its global testing approaches to the domain of workforce skills through the Programme for the International Assessment of Adult Competencies (PIAAC) and to the value-added effects of higher education through the planned Assessment of Higher Education Learning Outcomes (AHELO). These are new and emerging testing approaches in their early stages of development and implementation by the OECD. With PIAAC and AHELO, the OECD hopes to establish a position in relation to skills and higher education testing similar to that which PISA now holds in respect of international comparative school system performance. This testing is remaking and strengthening the education work of the OECD. Indeed, we would argue that the OECD and the Directorate for Education have become central to a 'globalizing empiricism' (Torrance, 2006) as 'centres of calculation' (Latour, 1987) for assisting national policy making in an age of evidence-informed policy (Wiseman, 2010) and audit cultures (Power, 1997). The central section of the chapter demonstrates how PISA, in conjunction with these new developments, is expanding its reach in terms of its *scope, scale* and *explanatory power*.

With PISA and the annual reporting of educational indicators in *Education at a Glance*, the OECD has become the recognized global center amongst international organizations for technical expertise in measurement of the schooling performance in member and non-member nations. While we acknowledge the importance of data in the OECD's work since its inception in 1961 (see Henry et al, 2001, ch. 5), we argue that globalization has strengthened the OECD's data role in education (Grek et al, 2009). Indeed, it was during the 1990s that member nations were pressing the OECD to develop such tests and databases as surrogate measures of the potential global competitiveness of national economies. As Brown et al (1997, p. 8) observe, 'the competitive advantage of nations is frequently redefined in terms of the quality of national education and training systems judged according to international standards'.

Woodward (2009, p. 99) suggests that the OECD has probably become, amongst the international organizations, including UNESCO, the 'premier supplier of educational statistics and sculptor of education policy agendas worldwide'. 'Sculptor' is a significant word here, as its picks up on the OECD's mode of operation, which is best seen as operating through 'soft power' and 'soft law'. Woodward (2009, pp. 5-9) describes four modes of governance pursued by the OECD – namely, 'cognitive', normative', 'legal' and 'palliative', with the latter referring to the multiple ways that the OECD 'greases the wheels of global governance' (p. 8). Our analysis will augment Woodward's account of how the OECD sculpts the policy work of nations through these modes of governance, adding two more specific modes of epistemological (spanning cognitive and normative) and infrastructural (a specific global form of palliative) governance. As we will demonstrate, PISA helps to create a global education policy field by constituting the globe as a commensurate space of measurement (Lingard & Rawolle, 2011), functioning through a global network of epistemic policy communities (Kallo, 2009), in effect 'harmonizing the globe' (Tröhler, 2010) and constituting a mode of global governance in education. We will also draw on the work of Jakobi and Martens (2010), who argue that with the enhanced significance of data in the OECD's education policy work from the 1990s, the OECD has enlarged its 'toolbox of governance mechanisms' through the production of what we would see as globalized education policy discourses (see also Rizvi & Lingard, 2010), through policy evaluation by peer review, through data generation, and through its impact upon the framing and stages of policy making and enactment within nations.

With Eccleston (2011, p. 248), we also recognize that the authority of an international organization such as the OECD has both 'rational-legal and moral dimensions'. Furthermore, we agree with Eccleston (2011, p. 248) when he suggests that an 'international organization's political authority is at its zenith when its rational/technical agenda aligns with prevailing social values and sentiments'. This offers an explanation, we would argue, of the enhanced significance of PISA, as nations demand international comparative measures of their human capital as a predictor of potential global economic competitiveness. As already noted, such a desire was also central to the creation of PISA and pressure on the OECD from the United States for indicators and testing in the long wake of the report *A Nation at Risk*. This enhanced significance also links to the audit culture (Power, 1997) and evidence-informed policy making (Head, 2008), which are part of the prevailing social values and sentiments in contemporary education policy making, manifest as what has been called 'policy as numbers' (Lingard, 2011). These numbers, at global (e.g. PISA) and national levels, enable comparison as a new mode of governance, where the 'global eye' and 'national eye' work together to facilitate educational governance (Nóvoa &

Yariv-Mashal, 2003). As Ozga (2009, p. 150) observes, 'data production and management' today 'are essential to the new governance turn'.

In our analysis, we draw on thirty-one semi-structured interviews conducted during recent visits to the OECD with personnel in various directorates, including that of education, and with policy makers in England and Australia (at federal and state levels, in systems and statutory authorities). As well, we draw on relevant policy documents, research reports and political statements from the OECD and various nations.

Our argument proceeds as follows. Initially we give a brief descriptive account of the OECD and education work in the OECD. We then turn specifically to consider the expanding place of PISA in the changing educational work of the OECD, including OECD ambitions to extend its *scope* (what is measured), its *scale* (the extent of coverage across the globe), and its *explanatory power* (to inform policy makers of what works). The conclusion provides an extension of Jakobi and Martens' (2010) and Woodward's (2009) modes of governance through which the OECD functions and has normative global and national effects (Breakspear, 2012) – namely, our concepts of epistemological and infrastructural governance. We also provide a contextualised account of the changing education work of PISA and the OECD and the enhanced significance of that education work inside the OECD, within the work of its broad range of directorates and globally.

## The OECD and Education

The OECD was established in 1961, emerging from the Organisation for European Economic Co-operation (OEEC), which was funded by the United States under the Marshall Plan to reconstruct post-war Europe and to serve as something of a bulwark against communism and as a showpiece for liberal democracy and capitalist market economies. Here the OECD can be seen as a part of the Bretton Woods agreement that established the post-war global infrastructure of international economic relations. However, the OECD stands in stark contrast to the other institutions that developed out of that agreement (e.g. the International Monetary Fund [IMF], World Trade Organization [WTO] and World Bank) due to its functioning through 'soft' rather than coercive power, through its 'technical expertise' and its unique positioning 'as an important node in a transgovernmental network where policy experts can meet, interact and devise coordinated responses to common policy challenges' (Eccleston, 2011, p. 246).

The OECD has been described as:

> a club of like-minded countries. It is rich, in that OECD countries produce two thirds of the world's goods and services, but it is not an exclusive club. Essentially membership is limited only by a country's commitment to a market economy and a pluralistic democracy. (OECD, 1994, p. 4)

The OECD also now explicitly characterizes its role as a response to globalization: 'The OECD is a unique forum where governments work together to address the economic, social and environmental challenges of globalization' (OECD, 1994, p. 7) Of course, in the context of the end of the Cold War and the collapse of the Soviet bloc, and with the emergence of a global economy, many more nations on the globe meet the Organization's membership criteria, to which has been more recently added a commitment to human rights.

The enhanced significance of the technical data work of the OECD globally, and within the OECD and across directorates, can be traced back to the soul searching of the organization following the end of the Cold War. The fall of the Soviet bloc also challenged a central *raison d'être* of the Organization. In that context, and also against the backdrop of the enhanced significance of supranational political units, particularly the EU and the related rise of new regionalisms (e.g. NAFTA, APEC), set against neo-liberal globalization, the OECD has worked hard to retain its relevance:

> The disintegration of authoritarianism and central planning in Eastern Europe was a victory for the OECD convictions about the superiority of capitalism and democracy as organizing principles for global governance, but bereft of plausible ideological adversaries the OECD looked anachronistic. ... [E]ven the Organization's sympathizers had misgivings about its suitability as a backdrop for fabricating the post-Cold War order. (Woodward 2009, pp. 32-33)

Economic globalization and the spread of both liberal democracy and commitment to human rights meant that more nations were eligible for accession to the OECD. Six nations have joined the OECD since the end of the Cold War and there are now thirty-four members.[2] However, the OECD increasingly has policy influence beyond this membership, working around development issues as well as with 'economies in transition' and the BRIC nations (Brazil, Russia, India, China).[3] The rise of the latter raises issues to do with enlargement of the OECD membership, given the increasing global significance of these nations in economic terms. In contrast to pressures for enlargement, some scholars have argued that the OECD's smallish and homogeneous membership has allowed it to retain coherence and has enhanced its effectiveness (Mahon & McBride, 2008; Woodward, 2009); yet, what will its influence be in the so-called Asian century, as power and influence of many kinds transit to Asia? However, we note here that the OECD's secretarial role in respect of the G8 and G20 nations enhances its potential influence with the BRICs, including China. In reconstituting its policy remit, the OECD now constructs itself as a center of policy expertise and comparative international data, based on its programmes of measurement, comparison and analysis. At a macro level it has been an important proselytizer of neo-liberal market capitalism, while at the same time documenting some of the negative social effects in the growth in inequality to flow from this paradigm (OECD, 2011).

Henry and colleagues (Henry et al, 2001, p. 7) describe the OECD as a 'geographic entity, an organizational structure, a policy-making forum, a network of policy makers, researchers and consultants, and a sphere of influence'. They also argue that, in respect of education, the OECD has become more of a policy actor in its own right during the post-Cold War era (see also Jakobi & Martens, 2010), with its technical expertise helping to constitute a global education policy field (Lingard & Rawolle, 2011) by establishing a commensurate space of measurement of national education performance, through what Lawn and Lingard (2002) call a 'magistrature of influence' above the nation. This influence, they suggest, works through, 'a new class of deterritorialized trans-national policy actors, ... a policy elite which act across borders, display a similar habitus, have the feel of the same policy game' (p. 292).

The place of education work within the OECD has changed dramatically since its establishment, moving from an initial 'inferred role' for education and no independent structural location (Papadopoulos, 1994) to its incorporation into the remit of the Directorate for Social Affairs, Manpower and Education in 1975, which was subsequently reconstituted as the Directorate for Education, Employment, Labour and Social Affairs (DEELSA) in 1991. However, the ascendency of education in the OECD began in earnest during the mid-1990s, with the emergence of neo-liberal global capitalism (Harvey, 2005), through a combination of developments, including: the ratification of new policy positions on education (e.g. lifelong learning and knowledge-based economies framed by human capital theory); the creation of the Indicators of Education Systems (INES) programme and the publication of *Education at a Glance* (Henry et al, 2001; Martens & Jakobi, 2010); the alignment of statistical data categories and data sets held by the OECD, UNESCO and Eurostat (Grek et al, 2009); and the emergence of PISA. At this time, member countries, particularly the United States under President Reagan and in the long aftermath of the *Nation at Risk* report, were demanding regular and reliable data on the comparative performance of their education systems, and the education work of the OECD evolved in response. As Eccleston (2011, p. 248) argues, the policy influence of an international organization such as the OECD is enhanced when its rational/technical agendas align closely with the prevailing political sentiments. The development of PISA began in the mid 1990s, and an assessment has taken place every three years since it was first administered in 2000. In 2002, the Education Directorate became autonomous, and as the data developments gathered apace, it has enhanced its influence within the OECD, across directorates and in global governance in education, taking on a preeminent role in this respect. Indeed, Rinne and colleagues (Rinne et al, 2004) speak of the OECD as an '*éminence grise*' in global education.

The rise of the OECD as an influential soft power in global education policy and global education governance is linked to the 'economization' of education policy and what we might see as the simultaneous 'educationizing' of economic policy, all linked to the growing significance of the skills agenda for the OECD across multiple directorates. As we suggested in the introduction, the recent publication of the cross-directorate OECD *Skills Strategy* (OECD, 2012) demonstrates the work being done on skills across the organization and the meta-policy status of the current skills agenda. The influence of human capital theory on the broad economic policy positions adopted and promoted by the OECD has led to education becoming a central concern in much of the organization's work. Indeed, the OECD (2012, p. 10) considers that 'skills have become the global currency of 21st-century economies'. This conception of skills draws theories of human capital, lifelong learning and knowledge-based economies into an overarching policy narrative that presents education and training as a primary site of policy intervention to improve, simultaneously, both the well-being of individuals and the economic strength of nations. There are forceful critiques of this narrative, which argue that the promise of more earning – for both individuals and nations – through more learning cannot be kept, given the complex empirical reality of contemporary global markets and changing modes of production (Brown et al, 2010). While there is recognition of these conditions within the OECD (e.g. Schleicher, 2010a), this policy narrative continues to exercise considerable influence as a global policy discourse.

One of our research interviewees in the Directorate for Employment, Labor and Social Affairs observed that the *Skills Strategy* is an attempt to 'bring together and leverage these different [skills] initiatives and pool together some common lessons coming out of all of these'. Another interviewee in the Directorate for Education described how the cross-directorate focus on skills has made their work increasingly central to the organization: '[F]or these past four or five years we have increasingly been working with the Economics Directorate, also with Employment, with Science and Technology ... So it is now one big OECD family and we have conquered a major pillar in it.' This cross-directorate role of education was recognized by another interviewee in the Economics Directorate, who outlined how education provides 'one of the best examples where [inter-directorate] communication is very good'. Here we can see how the *Skills Strategy* constitutes an important point of convergence around education across the organization's different domains of policy expertise.

The OECD's skills agenda is being reciprocally reinforced by the organization's capacity to measure skills through programs such as PISA and the more recent PIAAC. This also strengthens the internal positioning of the Education Directorate and its data work. For example, PISA data are now always used in the flagship national Economic Surveys produced by the Economics Directorate, which have been central to the work of the OECD since its inception in 1961. Further, PISA data are now included in the *Going for Growth* reports that contribute to the work of the G20. An interviewee from the Directorate for Employment, Labor and Social Affairs explained that PISA is now used 'in all of our reviews', while another observed that it has become, in terms of measuring skills, one 'incredibly important piece of the puzzle'. Further, the Directorate for Financial and Enterprise Affairs successfully lobbied to have financial literacy assessed as part of the 2012 PISA survey, which will further strengthen the cross-directorate usage of PISA and the position of the Education Directorate . The skills agenda is now at the very heart of the OECD's post-Cold War economic work and is linked to the role of the OECD in neo-liberal globalization. Rizvi and Lingard (2010, p. 131) have argued that the OECD actually 'ontologizes' the processes of neo-liberal globalization it describes and uses as rationales for programs and policy development. In Bourdieu's (2003) terms, and in relation to this 'ontologizing', we might see the OECD using a 'performative' semiotic construction of the concept of globalization, implying only neo-liberal globalization and denying other accounts in the process.

While PISA is currently being championed within the OECD, this has been made possible, at least in part, by demands from member countries for the educational data it provides. The increasing value placed on measurement, comparison and quantitative data as an evidence base for national policy making has driven interest in programs such as PISA from members. Countries opt into PISA and pay to participate, rather than the OECD holding expectations that countries participate. This opting in and paying to participate is indicative of the enhanced global significance today of PISA and the related use of international comparative systemic performance data in global governance in education and associated processes of policy development and enactment within nations (Jakobi & Martens, 2010). It is important to note, as well, that there is encouragement from the OECD for countries to participate in PISA and to use it to implement policy reform and to benchmark school system performance globally. An interviewee in the Education Directorate explained: '[PISA is] an offer and I think there is clearly, in many countries, the sense that we need to see ourselves in a global picture. So I expect take up to increase further but it sometimes has to be pushed.' There is a self-perpetuating dynamic here, whereby demand for and participation in PISA strengthens its influence and drives further expansion and promotion of the program. This is contributing to the expansion of the scope, scale and explanatory power of PISA, which is the focus of the subsequent sections of the chapter.

## Expanding the Influence of PISA and the OECD's Education Work

PISA has substantially expanded since it was first conducted in 2000. This expansion is taking place across three domains: (a) widening the *scope* of the assessment to measure a broader set of skills and capacities; (b) increasing the *scale* of the assessment to include a larger set of countries and economies; and (c) enhancing its *explanatory power*, or the relevance and usefulness of PISA-based analyses for policy makers and educators. The three domains of expansion have been derived from our analysis of research interviews and documents. These domains can be seen in Schleicher's (2010b) comments on the future of the program:

> The long-term future lies with multi-layered assessment systems that extend from classrooms to schools to regional to national to international levels [*scale*], that measure not just what students know but also how students progress, that are largely performance-based, that make student's thinking visible, and that allow for divergent thinking [*scope*]. Also, these assessments must generate data that teachers, administrators, and policy-makers can act upon [*explanatory power*]. (p. 434)

In this section of the chapter, we examine new developments across each of these domains, including the introduction of new programs that extend from and/or augment the work of PISA, such as the Program for International Assessment of Adult Competencies (PIAAC) and the current PISA-based Test for Schools pilot.

### Scope: measuring a broader set of skills and capacities

PISA provides a measure of human capital flows into economies. However, since the popularization of the concept in the middle of the last century, human capital has changed in response to related changes in the global economy and governance in advanced capitalist nations. Feher (2009) argues that the concept of human capital has come to incorporate a wider set of qualities beyond the skills and competencies gained through investments in education and training. Human capital now designates the entire ensemble of capacities embodied by individuals, and which are affected not just by education but by every facet of life: biology, psychology, economy, society, etc. Moreover, investment in these capacities is no longer made only during an initial period of education and training in anticipation of future returns. Investment strategies have evolved in response to economic globalization and the financialization of capital, in a manner analogous to corporate strategies:

> [I]n the neoliberal world of globalized and unregulated financial markets, corporate governance is concerned less with optimizing returns on investment over time than with maximizing the distribution of dividends in the short run. Accordingly, its major preoccupation is with capital growth or appreciation rather than income, stock value rather than commercial profit. ... [I]f we apply this major strategic shift in governance to human capital, it appears that an investor in his or her human capital is concerned less with maximizing the returns on his or her investments –

whether monetary or psychic –than with appreciating, that is, increasing the stock value of, the capital to which he or she is identified. (Feher, 2009, p. 27)

This change is illustrated in the shift of emphasis in the OECD's education work during the 1990s, toward the valorization of lifelong learning and knowledge economies in which education and training become a means for the perpetual appreciation of human capital rather than a one-off initial investment.

This change, coupled with the emphasis on innovation, presents at least two significant challenges to the measurement of human capital. First, it is no longer simply flows of human capital into economies that must be measured, but also the fluctuating value of human capital stocks in relation to changing economic conditions. An interviewee in the Economics Department explained:

> PISA is a measurement of the flow of human capital into the economy. What matters for innovation is not the first stock of human capital, it's the ability of the work force to come up with new products and new processes; but also to adopt new processes. ... PISA is just a flow, so the flow, it actually contributes to the stock, right? But it will take a long time, so we're interested to have a measurement of the stock, and I don't think we have a good way to measure the stock of our human capital.

Second, the dimensions of human capital that *might* have value for producing new products and processes in the future are less tangible than those that currently have value in the reproduction of existing products and processes. The measurement of human capital increasingly requires the quantification of the set of dispositions that are *potentially* valuable. These dispositions are often described in terms of creativity, motivation or collaboration and represent the potential for human capital appreciation, rather than the possession of actual skills that are susceptible to obsolescence with technological and economic change. An interviewee in the Education Directorate explained that their assessment work is increasingly focused on the relationships between these dispositions and future success: 'The evidence of these cognitive attributes might be ... determination, lateral thinking, creative thinking, those kinds of things.' Efforts to predict and quantify these more intangible qualities complicate the measurement of human capital. As Feher observes, human capital appreciation is 'especially difficult to predict, both because the future marketability of a conduct or a sentiment cannot easily be anticipated and because the correlation between financial and psychological forms of self-appreciation cannot be homogeneously established' (2009, p. 28).

The expanding scope of PISA is a partial response to these challenges and can be characterized as a *measurement expansion* whereby more dimensions of human being are subject to quantification and subsequent valuation. An interviewee within the Education Directorate explained the need for this expansion:

> We need to embrace a broader range of competencies ... you need to build in interpersonal competencies, problem solving; intrapersonal competencies and motivation, self-concept and so on, and these are things we just need to do better and need to work hard on to broaden the horizon.

Innovations in assessment methodology based on the use of computers and a new focus on collaborative problem solving to be included in PISA 2015 provide a good illustration of such expansion. Problem solving was first included in PISA 2003. In PISA 2012, participating countries and economies could opt into a computer-based assessment of problem-solving skills, which enables the dynamic measurement of the processes and strategies employed by students, as they work through tasks, and not simply assessment of their capacity to arrive at the correct outcome. In 2015 this dimension will be further extended to include collaborative problem solving, expanding the dimensions of human capital being assessed to incorporate both dynamic and interpersonal competencies.

PIAAC, the OECD's new program to measure human capital among adults (aged 16 to 64), provides another illustration of the evolution in OECD human capital metrics. The first round of data collection for PIAAC was conducted in early 2012 and the findings were scheduled to be published in October 2013. PIAAC responds to the proliferation of learning beyond the traditional times and spaces of schooling, providing a measure of fluctuating human capital stocks in the context of lifelong learning and the continual 'self-appreciation' or depreciation of human capital (Feher, 2009). As Rose observes:

> Education is no longer confined to 'schooling', with its specialized institutional sites and discrete biographical locus. The disciplinary utilization and normalization of the school sought to install, once and for all, the capacities and competencies for social citizenship. But a new set of educational obligations is emerging that are not confined in space and time in the same ways. The new citizen is required to engage in a ceaseless work of training and retraining, skilling and reskilling, enhancement of credentials and preparation for a life of incessant job seeking: life is to become a continuous economic capitalization of the self. (Rose, 1999, pp. 160-161)

Like PISA, PIAAC is assessing literacy, numeracy and problem-solving skills, and will be conducted as a largely computer-based survey, wherever individuals have the necessary technological competencies and access. However, PIAAC also incorporates, as part of a background questionnaire, the assessment of 'personal traits' such as 'grit' (persistence and self-discipline), social and cultural engagement, political efficacy and social trust

(OECD, n.d.). PIAAC represents, in part, a new effort to quantify 'sentiments' and 'conducts' that act as predictors of future human capital value.

An interviewee in the Education Directorate explained that the extension of PIAAC into the measurement of personal traits could increase the impact of PIAAC relative to PISA:

> We know how to measure income, employment, but we have no sense of things like self-concept in society, participation, political efficacy ... I think PIAAC will put those things on the map. Quantify it. Show that there are real differences among countries on this, that the potential for influencing the running of societies I think is really, really good.

The extension of PISA to assess dynamic and collaborative problem solving, and the augmentation of PISA by PIAAC, particularly its assessment of personality traits, both illustrate the contemporary expansion of OECD education metrics to assess more intangible aspects of human capital, which have an ambivalent ontological status between actual skills and 'potential' value. As a result, these metrics now seek to quantify *who* people are and who they could become, not simply *what* they know or can do.

### Scale: measuring a wider pool of human capital

The measurement expansion of PISA is being complemented by *spatio-temporal expansion* that is widening the pool of human capital assessed by the OECD. Since 2000, the global reach of PISA has increased significantly. At the same time, PISA-based tests are currently being trialed in schools for individual use by schools and global benchmarking of schools. These tests would introduce both a smaller unit and different frequency of assessment into the OECD's PISA-based benchmarking. The impetus for this spatiotemporal expansion was described by an interviewee in the Education Directorate who explained that the OECD aims to have 'the broadest possible picture of the global talent pool' (e.g. more nations participating) and to provide PISA as 'an open metric that people can subscribe to as they wish' (e.g. PISA for individual schools).

Participation in PISA has increased dramatically since the programme began. PISA 2000 included 28 OECD countries and 4 non-member countries, whereas PISA 2012 has covered all 34 OECD countries, plus an additional 31 non-member countries and economies – more than double the initial number of countries and economies participating in the 2000 assessment. Notably, all of the countries being targeted through the OECD's enhanced engagement program (Brazil, China, India, Indonesia and South Africa), except for South Africa, now have some degree of participation. Shanghai, China joined the assessments in 2009, and two provinces in India (Tamil Nadu and Himachel Pradesh) participated in the 2009 PISA+. PISA

2009+ assessed ten economies that were unable to meet the timelines for participation in PISA 2009, including Malaysia, Venezuela (Miranda) and United Arab Emirates. The reach of PISA now extends into new regions of Asia, South America, North Africa and the Arab Gulf, and includes each of the BRIC nations.

The effects of this spatial expansion of PISA were well illustrated by the inclusion of Shanghai in PISA 2009. Shanghai's top performance in its first assessment, along with the strong performance of other East Asian nations (such as Singapore, which also participated for the first time in 2009), has encouraged many nations to 'look East' for education policy ideas (Sellar & Lingard, 2012).The recent publication of the edited collection *Surpassing Shanghai: an agenda for American education built on the world's leading systems* (Tucker, 2011) signified a shift of perspective in global policy learning and the benchmarking of education systems. As Luke (2011) and others (e.g. Schleicher, 2010a) have noted, the United States is now looking outwards for education reform ideas, partly due to a new 'Sputnik moment' created by the surprisingly strong performance of Shanghai on PISA in the context of shifting geopolitics and economic power (see US President Obama's 2011 State of the Union Address). The value of PISA as a tool for comparison increases as the number of participating countries and economies expands, and the participation of new economic powers such as China and India is particularly important for its contemporary global relevance and impact.

While Finland's top PISA performance since the beginning of the program has made it a global education 'poster boy' (Sahlberg, 2011), PISA has also strengthened multilateral comparisons with neighboring nations and economic competitors. An interviewee in the Education Directorate emphasized the fact that 'one of the biggest things PISA has sparked is the [multilateral] interest of countries in other countries'. For example, the Grattan Institute in Australia recently published a report titled *Catching Up: learning from the best school systems in East Asia* (Jensen et al, 2012). This was coupled with public comment from Prime Minister Gillard, who observed that 'four of the top five performing school systems in the world are in our region and they are getting better and better' and that Australians cannot afford to become 'workers in an economy where we are kind of the runt of the litter in our region and we've slipped behind the standards and the high-skill, high-wage jobs are elsewhere in our region' (*The Australian*, 24 January 2012). Here we can see how the expansion of PISA increases the potential for intraregional comparisons and, with the strong performance of Asian economies, is shifting the global comparative gaze away from Europe for some countries.

Another interesting development in the OECD's education work is the development and trialing of PISA-based Tests for Schools in the United States, UK and Canada. This pilot program provides school-level assessments using PISA-based items and is designed to allow schools to compare their performance against other schools around the world. There has been great demand to participate in the trial, which was oversubscribed in the United States and generated high-level political interest in the UK. The test itself will likely be freely available to schools and able to be implemented at a time of the school's choosing. However, it is possible that schools would need to contract an approved provider of assessment and analysis services in order to have their results officially recognized. There will also likely be a market for secondary analysis and the provision of evidence-based advice to schools. This raises the possibility of edu-businesses such as Pearson finding a profitable niche in the delivery of this program (see Ball, 2012). The PISA-based Tests for Schools pilot provides another example of how PISA is being augmented on the basis of the replication and adaptation of its successful model. In this case, it will extend PISA-based assessments to smaller units of analysis (schools, school clusters) and will make them available at times driven by the user demand, rather than the logistics of developing and implementing large-scale global assessments. The extension of PISA-based tests to schools, in conjunction with the established practice of including sub-national units, is increasing the capacity for the OECD's measurement work to influence education policy and reform within nations at sub-national scales.[4]

### Explanatory Power: providing more influential analysis and ideas

The third domain of PISA expansion is *analytical*. This expansion extends from and culminates the previous two by drawing together the wider scope and increased coverage of the assessment to increase the explanatory power of PISA data and analyses. The primary objective here is to make PISA more relevant and useful for policy makers. Jakobi and Martens (2010, p. 7) argue that the soft power exerted by the OECD relies on persuasive argumentation, and they identify three mechanisms of OECD governance: idea production; policy evaluation; and data generation. We see the analytical expansion of PISA as an effort to strengthen the first mechanism – idea production and the framing of policy problems and solutions, and the promotion of policy ideas (e.g. knowledge-based economies) – by its leveraging of policy evaluation and data-generation work. As Jakobi and Martens (2010, p. 175) observe, '[t]he OECD today not only defines the problem, but also offers the solution, in contrast to its practice in the 1970s. With the new generation of indicators, the organization has therefore gained an important status in several stages of national policy-making, ranging from agenda setting to policy formulation and implementation'. That is, analytical expansion involves the strengthening of claims that can be made about the relationships between the factors and policy settings that drive particular educational outcomes, increasing their value for and influence on national policy making. Two examples of this expansion are current efforts to improve the quality of background data collected during PISA assessments, and to link PISA with findings from the OECD's Teaching and Learning International Survey (TALIS).

Much of the analytical power of PISA derives from the ability to identify relationships between testing outcomes and background data gathered as part of the assessment. A number of questionnaires are administered with PISA, including a standard student background questionnaire (used to gather data on socioeconomic status, student attitude, etc.) and a school principal questionnaire, as well as others that countries can opt to administer. An interviewee from the Education Directorate explained that 'we have to try and improve the measures in the background, otherwise we're not going to succeed in explaining what makes a difference to performance'. There is a clear relationship between increasing analytical power and increasing the scope, scale and quality of measurement and the data it generates.

A related issue, as noted by the following interviewee, is the absence of a teaching questionnaire and the gap this creates in explaining outcomes: 'the bit that is missing must have a lot to do with the teaching and teachers. ... So, we're looking over time to see how TALIS and PISA could be complementing each other more than they are now.' TALIS is the OECD's program to assess teacher working conditions and learning environments in schools through teacher questionnaires. The first round was conducted in 2008 and the second round was scheduled to be completed in 2013. Eight countries are currently experimenting with linking TALIS and PISA results, with alignment of the assessments possible in 2018 if these experiments succeed. This attempt to increase the analytical power of PISA through the inclusion of data on teachers' work has emerged from the contemporary global concern with teacher impact and effectiveness (e.g. OECD, 2005; Hattie, 2008). Indeed, an interviewee in the Centre for Education Research and Innovation (CERI) suggested that developing a 'measurement of teacher professional skills, competences [and] knowledge', which extends from TALIS to include teachers' practices in classrooms, is 'effectively the Holy Grail' for this aspect of the OECD's education work; this would particularly be the case if it can be linked to PISA.

Such efforts to increase the explanatory power of PISA raise questions concerning the evidence produced through the OECD's educational measurement and analyses. A significant issue for the OECD, as well as national users of their products, is that of causation. Burns and Schuller (2007, pp. 22-23) note:

> Causation is a particularly problematic concept, but one that
> demands attention from policy makers who are responsible for
> allocating resources accountable for the effects of these
> allocations. The debate reaches into the OECD's own work:
> OECD, and certainly the Education Directorate within it, would
> certainly claim to base policy recommendations on evidence, but
> the nature of evidence varies considerably. ... It would be fair to

acknowledge that there is no unanimity within OECD on where
exactly to draw the lines around what counts as evidence, nor how
it might best be used.

The analytical expansion of PISA raises questions about the claims it can
support about the relationship between policy settings, practices and
particular outcomes. The widespread and prominent media coverage that
PISA has enjoyed, including commentary from OECD staff in a variety of
national and international newspapers and magazines, often emphasizes the
reasons for a particular country's performance on PISA in order to promote
particular policy settings or education reform agendas. One prominent
example is the development, in conjunction with the Pearson Foundation, of
the *Strong Performers and Successful Reformers in Education* video series, which
is based on case studies with stakeholders in strong-performing or improving
countries and provides stories 'behind the data' about 'what works' in these
particular systems.[5] This is one way in which the OECD engages in the
first mode of governance described by Jakobi and Martens (2010) – idea
generation – and its significant impact to date is clearly spurring further
efforts to strengthen this approach. There has been some debate, however,
both within and beyond the OECD, about the claims that can be
substantiated on the basis of PISA data and analyses and the risk that its
popularity with nations is reducing support for other important OECD
programs of policy analysis in education.

## Conclusion

In this chapter we have demonstrated the growing significance of the work of
the Education Directorate within the OECD since the 1990s and particularly
this century. This has been framed by the meta-policy status granted to the
skills agenda at the OECD and what we have argued is the simultaneous
'economization' of education policy and 'educationalization' of economic
policy. Furthermore, we have shown how the OECD has searched for a new
*raison d'être* in the post-Cold War era of neo-liberal globalization, when most
nations are committed to market economics, to embracing or at least moving
towards liberal democracy, and to enacting or moving towards a human
rights agenda. Certainly, in the context of economic globalization, and with
education policy becoming central to the international competitiveness of
national economies, nations have demanded data on comparative schooling
performance as a surrogate measure of their potential and future global
competitiveness, and the OECD has been well positioned to redefine its role
in education to meet these demands. The OECD has also argued for the
necessity of such comparative data for effective national policy making. The
technical expertise of the OECD and the global demand for comparative
data, taken together, have witnessed the growing significance of PISA in the
OECD's education work. The success of PISA has been the prototype for the
expansion of OECD international comparative testing into other educational

and economic domains – namely, workforce skills (PIACC) and higher education (AHELO). We have also noted the cross-directorate use of PISA now, particularly its use in various kinds of reporting associated with the OECD's Economics Department.

Here we see the complementarity of global developments, the necessity of change at the OECD in the post-Cold War era of neo-liberal globalization, and national pressures on the OECD stemming from the reworking of the nation-state in the face of a global economy. The policy interests of the OECD and national economies have come together around education.

The changes we have documented in this chapter, including the moves to extend the *scope, scale* and *explanatory power* of PISA, have expressed and helped to create new forms of educational governance, both globally and nationally, with comparative data being very important in this respect. As we noted in the introduction to this chapter, Woodward (2009) talks of cognitive, normative, legal and palliative modes of governance, functioning through the OECD and contributing to global governance. Indeed, Woodward suggests that 'the OECD is a pivotal international organization because it sows the seeds of interstate consensus and cooperation that allow humankind to reap a greater capacity to manage our common affairs' (2009, p. 5). Normative governance functions through agreement about a set of values. This is in some ways comparable to Jakobi and Martens' (2010) description of the OECD's education policy work as generating ideas or global educational policy discourses, which help frame up national policy developments and contribute to policy convergence, at least at the meta discursive level. Cognitive governance refers, for Woodward (2009), to the advancement of a cooperative agenda across member and other nations through meetings and the circulation of these ideas. Legal governance is self-explanatory and has been less evident in education than in other areas of policy concern for the OECD, though overall it is the least prominent mode of governance. Palliative governance picks up on the work that the OECD does in 'lubricating' international relations (e.g. the secretariat work that the OECD does for the G8 and G20 meetings).

Our analysis has demonstrated the contribution of PISA and the OECD's education policy work to global governance and has also shown how PISA is helping constitute a global education policy field (as a mode of global governance in education) (Lingard & Rawolle, 2011), through the creation of the globe as a commensurate space of measurement of the comparative performance of schooling systems. In respect of that analysis, we would argue that what we are seeing in global educational governance is a form of 'epistemological governance', which spans both of Woodward's cognitive and normative modes. This works through policy discourses, peer evaluations and comparative data, as suggested by Jakobi and Martens (2010). The expanding scope and scale of PISA and the resultant increase in its analytical and explanatory power are serving to strengthen this mode of governance in education globally. Additionally, we would argue that this epistemological governance functions through an emergent global epistemic community of policy makers at the OECD and within nations (Kallo, 2009), often, but not exclusively, located at the national level. In Bourdieu's terms, what we see here is the alignment of policy habitus across the global and national scales of educational governance. This habitus accepts the reliability and validity and global (or universal) applicability of testing such as PISA, a case of global governance assuming the right to the universal in a globalized version of Bourdieu's (1999) account of the logics of practice of bureaucratic state structures (the assumption of the 'monopoly of the universal'). As Wiseman (2010) notes in this context of audit cultures and evidence-informed policy at national levels:

> what widely available international data on education has done is create an intellectual space where educational policymaking is not geographically or politically bounded but is instead bounded by the extent of the legitimated evidence used to support one decision or policy versus another. (Wiseman, 2010, p. 8)

Sassen (1997) sees globalization as the creation of a global infrastructure that facilitates transnational flows of multiple kinds. We see the ongoing spatio-temporal expansion of PISA, and other data work of the OECD, helping to create just such a global infrastructure. In respect of global governance, the OECD has helped to create a mode of 'infrastructural governance', which represents a specific form of Woodward's palliative or 'lubricant' governance. We speculate that while infrastructural governance helps constitute the global, palliative governance perhaps functions most often in multilateral ways.

We are very aware that we have worked largely, throughout this chapter, with a conceptualization of globalization from above. Indeed, that has been our focus in showing how the rise of the OECD's numbers works and how the expansion of PISA is helping to constitute new modes of global governance in education and a global education policy field, with associated effects in national governance and national education policy fields. At the same time, though, we need to acknowledge that nations and regions have their own histories, cultures and political differences and are positioned in a particular way in respect of the globalizing economy (e.g. Koh's [2010] discussion of Singapore and their strategy of 'tactical globalization'). To some extent, the OECD's concern for equity and human rights – more specifically, the focus in PISA on both quality and equity – reflects the underpinning assumption that all nations should be aiming for their schooling systems to be both high quality and high equity. This helps draw in the participation of nations with governments from across the political spectrum, thus enhancing PISA's role in instantiating global educational governance.

## Notes

[1] The research upon which this chapter is based has been developed from a Discovery Project (DP1094850), *Schooling the Nation in an Age of Globalisation: national curriculum, accountabilities and their effects*, funded by the Australian Research Council (ARC).

[2] Australia, Austria, Belgium, Canada, Chile, the Czech Republic, Denmark, Estonia, Finland, France, Germany, Greece, Hungary, Iceland, Ireland, Israel, Italy, Japan, Korea, Luxembourg, Mexico, the Netherlands, New Zealand, Norway, Poland, Portugal, the Slovak Republic, Slovenia, Spain, Sweden, Switzerland, Turkey, the United Kingdom and the United States.

[3] The slippage between the use of 'nations' and 'economies' in OECD discourse is symptomatic of its largely economic focus and the ways in which other policy domains, including education, are framed in this way.

[4] PISA already has sub-national applications through (a) the participation of cities such as Shanghai and Hong Kong; and (b) the oversampling of countries in the UK, or state systems in countries such as Australia and the United States, which enables internal comparisons based on PISA.

[5] See http://www.pearsonfoundation.org/oecd

## References

Ball, S.J. (2012) *Global Education Inc: new policy networks and the neo-liberal imaginary*. London: Routledge.

Bourdieu, P. (1999) *Practical Reason: on the theory of action*. Cambridge: Polity Press.

Bourdieu, P. (2003) *Firing Back against the Tyranny of the Market*. London: Verso.

Breakspear, S. (2012) *The Policy Impact of PISA: an exploration of the normative effects of international benchmarking in school system performance*. OECD Education Working Papers, no. 71. Paris: OECD Publishing.

Brown, P., Halsey, A.H., Lauder, H. & Wells, A.S. (1997) The Transformation of Education and Society: an introduction, in A.H. Halsey, H. Lauder, P. Brown & A. Stuart Wells (Eds) *Education: culture, economy and society*, pp. 1-44. Oxford: Oxford University Press.

Brown, P., Lauder, H. & Ashton, D. (2011) *The Global Auction: the broken promises of education, jobs and income*. Oxford: Oxford University Press.

Burns, T. & Schuller, T. (2007) The Evidence Agenda, in OECD (Ed.) *Evidence in Education: linking research and policy*. Paris: OECD Publishing.

Eccleston, R. (2011) The OECD and Global Economic Governance, *Australian Journal of International Affairs*, 65(2), 243-255.

Feher, M. (2009) Self-appreciation; or, the aspirations of human capital, *Public Culture*, 21(1), 21-41.

Grek, S., Lawn, M., Lingard, B., Ozga, J., Rinne, R., Segerholm, C. & Simola, H. (2009) National Policy Brokering and the Construction of the European Education Space in England, Sweden, Finland and Scotland, *Comparative Education*, 45(1), 5-21.

Harvey, D. (2005) *A Brief History of Neoliberalism*. Oxford: Oxford University Press.

Hattie, J. (2008) *Visible Learning: a synthesis of over 800 meta-analyses relating to achievement*. London: Routledge.

Head, B. (2008) Three Lenses of Evidence-based Policy, *Australian Journal of Public Administration*, 67(1), 1-11.

Henry, M., Lingard, B., Rizvi, F. & Taylor, S. (2001) *The OECD, Globalisation and Education Policy*. Amsterdam: Pergamon.

Jakobi, A.P. & Martens, K. (2010) Introduction: the OECD as an actor in international politics, in K. Martens & A.P. Jakobi (Eds) *Mechanisms of OECD Governance: international incentives for national policy-making?*, pp. 163-179. Oxford: Oxford University Press.

Jensen, B., Hunter, A., Sonneman, J. & Burns, T. (2012) *Catching Up: learning from the best school systems in East Asia*. Melbourne, Grattan Institute.

Kallo, J. (2009) *OECD Education Policy: a comparative and historical study focusing on the thematic reviews of tertiary education*. Jyväskylä: Jyväskylä University Press, Finnish Educational Research Association.

Koh, A. (2010) *Tactical Globalization: learning from the Singapore experiment*. Bern: Peter Lang.

Latour, B. (1987) *Science in Action: how to follow scientists and engineers through society*. Cambridge, MA: Harvard University Press.

Lawn, M. & Lingard, B. (2002) Constructing a European Policy Space in Educational Governance: the role of transnational policy actors, *European Educational Research Journal*, 1(2), 290-307.

Lingard, B. (2011) Policy as Numbers: ac/counting for educational research, *Australian Educational Researcher*, 38(4), 355-382.

Lingard, B. & Rawolle, S. (2011) New Scalar Politics: implications for education policy, *Comparative Education*, 47(4), 489-502.

Luke, A. (2011) Generalizing Across Borders: policy and the limits of educational science, *Educational Researcher*, 40, 367-377.

Mahon, Rianne & McBride, Stephen (Eds) (2008) *The OECD and Transnational Governance*. Vancouver: University of British Columbia Press.

Martens, K. & Jakobi, A.J. (2010) Expanding and Intensifying Governance: the OECD in education policy, in K. Martens & A.P. Jakobi (Eds) *Mechanisms of OECD Governance: international incentives for national policy-making?*, pp. 163-179. Oxford: Oxford University Press.

Nóvoa, A. & Yariv-Mashal, T. (2003) Comparative Research in Education: a mode of governance or historical journey? *Comparative Education*, 39(4), 423-438.

Obama, B. (2011) Remarks by the President in State of Union Address. http://www.whitehouse.gov/the-press-office/2011/01/25/remarks-president-state-union-address (accessed 25 April 2013).

Organisation for Economic Co-operation and Development (OECD) (n.d.) PIAAC BQ JRA V5.0 – Conceptual Framework. http://www.oecd.org/edu/48865373.pdf, accessed 9 October 2012.

Organisation for Economic Co-operation and Development (OECD) (1994) *OECD OCDE.* Paris: OECD.

Organisation for Economic Co-operation and Development (OECD) (2005) *Teachers Matter: attracting, retaining and developing effective teachers.* Paris: OECD.

Organisation for Economic Co-operation and Development (OECD) (2011) *Education at a Glance 2011: OECD indicators.* Paris: OECD.

Organisation for Economic Co-operation and Development (OECD) (2012) *Better Skills, Better Jobs, Better Lives: a strategic approach to skills policies.* Paris: OECD.

Ozga, J. (2009) Governing Education through Data In England: from regulation to self-evaluation, *Journal of Education Policy*, 24(2), 149-162.

Papadopoulos, G.S. (1994) *Education 1960-1990: the OECD perspective.* Paris: OECD Publishing.

Power, M. (1997) *The Audit Society: rituals of verification.* Oxford: Oxford University Press.

Rinne, R., Kallo, J. & Hokka, S. (2004) Too Eager to Comply? OECD Education Policies and the Finnish Response, *European Educational Research Journal*, 3(2), 454-485.

Rizvi, F. & Lingard, B. (2010) *Globalizing Education Policy.* London: Routledge.

Rose, N. (1999) *Powers of Freedom: reframing political thought.* Cambridge: Cambridge University Press.

Sahlberg, P. (2010) Rethinking Accountability in a Knowledge Society, *Journal of Educational Change*, 11(1), 45-61.

Sahlberg, P. (2011) *Finnish Lessons: what can the world learn from educational change in Finland?* New York, Teachers College Press.

Sassen, S. (2007) *Sociology of Globalization.* New York: W.W. Norton.

Schleicher, A. (2010a) The New Global Landscape of Educational Achievement, *Issues in Science and Technology*, 26(3), 81-85.

Schleicher, A. (2010b) Assessing Literacy across a Changing World, *Science*, 328(5977), 433-434.

Sellar, S. & Lingard, B. (2012) Looking East: Shanghai, PISA and the reconstitution of reference societies in the global education policy field. Paper presented at the 2012 Australian Association for Education Research Annual Conference, 3-6 December, in Sydney, Australia.

Torrance, H. (2006) Globalizing Empiricism: what, if anything, can be learned from international comparisons of educational achievement? In Hugh Lauder, Phillip Brown, Jo-Anne Dillabough and A.H. Halsey (Eds) *Education, Globalization and Social Change*, pp. 824-834. Oxford: Oxford University Press.

Tröhler, D. (2010) Harmonizing the Educational Globe: world polity, cultural features, and the challenges to educational research, *Studies in Philosophy and Education*, 29(1), 7-29.

Tucker, M. (Ed.) (2011) *Surpassing Shanghai: an agenda for American education built on the world's leading systems.* Cambridge, MA: Harvard Education Press.

Wiseman, A. (2010) The Uses of Evidence for Educational Policymaking: global contexts and international trends, in A. Luke, J. Green & G. Kelly (Eds) *What*

*Counts as Evidence and Equity? Review of Research in Education*, pp. 1-24. New York: AERA, Sage.

Woodward, R. (2009) *The Organization for Economic Cooperation and Development (OECD)*. Abingdon: Routledge.

CHAPTER 9

# Gauging the Role of Non-educational Effects in Large-scale Assessments: socio-economics, culture and PISA outcomes

## HEINZ-DIETER MEYER & KATHRYN SCHILLER

ABSTRACT In this chapter the authors explore the role of non-educational factors – specifically socio-economic and cultural variables – on Programme for International Student Assessment (PISA) outcomes. They suggest that non-educational factors like socio-economic and cultural variables have a strong, but largely unexplored, impact on PISA outcomes. They show that PISA scores increase with a country's socio-economic affluence, as well as with measures of human development (like the absence of child labor and Internet use). PISA outcomes also vary with cultural factors like individualism and obedience to authority (power distance). The authors argue that it is not warranted to attribute, without qualification, high scores on PISA to excellent schools and poor performance to weak schools. Specifically, they find that there seem to be two paths to the top of PISA rankings: relatively egalitarian and individualistic cultures (like those of Finland or Canada) or relatively collectivist and paternalistic cultures. A country's position on the global PISA ranking provides very little information about the quality of its schools. It is more meaningful to compare a country with meaningfully chosen peers – for example, those other countries with which one shares important socio-economic and cultural attributes.

## Introduction

How much of what happens in schools is the result of school-internal factors (teacher behavior, curriculum and testing, administration, etc.) and how much of it is the result of non-educational or 'out-of-school' forces? Most teachers know that a community's socio-economics, as well as attitudes like deference to authority and group norms, affect students' behavior in the classroom, even though there is very little that teachers can do about them. Students come to school with these 'background characteristics'. Most parents know how strongly the learning opportunities of their son or daughter are influenced by the composition of the peer group: how well behaved or unruly, how motivated to learn, how respectful towards teachers, how prone to violence. In the United States it is this knowledge that causes parents who can afford to do so to move from poorer to more affluent communities and school districts, or from public to private or parochial schools, hoping that the 'more upscale' community will provide a more conducive learning environment.

Many other educationally relevant dispositions and beliefs are likewise shaped by the larger socio-economic and cultural context. A country's wealth provides more resources to go into education, while economic development also tends to make education more important for productive employment in corporations and professions. The emphasis on the importance of education, the prestige of the teaching profession, the educational role of the family, not to mention factors like child labor, ethnic diversity, or racial segregation, can all be seen as 'inputs' that facilitate or complicate the work of the school without being under its control. These factors would affect school outcomes even in schools with otherwise identical teacher behavior, curriculum, testing, and administration systems.

There is no reason to expect that what plays out at the level of communities and school districts within a country would not also play out across countries. Are children expected to work after school or instead of school? Is school teaching a highly regarded profession, or is it a line of work seen as inferior to typical middle-class professions? Do teachers execute their work with pride, or are they absent from school much of the time, perhaps forced to work second jobs to make ends meet?

Evidence from single-country studies supports the notion that these non-educational factors can powerfully impact classroom learning. A sizable literature has documented the importance of culturally instilled beliefs (Bempechat & Drago-Severson, 1999; Black & Wiliam, 2005; Walker, 2009; Cheung & Chan, 2010; Strang, 2010). Parenting style, for example, has been found to vary across cultures (Dong & Zhou, 1997). Another frequent topic is the role of effort versus ability. Asian cultures tend to give greater weight to effort, while American students tend to see a larger portion of school success as being due to innate ability or 'intelligence' (Kim & Park, 2006). Cross-cultural psychologists have also found that children's 'action-control beliefs' and their habits of self-efficacy vary considerably across cultures. Kim and Park (2006) report that in South Korea, one of the top-scoring PISA countries, education is seen as self-cultivation, a lifelong pursuit that takes place in and out of school, with parents taking a great interest in their children's schooling, sacrificing much for the sake of it, and providing emotional support (see also Ma, Jong & Yuan, this volume).

The Finnish sociologist Hannu Simola (2005) has suggested that Finland has succeeded at PISA not because of, but *despite* a very conventional teaching culture that places teachers in front of the classroom as top-down lecturers. He cites a British study of pedagogy in 50 Finnish schools in which the dominant style was for a teacher to closely follow the textbook at a predictable pace (in Simola, 2005, p. 462). This is consistent with Andrew's comparison of math teaching in Finland and Belgium (in this volume). It is also consistent with the observations of the first author of this chapter during two weeks of visits to Finnish schools in 2011 and 2012 which offered evidence of solid but unspectacular teaching and pedagogical practice. At the same time, however, students on average seemed much more attentive and 'on task' than, say, their American counterparts.

That culturally shaped beliefs and forms of interaction would explain different performance levels of otherwise comparable schools is consistent with ideas invoked by sociologists about the importance of intangible aspects of community life. James Coleman (1988) pointed to the importance of 'social capital' – the degree to which members of a community could rely on other members to support the norms and expectations directed towards their children. Greater degrees of social capital would not only allow students of different ages to help and protect each other on the way to and from school, it would also supply a more cohesive network of norms for teachers and administrators to draw on, as comparisons of Catholic with public schools have shown (Bryk et al, 1993). Bourdieu (1977) has argued that cultural capital – the explicit or tacit understanding a student acquires in the home environment about cultural canons of knowledge and taste – will allow him or her to form an alliance with the teacher from which students who lack this capital are barred. DiMaggio (1982) has confirmed the power of cultural capital in a study of grades of American high school students. Annette Lareau (2000) has shown the significant role of the 'home advantage' – direct and indirect patterns of supporting a student's work that decrease as a family's poverty increases. Taken together, the work of these scholars suggests that schools are among the most socially 'embedded' institutions (Granovetter, 1985; Meyer & Rowan, 2006), dependent on myriad external influences they don't control.

It would be surprising if differences like these – relative poverty or affluence, integrity or erosion of the family, quality of early childhood education, cultural norms about teaching and learning, ethnic and racial homogeneity, social and cultural capital, and the overall embeddedness of education in the network of auxiliary institutions like college, vocational education and community organizations – did not affect the kind of learning and achievement gauged by tests like PISA.

*Attribution Problems*

But although theory and case evidence suggest that non-educational factors account for a great deal of the variance encountered in classrooms across countries, there is very little systematic research in this area. Some of this research, however, suggests that at least economic development is systematically related to gaps in educational outcomes between demographic subgroups within countries (Schiller et al, 2002). One of the consequences is a widespread over-attribution of school outcomes to school-internal factors. In the official presentation and reception of PISA data, non-educational factors are typically ignored or, at best, treated as 'residual noise'. Media, governments and school officials rush to praise a country's schools for good PISA outcomes, or to blame its curriculum or policies for bad ones (see also Wiseman, this volume). The high scores achieved in tests by countries like Finland and Korea have caused a flow of visitors to these countries seeking enlightenment not about their overall institutions, culture and history, but about their curriculum, finances or governance structures.

In this chapter we begin to address this gap between conventional wisdom and research by exploring the role of non-educational factors – specifically socio-economical and cultural variables – on PISA outcomes. We present a general argument and two examples showing how PISA outcomes vary with established socio-economic and cultural measures. We then consider association effects between economic and cultural development and PISA outcomes. Following that, we zero in on how two cultural characteristics – individualism and power distance – are related to PISA outcomes. Finally, we discuss implications of this chapter. One of them is to de-emphasize global league tables and instead focus on more meaningful comparisons of 'peer groups' which share similar out-of-school factors. For many countries, doing so may change how we view PISA outcomes. For example, when compared with peer nations like Canada, Australia or the United Kingdom, the US performance appears different from how it seems when merely noting its position in the league table.

## Socio-economic and Socio-cultural Development and PISA

In this section we consider associations between PISA outcomes and indicators of economic and social and cultural development. We begin with economic development.

*Socio-economic Development and PISA*

Two economic indicators – per-capita gross domestic product (GDP) and per-pupil spending in secondary schools – were obtained from the UNESCO Institute for Statistics. Both measures were averaged over 2005 to 2010 and the second measure, per-pupil spending in secondary schools, was scaled as a percentage of GDP.

The regression results in Table I show that, together, GDP and per-pupil spending in secondary schools accounted for around two thirds of the variation in mean PISA scores across countries. The standardized coefficients indicate that a standard-deviation change in GDP was related to just under or over .63 of a standard-deviation difference in mean PISA scores. While less dramatic, per-pupil spending also accounted for a significant difference in the average performance on PISA of nations' youth. These results suggest that a country's economic wealth is correlated with PISA outcomes *independently* of how much is spent on schooling, supporting the notion that economic resources are an important out-of-school factor impacting PISA performance.

| Independent variables | Reading | | Mathematics | | Science | |
|---|---|---|---|---|---|---|
| GDP | .629 | ★★★ | .658 | ★★★ | .632 | ★★★ |
| Per-pupil spending in secondary schooling | .290 | ★★ | .243 | ★ | .278 | ★★ |
| R-square | .643 | | .635 | | .633 | |

$*p < .05; **p < .01; ***p < .001.$

Table I. Standardized regression coefficients predicting mean PISA scores.

## Socio-cultural Development and PISA

Table II combines OECD's PISA scores on reading literacy with UNESCO data on human development, including Internet use, child mortality, secondary school attendance, and child labor. We also include for inspection GINI index data, indicating a country's income inequality. We present these data to draw attention to the drastic differences between the two top and the two bottom PISA performance levels. The fact that the countries in the two bottom performance levels – Kyrgyzstan, Azerbaijan, Peru, Panama, Qatar, Albania, Kazakhstan, Argentina, Indonesia, Tunisia, Jordan, Montenegro, Brazil, Colombia, Trinidad-Tobago, Thailand, Romania, Mexico, Uruguay, Bulgaria, Serbia and Chile – differ from the top performers by several orders of magnitude on indices like child labor, secondary school attendance, child mortality and Internet use makes one wonder about the wisdom of and justification for measuring and ranking these countries using the same test. How should we interpret Peru's reading score of 370, compared with Germany's of 487 or Finland's of 536, knowing that a third of Peru's children are engaged in child labor (compared with 0% in the top-performing countries), that only a quarter of Peruvian households have Internet access (compared with 80% in the top performers), that only 70% of Peru's secondary-school-age children attend school, and that Peru's child mortality is four times that of the top-performing countries?

| Country | PISA Reading | GINI | 2008 Internet Users | 2009 Mortality Rate | Secondary School Attendance Ratio Male | Secondary School Attendance Ratio Female | % Child Labor |
|---|---|---|---|---|---|---|---|
| Korea | 539 | 31.4 | 77 | 5 | 0 | 0 | 0 |
| Finland | 536 | 26.8 | 83 | 3 | 0 | 0 | 0 |
| Hong Kong | 533 | 53.3 | | | 0 | 0 | 0 |
| Singapore | 526 | 47.8 | 73 | 3 | 0 | 0 | 0 |
| Canada | 524 | 32.1 | 75 | 6 | 0 | 0 | 0 |
| New Zealand | 521 | 36.2 | 72 | 6 | 0 | 0 | 0 |
| Japan | 520 | 37.6 | 75 | 3 | 0 | 0 | 0 |
| Australia | 515 | 305.0 | 72 | 5 | 0 | 0 | 0 |
| Netherlands | 508 | 309.0 | 87 | 4 | 0 | 0 | 0 |
| Belgium | 506 | 28.0 | 69 | 5 | 0 | 0 | 0 |
| Norway | 503 | 25.0 | 83 | 3 | 0 | 0 | 0 |
| Estonia | 501 | 31.4 | 66 | 6 | 0 | 0 | 0 |
| Switzerland | 501 | 33.7 | 77 | 4 | 0 | 0 | 0 |
| Iceland | 500 | 28.0 | 91 | 3 | 0 | 0 | 0 |
| Poland | 500 | 34.2 | 49 | 7 | 0 | 0 | 0 |
| United States | 500 | 45.0 | 74 | 8 | 0 | 0 | 0 |
| Liechtenstein | 499 | | 66 | 2 | 0 | 0 | 0 |
| Germany | 497 | 27.0 | 75 | 4 | 0 | 0 | 0 |
| Sweden | 497 | 23.0 | 88 | 3 | 0 | 0 | 0 |
| France | 496 | 32.7 | 68 | 4 | 0 | 0 | 0 |
| Ireland | 496 | 29.3 | 63 | 4 | 0 | 0 | 0 |
| Denmark | 495 | 29.0 | 84 | 4 | 0 | 0 | 0 |
| Hungary | 494 | 24.7 | 59 | 6 | 0 | 0 | 0 |
| United Kingdom | 494 | 34.0 | 76 | 6 | 0 | 0 | 0 |
| Portugal | 489 | 38.5 | 42 | 4 | 0 | 0 | 3 |
| Italy | 486 | 32.0 | 42 | 4 | 0 | 0 | 0 |
| Latvia | 484 | 35.7 | 61 | 8 | 0 | 0 | 0 |
| Greece | 483 | 33.0 | 44 | 3 | 0 | 0 | 0 |
| Slovenia | 483 | 28.4 | 56 | 3 | 0 | 0 | 0 |
| Spain | 481 | 32.0 | 57 | 4 | 0 | 0 | 0 |
| Czech Republic | 478 | 26.0 | 58 | 4 | 0 | 0 | 0 |
| Slovak Republic | 477 | 26.0 | 66 | 7 | 0 | 0 | 0 |
| Croatia | 476 | 33.7 | 51 | 5 | 0 | 0 | 0 |
| Israel | 474 | 39.2 | 50 | 4 | 0 | 0 | 0 |
| Luxembourg | 472 | 26.0 | 81 | 3 | 0 | 0 | 0 |

| | | | | | | |
|---|---|---|---|---|---|---|
| Austria | 470 | 26.0 | 71 | 4 | 0 | 0 | 0 |
| Lithuania | 468 | 37.6 | 55 | 6 | 0 | 0 | 0 |
| Turkey | 464 | 39.7 | 34 | 20 | 52 | 43 | 3 |
| Russian Federation | 459 | 42.2 | 32 | 12 | 0 | 0 | 0 |
| Chile | 449 | 52.1 | 32 | 9 | 0 | 0 | 3 |
| Serbia | 442 | 28.2 | 34 | 7 | 81 | 87 | 4 |
| Bulgaria | 429 | 45.3 | 35 | 10 | 0 | 0 | 0 |
| Uruguay | 426 | 42.4 | 40 | 13 | 0 | 0 | 8 |
| Mexico | 425 | 51.7 | 22 | 17 | 0 | 0 | 5 |
| Romania | 424 | 31.2 | 29 | 12 | 0 | 0 | 1 |
| Thailand | 421 | 53.6 | 24 | 14 | 77 | 84 | 8 |
| Trinidad/Tobago | 416 | - | 17 | 35 | 84 | 90 | 1 |
| Colombia | 413 | 58.5 | 39 | 19 | 64 | 72 | 9 |
| Brazil | 412 | 53.9 | 38 | 21 | 74 | 80 | 3 |
| Montenegro | 408 | 30.0 | 47 | 9 | 90 | 92 | 10 |
| Jordan | 405 | 39.7 | 26 | 25 | 85 | 89 | 0 |
| Tunisia | 404 | 40.0 | 28 | 21 | 0 | 0 | 0 |
| Indonesia | 402 | 36.8 | 8 | 39 | 57 | 59 | 7 |
| Argentina | 398 | 45.8 | 28 | 14 | 0 | 0 | 7 |
| Kazakhstan | 390 | 26.7 | 11 | 29 | 97 | 97 | 2 |
| Albania | 385 | 34.5 | 24 | 15 | 79 | 77 | 0 |
| Qatar | 372 | 41.1 | 34 | 11 | 0 | 0 | 0 |
| Panama | 371 | 51.0 | 27 | 23 | 0 | 0 | 7 |
| Peru | 370 | 48.0 | 25 | 21 | 70 | 70 | 34 |
| Azerbaijan | 362 | 33.7 | 28 | 34 | 82 | 80 | 7 |
| Kyrgyzstan | 314 | 33.4 | 16 | 37 | 90 | 92 | 4 |

Table II. PISA reading scores and socio-cultural development.
Source: OECD and UNESCO.

## Individualism, Power Distance and PISA Outcomes

Linking culture and the performance of educational institutions (LeTendre, 2002; von Kopp, 2003) has been the subject of much debate. Some have argued that without understanding a country's culture there is no way to understand the educational achievement of that country (Purves, 1987). Advocates for this position can draw on a strong sociological tradition that sees society's use of education as a mechanism to reproduce a society's culture and values (Durkheim, 1956). Others have wondered whether the concept is not too amorphous to be of much use (LeTendre, 2002). Yet others have argued that the globalization is causing educational experiences of different countries increasingly to converge (Meyer et al, 1997).

Without denying the difficulty inherent in the concept of culture when used as a catch-all for behavioral traits, historical traditions and shared values (Meyer, 2003), we focus here on cultural characteristics that are both well established and for which quantitative data are available: individualism and acceptance of status inequality or 'power distance'. In addition, we use data on ethnic homogeneity to gauge the impact of a country's relative fractionalization along ethnic lines.

### Individualism

The individualism/collectivism distinction (Lodge & Vogel, 1987; Triandis, 1990; Hofstede, 2001; Hofstede & Hofstede, 2005; Schimmack et al, 2005) reflects a fundamental issue that all cultures must resolve: how to weigh the claims of the individual self against those of the group, especially when they conflict. Individualist cultures tend to give priority to the claims of the individual, refuting the idea that the group has legitimate claims over the individual. In collectivist cultures the claims of the group (family, peers, work group, company, nation) trump those of the individual. Greif (1994) builds his definition of individualist and collectivist cultures around the concepts of integration and segregation: in a collectivist society, 'the social structure is "segregated" in the sense that each individual socially and economically interacts mainly with members of a specific religious, ethnic or familial group' (p. 913). Enforcement is achieved mainly through '"informal" economic and social institutions, and members of collectivist societies feel involved in the lives of other members of their group'. In individualist societies, 'the social structure is "integrated" in the sense that economic transactions are conducted among people from different groups and individuals shift frequently from one group to another' (Greif, 1994, p. 913).

The norm of individualism will direct the behavior of actors toward the pursuit of self-interest, where collectivist norms will stipulate individuals' subordination under collectively imposed norms. Individualism may be associated with an attitude towards education and learning that emphasizes upward mobility and one's right to shape one's own future.

### Power Distance

Similarly, deference toward authority will make certain kinds of teaching and learning easier, as children will accept a teacher's authority without challenge or contradiction. This disposition is captured by what Hofstede has dubbed 'power distance', which reflects the degree to which a hierarchical social order is accepted by the less powerful without needing justification. Higher values on this scale indicate acceptance of authority, while lower values reflect a society in which people prefer more equal distributions of power. Hofstede's data suggest that eastern cultures tend to have a high tolerance for power distance, while western cultures do not.

We expect that countries with high values on the scale will have fewer problems of discipline in the classroom and an easier time of rote learning. As a general rule, one might postulate that the greater the respect for authority, the greater the respect for teachers, and the fewer discipline problems teachers will have in the classroom. Similarly, culture may affect the degree of respect shown to the teacher by parents. In 'high power distance' cultures, teachers will enjoy more autonomy and fewer interruptions from parents.

### Ethnic Homogeneity

In his study about ethnic diversity and social trust, Robert Putnam (2007) found ethnic diversity to be negatively associated with trust. Homogeneous societies invest more in public goods, indicating a higher level of public altruism. For example, ethnic homogeneity correlates with the government's share of gross domestic product as well as with the average wealth of citizens (Calhoun, 1993).

To gauge the impact of individualism, power distance and ethnic homogeneity, information concerning nations' performance on PISA was combined with indicators of cultural and economic characteristics from several established international databases. The purpose of this analysis was to examine the extent to which individualism, power distance and ethnic heterogeneity were associated with variation in PISA scores. The analytical strategy was to first identify groups of similarly performing countries, then examine the cultural characteristics of countries across performance levels, and lastly examine a possible pathway through which cultural characteristics may impact literacy levels of a nation's youth. While the results only show statistical associations, logically any causal influences that exist would flow from relatively stable cultural characteristics through educational practices and policies to performance on PISA, rather than the reverse.

### Identifying Performance Levels

PISA assesses three types of literacy: ability to understand, reflect on, and engage with written texts (*reading literacy*); capacity to formulate and solve mathematical problems (*mathematics literacy*); and knowledge of scientific phenomena and scientific reasoning (*scientific literacy*). Since the scores on each literacy assessment were independently scaled for PISA to have a mean of 500 (with a standard deviation of 100), we could not simply add the PISA scores in each of the three test areas. To incorporate all three types of literacy, the first step in this analysis was to develop an indicator that incorporated PISA's three indices of literacy. To classify countries into performance-level groups, we wanted to take into account how 15-year-olds performed on all three PISA assessments. For this analysis, mean scores for each assessment were used to capture relative differences in literacy across countries.

While the scores in the three literacy assessments were highly correlated (between .948 and .982), we will see later that each type of literacy played a distinct role in classifying countries into overall performance categories.

The cluster analysis using PISA literacy indicators identified five distinct groups of countries, which we call 'performance levels' ranging from F (lowest) to A (highest). Table III shows the countries classified in each performance level and provides a description of the groups' performance characteristics.

| Performance level | Countries | Trends in PISA scores | Threshold with next lowest group |
|---|---|---|---|
| Group A | Finland, Hong Kong, Korea, Shanghai & Singapore | Higher mean scores and percentages of high performers in all subjects, and the greatest consistency in high performers across subjects. | Reading: 527 Math: 544 Science: 539 |
| Group B | Macao-China, Chinese Taipei, Germany, Liechtenstein, Switzerland, Estonia, Belgium, Netherlands, Australia, Japan, New Zealand & Canada | Relatively high mean scores in all subjects, particularly math and science, but moderate percentages of high performers, suggesting that they also tended to have fewer extremely low performers. | Reading: 501 Math: 510 Science: 513 |
| Group C | Russian Federation, Dubai (UAE), Turkey, Lithuania, Austria, Luxembourg, Israel, Croatia, Slovak Republic, Czech Republic, Spain, Greece, Slovenia, Latvia, Italy, Portugal, Hungary, United Kingdom, Denmark, France, Ireland, Sweden, United States, Iceland, Poland & Norway | Moderate mean scores, particularly in math and science. Larger percentages of high performers than those in Group B, suggesting that they had greater diversity in performance within a country. | Reading: 452 Math: 442 Science: 451 |

| Group D | Albania, Kazakhstan, Argentina, Indonesia, Tunisia, Jordan, Montenegro, Brazil, Colombia, Trinidad-Tobago, Thailand, Romania, Mexico, Uruguay, Bulgaria, Serbia & Chile | Lower mean scores for each subject and smaller percentages of high scorers than Group C. | Reading: 382 Math: 372 Science: 384 |
|---|---|---|---|
| Group F | Kyrgyzstan, Azerbaijan, Peru, Panama & Qatar | Lowest mean scores for all three subjects and small percentages of high scorers. | |

Table III. PISA performance levels.

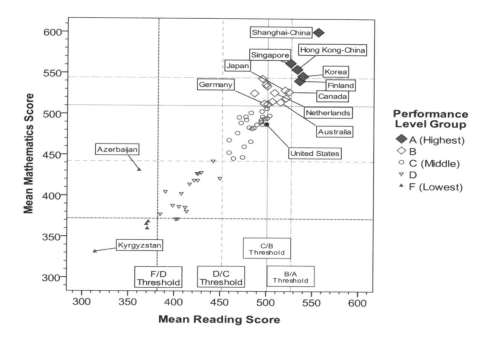

Figure 1. Relationship between countries' mean reading and mathematics scores on PISA by performance level.

Table III also reports the threshold scores between performance levels, estimated using ordinal multinomial logistic regression, for each of the PISA assessments. The thresholds between levels for mathematics and reading are also indicated in Figure 1, which shows how countries' mean scores on these assessments were related to their performance classification.

While those countries with higher reading scores also tended to have higher mathematics scores, the correlation is not perfect as some countries with the same mean reading scores had different mean mathematics scores. The role mathematics played in distinguishing the middle-performing countries from the high-performing ones is clear in Figure 1, which shows substantial overlap in mean reading scores between the C and B groups but no overlap in mean mathematics scores. For example, Germany had a reading score just below the B/C threshold but is classified as a B-group country by virtue of its having mathematics and science scores over the B-group thresholds for those subjects. Some overlap in mean science scores was also found between the C and B groups, but to a lesser extent than for reading. Thus, a key contributor to what made the B group distinctive compared with the C group was higher levels of mathematics literacy.

## Individualism and Power Distance in High-performing Countries

We now turn to examining cultural differences across countries across performance levels to gain insight into what factors may promote higher test scores among nations' youth. In particular, we are interested in uncovering whether cultural characteristics such as individualistic orientation or ethnic homogeneity are related to PISA scores.

### Measures and Data

The cultural and economic indicators used in this chapter were obtained from three published sources. Two indicators of cultural orientations – individualism and power distance – were obtained from Hofstede et al (2010).

Higher values on the 'individualism' scale indicate stronger cultural expectations that individuals should take care of themselves and their immediate families, while lower values indicate a more collectivist orientation in which relatives and others in authority are expected to provide assistance in exchange for loyalty. Higher values on the 'power distance' scale indicate societies in which a hierarchical social order is accepted by the less powerful without needing justification. A third cultural indicator – ethnic fractionalization – was obtained from Fearon (2003). Higher values on the ethnic fractionalization index indicate greater ethnic diversity measured by calculating the probability that two individuals selected at random in a country are from different ethnic groups.

*Analysis*

We started the analysis of cultural orientations by examining the relationships between the three main cultural variables, individualism, power distance, and ethnic fractionalization. Ethnic fractionalization was at best moderately correlated (r. < .309) with individualism and power distance. Individualism and power distance, however, were strongly correlated (r = -.665) with each other, as illustrated in Figure 2. The large majority of countries with values above the median on the power distance index (the *x*-axis in Figure 2) had values below the median on the individualism index; similarly, the large majority of countries above the median on individualism were below the mean on power distance.

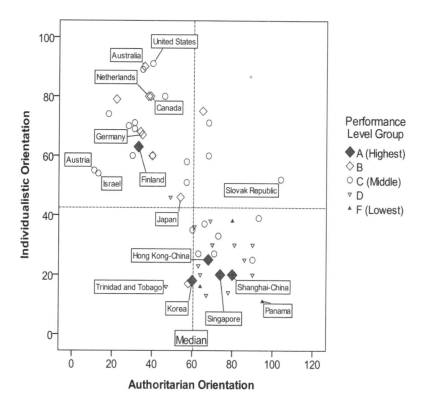

Figure 2. Relationship between authoritarian and individualistic orientations by countries' PISA performance level.

Figure 2 shows that countries in the A and B performance levels tended to have a more individualistic orientation (Finland, Canada, Australia, Netherlands), with the notable exceptions of Korea, Hong Kong, Singapore and Shanghai. These four countries are culturally distinct from other A and B group members. Closer inspection of the data in conjunction with socio-economic data suggests that there are two distinct paths to the top: an individualistic-egalitarian one, and a high tolerance for power distance. For western nations to score high on PISA requires that they exhibit a pronounced tendency toward individualism, combined with a low-to-moderate degree of social inequality. For eastern nations to score high on PISA requires high tolerance for power distance.

### The Position of the United States

Weaker performance in mathematics and science, in particular, were the reason that the United States was classified as a middle-performing (C-group) country by the cluster analysis. The United States' mean reading score (just under 500) was only one point from the B-group threshold of 501 for reading, which is within the margin of error for the mean, indicating that the difference could be due random factors related to sampling and measurement. However, the United States would need to improve its mathematics performance by more than 20 points in order to approach the B-group threshold of 510 for mathematics. This difference would be a statistically significant ($t = -6.324$) gain over the United States' mean mathematics score of 487. Even if the United States' mean mathematics score was 506, which would be commensurate with its mean reading scores, the country would fail to cross the B-group threshold in this subject. The United States' mean science score of 502 was also below the B-group threshold of 513 for this subject, and a statistically significant ($t = -3.018$) improvement would be needed to exceed that threshold. Thus, while 15-year-olds in the United States tend to read well enough for the country to be grouped among the B group of high-performing countries, its performance on mathematics in particular keeps the country classified as a C group of middle performers.

### High-scoring PISA Countries: two ways to the top

The majority of above-average PISA countries belong to either an eastern pattern (Korea, Singapore, Hong Kong and China [Shanghai]) or a western pattern (Finland, Canada, Australia). The eastern pattern exhibits low individualism and high power distance. The western pattern exhibits the converse: high individualism and low power distance. Eastern countries tend to do well even in the absence of factors like individualism or high per-pupil spending. They score about ONE standard deviation above western countries on PISA. These patterns hold strong, with no exceptions in the eastern group, and very few in the western one. According to these data, there are only two paths to performing significantly above average on PISA: an eastern and a western path. How are they different?

To be successful on PISA a country has to be relatively affluent, individualistic and relatively egalitarian (the western pattern), or affluent and accepting of pronounced power differentials (the eastern pattern). Ethnic homogeneity is a further plus in both groups.

On the basis of those results, the United States would seem barred from reaching the first tier of the PISA scale. While it has two strikes in its favor – affluence and individualism – it also has two strikes against it: ethnic heterogeneity and inequality.

### Peers and Aspirational Peers for the United States

More specifically, the United States is in the same performance tier as France, the UK and Norway (besting countries like Austria, Italy and Ireland). The 'aspirational peers' of the United States are countries like Germany, the Netherlands, Australia and Canada. Of these, the latter two, Canada and Australia, would seem to qualify as the most interesting and relevant comparison group. The United States shares with these countries similarity in population size (relatively speaking), affluence, individualism and ethnic heterogeneity (as well as a dominant religious tradition of Protestantism). Where it differs from both is the high degree of social inequality. On the GINI index (see Table II), the United States scores 40.8, compared with Canada's 32.1 and Australia's 35.2. The United States is also more unequal than any of its western peers or aspirational peers: Germany scores 28.3, the Netherlands 30.9, Finland 26.8, and France 32.7. Even to reduce social inequality to levels of Australia would require a return to social conditions of the 1960s and 1970s – a formidable goal.

### Context-sensitive Readings of PISA

More generally, our analysis suggests that a different (and for many countries more optimistic) reading of PISA scores results from an analysis that takes a country's structural and cultural conditions into account. Rather than the context-indifferent presentation of PISA data in a global ranking (in which, by definition, about two thirds of all countries perform less than satisfactorily), a context-sensitive presentation would take socio-economic and socio-cultural factors into account. In such a reading it makes little sense to compare the United States with, say, Korea or Singapore. Much more informative are comparisons with countries sharing key social attributes.

One may notice, for example, that the United States performs in the same tier as Sweden, Norway, France and Denmark – countries that are known to take the education of their young seriously. Second, the United States comes within 20 points of western top performers like Canada and Australia. These results hardly support the self-flagellating cries of woe and mediocrity that have come to be the standard tri-annual ritual of media editors and corporate advocates of school reform following the publication of the PISA tables.

## Conclusion

In this chapter we argue that non-educational factors influence the educational achievement captured by tests like PISA. It is therefore not warranted to attribute, without qualification, high scores on PISA to excellent schools and poor performance to weak schools. Nor is it warranted to seek to redress poor performance by reforming school-internal factors like curriculum, funding or school organization. A more nuanced reflection on the causes of educational achievement will include non-educational factors such as economic resources and cultural beliefs, which are either beyond the reach of government action or, at any rate, immune to the kind of 'quick fixes' dictated by PISA's three-year testing cycle. Another corollary is that a country's position on the global PISA ranking provides very little information about the quality of its schools. Instead, we should compare a country with those other countries with which it shares a meaningful set of socio-economic and cultural attributes.

In particular we have pointed out two patterns of high-performing countries – a western 'individualistic' pattern (including Finland, Canada and Australia, among others), and an eastern 'paternalistic' group (including Korea, Singapore, Hong Kong and China). Since paternalism is a system of cultural norms and beliefs that is inconsistent with US cultural beliefs, it makes little sense to compare American PISA outcomes with those of Korea or Singapore – all the more since paternalism may be negatively associated with one of the most cherished American abilities: innovation and entrepreneurialism (see Zhao & Meyer, this volume). More realistic and informative peers would include Australia and Canada, which are socio-economically and culturally closer to the United States.

A more fine-tuned comparison of the United States with its more relevant western peers brings the United States' high degree of social inequality into focus. Inequality often means erosion of the middle class, which results in a more polarized class structure in which hard work at school is no longer the trusted lever of upward mobility. Combined with greater ethnic diversity and minority status, social inequality may well produce a mix of discrimination and low expectations for large numbers of students from groups with multiple disadvantages. This interpretation is consistent with comparisons with PISA peers which show that while the percentage of high-scoring students is as large for the United States as it is for its aspirational peers, the United States' share of students in the lower-performing rungs is much larger than that of these peers – and exhibits a much stronger connection with social disadvantage (Schleicher, 2009).

On the positive side, we note that the improvement horizon for the United States is real. A gain of some 15 points on the PISA scale would bring

US schools to the level of Australia and close to that of Canada. Alas, reaching those levels may be more effectively influenced by policies that lower inequality than by the imposition of punishing testing regimes and the disempowerment of teachers.

## References

Bempechat, J. & Drago-Severson, E. (1999) Cross-national Differences in Academic Achievement: beyond etic conceptions of children's understandings, *Review of Educational Research*, 69(3), 287-314.

Black, P. & Wiliam, D. (2005) Lessons from Around the World: how policies, politics and cultures constrain and afford assessment practices, *Curriculum Journal*, 16(2), 249-261.

Bourdieu, Pierre (1977) Cultural Reproduction and Social Reproduction, in J. Karabel & A.H. Halsey (Eds) *Power and Ideology in Education*, pp. 487-511. New York: Oxford University Press.

Bryk, Anthony S., Lee, Valerie E. & Holland, Peter B. (1993) *Catholic Schools and the Common Good*. Cambridge, MA: Harvard University Press.

Calhoun, C. (1993) Nationalism and Ethnicity, *Annual Review of Sociology*, 19(1), 211-239.

Cheung, H. & Chan, A. (2010) Education and Competitive Economy: how do cultural dimensions fit in? *Higher Education*, 59 (5), 525-541.

Coleman, James S. (1988) Social Capital in the Creation of Human Capital, *American Journal of Sociology*, 94, Supplement, 95-120.

DiMaggio, Paul (1982) Cultural Capital and School Success: the impact of status culture participation on the grades of US high school students, *American Sociological Review*, 47(2), 189-201.

Dong, X. & Zhou, H. (1997) Authoritative and Authoritarian Parenting Practices and Social and School Performance in Chinese Children, *International Journal of Behavioral Development*, 21(4), 855-874.

Durkheim, Emile (1956) *Education and Sociology*. Glencoe, IL: The Free Press.

Fearon, James D. (2003) Ethnic and Cultural Diversity by Country, *Journal of Economic Growth*, 8, 1995-222.

Granovetter, M. (1985) Economic Action and Social Structure: the problem of embeddedness, *American Journal of Sociology*, 91(3), 481-510.

Greif, Avner (1994) Cultural Beliefs and the Organization of Society: a historical and theoretical reflection on collectivist and individualist societies, *Journal of Political Economy*, 102, 912-950.

Hofstede, Geert (2001) *Culture's Consequences: comparing values, behaviors, institutions, and organizations across nations*. Thousand Oaks, CA: Sage.

Hofstede, Geert & Hofstede, Gert Jan (2005) *Cultures and Organizations: software of the mind*. New York: McGraw-Hill.

Hofstede, G., Hofstede, Gert Jan & Minkov, Michael (2010) *Cultures and Organizations: software of the mind*, rev. & expanded 3rd edn. New York: McGraw-Hill.

Kim, U. & Park, Y-S. (2006) Indigenous Psychological Analysis of Academic Achievement in Korea: the influence of self-efficacy, parents, and culture, *International Journal of Psychology*, 41(4), 287-292.

Lareau, Annette (2000) *Home Advantage: social class and parental intervention in elementary education*. New York: Rowman and Littlefield.

LeTendre, Gerald K. (2002) Advancements in Conceptualizing and Analyzing Cultural Effects in Cross-national Studies of Educational Achievement, in Andrew C. Porter & Adam Gamoran (Eds) *Methodological Advances in Cross-national Surveys of Educational Achievement*. Washington, DC: National Academy Press (National Research Council).

Lodge, George & Vogel, Ezra (1987) *Ideology and National Competitiveness*. Boston: Harvard University Business School Press.

Meyer, Heinz-Dieter (2003) Tocqueville's Cultural Institutionalism, *Journal of Classical Sociology*, 3(2), 197-220.

Meyer, Heinz-Dieter & Rowan, Brian (2006) *The New Institutionalism in Education*. Albany: SUNY Press.

Meyer, John W., Boli, John, Thomas, George M. & Ramirez, Francisco O. (1997) World Society and the Nation State, *American Journal of Sociology*, 103(1), 144-181.

Purves, A. (1987) IEA Agenda for the Future, *International Review of Education*, 33, 103-107.

Putnam, Robert (2007) *E Pluribus Unum:* diversity and community in the twenty-first century. The 2006 Johan Skytte Prize Lecture, *Scandinavian Political Studies*, 30(2) (June), 137-174.

Schimmack, Ulrich, Oishi, Shigehiro & Diener, Ed (2005) Individualism: a valid and important dimension of cultural differences between nations, *Personality and Social Psychology Review*, 9, 17-31.

Schiller, Kathryn, Khmelkov, Vladimir T. & Wang, Xiao-qing (2002) Economic Development and the Effects of Family Characteristics on Mathematics Achievement, *Journal of Marriage and Family*, August, 730-742.

Schleicher, A. (2009) Securing Quality and Equity in Education: lessons from PISA, *Prospects: quarterly review of comparative education*, 39(3), 251-263.

Simola, H. (2005) The Finnish Miracle of PISA: historical and sociological remarks on teaching and teacher education, *Comparative Education*, 41(4), 455-470.

Strang, K. (2010) Global Culture, Learning Style, and Outcome: an interdisciplinary empirical study of international university students,. *Intercultural Education*, 21(6), 519-533.

Triandis, Harry C. 1990. Cross-cultural Studies of Individualism and Collectivism, in J.J. Berman (Ed.) *Nebraska Symposium on Motivation*, vol. 37. Lincoln: University of Nebraska Press.

von Kopp, B. (2003) On the Question of Cultural Context as a Factor in International Academic Achievement, *European Education*, 35(4), 70-98.

Walker, J.T. (2009) Authoritative Classroom Management: how control and nurturance work together, *Theory Into Practice*, 48(2), 122-129.

CHAPTER 10

# Exploring Reasons for the East Asian Success in PISA

## XIN MA, CINDY JONG & JING YUAN

ABSTRACT This chapter explores the success of six top-performing East Asian countries (regions) in PISA 2009 – Hong Kong (China), Japan, Korea, Shanghai (China), Singapore and Taipei (China). For each of these countries (regions), a two-level hierarchical linear model (HLM) was specified to examine student performance in reading, mathematics and science respectively. The search for reasons for success focused on (a) student academic behaviors; and (b) school climatic attributes. At the student level, there were striking total consistencies across all academic areas and across all countries (regions) in terms of highly successful students (a) being skillful users of control strategies in their learning, and (b) knowing how to utilize meta-cognitive skills in the process of their learning. Not only are these positive effects comprehensive, but they also universally demonstrate the strongest effects among all statistically significant student academic behaviors. At the school level, a nearly perfect occurrence was identified across academic areas and across countries (regions) of school disciplinary climate being the most important school climatic attribute to academic performance of students.

### Literature Review

Over the years, international achievement test results have consistently shown that East Asian countries are among the top performers. This is the case for all of the major international achievement tests (i.e. the Programme for International Student Assessment, or PISA; the Third International Mathematics and Science Study, or TIMSS; and the Progress in International Reading Literacy Study, or PIRLS), where East Asian countries scored well above average. In addition to high achievement in mathematics and science, East Asian countries have high scores in reading and literacy tests (Topping, 2006; Chiu & McBride-Chang, 2010). These results have heightened educators', researchers' and policymakers' interest in understanding the factors that have influenced the consistent high achievement in East Asian countries. Thus, there have been several attempts to examine which factors are salient in contributing to academic achievement in East Asia.

Factors examined on various international achievement tests are student-, teacher-, school- and family-related variables. However, it is not a simple process to zero in on the most influential variables, especially when comparing results across multiple countries. While there are similarities across some East Asian cultures in terms of educational values, studies indicate that much contextual variation exists (Valverde & Schmidt, 2000; Leung, 2002; Shin et al, 2009).

*Student Characteristics*

Perhaps one of the most contested perceptions of East Asian cultures is the amount of emphasis placed on effort over ability. The influential work of Stevenson and his colleagues (Stevenson et al, 1986, Stevenson, 1987; Stevenson & Stigler, 1992) has suggested that high achievement of East Asian students is the result of strong beliefs in the value of hard work. A similar idea of effort emphasized over ability is supported in current literature (Kim, 2005; Jeynes, 2008). However, other researchers have made contrasting claims that ability is responsible for success in East Asia (Weiner, 1985, 1994; Eccles & Wigfield, 1995). Ho and Hau (2008) examined Chinese students' achievement in mathematics using PISA 2000 data and found that their achievement was a result of their strong desire to learn as well as their own abilities in mathematics. Bempechat and Drago-Severson (1999) also considered both sides of the debate and recommended that researchers take a social cognitive approach and make more meaningful attempts to understand culture and context.

Zhu and Leung (2011) examined whether an East Asian model of motivation exists by using the TIMSS 2003 eighth-grade mathematics data across nine countries – Hong Kong, Japan, Korea, Singapore, (Chinese) Taipei, Australia, England, the Netherlands, and the USA. They examined intrinsic motivational factors (students' enjoyment and preference for mathematics) and extrinsic ones (students' perceived usefulness of mathematics) across the countries. They found that both forms of motivation had positive influences on East Asian students' achievement, with the exception of Singapore, which showed a negative relationship with extrinsic motivation.

More recent studies examining student factors have primarily focused on attitudes rather than behaviors (Kaya & Rice, 2010; Zhu & Leung, 2011). Bybee and McCrae (2011) argue that 'attitudes represent a complex system of cognitions, feelings, and inclinations towards action, and they ultimately influence students' continuing interest in and dispositions for positive and constructive responses' (p. 23). They used PISA 2006 data to examine scientific literacy and attitudes toward science and found that while general interest in science learning was positively related to performance, there was a negative relationship between science performance and students' science topic interest at the country level. Interestingly, East Asian countries had a significantly higher interest level in learning science topics than other highly developed countries. Over the past two decades, researchers have specifically studied the high achievement of Japanese students and found that while emphasis is typically placed on effort, important teacher and school variables should also be taken into consideration (Holloway, 1988; Kinney, 1998; Schumer, 1999; Jacobs & Morita, 2002; Woodward & Ono, 2004).

*School Factors*

Currently, researchers have used international data sets to examine multilevel effects of both student- and school-based factors across various countries, but typically focus on one content area (Shin et al, 2009; Chiu & McBride-Chang, 2010; Kaya & Rice, 2010). Kaya and Rice (2010) examined multilevel effects of student and classroom factors on elementary science achievement in Singapore, Japan, the USA, Australia and Scotland using the TIMSS 2003 data. Self-confidence and home resources had positive influences on science achievement, but school-related factors varied across countries. The researchers found that Japan had the smallest between-class variance, while Singapore had the largest between-class variance, showing a contrast in school uniformity between the two East Asian countries in this study. Shin et al (2009) investigated multilevel student and school factors affecting mathematics achievement of Korean, Japanese and American students using PISA 2003 data. Results indicated that Korean and Japanese students' competitive learning preferences were positively correlated with mathematics achievement at a statistically significant level. The student-level variables of instrumental motivation and mathematics interest both positively affected mathematics achievement in all countries, with the USA having the lowest correlations. However, countries differed on the variables that were the strongest predictors. School-level variables of student-teacher relationship and school disciplinary climate were all positively related to mathematics achievement, with Japan having the highest correlation in both areas. The student–teacher relationship variables are based on students' perceptions of their teachers, such as whether their teachers are helpful, listen to them, and treat them fairly. East Asian students are viewed as being very respectful toward teachers (Stevenson & Stigler, 1992), but some researchers suggest that such an elevated level of respect can interfere with learning when students do not feel comfortable questioning what teachers say (Kim, 2005; Jeynes, 2008).

The high achievement in mathematics and science of East Asian countries has also been attributed to high national standards and expectations (Schumer, 1999; Valverde & Schmidt, 2000). Research suggests that standards in mathematics and science in East Asian countries appear to be more coherent and focused (Valverde & Schmidt, 2000). It is possible that standards are an aspect of uniformity that exists in schools as a result of the centralized system in some East Asia countries (e.g. Korea, Japan, China) (Leung, 2002; Kim, 2005; Kaya & Rice, 2010). The literature also suggests that more depth and less breadth exist in mathematics and science content in East Asian countries (Geary, 1996; Li, 2000; Leung, 2005; Kaya & Rice, 2010).

### Teacher Factors

In addition to high content standards, there is an expectation placed on teachers – they need to be highly skilled in order for students to learn and be successful. Liping Ma's (1999) influential study showed that Chinese teachers had a deeper understanding of mathematics content taught at the elementary level than American teachers. Results from video studies have also indicated that teachers in East Asian countries present clearer lessons and have more student engagement (Hiebert & Stigler, 2000; Jacobs & Morita, 2002; Leung, 2005). Several researchers suggest that professional development plays a central role in East Asian teachers' success (Stigler & Stevenson, 1991; Kinney, 1998; Stevenson, 1998; Stigler & Hiebert, 1998; Hiebert & Stigler, 2000; Jacobs & Morita, 2002; Fernandez et al, 2003). For example, lesson study is one common form of professional development in Japan where teachers engage in a collaborative lesson design, implementation and reflection process (Fernandez et al, 2003). However, two characteristics of East Asian classrooms that are somewhat puzzling to researchers are the large class sizes and the whole-group teaching norm (Leung 2002, 2005; Kim 2005; Jeynes, 2008). It does, however, make sense that clear lessons and good school disciplinary climates would be necessary to engage students (Shin et al, 2009).

### Family Factors

Literature on international studies has also shed light on factors beyond schools to include family backgrounds. For example, a recent PISA reading study including 41 countries revealed that while family characteristics can influence literacy skills, the connections are not universal but can be somewhat predictable depending on the countries' economic and cultural characteristics (Chiu & McBride-Chang, 2010). Many scholars have suggested that strong family values and support have positive influences on East Asian student achievement (Kim 2005; Wang & Lin, 2005; Jeynes, 2008; Chiu & McBride-Chang, 2010). Family resources and parental educational levels appear to be strong predictors of student achievement (Wößmann, 2005; Marks et al, 2006; Anderson et al, 2007; Hojo & Oshio,

2009). Results of these studies raise important questions about socioeconomic inequalities around the world (Marks et al, 2006). Due to family backgrounds being such strong predictors of student achievement, it is recommended that multilevel studies control for this factor to gain a better understanding of other variables.

*Our Position*

In the research literature, apart from effort, ability, teacher quality, family support and culturally encoded respectfulness, there are other accounts (factors) for East Asian success as the result of high levels of pressure to perform well on exit exams and additional outside schooling that students receive (Bishop, 1998; Watanabe, 2000; Baker et al, 2001; Cave, 2001; Bray, 2010). Our position is that academic success can never be the consequence of a single factor (let alone the inconclusiveness of research findings on every factor examined). We seek the interaction among those factors as providing reasons for success. Adopting the mainstream theoretical framework of school effects, our search focused on student academic behaviors (students' daily academic actions or activities), with control for student background characteristics at the student level, and on school climatic attributes (schools' daily learning climate or environment), with control for school contextual characteristics at the school level. Student academic behaviors reflect effort, ability, family support and outside schooling; and school climatic attributes reflect teacher quality, culturally encoded respectfulness, and pressure on exit exams.

In particular, we emphasize the lack of attention in the research literature to the way East Asian students manage their learning – clearly a matter of effort and ability – in relation to their success. Students employ various cognitive and meta-cognitive processes (skills) in their learning that effectively single out competent learners who are aware of and able to use a variety of appropriate strategies to regulate their independent learning to produce favorable learning outcomes (e.g. Willoughby & Wood, 1994; Zimmerman & Schunk, 2001). According to the Organisation for Economic Co-operation and Development (OECD, 2010c, p. 9), 'learning strategies are an important area of educational policy and practice'. By including learning strategies and meta-cognitive processes as part of student academic behaviors, we attempted to investigate whether these variables are overlooked factors in explaining East Asian educational success, and to test the validity of the interaction between effort and ability.

Students who employ memorization (rehearsal) strategies learn through repeating and storing in their memory facts and procedures without further information processing. These strategies allow students to recall and retrieve information. Students who employ elaboration strategies learn by acquiring understanding through connecting related knowledge, searching for alternative solutions, and exploring knowledge in other contexts. Students who employ control strategies learn by regulating their learning through setting up clear goals for learning, monitoring progress in achieving those goals, and making efforts to accomplish what is still to be achieved.

Students who engage in meta-cognitive processes attempt to reflect on and gain control over their cognitive processes. Students who employ summarizing, an important meta-cognitive process, generalize knowledge by inferring common principles that underlie certain knowledge or by identifying main aspects of certain knowledge. Students who employ understanding and remembering, another important meta-cognitive process, retrieve knowledge on the basis of a good understanding of certain knowledge. Such understanding often comes from searching for information to fill in gaps or extend knowledge, detecting errors in the presentation of knowledge, breaking knowledge down into a sequence of meaningful components, self-monitoring (i.e. analyzing progress and differentiating learning strategies), and self-explaining.

## Research Design

This chapter explores the success of six top-performing East Asian countries (regions) in PISA 2009: Hong Kong (China) – 4837 students from 151 schools; Japan – 6077 students from 185 schools; Korea – 4989 students from 157 schools; Shanghai (China) – 5115 students from 152 schools; Singapore – 5283 students from 171 schools; and Taipei (China) – 5831 students from 158 schools (see OECD, 2010a). OECD (2011) contains detailed information on the PISA sample design (see Chapter 4). For each country (region), a two-level hierarchical linear model (HLM) was specified, with students (level 1) nested within schools (level 2), to examine student performance in reading, mathematics and science respectively. With control over student background, this model attempted to identify which student academic behaviors contribute to high performance; meanwhile, with control over school context, this model attempted to identify which school climatic attributes contribute to high performance over and above the contribution of student academic behaviors.

Student academic behaviors included time spent in learning, use of learning strategies, use of meta-cognitive skills, attitude and use of learning resources. Time spent in learning refers to learning time in school and out of school lessons. Learning strategies refer to memorization (rehearsal), elaboration and control strategies. Meta-cognition pertains to summarizing as well as understanding and remembering. Attitude describes students' general disposition towards education. Finally, use of learning resources refers to use of libraries. These behavioral variables capture the essence of students' daily academic activities. Student background characteristics included gender, age, father and mother's SES (socioeconomic status), and family structure (i.e. both parents vs. single parent).

School climatic attributes included parental academic pressure, school disciplinary climate, teacher–student relationship, student behaviors, teacher behaviors, principal leadership, teacher participation, ability grouping, school educational resources and extra-curricular activities. These climatic variables capture almost all key dimensions of school effects (see Teddlie & Reynolds, 2000). School contextual characteristics included school (enrollment) size, school mean father and mother SES, number of competing schools in nearby area, student-teacher ratio and proportion of certified teachers. See OECD, 2010b for detailed information on PISA variables, including all that we used in our analysis (see Annex A1).

Results of statistical analyses reveal what can be counted as the most important student academic behaviors and school climatic attributes contributing to academic success in those East Asian countries (regions). In other words, the findings describe the behavioral characteristics of highly successful students and the climatic characteristics of their schools that relate to the East Asian countries (regions) they are in.

## Results

In Tables I to VI, we present the most important analytical results of our HLM analyses (the full results are available from the authors) for each country (region). Each table contains three sets of data analyses, one for each academic area (reading, mathematics and science). Due to space limitations, we omitted analytical results associated with student background characteristics and school contextual characteristics (both functioned as control variables). We used the same HLM model across all six countries (regions), which allowed us to identify and compare critically important variables and the magnitude of effects associated with those variables.

### *Effects of Student Academic Behaviors*

At the student level, highly successful students in reading spent statistically significantly more time in reading in school (per week) in Japan and Shanghai. Highly successful students in mathematics spent statistically significantly more time in mathematics in Hong Kong, Japan, Singapore and Taipei. Highly successful students in science spent statistically significantly more time in science in Hong Kong, Korea, Shanghai and Singapore. Given that PISA achievement tests have a mean of 500 and a standard deviation (SD) of 100, statistically significant effects can be easily turned into an effect size measure that uses the percentage of an SD to demonstrate the (comparable) magnitude of the effects within and across academic areas. For example, one SD increase in learning time in school was associated with an increase in performance about 7% of an SD in mathematics and about 9% of an SD in science in Hong Kong (see Table I).

For out-of-school lessons in reading, the statistically significant negative effects in Hong Kong and Singapore indicate that better-performing students took statistically significantly fewer out-of-school lessons in reading than poorer-performing students. In other words, out-of-school lessons in reading were more of a means for poorer-performing students to catch up rather than for better-performing students to excel further. In mathematics, out-of-school lessons were for low-performing students to catch up in Shanghai but for high-performing students to excel further in Korea.

| | Reading | | Mathematics | | Science | |
|---|---|---|---|---|---|---|
| | Effect | SE | Effect | SE | Effect | SE |
| *Student academic behaviors* | | | | | | |
| Learning time in school | -3.11 | 2.18 | 7.41* | 2.22 | 8.80* | 1.47 |
| Out of school lessons | -4.56* | 1.42 | -4.77* | 1.18 | -0.59 | 1.07 |
| Use of memorization strategies | -9.49* | 1.82 | -17.67* | 2.80 | -10.31* | 2.57 |
| Use of elaboration strategies | -3.65* | 1.55 | -0.76 | 1.89 | -4.02 | 2.50 |
| Use of control strategies | 19.15* | 1.97 | 23.10* | 2.62 | 20.37* | 2.91 |
| Meta-cognition of summarizing | 11.85* | 1.23 | 13.90* | 1.62 | 13.65* | 1.98 |
| Meta-cognition of understanding and remembering | 7.67* | 1.44 | 6.92* | 1.84 | 6.08* | 2.18 |
| *School climatic attributes* | | | | | | |
| Disciplinary climate | 28.91* | 10.91 | 30.97* | 11.81 | 30.37* | 12.22 |
| Principal leadership | -4.65* | 2.22 | -5.67* | 2.61 | -7.59* | 2.65 |
| *Proportion of variance explained* ($R^2$) | B over N | F over B | B over N | F over B | B over N | F over B |
| Level 1 | 0.10 | 0.18 | 0.07 | 0.19 | 0.07 | 0.18 |
| Level 2 | 0.68 | 0.43 | 0.71 | 0.44 | 0.65 | 0.52 |

*$p < .05$. *Note.* N = null model; B = base model; F = full model.

Table I. Effects of student academic behaviors and school climatic attributes on academic achievement with control over student background and school context: the case of Hong Kong.

As indicated by the statistically significant negative effects, students who relied on memorization (rehearsal) strategies to learn were disadvantaged in academic performance across all three areas in Hong Kong, Japan, Shanghai and Singapore, as well as in one area (mathematics) in Taipei, though there were no statistically significant effects of using memorization (rehearsal) strategies on academic performance in any of the three areas in Korea. In Hong Kong, for example, one SD increase in use of memorization (rehearsal) strategies was associated with a decrease in academic performance about 9% of an SD in reading, about 18% of an SD in mathematics, and about 10% of an SD in science (see Table I).

There was also some statistically significant disadvantage in reading performance from use of elaboration strategies in Hong Kong. There were no statistically significant effects of using elaboration strategies on academic performance in any of the three areas in Korea, Singapore or Taipei. There was some statistically significant advantage in academic performance from use of elaboration strategies in mathematics and science in Japan and in mathematics in Shanghai. In Hong Kong, for example, one SD increase in use of elaboration strategies was associated with a decrease about 4% of an SD in reading performance (see Table I).

| | Reading | | Mathematics | | Science | |
|---|---|---|---|---|---|---|
| | Effect | SE | Effect | SE | Effect | SE |
| *Student academic behaviors* | | | | | | |
| Learning time in school | 8.19★ | 3.36 | 8.15★ | 2.95 | 6.73 | 3.69 |
| Use of memorization strategies | -5.43★ | 1.99 | -11.44★ | 1.95 | -9.67★ | 1.75 |
| Use of elaboration strategies | 1.27 | 1.63 | 4.13★ | 1.79 | 5.35★ | 1.76 |
| Use of control strategies | 14.57★ | 2.29 | 12.24★ | 2.38 | 13.44★ | 2.42 |
| Meta-cognition of summarizing | 21.59★ | 2.26 | 17.32★ | 2.07 | 24.13★ | 2.08 |
| Meta-cognition of understanding and remembering | 8.40★ | 1.89 | 5.40★ | 1.90 | 8.77★ | 2.00 |
| *School climatic attributes* | | | | | | |
| Disciplinary climate | 24.35★ | 7.68 | 22.08★ | 8.50 | 24.48★ | 7.24 |
| Teacher–student relations | 38.89★ | 9.98 | 9.56 | 14.58 | 22.92★ | 11.31 |
| Student behaviors | 19.13★ | 4.73 | 22.30★ | 5.42 | 12.01 | 6.15 |
| Teacher behaviors | -9.74★ | 4.04 | -9.28★ | 4.58 | -3.52 | 5.22 |
| *Proportion of variance explained* ($R^2$) | B over N | F over B | B over N | F over B | B over N | F over B |
| Level 1 | 0.12 | 0.19 | 0.11 | 0.17 | 0.10 | 0.23 |
| Level 2 | 0.64 | 0.77 | 0.65 | 0.71 | 0.64 | 0.70 |

★$p < .05$. *Note.* N = null model. B = base model. F = full model.

Table II. Effects of student academic behaviors and school climatic attributes on academic achievement with control over student background and school context: the case of Japan.

In contrast, students who employed control strategies to learn demonstrated statistically significant advantage in academic performance across all three areas in each and every country (region). Therefore, it is common that highly successful students were skillful users of control strategies in learning across all six East Asian countries (regions). In Hong Kong, for example, one SD increase in use of control strategies was associated with an increase in academic performance of about 19% of an SD in reading, about 23% of an SD in mathematics, and about 20% of an SD in science (see Table I).

Meta-cognition also demonstrated statistically significant positive effects on academic performance across all three areas in each and every country (region). Therefore, it was also common that highly successful students knew how to utilize meta-cognitive skills in their learning across all six East Asian countries (regions). In Hong Kong, for example, one SD increase in using summarizing as a meta-cognitive process was associated with an increase in academic performance of about 12% of an SD in reading and of about 14% of an SD in both mathematics and science. Meanwhile, one SD increase in using understanding and remembering as a meta-cognitive process was associated with an increase in academic performance of about 8% of an SD in reading, about 7% of an SD in mathematics, and about 6% of an SD in science (see Table I).

| | Reading | | Mathematics | | Science | |
|---|---|---|---|---|---|---|
| | Effect | SE | Effect | SE | Effect | SE |
| *Student academic behaviors* | | | | | | |
| Use of memorization strategies | 3.15 | 2.28 | -6.70 | 3.47 | -0.79 | 2.94 |
| Use of elaboration strategies | 4.38 | 2.98 | 5.39 | 3.89 | 4.45 | 3.16 |
| Use of control strategies | 11.40* | 2.52 | 14.47* | 3.23 | 12.87* | 2.72 |
| Meta-cognition of summarizing | 20.65* | 2.41 | 15.16* | 2.94 | 21.55* | 2.59 |
| Meta-cognition of understanding and remembering | 10.77* | 2.69 | 12.83* | 3.09 | 13.88* | 3.09 |
| *School climatic attributes* | | | | | | |
| Academic pressure (many parents vs. none) | 28.11* | 9.69 | 34.59* | 13.04 | 18.35 | 11.12 |
| Disciplinary climate | 20.48* | 9.01 | 6.59 | 11.93 | 19.99* | 8.82 |
| *Proportion of variance explained* ($R^2$) | B over N | F over B | B over N | F over B | B over N | F over B |
| Level 1 | 0.17 | 0.39 | 0.16 | 0.31 | 0.08 | 0.43 |
| Level 2 | 0.60 | 0.85 | 0.59 | 0.71 | 0.50 | 0.84 |

*$p < .05$. *Note.* N = null model. B = base model. F = full model.

Table III. Effects of student academic behaviors and school climatic attributes on academic achievement with control over student background and school context: the case of Korea.

Higher-performing students in reading in Japan and Shanghai and higher-performing students in science in Korea and Shanghai demonstrated a significantly more negative attitude toward school statistically than their lower-performing counterparts. Only in Singapore did higher-performing students in science demonstrate a significantly more positive attitude toward school statistically than their lower-performing counterparts.

Finally, higher-performing students in all three areas used libraries as their learning resources significantly less statistically than their lower-performing counterparts in Shanghai, Singapore and Taipei – as did higher-performing students in mathematics in Hong Kong. Only in Japan did higher-performing students in science use libraries as their learning resources significantly more statistically than their lower-performing counterparts.

*Effects of School Climatic Attributes*

We now turn to the school level to examine the effects of school climatic attributes on academic performance over and above the effects of student academic behaviors (and student background characteristics), with control over school contextual characteristics. The most striking variable among all school climatic attributes is school disciplinary climate, with statistically significant positive effects on academic performance across all three areas in Hong Kong, Japan and Taipei. Statistically significant positive effects of disciplinary climate appeared in two areas in Korea (reading and science) and in Singapore (reading and mathematics). There were also statistically significant positive effects of disciplinary climate on mathematics performance in Shanghai. In terms of magnitude, consider two schools with a measure of disciplinary climate one SD apart. In Hong Kong, for example, students in the school with the better disciplinary climate achieved a higher level in reading of about 29% of an SD, a higher level in mathematics of about 31% of an SD, and a higher level in science of about 30% of an SD than students in the school with the poorer disciplinary climate (see Table I).

| | Reading | | Mathematics | | Science | |
|---|---|---|---|---|---|---|
| | Effect | SE | Effect | SE | Effect | SE |
| *Student academic behaviors* | | | | | | |
| Learning time in school | 5.00* | 2.31 | 3.66 | 2.94 | 4.12* | 1.70 |
| Use of memorization strategies | -7.90* | 2.12 | -10.14* | 3.32 | -7.19* | 3.06 |
| Use of elaboration strategies | 2.65 | 2.12 | 8.38* | 3.25 | 2.50 | 3.46 |
| Use of control strategies | 16.49* | 2.26 | 18.39* | 3.44 | 18.00* | 3.76 |
| Meta-cognition of summarizing | 13.58* | 1.93 | 18.71* | 2.18 | 16.79* | 2.75 |
| Meta-cognition of understanding and remembering | 9.68* | 1.32 | 9.23* | 1.95 | 8.49* | 2.02 |
| Attitude towards school | -4.27* | 1.63 | -4.42 | 2.69 | -4.94* | 2.26 |
| Use of libraries | -8.86* | 1.22 | -12.56* | 1.73 | -6.03* | 2.45 |
| *School climatic attributes* | | | | | | |
| Disciplinary climate | 12.69 | 8.56 | 43.36* | 11.59 | 12.27 | 10.29 |
| Student behaviors | 7.63* | 2.15 | 11.30* | 3.46 | 8.97* | 3.49 |
| Teacher behaviors | -9.37* | 3.24 | -10.73* | 5.09 | -8.36 | 4.52 |
| Teacher participation | -4.07* | 1.69 | -4.09 | 2.33 | -4.00* | 1.78 |
| Extra-curricular activities | 6.92* | 2.46 | 8.89* | 3.09 | 8.49* | 2.85 |
| *Proportion of variance explained ($R^2$)* | B over N | F over B | B over N | F over B | B over N | F over B |
| Level 1 | 0.13 | 0.22 | 0.08 | 0.20 | 0.08 | 0.23 |
| Level 2 | 0.65 | 0.53 | 0.61 | 0.56 | 0.57 | 0.57 |

*$p < .05$. *Note.* ICT = information and communication technology; N = null model; B = base model; F = full model.

Table IV. Effects of student academic behaviors and school climatic attributes on academic achievement with control over student background and school context: the case of Shanghai.

Other statistically significant school climatic attributes lacked sufficiently consistent patterns across areas and countries (regions) to be important. Parental academic pressure showed statistically significant positive effects on academic performance in reading and mathematics in Korea only. The teacher-student relationship demonstrated statistically significant positive effects on academic performance in reading in Japan and Shanghai, and in science in Japan. Student behaviors indicated statistically significant positive effects on academic performance in Japan (in reading and mathematics) and in Shanghai (across all three areas).

| | Reading | | Mathematics | | Science | |
|---|---|---|---|---|---|---|
| | Effect | SE | Effect | SE | Effect | SE |
| *Student academic behaviors* | | | | | | |
| Learning time in school | -4.89* | 1.19 | 2.29* | 1.00 | 4.87* | 1.15 |
| Use of memorization strategies | -9.28* | 1.61 | -9.91* | 1.99 | -11.78* | 1.69 |
| Use of elaboration strategies | -2.95 | 1.62 | 0.37 | 1.83 | -1.21 | 2.01 |
| Use of control strategies | 11.76* | 1.77 | 11.65* | 2.24 | 10.66* | 2.05 |
| Meta-cognition of summarizing | 23.23* | 1.60 | 19.75* | 1.86 | 22.72* | 1.77 |
| Meta-cognition of understanding and remembering | 5.99* | 1.46 | 6.22* | 1.69 | 7.75* | 1.57 |
| Use of libraries | -5.60* | 2.08 | -13.43* | 2.53 | -10.00* | 2.31 |
| *School climatic attributes* | | | | | | |
| Disciplinary climate | 23.11* | 7.93 | 19.98* | 9.44 | 15.41 | 8.71 |
| *Proportion of variance explained* ($R^2$) | B over N | F over B | B over N | F over B | B over N | F over B |
| Level 1 | 0.16 | 0.28 | 0.13 | 0.23 | 0.13 | 0.29 |
| Level 2 | 0.74 | 0.51 | 0.74 | 0.45 | 0.75 | 0.45 |

*$p < .05$. *Note.* N = null model; B = base model; F = full model.

Table V. Effects of student academic behaviors and school climatic attributes on academic achievement with control over student background and school context: the case of Singapore.

There were statistically significant positive effects of teacher behaviors on academic performance across all three areas in Taipei but statistically significant negative effects on academic performance in reading and mathematics in Japan and Shanghai. There were also statistically significant negative effects of principal leadership on academic performance across all three areas in Hong Kong only. Teacher participation showed statistically significant effects in Korea (positive on mathematics performance) and Shanghai (negative on performance in reading and science). Finally, extra-curricular activities demonstrated statistically significant positive effects on academic performance in Shanghai (across all three areas) and Taipei (in mathematics).

The few statistically significant negative effects on academic performance need some caution when interpreting them. For example, instead of concluding that in Hong Kong, students in schools with a strong principal leadership performed significantly poorer statistically than students in schools with a weak principal leadership (see Table I), we think that the statistically significant negative effects may represent a case of invisible leadership. That is, principals become more or less invisible in leadership when they enable smooth functioning of their schools without much overt heavy lifting. These principals may not be considered strong in leadership because they are not heavy handed. A similar idea also applies well to other statistically significant negative effects (e.g. teacher participation).

| | Reading | | Mathematics | | Science | |
|---|---|---|---|---|---|---|
| | Effect | SE | Effect | SE | Effect | SE |
| *Student academic behaviors* | | | | | | |
| Use of memorization strategies | -3.12 | 2.58 | -9.29* | 3.04 | -4.65 | 2.50 |
| Use of elaboration strategies | 1.93 | 2.20 | 1.46 | 3.32 | 4.56 | 3.31 |
| Use of control strategies | 21.27* | 2.88 | 24.83* | 3.52 | 19.09* | 2.90 |
| Meta-cognition of summarizing | 12.92* | 1.75 | 11.20* | 2.52 | 12.59* | 2.07 |
| Meta-cognition of understanding and remembering | 9.14* | 2.66 | 12.82* | 3.25 | 9.10* | 2.68 |
| Use of libraries | -10.08* | 2.69 | -16.27* | 2.88 | -11.62* | 2.29 |
| *School climatic attributes* | | | | | | |
| Disciplinary climate | 19.01* | 8.40 | 27.36* | 13.76 | 19.84* | 8.94 |
| Teacher behaviors | 9.52* | 3.07 | 14.37* | 4.91 | 8.46* | 3.13 |
| *Proportion of variance explained ($R^2$)* | B over N | F over B | B over N | F over B | B over N | F over B |
| Level 1 | 0.23 | 0.30 | 0.13 | 0.30 | 0.15 | 0.31 |
| Level 2 | 0.71 | 0.71 | 0.66 | 0.59 | 0.66 | 0.69 |

*$p < .05$. *Note.* N = null model; B = base model; F = full model.

Table VI. Effects of student academic behaviors and school climatic attributes on academic achievement with control over student background and school context: the case of Taipei.

### Adequacy of HLM Models

Tables I to VI all contain a small section (at the bottom) with statistical estimates on the adequacy of our HLM models across the three areas. We compared three models. The null model has no variables at either student or school level; the base model has student background variables at the student level and school contextual variables at the school level; and the full model has student academic behaviors added to the student level and school climatic attributes added to the school level.

In the case of reading achievement in Hong Kong, the base model containing our control variables at the student and school levels accounted for about 10% of the variance at the student level and about 68% of the variance at the school level (see Table I). The full model containing our key variables at the student and school levels explained on top of the base model about 18% of the remaining variance at the student level and about 43% of the remaining variance at the school level. These percentages are all sound indicators of the adequacy of our HLM models on reading performance. The adequacy of our HLM models on mathematics and science performance is equally sound. These sound statistics increase our confidence in making knowledge claims regarding student academic performance in Hong Kong. Similarly, we found sound statistical estimates on the adequacy of our HLM models across all three areas in all other countries (regions).

## Discussion

In searching for 'universal' success factors in the six top-performing East Asian countries (regions) in PISA 2009, our strategy is to look for consistency on reasons for (indicators of) success across academic areas and across countries (regions) as a way to triangulate East Asian success. We believe that in order for the education of the world to progress forward, we must learn educational lessons from top-performing countries (regions). We believe that the issues at hand are what factors have made a student effective in learning and a school effective in teaching in those top-performing countries (regions). These factors, as we have identified, are often educational goals, emphases and pursuits (either explicitly or implicitly) in those countries (regions) because they distinguish between effective and ineffective students and schools in learning and teaching. The same factors may provide valuable insights into various educational reforms aimed at improving learning outcomes of students in other countries (regions).

### Which Student Academic Behaviors Count in Top-performing East Asian Countries (Regions)?

It is rather convincing that among the five categories of student academic behaviors (time spent in learning; use of learning strategies; use of meta-cognitive skills; general attitude; and use of learning resources), both use of learning strategies and use of meta-cognitive skills have shown amazingly consistent results across academic areas and across countries (regions). In terms of learning strategies, use of memorization (rehearsal) strategies to learn does harm to academic performance whenever it has statistically significant effects. Use of elaboration strategies functions as a 'transition point' in that use of these strategies begins to demonstrate some quite limited advantage in academic performance.

What is striking is the total consistency across the six top-performing East Asian countries (regions) in terms of highly successful students being skillful users of control strategies in their learning. What is equally striking is another total consistency across the six top-performing East Asian countries (regions), in that highly successful students knew how to utilize meta-cognitive skills in the process of their learning. Not only are these positive effects comprehensive across all academic areas and across all countries (regions), but also they universally demonstrate the strongest effects among all statistically significant student academic behaviors.

It is credible to infer that these learning strategies and meta-cognitive skills are present commonly among highly successful students across the six top-performing East Asian countries (regions). In their pursuit of excellence in core academic areas, many East Asian students have become effective learners skillfully utilizing the most sophisticated learning strategies and meta-cognitive skills to manage their learning. To a large extent, these East Asian countries (regions) perform at the very top internationally because there are many students in each of these countries (regions) who are highly effective learners (i.e. they know very well how to learn).

Relating to education around the world, how to teach rather than how to learn is usually a societal concern in education. Teachers all over the world are trained vigorously on the methods of teaching. It is not untypical that teacher education programs across the world pay little attention to the methods of learning. We believe that even though we are not sure whether it is due to teachers or parents, students are taught, or at very least influenced on, how to learn effectively in the six East Asian countries (regions). Overall, these top-performing East Asian countries (regions) have offered a convincing common clue to education around the world with regard to the academic success of their students.

### *Which School Climatic Attributes Count in Top-performing East Asian Countries (Regions)?*

In general, patterns regarding the effects of school climatic attributes on academic performance are not as strong and invariable as those of student academic behaviors. Still, we have identified a nearly perfect occurrence of school disciplinary climate as the most important school climatic attribute affecting academic performance. The effects of disciplinary climate are comprehensive across all academic areas in Hong Kong, Japan and Taipei. The effects of disciplinary climate are statistically significant in two academic areas in Korea and Singapore and in one academic area in Shanghai. The magnitude of these effects is largest among all statistically significant school climatic attributes across all countries (regions). In fact, disciplinary climate demonstrates larger effects on academic performance than any statistically significant student academic behavior. Such a finding speaks volumes because school effects are effects above and beyond student effects and thus are typically smaller than student effects. The magnitude concerning the effects of disciplinary climate strongly indicates that disciplinary climate is a universally powerful factor for the academic success in the six top-performing East Asian countries (regions).

The literature on school effects emphasizes school disciplinary climate as one of the most essential aspects of school life (see Teddlie & Reynolds, 2000). An orderly learning environment is definitely the most common (and important) climatic attribute of schools that highly successful students attend in the six top-performing East Asian countries (regions). It is quite common in East Asian schools that discipline is taught as a virtue and that it is reinforced jointly by administrators, teachers and parents. Overall, these top-performing East Asian countries (regions) have offered another convincing common clue to education around the world about the academic success of their students– conducive disciplinary climate establishes an environment that helps students achieve academic success. This finding is not necessarily new to the research literature, but the results of our data analysis concerning the importance of disciplinary climate been of a magnitude and consistency that is rather rare in the research literature.

*Reflection on Literature*

On the basis of the results of our data analysis, we address a couple of key issues (debates) in the research literature on East Asian academic success. Our research is not designed to discern what relative roles effort and ability play in academic success (e.g. Ho & Hau, 2008; Jeynes, 2008) in the six top-performing East Asian countries (regions). Nevertheless, our consistent results across all these countries (regions) revealed that highly successful students in these countries (regions) were effective learners who were able to skillfully employ the most sophisticated learning strategies and meta-cognitive skills to manage and regulate their learning. We offer a third alternative to explain the East Asian success in academic performance (i.e. our interaction argument); that is, many students in East Asian countries (regions) know well how to learn. We suggest that this crossroads (i.e. interaction) between effort and ability produces extraordinary academic performance.

We question the concern in the research literature about East Asian students' elevated respect for teachers interfering with their critical thinking (e.g. Kim, 2005; Jeynes, 2008). Again, even though our research is not designed to test this proposition, we infer from our findings that unless students are able to detect errors in the presentation of knowledge by others such as teachers, peers and parents (i.e. distinguish between right and wrong in knowledge claims), it is simply impossible for them to become effective learners skillfully applying meta-cognitive skills to regulate their learning. We confidently suspect that East Asian students may not explicitly question what their teachers say but do check through other avenues for any potential errors in the knowledge presented by their teachers. For example, our personal experiences with Chinese students do suggest that some of them respectfully present their cases as alternative solutions to their teachers and would like their teachers to evaluate whether or not their cases are correct. The result improves the understanding of both students and teachers in a non-offensive manner.

Our findings do not support the criticism of East Asian achievement whereby it is deemed to be a pure result of endless outside schooling or tutoring that students receive for the purpose of excelling on exit or entrance exams (e.g. Baker et al, 2001; Cave, 2001; Bray, 2010). We found that learning time in school showed far more cases of statistical significance on academic performance than out-of-school lessons did. In fact, we found cases of East Asian countries (regions) in which out-of-school lessons were more of a means for low-performing students to catch up rather than for high-performing students to excel further (e.g. Hong Kong). Although it may be true that many East Asian students are under greater pressure to achieve, we confidently suspect that many of them have also found an effective way to cope with this pressure. They resort to more effective learning strategies and meta-cognitive skills to excel in academic performance.

It is intriguing to us that the research literature has not given school disciplinary climate a predominant position as the most distinct school climatic attribute of East Asian schools even though there are some researchers who bring this issue up for discussion (e.g. Shin et al, 2009). The complication regarding this issue is the fact that the PISA definition of disciplinary climate pertains to environment or order of classroom learning (see OECD, 2011). What is often referred to as disciplinary climate in the literature is actually what PISA refers to as student behaviors (see OECD, 2011). Therefore, what East Asian schools have achieved is actually more on-task time (in classroom instruction). Our comprehensive results have revealed the critical importance to academic success of the orderly classroom learning environment over all other school climatic attributes.

Finally, we briefly comment on the notion of Zhu and Leung (2011) regarding whether an East Asian model of learning (motivation in their case) exists. Even though we are not addressing the same research issue as theirs, we believe that an East Asian model of education must be based on fairly consistent results across East Asian countries (regions). If, indeed, the pursuit of such a model is fruitful, then the results of our data analyses have added some credible substance to the model. We have shown consistency across all six East Asian countries (regions) regarding highly successful students being effective learners, and school disciplinary climate (precisely, orderly classroom learning environment) being the most important climatic attribute of schools that highly successful students attend.

*Cultural Explanations*

Returning to the aforementioned East Asian model of learning, we suggest that our findings represent a move towards an East Asian model of cultural learning or cultural explanations. Clearly, learning strategies, meta-cognitive skills and school disciplinary climate are all expected to be shaped by cultural influence and cultural practice. For example, the East Asian cultural emphasis on harmony would particularly impact disciplinary climate. Intrinsic intellectual challenges of East Asian languages may dispose students to acquire different procedural and conceptual skills. Faced with a strong cultural emphasis on effort and increasingly sophisticated challenges in learning reading, mathematics and science that require strong ability more than effort, East Asian young people could seek to strategize their learning.

Overall, without going beyond what our data can afford us, it is reasonable to conclude that our results appear quite compatible with cultural explanations.

## Final Remarks

Using national (regional) data from six top-performing countries (regions) in PISA 2009, we have established the substantial importance of learning strategies and meta-cognitive skills (belonging to student academic behaviors) as well as of school disciplinary climate (belonging to school climatic attributes) to student academic success. We are highly confident about this knowledge claim because of our careful control over student background characteristics (at the student level) and school contextual characteristics (at the school level). Again, from an academic perspective, these findings may not necessarily be new. Nevertheless, these six top-performing East Asian countries (regions) have really put theory into practice and have benefited from this effort tremendously. Although how they put theory into practice may not be entirely applicable to other parts of the world, results concerning East Asian student achievement have revealed a promising direction for education around the world to take to meaningfully improve student learning outcomes.

## References

Anderson, John O., Lin, Huann-Shyang, Treagust, David F., Ross, Shelley P., & Yore, Larry D. (2007) Using Large-scale Assessment Datasets for Research in Science and Mathematics Education: Programme for International Student Assessment (PISA), *International Journal of Science and Mathematics Education*, 5, 591-614.

Baker, David P., Akiba, Motoko, LeTendre, Gerald K. & Wiseman, Alexander W. (2001) Worldwide Shadow Education: outside-school learning, institutional quality of schooling, and cross-national mathematics achievement, *Educational Evaluation and Policy Analysis*, 23, 1-17.

Bempechat, Janine & Drago-Severson, Eleanor (1999) Cross-national Differences in Academic Achievement: beyond etic conceptions of children's understandings, *Review of Educational Research*, 69 (Autumn), 287-314.

Bishop, John H. (1998) The Effect of Curriculum-based External Exit Exam Systems on Student Achievement, *Journal of Economic Education*, 29 (Spring), 171-182.

Bray, Mark (2010) Researching Shadow Education: methodological challenges and directions, *Asia Pacific Education Review*, 11, 3-13.

Bybee, Rodger & McCrae, Barry (2011) Scientific Literacy and Student Attitudes: perspectives from PISA 2006 Science, *International Journal of Science Education*, 33 (January), 7-26.

Cave, Peter (2001) Educational Reform in Japan in the 1990s: 'individuality' and other uncertainties, *Comparative Education*, 37 (May), 173-191.

Chiu, Ming M. & McBride-Chang, Catherine (2010) Family and Reading in 41 Countries: differences across cultures and students, *Scientific Studies of Reading*, 14, 514-543.

Eccles, Jacquelynne & Wigfield, Allan (1995) In the Mind of the Actor: the structure of adolescents' achievement task values and expectancy-related beliefs, *Personality and Social Psychology Bulletin*, 21, 215-225.

Fernandez, Clea, Cannon, Joanna & Chokshi, Sonal (2003) A US-Japan Lesson Study Collaboration Reveals Critical Lenses for Examining Practice, *Teaching and Teacher Education*, 19, 171-185.

Geary, David (1996) International Differences in Mathematical Achievement: their nature, causes, and consequences, *Current Directions in Psychological Science*, 5 (October), 133-137.

Hiebert, James & Stigler, James W. (2000) A Proposal for Improving Classroom Teaching: Lessons from the TIMSS Video Study, *Elementary School Journal*, 101, 3-20.

Ho, Irene T., & Hau, Kit-Tai (2008) Academic Achievement in the Chinese Context: the role of goals, strategies, and effort, *International Journal of Psychology*, 43, 892-897.

Hojo, Masakazu & Oshio, Takashi (2009) What Factors Determine Student Performance in East Asia? New Evidence from TIMSS 2007. Technical report. Niigata University.

Holloway, Susan D. (1988) Concepts of Ability and Effort in Japan and the United States, *Review of Education Research*, 58 (Fall), 327-345.

Jacobs, Jennifer K. & Morita, Eiji (2002) Japanese and American Teachers' Evaluations of Videotaped Mathematics Lessons, *Journal for Research in Mathematics Education*, 33, 154-175.

Jeynes, William (2008) What We Should and Should Not Learn from the Japanese and Other East Asian Educational Systems, *Educational Policy*, 22 (November), 900-927.

Kaya, Sibel & Rice, Diana C. (2010) Multilevel Effects of Student and Classroom Factors on Elementary Science Achievement in Five Countries, *International Journal of Science Education*, 32 (July), 1337-1363.

Kim, Kyung H. (2005) Learning from Each Other: creativity in East Asian and American education, *Creativity Research Journal*, 17, 337-347.

Kinney, Carol J. (1998) Building an Excellent Teacher Corps: how Japan does it, *American Educator*, 21 (Winter), 16-23.

Leung, Frederick K.S. (2002) Behind the High Achievement of East Asian Students, *Educational Research and Evaluation*, 8, 87-108.

Leung, Frederick K.S. (2005) Some Characteristics of East Asian Mathematics Classrooms Based on Data from the TIMSS 1999 Video Study, *Educational Studies in Mathematics*, 60, 199-215.

Li, Yeping (2000) A Comparison of Problems that Follow Selected Content Presentations in American and Chinese Mathematics Textbooks, *Journal for Research in Mathematics Education*, 31, 234-241.

Ma, Liping (1999) *Knowing and Teaching Elementary Mathematics*. Mahwah, NJ: Lawrence Erlbaum Associates.

Marks, Gary N., Cresswell, John & Ainley, John (2006) Explaining Socioeconomic Inequalities in Student Achievement: the role of home and school factors, *Educational Research and Evaluation*, 12 (April), 105-128.

Organisation for Economic Co-operation and Development (OECD) (2010a) *PISA 2009 Results: what students know and can do – student performance in reading, mathematics, and science*, vol. 1. Paris: OECD.

Organisation for Economic Co-operation and Development (OECD) (2010b) *PISA 2009 Results: what makes a school successful*, vol. 4. Paris: OECD.

Organisation for Economic Co-operation and Development (OECD) (2010c) *Mathematics Teaching and Learning Strategies in PISA*. Paris: OECD.

Organisation for Economic Co-operation and Development (OECD) (2011) *PISA 2009 Technical Report*. Paris: OECD.

Schumer, Gundel (1999) Mathematics Education in Japan, *Journal of Curriculum Studies*, 31, 399-427.

Shin, Jongho, Lee, Hyunjoo & Kim, Yongnam (2009) Student and School Factors Affecting Mathematics Achievement International Comparisons between Korea, Japan and the USA, *School Psychology International*, 30, 520-537.

Stevenson, Harold (1987) The Asian Advantage: the case of mathematics, *American Educator*, Summer, 26-31, 47-48.

Stevenson, Harold W. (1998) A Study of Three Cultures: Germany, Japan and the United States. An Overview of the TIMSS Case Study Project, *Phi Delta Kappan*, 79, 524-529.

Stevenson, Harold W., Lee, Shin-Ying & Stigler, James W. (1986) Mathematics Achievement of Chinese, Japanese and American Children, *Science*, 231, 693-699.

Stevenson, Harold & Stigler, James W. (1992) *The Learning Gap*. New York: Summit Books.

Stigler, James W. & Hiebert, James (1998) The TIMSS Videotape Study, *American Educator*, 22, 43-45.

Stigler, James W. & Stevenson, Harold W. (1991) How Asian Teachers Polish Each Lesson to Perfection, *American Educator: the professional journal of the American Federation of Teachers*, 15, 12-20, 43-47.

Teddlie, Charles & Reynolds, David (Eds) (2000) *The International Handbook of School Effectiveness Research*. London: Falmer.

Topping, Keith (2006) PISA/PIRLS Data on Reading Achievement: transfer into international policy and practice, *The Reading Teacher*, 59 (March), 588-590.

Valverde, Gilbert A. & Schmidt, William H. (2000) Greater Expectations: learning from other nations in the quest for 'world-class standards' in US school mathematics and science, *Journal of Curriculum Studies*, 32, 651-687.

Wang, Jian & Lin, Emily (2005) Comparative Studies on US and Chinese Mathematics Learning and the Implications for Standards-based Mathematics Teaching Reform, *Educational Researcher*, 34 (June/July), 3-13.

Watanabe, Ted (2000) Japanese High School Entrance Examinations, *Mathematics Teacher*, 93 (January), 30-35.

Weiner, Bernard (1985) Principles for a Theory of Student Motivation and Their Application within an Attributional Framework, in R. Ames & C. Ames (Eds) *Research on Motivation in Education. Vol. 1: Student Motivation.* New York: Academic Press.

Weiner, Bernard (1994) Integrating Social and Personal Theories of Achievement Strivings, *Review of Educational Research*, 64, 557-573.

Willoughby, Teena & Wood, Eileen (1994) Elaborative Interrogation Examined at Encoding and Retrieval, *Learning and Instruction*, 4, 139-149.

Woodward, John & Ono, Yumiko (2004) Mathematics and Academic Diversity in Japan, *Journal of Learning Disabilities*, 37 (January/February), 74-82.

Wößmann, Ludger (2005) Educational Production in East Asia: the impact of family background and schooling policies on student performance, *German Economic Review*, 6, 331-353.

Zhu, Yan & Leung, Frederick K.S. (2011) Motivation and Achievement: is there an East Asian model? *International Journal of Science and Mathematics Education*, 9, 1189-1212.

Zimmerman, Barry J. & Schunk, Dale H. (2001) *Self-regulated Learning and Academic Achievement: theoretical perspectives*, 2nd edn. Mahwah, NJ: Lawrence Erlbaum Associates.

CHAPTER 11

# Immigrant Children's Academic Performance: the influence of origin, destination and community[1]

## JAAP DRONKERS & MANON DE HEUS

ABSTRACT This chapter studies the scientific literacy of migrant children in a cross-classified multilevel framework. Using data from the 2006 PISA survey, features of migrant children's origin countries, destination countries and communities (the specific origin–destination combination) are taken into account in order to explain macro-level differences in migrants' educational performance. The sample consists of 9414 15-year-old migrant children, originating from 46 different countries, living in 16 western destination countries. The results show that differences in scientific performance between migrant children from different origins and between children living in different destination countries cannot be fully explained by compositional differences. Contextual attributes of origin countries, destination countries and communities matter as well. It is shown, for instance, that the better educational performance of migrant children living in traditional immigration receiving countries cannot be explained by these children's favourable background characteristics. The economic features of the origin countries did not influence the science performance, in contrast with the origin countries' prevailing religions.

## Introduction

The educational position of migrant children with different origins has been well documented. Research conducted in the United States has shown that major variation exists in educational outcomes of different ethnic groups: Mexican Americans and blacks obtain lower average grades than Asians and native Americans, and they are more likely to drop out of high school and less likely to earn a college degree. Similar gaps in educational success between different migrant groups have been observed in other western countries, such as the Netherlands, Belgium and Germany. In order to understand these migrant group differences, research has often relied on classic individual-level determinants (Kao & Thompson, 2003). Overall, these individual-level explanations have focused on the cultural position (e.g. their motivation to perform) and the structural characteristics (e.g. parental capital and the time of arrival) of different migrant groups.

Next to the study of the educational performance of different migrant groups in a single country, cross-national research has been conducted. Cross-national studies such as the Trends in International Mathematics and Science Study (TIMMS), the Programme for International Student Assessment (PISA) and the Progress in International Reading Literacy Study (PIRLS) that focus on children's performances in numerous subjects have allowed comparisons to be made between the educational performance of migrant and non-migrant pupils in different destination countries. Individual- and school-level characteristics have been taken into account with PISA 2000 to explain differences in educational performance between first- and second-generation migrant pupils and natives (Marks, 2005; Schnepf, 2006). Interestingly, these effects vary substantially between countries. Although not tested, they suggest that these differential effects stem from differences in destination countries' educational systems or immigration policies.

However, since immigration is intrinsically a transnational phenomenon, it should be studied accordingly (Portes, 1999). Migrant parents and children from various origin countries move to various destination countries. In order to fully capture the complexity of the migration process, the use of a so-called cross-classified multilevel design (or double comparative design) has been proposed (van Tubergen et al, 2004). Instead of relying on observation of multiple-origin groups in a single destination or a single-origin group in multiple destinations, the cross-classified design allows a comparison of multiple origins in multiple destinations simultaneously. Since this design disentangles effects of characteristics of countries migrants come from ('origin effects'), characteristics of the countries to which they migrate ('destination effects'), and characteristics of their specific community (the origin–destination combination), it is extremely useful for attempts to gain insights into migrants' outcomes such as educational performance. Analyzing migrants' integration into host societies without properly taking into account these origin effects will indeed lead to flawed results. Depending on the composition of the migrant population in a certain society, results may be too optimistic or too pessimistic. Levels et al (2008) conclude, using the PISA 2003 data, that both origin and destination of migration have substantial effects on scholastic achievement, and that these effects influence in important ways differences in scholastic knowledge between native pupils, first-generation migrants and second-generation migrants.

The PISA 2006 data, which will be used in this chapter, show both origin and destination variance in educational outcome (see Table I). The migrants' average score of 468 for scientific literacy conceals the considerable variation by origin country, ranging from a score of 404 for the Albanian migrants to a score of 571 for the US migrant pupils. Other high performers are the Chinese and Australian migrants (552 and 548 respectively). Next to those apparent origin effects, destination effects seem to exist as well. Whereas migrant pupils in Australia outperform their native counterparts with an average scientific literacy score of 536, the Danish migrant pupils have a score of no higher than 388. So, irrespective of origin country, average science performance of migrants also differs across different destination countries. The specific combinations of origin and destination need to be taken into account as well. For instance, whereas the Turkish migrants in Germany have a score of 411, their Turkish counterparts in Austria have a score of 380, and of 374 in Denmark.

The main question of this chapter concerns the explanation of this variance of educational performance of migrant pupils by the macro-characteristics of their origin and destination countries.

## Why Countries' Macro-characteristics Might Matter

### Contextual and Composition Effects

Differences in average scientific performance between different origin groups and different destination countries can be due to either compositional or contextual effects. The former occurs whenever the composition of groups (e.g. origin groups, destination countries), with respect to individual background variables, differs. Migrant children in some destination countries might outperform migrant children in others because some destination countries attract migrants with more favourable individual background characteristics. In a similar vein, different compositions of origin groups may explain part of the variance in educational attainment between these origin groups. Contextual effects refer to origin and destination countries' distinct properties that surpass compositional differences. In order to rule out compositional effects and determine which origin and destination countries' contextual characteristics influence scientific achievement, we control for a range of individual background variables.

### Destination-country Characteristics

In order to evaluate destination countries' immigration policies, we use the migrant integration policy index (MIPEX). This index takes into account over a hundred legal policy indicators in order to determine to what extent migrants living in a European Union (EU) member state profit from legal policies on long-term residence, access to nationality, anti-discrimination, family reunion, political participation and labour market access (Niessen et al, 2007). Since countries that score high on these policy dimensions are expected to have a positive influence on their migrant population's economic, political and social integration, performing well at school pays off for migrant children. We therefore hypothesize that *migrant children living in countries that have more favourable migrant policies outperform migrant children in countries with less favourable migrant policies (hypothesis 1)*.

Destination countries also differ in their immigration admission policies. During the past 50 years, traditional migrant-receiving countries such as Australia, Canada and New Zealand have instituted skills-based 'point systems' that reward certain socio-economic traits in the admission formula. In general, people with higher educational levels, more job experience and a better command of English have higher chances of being admitted. In doing this, these countries match migrant skills with labour market needs and reduce the fiscal burden that immigration would place on the host country's system of social assistance (Borjas, 2001). Although selective admission is directed towards adult migrants, traditional migrant-receiving countries also make more serious efforts to secure the economic viability of migrant children than European countries. Following the above line of argument, we expect both composition and contextual characteristics to cause superior scientific performance of migrant children living in traditional migrant-receiving countries. Although their higher educational performance will be partly caused by favourable parental background characteristics, positive sentiments towards migrants and an educational system adapted to the needs of migrant children are likely to positively affect the scientific performance of migrant children in traditional migrant-receiving countries on top of compositional differences: *migrant children living in traditional migrant-receiving countries outperform migrant children in non-traditional migrant-receiving countries, also after controlling for composition effects (hypothesis 2)*. Given the selective nature of the immigration policy and the openness to migrants of these traditional migrant-receiving countries, we assume that migrants with high socio-economic status profit more from migration to these traditional migrant-receiving countries. For that reason we expect that *migrant children living in traditional migrant-receiving countries with parents with high socio-economic status outperform both comparable migrant children in non-traditional migrant-receiving countries and migrant children living in traditional migrant-receiving countries but with parents with low socio-economic status (hypothesis 2a)*.

### Origin-country Characteristics

Next to differences in average scientific performance between migrants' in different destination countries, we expect differences between children from different origins regardless of their destination country.

Van Tubergen et al (2004) have argued that migrants originating from economically developed countries generally have more human capital skills than migrants from developing countries. Since the education systems of economically developed countries transfer skills and diplomas that are also of value in migrants' new economically developed destination countries, migrants from economically more developed countries are likely to have more favourable background characteristics than migrants from less economically developed countries. Jasso and Rosenzweig (1990) have, for instance, shown that migrants in the United States from economically developed countries have a better command of English. So, although we expect a positive effect of origin countries' economic development on children's educational performance, we expect this to result fully from compositional differences. So we argue that *after taking into account composition effects, the positive effect of origin countries' economic development will disappear (hypothesis 3)*.

Next to political and economic factors of origin countries, the degree of social distance between origin and destination cultures is likely to influence educational performance. It was Bogardus who originally advanced the idea that people feel more distant and less understanding towards some groups of people than towards others. According to Portes and Rumbaut (2001), the ranking of social distance is based on differences in cultural values, socio-economic background and physical appearance. Greater social distance between natives and migrant groups has often been related to labour-market discrimination, but very likely also translates into lower educational performance of those migrant pupils that differ culturally and economically from native pupils. We examine this idea by taking into account one dimension of migrant children's origin cultures: their origin countries' dominant religion. Since all destination countries analyzed in this chapter are predominantly Christian, *we expect migrant children originating from Christian origin countries to outperform migrant children from countries with other prevailing religions (hypothesis 4)*. Distance in religion between destination country and origin country might be mitigated or even neutralized if the migrants have a higher socio-economic status. For that reason, *we expect that hypothesis 4 is only true for migrant children originating from non-Christian countries with parents with low socio-economic status (hypothesis 5a)*.

*Community Characteristics*

Next to using religion as a measure of cultural distance, we take into account differences in value orientations between migrants' origins and destinations.

According to Portes and Rumbaut (2001), social distance between natives and migrants is not only based on differences in cultural values, but also on differences in socio-economic background. Adults from migrant communities with more socio-economic and cultural capital relative to the native population are less likely to be regarded with prejudice by natives, they have better chances of providing their children with resources that stimulate upward mobility, and they are more likely to convince their children that upward mobility is possible. Levels et al (2008) found a significant effect of social distance between natives and migrants differing in socio-economic background. We therefore hypothesize that *migrant children from communities with higher levels of socio-economic and cultural capital than the native population outperform those from communities with lower levels of capital (hypothesis 5)*.

## PISA 2006 and Its Focus on Scientific Literacy

Since 2000, the Organisation for Economic Co-operation and Development (OECD) has tri-annually conducted large-scale tests among 15-year-olds living in its member states and partner states in order to assess pupils' mathematical, reading and scientific literacy. In doing so, the OECD has aimed to find out to which extent pupils near the end of compulsory education have acquired some of the knowledge and skills essential for full participation in society. Alongside information on pupils' educational performance, PISA also provides information on their individual characteristics (e.g. on parental education and careers, resources that are available in the child's home, the language spoken at home, the birth countries of both the parents and the student) and the school they attend (e.g. the teacher-student ratio, the number of vacant science positions, the school's location) through respectively administering a student and a principal questionnaire. The dependent variable of this study is scientific literacy, which was the main focus of the PISA 2006 wave.

## Determining Pupils' Origin Country and Migrant Status

Since specific information on the country of birth of both the parents and the student is necessary to be able to determine a pupil's origin country, countries that did not allow enough specificity in birth countries could not be taken into account. Therefore, although no less than 57 countries participated in the 2006 PISA wave, only data from the following 16 developed countries are suited to test the hypotheses: Australia, Austria, Belgium, Denmark, Finland, Germany, Greece, Latvia, Liechtenstein, Luxembourg, the Netherlands, New Zealand, Norway, Portugal, Switzerland and Scotland.

In order to determine pupils' origin country, several decision rules have been used based upon their own birth country and the birth countries of both of their parents. Next to the pupil's origin country, we identified his/her migrant status. Students of whom at least one of the parents was born in a country different from the destination country were identified as migrants. Migrant students were either classified as first- or second-generation migrants, with the former being those students who were born abroad themselves as well. Finally, the decision rules used to identify pupils' origin country and migrant status gave a final sample of 9414 migrant students, originating from 46 different origin countries.

Table I provides a first insight into the variation in scientific literacy between migrant children from different origin groups in various destination countries.

(a)

| Origin countries | Destination countries | | | | | | | | |
|---|---|---|---|---|---|---|---|---|---|
| | AU | AT | BE | CH | DE | DK | EL | FI | Mean |
| Albania | 0 | 412 | 0 | 359 | 0 | 0 | 434 | 0 | 404 |
| Australia | 0 | 0 | 0 | 0 | 0 | 0 | 0 | 0 | 548 |
| Austria | 0 | 0 | 0 | 495 | 0 | 0 | 0 | 0 | 519 |
| Bangladesh | 0 | 0 | 0 | 0 | 0 | 0 | 0 | 0 | 476 |
| Belarus | 0 | 0 | 0 | 0 | 0 | 0 | 0 | 0 | 504 |
| Belgium | 0 | 0 | 0 | 0 | 0 | 0 | 0 | 0 | 528 |
| Bosnia Herzegovina | 0 | 445 | 0 | 0 | 451 | 421 | 0 | 0 | 440 |
| Brazil | 0 | 0 | 0 | 0 | 0 | 0 | 0 | 0 | 464 |
| Cap Verde | 0 | 0 | 0 | 0 | 0 | 0 | 0 | 0 | 380 |
| China | 562 | 518 | 0 | 0 | 0 | 0 | 0 | 0 | 552 |
| Congo | 0 | 0 | 427 | 0 | 0 | 0 | 0 | 0 | 427 |
| Croatia | 0 | 458 | 0 | 0 | 433 | 0 | 0 | 0 | 451 |
| Czech Republic | 0 | 569 | 0 | 0 | 0 | 0 | 0 | 0 | 569 |
| Denmark | 0 | 0 | 0 | 0 | 0 | 0 | 0 | 0 | 411 |
| Estonia | 0 | 0 | 0 | 0 | 0 | 0 | 0 | 437 | 437 |
| France | 0 | 0 | 448 | 507 | 0 | 0 | 0 | 0 | 488 |
| Germany | 0 | 521 | 508 | 549 | 0 | 0 | 0 | 0 | 526 |
| Greece | 0 | 0 | 0 | 0 | 419 | 0 | 0 | 0 | 419 |
| Hungary | 0 | 561 | 0 | 0 | 0 | 0 | 0 | 0 | 561 |
| India | 551 | 0 | 0 | 0 | 0 | 0 | 0 | 0 | 551 |
| Italy | 0 | 0 | 0 | 443 | 415 | 0 | 0 | 0 | 438 |
| Rep. of Korea | 514 | 0 | 0 | 0 | 0 | 0 | 0 | 0 | 521 |
| Liechtenstein | 0 | 0 | 0 | 496 | 0 | 0 | 0 | 0 | 496 |
| Macedonia | 0 | 407 | 0 | 0 | 433 | 0 | 0 | 0 | 411 |
| Morocco | 0 | 0 | 438 | 0 | 0 | 0 | 0 | 0 | 438 |
| Netherlands | 0 | 0 | 522 | 0 | 0 | 0 | 0 | 0 | 522 |
| New Zealand | 508 | 0 | 0 | 0 | 0 | 0 | 0 | 0 | 508 |
| Pakistan | 0 | 0 | 0 | 0 | 0 | 383 | 0 | 0 | 412 |
| Philippines | 512 | 0 | 0 | 0 | 0 | 0 | 0 | 0 | 512 |
| Portugal | 0 | 0 | 0 | 454 | 0 | 0 | 0 | 0 | 428 |
| Romania | 0 | 439 | 0 | 0 | 0 | 0 | 0 | 0 | 539 |
| Russia | 0 | 0 | 0 | 0 | 466 | 0 | 0 | 550 | 493 |
| Samoa | 0 | 0 | 0 | 0 | 0 | 0 | 0 | 0 | 425 |
| Serbia Montenegro | 0 | 426 | 0 | 427 | 414 | 0 | 0 | 0 | 420 |
| Slovakia | 0 | 507 | 0 | 0 | 0 | 0 | 0 | 0 | 507 |
| Slovenia | 0 | 416 | 0 | 0 | 435 | 0 | 0 | 0 | 420 |
| South Africa | 541 | 0 | 0 | 0 | 0 | 0 | 0 | 0 | 541 |
| Spain | 0 | 0 | 0 | 466 | 0 | 0 | 0 | 0 | 467 |

| | | | | | | | | | |
|---|---|---|---|---|---|---|---|---|---|
| Sweden | 0 | 0 | 0 | 0 | 0 | 0 | 0 | 522 | 477 |
| Switzerland | 0 | 0 | 0 | 0 | 0 | 0 | 0 | 0 | 521 |
| Turkey | 0 | 380 | 414 | 425 | 411 | 374 | 0 | 0 | 429 |
| Ukraine | 0 | 0 | 0 | 0 | 0 | 0 | 0 | 0 | 472 |
| United Kingdom | 542 | 0 | 0 | 0 | 0 | 0 | 0 | 0 | 550 |
| United States | 571 | 0 | 0 | 0 | 0 | 0 | 0 | 0 | 571 |
| Vietnam | 518 | 0 | 0 | 0 | 0 | 0 | 0 | 0 | 518 |
| | | | | | | | | | |
| Mean migrants | 536 | 437 | 453 | 444 | 438 | 388 | 434 | 522 | 468 |
| Mean natives | 524 | 525 | 527 | 527 | 531 | 501 | 480 | 565 | 518 |
| Difference (I-N) | 12 | -88 | -74 | -83 | -93 | -113 | -46 | -43 | -50 |

(b)

| | Destination countries | | | | | | | | |
|---|---|---|---|---|---|---|---|---|---|
| *Origin countries* | LI | LU | LV | NL | NO | NZ | PT | SC | Mean |
| Albania | 358 | 0 | 0 | 0 | 0 | 0 | 0 | 0 | 404 |
| Australia | 0 | 0 | 0 | 0 | 0 | 548 | 0 | 0 | 548 |
| Austria | 554 | 0 | 0 | 0 | 0 | 0 | 0 | 0 | 519 |
| Bangladesh | 0 | 0 | 0 | 0 | 0 | 0 | 0 | 476 | 476 |
| Belarus | 0 | 0 | 504 | 0 | 0 | 0 | 0 | 0 | 504 |
| Belgium | 0 | 528 | 0 | 0 | 0 | 0 | 0 | 0 | 528 |
| Bosnia Herzegovina | 0 | 0 | 0 | 0 | 0 | 0 | 0 | 0 | 440 |
| Brazil | 0 | 0 | 0 | 0 | 0 | 0 | 464 | 0 | 464 |
| Cap Verde | 0 | 380 | 0 | 0 | 0 | 0 | 0 | 0 | 380 |
| China | 0 | 0 | 0 | 0 | 0 | 547 | 458 | 483 | 552 |
| Congo | 0 | 0 | 0 | 0 | 0 | 0 | 0 | 0 | 427 |
| Croatia | 0 | 0 | 0 | 0 | 0 | 0 | 0 | 0 | 451 |
| Czech Republic | 0 | 0 | 0 | 0 | 0 | 0 | 0 | 0 | 569 |
| Denmark | 0 | 0 | 0 | 0 | 411 | 0 | 0 | 0 | 411 |
| Estonia | 0 | 0 | 0 | 0 | 0 | 0 | 0 | 0 | 437 |
| France | 446 | 505 | 0 | 0 | 0 | 0 | 0 | 0 | 488 |
| Germany | 550 | 532 | 0 | 504 | 0 | 0 | 0 | 0 | 526 |
| Greece | 0 | 0 | 0 | 0 | 0 | 0 | 0 | 0 | 419 |
| Hungary | 0 | 0 | 0 | 0 | 0 | 0 | 0 | 0 | 561 |
| India | 0 | 0 | 0 | 0 | 0 | 0 | 0 | 541 | 551 |
| Italy | 445 | 430 | 0 | 0 | 0 | 0 | 0 | 0 | 438 |
| Rep. of Korea | 0 | 0 | 0 | 0 | 0 | 528 | 0 | 0 | 521 |
| Liechtenstein | 0 | 0 | 0 | 0 | 0 | 0 | 0 | 0 | 496 |
| Macedonia | 0 | 0 | 0 | 0 | 0 | 0 | 0 | 0 | 411 |
| Morocco | 0 | 0 | 0 | 0 | 0 | 0 | 0 | 0 | 438 |
| Netherlands | 0 | 0 | 0 | 0 | 0 | 0 | 0 | 0 | 522 |
| New Zealand | 0 | 0 | 0 | 0 | 0 | 0 | 0 | 0 | 508 |
| Pakistan | 0 | 0 | 0 | 0 | 0 | 0 | 0 | 454 | 412 |
| Philippines | 0 | 0 | 0 | 0 | 0 | 0 | 0 | 0 | 512 |
| Portugal | 445 | 420 | 0 | 0 | 0 | 0 | 0 | 0 | 428 |
| Romania | 0 | 0 | 0 | 0 | 0 | 0 | 0 | 0 | 539 |
| Russia | 0 | 0 | 496 | 0 | 0 | 0 | 0 | 0 | 493 |
| Samoa | 0 | 0 | 0 | 0 | 0 | 425 | 0 | 0 | 425 |

| | | | | | | | | |
|---|---|---|---|---|---|---|---|---|
| Serbia Montenegro | 417 | 0 | 0 | 0 | 0 | 0 | 0 | 0 | 420 |
| Slovakia | 0 | 0 | 0 | 0 | 0 | 0 | 0 | 0 | 507 |
| Slovenia | 0 | 0 | 0 | 0 | 0 | 0 | 0 | 0 | 420 |
| South Africa | 0 | 0 | 0 | 0 | 0 | 0 | 0 | 0 | 541 |
| Spain | 516 | 0 | 0 | 0 | 0 | 0 | 0 | 0 | 467 |
| Sweden | 0 | 0 | 0 | 0 | 465 | 0 | 0 | 0 | 477 |
| Switzerland | 521 | 0 | 0 | 0 | 0 | 0 | 0 | 0 | 521 |
| Turkey | 389 | 0 | 0 | 466 | 0 | 0 | 0 | 0 | 429 |
| Ukraine | 0 | 0 | 472 | 0 | 0 | 0 | 0 | 0 | 472 |
| United Kingdom | 0 | 0 | 0 | 0 | 0 | 569 | 0 | 0 | 550 |
| United States | 0 | 0 | 0 | 0 | 0 | 0 | 0 | 0 | 571 |
| Vietnam | 0 | 0 | 0 | 0 | 0 | 0 | 0 | 0 | 518 |
| | | | | | | | | | |
| Mean migrants | 498 | 455 | 492 | 472 | 444 | 525 | 464 | 474 | 468 |
| Mean natives | 540 | 512 | 495 | 540 | 492 | 537 | 482 | 516 | 518 |
| Difference (I-N) | -42 | -67 | -3 | -68 | -48 | -12 | -18 | -42 | -50 |

*Notes:* AU = Australia; AT = Austria; BE = Belgium; CH = Switzerland; DE = Germany; DK = Denmark; EL = Greece; FI = Finland; LI = Liechtenstein; LU = Luxembourg; LV = Latvia: NL = Netherlands; NO = Norway; NZ = New Zealand; PT = Portugal; SC = Scotland. *Source:* Authors' own computation of PISA 2006.

Table I. Average scientific literacy of migrant pupils per destination country and origin country ($n$ = 9414).

On average, the 9414 migrant pupils living in our 16 destination countries have a scientific literacy score of 468, which is 50 points below the average science score of their native counterparts. Except for Australia, natives in all destination countries surpass the migrant pupils in scientific performance, ranging from a difference of 3 points in Latvia to no less than 113 points in Denmark.

### Independent Variables

*Destination Variables*

Australia and New Zealand are the only *traditional immigration countries* that have received large inflows of immigration from the nineteenth century onwards, from the European destination countries where immigration became important after World War II.

A measure of destination countries' migrant policies is the migrant integration policy index (MIPEX), which displays on a scale from 0 to 100 to what degree a country's migrant policies foster integration (Niessen et al, 2007). Next to the overall score, we take into account the degree to which policies encourage integration in the sub-areas of long-term residence; their provision of access to nationality; their anti-discrimination policy; family reunion; political participation; and labour-market access (all on a scale from 0 to 100).

### Origin Variables

An origin country's level of economic development was approached by its human development index (HDI). Whereas a country's gross domestic product (GDP) per capita merely refers to a country's economic development level in taking into account the total amount of final goods and services, the HDI (2007) provides a broader picture of a county's human development level. Ranging from 0 to 1, the HDI (2007/2008) combines information on countries' life expectancies, adult literacy rates, gross enrolment ratios in primary, secondary and tertiary education, and GDPs in order to measure countries' levels of human development.

Last, we include several measures of social distance. In order to take into account *origin countries' religious backgrounds*, dummy variables were created to indicate whether at least 50% of the countries' inhabitants are Catholic (like Austria or France), Protestant (Scandinavia), Christian (mixed Catholic and Protestant like the Netherlands or the USA), Eastern Orthodox, Eastern religious (India; Vietnam) or Islamic; non-religious countries in which no religious denomination has the support of at least 50% of the population were classified as 'no prevailing religion' (like Russia and China). In our analysis, the first four categories will be regarded as Christian origin countries.

### Community Variable

*Community-relative socio-economic and cultural capital* refers to the differences in the average socio-economic and cultural capital of natives and migrant children from each origin country in each destination country. We have used the individual-level variable 'parental socio-economic and cultural capital' (to be described below) to construct this variable. Positive values refer to communities that have more socio-economic and cultural resources than the natives in the respective destination country; negative values indicate communities that have fewer resources than the native population.

### Individual Variables

To account for compositional differences, we controlled for individual characteristics:

- *Second-generation migrant; An migrant generation missing variable* distinguishes migrants with an unknown generation from first-generation migrants;
- *One native parent* identifies pupils who had one migrant and one native-born parent;

- *Official language of destination country spoken at home. A language missing variable* was taken into account in order to compare pupils whose language spoken at home is unknown;
- *Arrival age* is a continuous variable, ranging from 0 to 16 years of age;
- *Parental socio-economic and cultural capital* is a combined standardized scale of the highest international socio-economic index of occupational status of the father or mother, the highest educational level of parents converted into years of schooling and the index of home possessions (OECD, 2007);
- *Female.*

## Results

### Multilevel Analysis

By using individual-level techniques on data with multiple levels, standard errors of the macro-level effects will be underestimated, and consequently parameters may unjustly appear to be significant (Snijders & Bosker, 1999; Raudenbush & Bryk, 2002). To analyze non-hierarchically structured data, cross-classified multilevel regression analyses are appropriate. Although originally designed to fit hierarchical models, IGLS (iterative generalized lest squares) can also be adapted to non-hierarchical data structures.

### Test of Hypotheses

Table II displays the results of our cross-classified multilevel analyses. As can be seen from the table, characteristics of the four different levels were added in a stepwise manner and finally combined in model 5. Model 6 differs from model 5 in that it takes into account characteristics at the destination, origin and community level, but leaves out individual-level characteristics.

In order to rule out compositional differences between origin groups and destination countries, model 1 starts by adding individual-level predictors to the initial empty model. Considering these possible compositional effects is important, since not doing so would overestimate the influence of countries' contextual features. Overall, the influence of individual-level characteristics is in line with previous research: parental resources positively influence migrant children's performance, second-generation migrants perform better than first-generation migrants, and the later migrant children have arrived in their new host country, the worse they perform in school (Kao & Thompson, 2003).

Models 2, 3 and 4 respectively add variables at the destination, origin and community level. First, at the destination level, countries' migrant policies do not have an influence on the educational performance of migrant children. A possible explanation for this might be that since migrant policies are overall aimed at affecting migrant children's parents, migrant children are only indirectly affected by them. However, leaving parental socio-economic and cultural capital out of the equation does not change the insignificant effects of immigration policies. Hypothesis 1 has to be rejected. The second hypothesis, on the other hand, is confirmed by our results. As expected under hypothesis 2, migrants living in the traditional immigration countries New Zealand and Australia outperform migrants living in the other countries that have a shorter history of immigration. As becomes clear from comparing the coefficient for traditional immigration countries in models 5 ($b = 35.27^{\star}$) and 6 ($b = 32.91^{\star}$), the relatively high average educational performance of migrant children in these countries cannot be explained by their favourable background characteristics. Even if New Zealand and Australia attracted migrants with less advantageous background characteristics, migrant children in these countries would still outperform their counterparts in other western countries. This finding suggests that the traditional migrant-receiving countries might indeed be better adapted to meeting the specific needs of migrants and their children.

| | Model 1 | Model 2 | Model 3 | Model 4 | Model 5 | Model 6 |
|---|---|---|---|---|---|---|
| Intercept | 467.48* | 471.47* | 439.59* | 498.43* | 151.81* | 122.57* |
| | (7.35) | (3.60) | (32.95) | (6.46) | (88.82) | (100.7) |
| *Destination effects* | | | | | | |
| Average science performance by native pupils | | 0.50* (0.24) | | | 0.57* (0.17) | 0.60* (0.19) |
| Traditional migrant receiving country | | 59.36* (9.35) | | | 35.27* (8.31) | 32.91* (9.47) |
| *Origin effects* | | | | | | |
| Catholic country | | | ref. | | ref. | ref. |
| Protestant country | | | 8.87 (12.84) | | -1.44 (9.85) | -1.69 (11.25) |
| Eastern orthodox country | | | -18.58 (10.37) | | -3.17 (7.71) | -0.61 (8.81) |
| Prevalently Christian country | | | -63.49* (26.98) | | -47.51* (21.7) | -51.30* (25.07) |
| Islamic country | | | -32.70* (9.715) | | -8.96 (8.26) | -9.362 (9.50) |
| Eastern religious country | | | 43.52* (13.96) | | 37.97* (11.82) | 28.05* (13.42) |
| Country without prevalent religion | | | -1.68 (17.96) | | -12.01 (15.21) | -31.21* (17.24) |
| Country without religious affiliation | | | 50.08* (23.77) | | 56.85* (21.09) | 52.18* (23.59) |
| Human Development Index | | | 59.91 (36.71) | | 50.25 (28.3) | 67.57* (32.49) |
| Community effects | | | | | | |
| Relative communal economic and socio-cultural capital | | | | 46.52* (6.40) | 35.06* (6.09) | 68.45* (6.81) |

*Individual effects*

| | | | | | |
|---|---|---|---|---|---|
| Second generation migrant | 7.01* | 6.95* | 7.16* | 7.26* | 7.47* |
| | (2.06) | (2.06) | (2.06) | (2.06) | (2.04) |
| Migrant generation unknown | -18.05* | -18.12* | -18.19* | -18.14* | -18.09* |
| | (4.59) | (4.59) | (4.59) | (4.59) | (4.58) |
| One native parent | 5.39 | 5.51 | 4.91 | 4.50 | 4.50 |
| | (4.10) | (4.10) | (4.10) | (4.09) | (4.09) |
| Language of test country spoken at home | 17.62* | 17.96* | 17.54* | 15.96* | 16.70* |
| | (2.44) | (2.43) | (2.43) | (2.44) | (2.43) |
| Language spoken at home unknown | -28.50* | -28.51* | -28.45* | -29.06* | -28.79* |
| | (3.06) | (3.05) | (3.05) | (3.05) | (3.05) |
| Arrival age | -2.79* | -2.81* | -2.80* | -2.83* | -2.84* |
| | (0.29) | (0.29) | (0.29) | (0.29) | (0.29) |
| Parental economic and socio-cultural status | 29.72* | 29.75* | 29.66* | 29.15* | 29.15* |
| | (1.0) | (1.0) | (1.00) | (1.01) | (1.00) |
| Girls | -2.38 | -2.39 | -2.40 | -2.40 | -2.44 |
| | (1.72) | (1.72) | (1.72) | (1.72) | (1.72) |

*Variance components*

| | | | | | | |
|---|---|---|---|---|---|---|
| Destinations | 566 | 0 | 358 | 294 | 0 | 0 |
| | (300.24) | (0) | (187.2) | (166.61) | (0) | (0) |
| Origins | 962 | 896 | 509 | 553 | 328 | 451 |
| | (193.86) | (164.62) | (112.52) | (120.34) | (70.78) | (93.36) |
| Communities | 0 | 0 | 0 | 0 | 0 | 0 |
| | (0) | (0) | (0) | (0) | (0) | (0) |
| Individuals | 6910 | 6910 | 6910 | 6908 | 6905 | 7850 |
| | (101.17) | (101.17) | (101.15) | (101.13) | (101.06) | (114.91) |
| Total unexplained variance | 8438 | 7706 | 7777 | 7755 | 7233 | 8310 |
| Deviance (IGLS; -2*LL) | 110152 | 110129 | 110110 | 110110 | 110058 | 111276 |

Table II. Cross-classified regression of societal characteristics of countries of origin and destination, community characteristics, and individual characteristics on the scientific literacy of migrant pupils ($N_d$ = 16, $N_o$ = 46, $N_c$ = 91, $N_i$ = 9414).
*Source:* Authors' own computation of PISA 2006.

At the origin level, an insignificant effect has also been detected for origin countries' level of human development (HDI). Although children from more economically developed countries have on average higher science scores than children from less economically developed countries, this can be fully explained by compositional differences. In fact, it can be fully explained by a difference in average arrival age in the new host country. Consequently, hypothesis 3 can be confirmed. Last, in contrast to hypothesis 4, which stated that migrant children from predominantly Christian countries perform better than their counterparts from other religious origins, results show that children originating from prevalently Catholic, Protestant or Eastern

Orthodox countries perform less well than children originating from Eastern religious or non-religious countries. The lowest performers (*ceteris paribus*) are the migrant children from other Christian countries, thereby clearly rejecting hypothesis 4. Interesting is the finding that the positive effect of originating from an Eastern religious country is even stronger after taking into account individual-level characteristics. This indicates that despite their relatively unfavourable background characteristics (an increase from 28.05* in model 6 to 37.97* in model 5), children from Eastern religious countries (in our case, the Asian countries India and China) outperform children from other origins. This finding is in line with former research that has shown that children originating from Asian countries are extremely motivated to perform (Baker et al, 2001).

At the community level, in line with the expectations, migrant pupils from communities with higher levels of socio-economic and cultural capital than the native population outperform those from communities with lower levels of capital. Although much of this positive effect can be explained by compositional differences between these communities ($b$ = 35.06* in model 5 versus $b$ = 68.45* in model 6), the effect of communities' relative socio-economic and cultural capital supersedes the effect of composition. Hypothesis 5 can be confirmed.

### Cross-level Interactions

With regard to hypotheses 2a and 4a, the significant cross-level interactions reveal some interesting additional insights. First, as can be seen from the significant interaction between parental socio-economic status and traditional migrant-receiving countries ($b$ = 9.71*), the positive effect of living in traditional migrant countries is strongest for migrant children from the highest-status families ($b$ = 32.43 + (3*9.71) = 61.56). Although migrant children with an average parental status (0) still profit from living in traditional migrant-receiving countries ($b$ = 32.43), children from the lowest-class families do not ($b$ = 32.43 – (4.4*9.71) = -10.29). Our hypothesis 2a is accepted: the traditional migrant-receiving countries are most open and profitable for migrants with higher socio-economic status. Second, the significant cross-level interaction between parental socio-economic status and Islamic origin countries ($b$ = -11.08*) indicates that originating from an Islamic country on educational performance only has a negative effect for children from the highest-status families ($b$ = -15.93 + (3*-11.08) = -49.17). That is to say, children from high-status families who originate from an Islamic country perform less well in school than comparable children from high-status families who have originated from Catholic, Protestant, or Eastern Orthodox origin countries. This result (the only significant interaction term between parent socio-economic status and non-Christian origin country) runs against our hypothesis 4a. Higher socio-economic status of migrants does not mitigate or neutralize religious distance between origin and destination country, especially when Islam is the prevalent religion in the origin country.

| Main effects | |
| --- | --- |
| Parental economic and socio-cultural status | 30.39* (1.33) |
| Traditional migrant-receiving country | 32.43* (8.39) |
| Islamic country | -15.93 (8.42) |
| Cross-level interactions | |
| Parental economic and socio-cultural status* Traditional migrant-receiving country | 9.71* (2.73) |
| Parental economic and socio-cultural status* Islamic country | -11.08 (2.33) |
| Variance components | |
| Destinations | 0 (0) |
| Origins | 334 (71.20) |
| Communities | 0 (0) |
| Individuals | 6869 |
| Total unexplained variance | 7203 |
| Deviance (IGLS; -2*LL) | 110010 |

Table III. Cross-level interactions, controlled for all variables in model 5.
*Source:* Authors' own computation of PISA 2006.

### Conclusion and Discussion

Multiple studies have shown that individual pupils' educational achievement is influenced by numerous (multilevel) factors, such as their family characteristics, their peers, the schools they attend and their educational system's features. For migrant pupils, this web of influence is even more complex. Next to their being shaped and socialized within the context of their new destination country, their former home countries should be regarded as well. Only then is the transnational character of the migration process fully captured and a better understanding of the multilevel factors influencing migrant children's educational performance gained. We conducted cross-classified multilevel analysis on PISA 2006 data concerning 9414 migrant pupils, originating from 46 origin countries, living in 16 destination countries in order to establish which individual-, community- and macro-level features affect migrant children's performance.

To explain differences in educational achievement between migrants in our 16 destination countries, we have focused on two specific sets of policies: the policies regulating the inflow of migrants (distinguishing traditional migrant-receiving countries from non-traditional migrant-receiving countries); and the policies designed to facilitate the integration of migrants after migration (using the MIPEX policy measures). With regard to the former, our analyses have indeed shown that migrant children living in the highly selective traditional migrant-receiving countries of Australia and New Zealand outperform migrant children in the other destination countries.

However, our analyses have also shown that this higher performance is not related to these countries' selective admission process: migrant children living in these two countries would still outperform their migrant counterparts in other countries if they had the same individual background composition. This finding is in line with research suggesting that migrants living in traditional migrant-receiving countries profit from a relatively favourable view of non-migrants toward migrants, because, for instance, the educational system is better able to cope with the specific educational needs of migrant children or the migrant policies of these two countries are far more inclusive than those of the European countries. However, our finding that lower-status migrant pupils living in traditional immigration countries do not outperform their counterparts in non-traditional immigration countries suggests that these merits are not effective for lower-class migrants. A reason might be that because of the historical selection of and focus on prosperous migrants, these countries are less willing to support the few lower-status migrants they attract. However, since this study was merely able to take into account only two traditional immigration countries, future research taking into account other traditional migrant-receiving countries (Canada and the United States) and more direct measures of these countries' educational systems and migrant attitudes would be necessary to better understand what it is exactly that makes higher-status migrants gain and lower-status migrants lose in the traditional immigration countries.

With regard to destination countries' policies designed to facilitate legally the integration of migrants after migration, our analyses have revealed that these policies cannot explain differences in migrants' educational achievement, at least not for the European destination countries. The degree to which countries legally encourage migrants' integration through supporting, among other things, political participation, labour-market access and long-term residence is unrelated to migrant children's educational performance. Although this lack of policy influence might seem surprising, earlier studies have revealed that the influence of policy indicators on migrants' labour-market integration is meagre at best as well (Fleischmann & Dronkers, 2010). This possibly hints at a gap between countries' intended legal policies and their actual implementation.

At the origin level, political and economic features were shown not to influence the educational performance of migrant children originating from these countries. That is to say, no support was found for the idea that migrant children from politically unstable countries perform less well in science than their counterparts from politically stable countries. Moreover, as expected, the positive effect of origin countries' economic development was completely due to a composition effect: children originating from economically developed countries outperform children from less-developed countries, not because of contextual features of these countries, but because these children have been living in their new destination countries for a longer period. The strongest origin effects were found for countries' prevailing religions. Contrary to what was expected, everything else being equal, migrant children originating from Catholic, Protestant or other Christian countries are not the highest performers. Instead, migrant children from non-religious countries (China, Russia) and eastern religious countries (India, Vietnam) have the highest scientific literacy. This finding is not in line with social distance theory that relates social distance (being either cultural, socio-economic or physical) to feelings of discrimination and misunderstanding, and, consequently, lower educational performance. Interesting in this light is the finding that children from high-status families who originate from an Islamic country perform less well in school than comparable migrant children from high-status families who originate from Catholic, Protestant or Eastern Orthodox origin countries. A possible explanation is the current negative societal view towards migrants originating from Islamic countries. Other possible explanations are: the negative selectivity of guest-worker programs, which brought many Islamic migrants to Europe; or some values in Islamic religion which contradict conditions of success in education in western societies (e.g. gender inequality; honour; authoritarianism). However, since PISA does not allow migrant pupils' individual religious affiliation to be determined, it is not possible to state to what extent the negative Islam effect is due to contextual features of the Islamic countries and to what extent to the individual religious views of the (high-status) children originating from them. But using the European Social Surveys, Dronkers and Fleischmann (2009) found significant effects of individual religion on educational outcomes of second-generation male migrants in the EU.

Last, our results have shown that not only does it matter which country migrant children come from (irrespective of which country they migrate to) or which country they migrate to (irrespective of which country they come from), but the specific origin-destination combination matters too. Children from migrant communities that have higher levels of socio-economic capital than the native population outperform comparable children from communities with relatively lower levels of capital. This is to a large extent the case because children from these relatively high-status communities have higher levels of parental socio-economic capital and a better command of their destination country's language (composition effect). However, on top of that, the community's relative position matters too, suggesting that a favourable socio-economic distance between migrant communities and the native population leads to a stronger position in the destination country and a more positive outlook on migrants' future chances in school.

In sum, our analyses have offered meaningful explanations for macro-level differences in migrant children's educational performance. Although most variance in scientific performance occurs at the individual level, origin, destination and community characteristics influence educational performance on top of individual characteristics. Moreover, the variance at the origin level is more important than that at the destination or community level. We therefore once more underscore the added value of studying migrant performance in a cross-classified multilevel design.

## Note

[1] A more extensive version of this chapter, which also includes macro-variables (like Hofstede's cultural dimensions) that had no significant effect, is available on the Internet (http://www.cream-migration.org/publ_uploads/CDP_13_12.pdf).

## References

Baker, D.P., Akiba, M., LeTendre, G.K. & Weiseman, W.A. (2001) Worldwide Shadow Education: outside-school learning, institutional quality of schooling, and cross-national mathematics achievement, *Educational Evaluation and Policy Analysis*, 23, 1-17.

Borjas, G.J. (2001) Immigration Policy: a proposal, in R.D. Lamm & A. Simpson (Eds) *Blueprints for an Ideal Legal Immigration Policy*. Washington, DC: Centre for Immigration Studies.

Dronkers, J. & Fleischmann, F. (2009) The Educational Attainment of Second Generation Migrants from Different Countries of Origin in the EU Member-states, in J. Dronkers (Ed.) *Quality and Inequality of Education: cross-national perspectives*. Dordrecht: Springer.

Fleischmann, F. & Dronkers, J. (2010) The Socio-economic Integration of Migrants in the EU: effects of characteristics of origin and destination countries on the first and second generation, in P. Attewell & K.S. Newman (Eds) *Growing Gaps: educational inequality around the world*. Oxford: Oxford University Press.

Human Development Index (2007) http://hdr.undp.org/hdr2006/statistics

Jasso, G. & Rosenzweig, M.R. (1990) *The New Chosen People: migrants in the United States*. New York: Russell Sage.

Kao, G. & Thompson, J.S. (2003) Racial and Ethnic Stratification in Educational Achievement and Attainment, *Annual Review of Sociology*, 29, 417-442.

Levels, M., Dronkers, J. & Kraaykamp, G. (2008) Migrant Children's Educational Achievement in Western Countries: origin, destination, and community effects on mathematical performance, *American Sociological Review*, 73, 835-853.

Marks, G.N. (2005) Accounting for Migrant Non-migrant Differences in Reading and Mathematics in Twenty Countries, *Ethnic and Racial Studies*, 28, 925-946.

Niessen, J., Huddleston, T. & Citron, L. (2007) *Migrant Integration Policy Index*. http://www.britishcouncil.org/netherlands-networks-mipex-report.pdf

Organisation for Economic Co-operation and Development (OECD) (2007) *PISA 2006. Science Competencies for Tomorrow's World: analysis*. Paris: OECD.

Portes, A. (1999) Conclusion: towards a new world – the origins and effects of transnational activities, *Ethnic and Racial Studies*, 22(2), 463-477.

Portes, A. & Rumbaut, R.G. (2001) *Legacies: the story of the migrant second generation*. Berkeley: University of California Press.

Raudenbush, S.W. & Bryk, A.S. (2002) *Hierarchical Linear Models: applications and data analysis methods*, 2nd edn. Newbury Park, CA: Sage.

Schnepf, S.V. (2006) How Different are Migrants? A Cross-country and Cross-survey Analysis of Educational Achievement, in C. Parsons & T. Smeeding (Eds) *Immigration and the Transformation of Europe.* Cambridge: Cambridge University Press.

Snijders, T.A.B. & Bosker, R.J. (1999) *Multilevel Analysis. An Introduction to Basic and Advanced Multilevel Modeling.* London: Sage.

van Tubergen, F., Maas, I. & Flap, H. (2004) The Economic Incorporation of Migrants in 18 Western Societies: origin, destination, and community effects, *American Sociological Review*, 69, 704-707.

CHAPTER 12

# High on PISA, Low on Entrepreneurship? What PISA Does Not Measure

## YONG ZHAO & HEINZ-DIETER MEYER

ABSTRACT The authors discuss the hypothesis that high achievements on standardized tests may reflect a school system's efficient functioning as a disciplinary mechanism, representing the absence of independent and creative thinking. To focus the debate, they concentrate on entrepreneurialism, a key indicator of a person's ability and willingness to take risks in the pursuit of innovation, and a key prerequisite for economic prosperity. Entrepreneurialism, they argue, is not only unrelated to the attitudes and dispositions that may produce high scores on standardized tests like the Programme for International Student Assessment (PISA), it is often their exact opposite. For illustration they focus on East Asian countries often touted as paragons of high educational achievements. They find that individualist and collectivist cultural dispositions produce opposite effects on tests like PISA on the one hand and entrepreneurialism on the other. Individualism is often positively related with entrepreneurialism, but not necessarily with the disciplined obedience that produces above-average test scores. By contrast, countries whose cultural traditions emphasize the individual's subordination to the collective are naturally less well suited to preparing students for entrepreneurial careers, while the norm to subordinate oneself to the group makes the teacher's job much easier.

## Introduction

Education is a better safeguard of
liberty than a standing army. (Edward Everett)

An educated people can be easily governed.
(Frederick the Great)

The two quotes above point to a deeply ambiguous relationship between education and freedom. The Harvard-educated Edward Everett emphasizes education's emancipatory potential, while the Prussian autocrat Frederick the Great sees education as a tool to govern and control a people. In the current policy climate, analysts and administrators tend to automatically assume that the democratic function prevails in modern education systems and that high scores on tests like the Programme for International Student Assessment (PISA) reflect a nation's progress in that direction. This chapter challenges that assumption. We argue that high achievements on standardized tests may also reflect a school system's efficient functioning as a disciplinary mechanism, representing the absence of independent and creative thinking. To focus the debate, we concentrate on entrepreneurialism, a key indicator of a person's ability and willingness to take risks in the pursuit of innovation, and a key prerequisite for economic prosperity. Entrepreneurialism, we argue, is not only unrelated to the attitudes and dispositions that may produce high scores on standardized tests like PISA, it is often their exact opposite. For illustration we focus on East Asian countries often touted as paragons of high educational achievement. To take the reader inside countries like China or Singapore, where opinion is often heavily censored, we draw on non-traditional sources like blogs and web pages.

## Chinese Discontent with a Weak Entrepreneurial Tradition

'China needs (Steve) Jobs,' China's Premier Wen Jiabao told a group of business leaders in Jiangshu during his tour of one of the most developed provinces in China in December 2011. 'We must have products like Apple's that can dominate the world's markets.' Wen's comments reflect China's desire for innovative and entrepreneurial talents. A few days after Job's passing, China's Ningbo City of Zhejiang Province, for example, announced that it planned to spend 50 million *yuan* to cultivate innovative entrepreneurial talents in October 2011. The city government planned to produce 1400 top entrepreneurs in five years, according to the *Ningbo Evening News*, a local paper of the city (Luo et al, 2011).

The news added fuel to an already raging discussion about China's lack of entrepreneurs. Kai-fu Lee, one of the most influential Chinese-American technology gurus, who has dedicated himself to incubating young entrepreneurs in China, remarked that 'the next Apple, the next Google will come, but probably not in China'. Kai-fu Lee is founder of Innovation Works, an investment company aimed at cultivating innovative entrepreneurship in China. Lee was former founding president of Google China and former vice president of Interactive Services of Microsoft after working at Apple as a research and development executive (Caijing, 2010). 'At least not in the next 50 years or 100 years there will not be an Apple or Google in China,' he said at the World Economic Forum's Summer Davos in Tianjin, China, in September 2010. Lee migrated from Taiwan to the United

States at 11 and received his undergraduate education at Columbia and earned a PhD from Carnegie Mellon University.

Lee's message was echoed in another round of heated discussion ignited by the passing of Steve Jobs a year later. 'Searching for Jobs', 'Can China Produce Steve Jobs?', 'Why Cannot China Have Jobs?' headlined blog posts and commentaries in traditional media. Education, again, was identified as the culprit. One of the most reposted articles on blogs, online forums and websites was titled 'Had Steve Jobs Been Born in China'. In this article, whose original author cannot be traced because of numerous reposts and modifications, the author or authors ponder what would have happened to Steve Jobs if he had been born in China:

> If Jobs had been born in China, he would have had a very low self-esteem because he was born out-of-wedlock. He would have been mocked by his classmates all the time. To defend his dignity, Jobs would have been involved in daily fights with his classmates. As a result, his parents would have been forced to transfer him to a different school. But thanks to his talents, he had good grades and passed the exam to a decent middle school.
>
> Jobs would not have had any interest in rote memorization of the textbooks in middle school and told his parents that he decided to quit school. His parents would have beaten him to submission after having failed to convince him with words. Jobs would have had no choice but to go on. But because he had no interest in studying, his grades would have become so bad, and he did not do well on the exam, so he ended up in a third rate high school.
>
> In high school, Jobs met Steve Wozniak. The pair had a great passion for electronic products. They won first prize in the national innovation contest. Nevertheless, because of his poor test scores in English, Chinese, and Chemistry, both Jobs and Wozniak ended in a no-name three-year college.

Ironically, many of the details in this hypothetical story are reinforced by the picture Jobs' biographer, Isaacson, draws of him in his recent biography (Isaacson, 2011). There he points out that Steve Jobs, who was often bored by the mechanical routine of the school day, was best known in his school for pulling ingenious pranks that, more often than not, got him into trouble with teachers and administrators.

The above criticism stands in sharp contrast to China's reputation derived from results at international tests. Its stunning No. 1 showing on the most recent PISA in math, sciences and reading has convinced many that it is an 'education giant' (Tucker, 2011b). 'Surpassing Shanghai' has become a goal of American educators, as suggested by the title of a recent book authored by leading experts in the United States and published by Harvard Education Press (Tucker, 2011a). But why is such an 'excellent education system' held responsible for China's failure to produce entrepreneurial talent? Apparently there is a mismatch of understanding of educational excellence.

### The Singapore Puzzle: education giant, entrepreneurial dwarf

The mismatch goes beyond China. The passing of Steve Jobs also incited a round discussion about creativity and entrepreneurship in another Asian country. On 14 December 2011, Steve Wozniak, who founded Apple with Steve Jobs, said during an interview on the UK radio network BBC that a company like Apple could not emerge in structured countries like Singapore:

> When you're very structured almost like a religion ... Uniforms, uniforms, uniforms ... everybody is the same. Look at structured societies like Singapore where bad behavior isn't tolerated. You are extremely punished. Where are the creative people? Where are the great artists? Where are the great musicians? Where are the great singers? Where are the great writers? Where are the athletes? All the creative elements seem to disappear. (Wozniak, 2011)

Wozniak's comments quickly got the attention of Singaporeans, who have been working hard at promoting creativity and entrepreneurship (Mahtani & Holmes, 2011; Wee, 2011; Ong, 2012). As expected, there are some who disagreed with Wozniak's assessment, but the overall reaction is that he told the truth. Singaporean entrepreneur Willis Wee wrote:

> I'm not sure how much Wozniak knows about Singapore and its system. But as a Singaporean, who grew up in this tiny island, I have to agree with his words ...
>
> We're big thinkers and very ambitious. What's really lacking is the guts to do things. Only few have the balls to do what they really want. And unfortunately, most Singaporeans who aren't that courageous end up as Thank-God-Its-Friday laborers, or folks who are always looking forward to Friday and the paycheck. They are the people who complain about their lives the most, not the entrepreneurs and creative minds. (Wee, 2011)

Alexis Ong, a Singaporean journalist, wrote on CNN in January 2012, 'At first glance, it made the small pseudo-patriot in me annoyed, but for the most part, the great and mighty Woz speaks the truth.' Ong goes on to suggest that it is Singapore's education system that is to blame:

> Wozniak's comments are really a scathing indictment of the Singapore education system, its strictly regimented curriculum and by-rote study techniques that sustain the city's 'formal culture.' He points out that everybody is 'educated,' but clearly the Singaporean education isn't the kind of education that gives rise to the people like Sergey Brin and Mark Zuckerberg ... This mindset is cultivated from youth. But in Singapore, where

children are streamed into different academic tracks and under pressure to get into a reputable school before the age of 12, the push to conform is enormous. (Ong, 2012)

Singapore is supposed to have an excellent education system as well. Like China, Singapore has been a country of envy and admiration by outsiders for its consistent high performance in international tests. Since the early 1990s, Singapore has ranked in the top five in the Trends in International Mathematics and Science Study (TIMSS). In the most recent PISA, Singapore took the second place in math, fourth place in sciences, and fifth in reading, whereas China was first in all three areas. Singapore thus represents another case of contradiction between test scores and creative entrepreneurship.

## The Inverse Relationship of Test Scores and Entrepreneurial Attitudes

This contradiction also exists in other high-performing countries. Korea and Japan are two other Asian countries that have consistently produced outstanding scores in international tests. In the most recent PISA administered in 2009 in over 60 countries, Korea ranked fourth in math, sixth in sciences and second in reading, while Japan was ninth in math, fifth in sciences and eighth in reading. As impressive as their test scores, these countries have not traditionally shown a level of creativity and innovation-driven entrepreneurship that matched their test scores. According to the 2010 Global Entrepreneurship Monitor (GEM) report, out of the 22 innovation-driven, economically developed countries (which China is not part of; also, Singapore did not participate in the GEM study), Korea and Japan were at the bottom, taking 19th and 21st place, respectively, in terms of 'nascent entrepreneurship rate' or percentage of people actively seeking to establish businesses in the next three years. In terms of 'total early entrepreneurship ownership rate', or percentage of individuals who started and are still managing a business, Korea ranked seventh and Japan 21st. The same pattern was found in the 2011 GEM report.

An even more telling figure is the small proportion of opportunity entrepreneurship that exists among the total number of early entrepreneurs. Less than half of all the early entrepreneurship activities in Korea and Japan were driven by opportunity and improvement; the rest were driven by necessity. In this category, Korea ranked 16th and Japan 18th.

The contradictory relationship between test scores and entrepreneurship activities is further affirmed by an analysis of PISA performance and entrepreneurship activities of nations. Thirty-eight out of the 53 countries surveyed by the Global Entrepreneurship Monitor in 2010 also participated in the 2009 PISA. Thirty-nine countries out of the 54 economies surveyed by the GEM in 2011 participated in the 2009

PISA. Table I displays the correlation between PISA raw scores and new entrepreneurship activities in these countries.

| | Reading | | Math | | Sciences | |
|---|---|---|---|---|---|---|
| | 2010 | 2011 | 2010 | 2011 | 2010 | 2011 |
| Entrepreneurial intentions | -.57** | -.71** | -.52** | -.72** | -.59** | -.73** |
| Nascent entrepreneurship rate | -.69** | -.73** | -.64** | -.74** | -.68** | -.73** |
| New business ownership rate | -.37* | -.73** | -.37* | -.70** | -.39* | -.66** |
| Total entrepreneurial activity | -.66** | -.77** | -.62** | -.79** | -.66** | -.78** |
| Discontinuation of business | -.58** | -.53** | -.57** | -.54** | -.61** | -.56** |

$**p < .01; *p < .05.$

Table I. Correlations between PISA raw scores and new entrepreneurship activities.

As Table I shows, PISA scores in all three areas – reading, math and sciences – are negatively correlated with entrepreneurship indicators in almost every category at statistically significant levels. In other words, countries that have higher PISA scores have lower entrepreneurship attitudes. Specifically, those countries that show better performance on the PISA tend to have fewer people who intend to or plan to start businesses and fewer people who have started new businesses.

The inverse relationship between PISA scores, often perceived as the measure of a nation's education quality and its students' academic abilities, and entrepreneurship activities, an indicator of a nation's entrepreneurial actions, seems to affirm the contradiction exemplified by Singapore and China. That is, the commonly used measures of educational quality have negative or no relationships with entrepreneurship.

Additional data suggest that entrepreneurship activity may be related to schooling. For example, the Kauffman Index of Entrepreneurial Activity produced by the Kauffman Foundation shows that during the period from 1996 to 2010, the group with less than high school education showed a consistently higher rate of entrepreneurial activity than all other groups (high school graduates, those with some college, and college graduates) in the United States (Fairlie, 2011). A Harris Poll conducted in 2010 for the Kauffman Foundation found that although there is no difference in the percentage of individuals who said they may start a business someday among three youth groups – 8-12-year-olds, 13-17-year-olds, and 18-24-year-olds – a lot more 18-24-year-olds (29%) than 8-12-year-olds (15%) said no. The 18-24-year-olds certainly have more schooling than the 8-12-year-olds (Harris Interactive, 2010).

The Global Entrepreneurship Monitor report included data concerning entrepreneurial qualities – that is, personal factors that affect people's potential engagement in entrepreneurial activities. These factors have been established to predict to what degree one may decide to start a business. They include personal perceptions of the availability of entrepreneurship opportunities, to what degree a person has the capability to succeed in business, the degree of fear of failure, whether entrepreneurship is a good career choice, whether successful entrepreneurs enjoy high social status, and how much the media pays attention to entrepreneurship. Table II summarizes the correlations between these factors and the 2009 PISA results of 38 countries that participated in both PISA and GEM in 2010 and 39 countries that participated in both the 2009 PISA and the 2011 GEM.

|  | Reading | | Math | | Sciences | |
|---|---|---|---|---|---|---|
|  | 2010 | 2011 | 2010 | 2011 | 2010 | 2011 |
| Perceived opportunities | -.35* | -.40* | -.33* | -.39* | -.38* | -.43** |
| Perceived capabilities | -.60** | -69** | -.59** | -72** | -.61** | -.72** |
| Entrepreneurship as a good career choice | -.50** | -.64** | -.45** | -.63** | -.53** | -.66** |

Table II. Correlation between PISA raw scores and entrepreneurial qualities (all countries).

The results show a clear pattern of negative correlations between countries' PISA performance and entrepreneurial qualities. In countries that have higher PISA scores in math, reading and sciences, fewer people believe there are entrepreneurial opportunities, fewer people believe they have the capability to start and succeed in entrepreneurship, and fewer people believe entrepreneurship is a good career choice.

Educational practices and societal factors that help students to achieve academically may hamper entrepreneurial qualities, making them believe there are few entrepreneurial opportunities or that they do not have entrepreneurial capability. Standardized testing and a focus on rote memorization, for example, are perhaps the biggest enemies of entrepreneurial capability.

A contrast between Finland and the East Asian countries illustrates this point. Since the end of the Cold War, which also ended decades during which Finland lived economically and socially in the shadow of its mighty neighbor, the Soviet Union, entrepreneurial innovation has risen dramatically, with companies like Nokia taking the lead. Not coincidentally, the Finns possess a much higher level of perceived entrepreneurial capability than the East Asian countries. In the 2011 Global Entrepreneurship Monitor Survey, 37.3% of Finns reported having the capability for entrepreneurship, more than 20 percentage points higher than the Japanese (13.7%), more than 10 percentage points higher than the Koreans (26.7%) and Singaporeans (24.1%), and nearly 10 percentage points higher than the Taiwanese (28.6%). This difference may come from the different style of education in Finland compared with the East Asian countries. Unlike the high-performing education systems in East Asia that have a well-known reputation for authoritarian and standardized-test-driven education that emphasizes rote memorization, Finnish students do not take standardized tests until the end of high school. Finnish schools are a standardized-test-free zone, according to Pasi Sahlberg in his book *Finnish Lessons: what can the world learn from educational change in Finland?* (Sahlberg, 2011). As a result, students in Finland are not pushed toward rote memorization. Finnish education is certainly not nearly as authoritarian as its Asian counterparts. Most important, as education historian Diane Ravitch observed, 'the central aim of Finnish education is the development of each child as a thinking, active, creative person, not the attainment of higher test scores, and the primary strategy of Finnish education is cooperation, not competition (Ravitch, 2012).

The data suggest that high PISA scores may be the result of 'forced excellence'.

### Early Childhood Socialization: 'the nail that sticks out ...'

In this section we provide evidence for the idea that the above-documented differences are not the result of teaching styles, but are, in fact, deeply rooted in culture and, in particular, early childhood socialization. Research documents the differences in early childhood socialization that produce an individualistic habitus in countries like the United States and a conforming, harmony-seeking habitus in many Asian cultures. A good example is the study *Pre-school in Three Cultures* by Tobin et al (1989). They describe how patterns of collectivism and individualism are instilled in children via pre-school teaching practices early on. Their study focuses on China, Japan and the United States. In the case of China it shows high degrees of regimentation of the pre-schooler's life. Not only do these children learn, eat and sleep together, they even go to the bathroom as a group and in lockstep.

The book also shows the case of Hiroki – a five-year-old boy in a Japanese pre-school. Hiroki tends to keep to himself, rejects attempts to include him in activities, and interacts with his peers only to start a fight. The Japanese pre-school teachers not only refused to give special treatment to him, they also encouraged the group to find ways of coping with the boy and the problems he created (pp. 16-17). In stark contrast to American practice, Japanese teachers focused their efforts on assisting the group to integrate their various members – however much they might at first resist conforming.

These examples illustrate the emphasis on integrating themselves with and subordinating themselves to the larger group. In the context of the present study, we also note the propensity of collectivist cultures not to individualize certain students by attaching labels to them ('emotionally disturbed,' 'learning difficulty') or by segregating them from the majority of their peers. Instead, Japanese or Chinese educators expect that even 'difficult' students can be brought in line with the group.

Hiroki's case forms an interesting contrast to a similarly 'difficult' child in an American pre-school. In that case the teachers isolate the child from the group, and treat him with a mixture of warnings and punishment ('time out').

Cases like these illustrate how collectivist and individualist cultures instill norms about the self/group relationship early on, minimizing individual differences in one case, and reinforcing them in the other; subjecting the child to the discipline of the group in the former, while isolating him from the group in the latter; applying group norms in the former, while reasoning with the child in the latter.

In fact, anthropological researchers have identified 'harmonious interdependence' (Markus & Kitayama, 1991), cooperation, solidarity and social conformity (Frager, 1970) as characteristics of *collectivism*. Members of collectivist cultures feel secure when they are well integrated into their community because it leads them to believe they might achieve harmony, while members of individualist cultures always reserve the right to 'go their own way'.

The pursuit of harmony has both positive and negative effects. While providing a sense of belonging, it also leads to devaluing what is new, different or unfamiliar. Those who are not like others in their community may become the object of discrimination. Robert LeVine, a prominent researcher on comparative early childhood socialization, has pointed out how 'separateness, self-sufficiency, and self-confidence' are 'pervasive theme[s] of American child rearing ideology' (LeVine, 2003, p. 93). 'The emphasis on separateness begins at birth among middle-class Americans...'

## Discussion: individualism, collectivism and 'forced excellence'

Cultures shape behavior. Through intermediary institutions like schools, pre-schools and the family, they instill lasting differences among the normative orientations of students (Meyer, 2002). Countries like the United States, which tend to garner 'mediocre' scores on tests like PISA, are high on traits like individualism and low on traits like collectivism (Triandis, 1990; Hofstede, 2001; Schimmack et al, 2005). Individualism goes along with the willingness to stand out from the group. It also is associated with a stronger sense of self-confidence. Both the willingness to engage in non-conformism and the willingness to believe in oneself are characteristics of entrepreneurialism, as entrepreneurs must be ready to take risks and to deviate from the beaten path.

Confidence is a key factor in entrepreneurship, as Gary Rabbior, longtime entrepreneurship educator and executive director of the Canadian Foundation for Economic Education, writes:

> There is no more important attribute of entrepreneurship than a
> sense of self-confidence, the belief in oneself and one's own ideas.
> Entrepreneurs are agents of change, and change is usually resisted.
> Entrepreneurs will continually confront roadblocks and resistance

from individuals who do not support or believe in their ideas. ...
To confront and overcome the resistance they will encounter, it is
imperative that entrepreneurs have a sense of self-confidence.
(Rabbior, 1990, p. 61)

By contrast, countries whose cultural traditions emphasize the individual's
subordination to the collective (DeBarry 1991; Greif, 1994; Weber, 1988)
are naturally less well suited to prepare students for entrepreneurial careers.
On the other hand, the norm to subordinate oneself to the group makes the
teacher's job infinitely easier. Students are compliant and even docile,
exhibiting reverence and deference for their teacher in and out of the
classroom. To challenge the teacher is largely unheard of.

Nations' scores in international tests do not go the same way as their
entrepreneurship activities, their perceived entrepreneurial capabilities, and
their students' self-confidence. In other words, superior test scores do not
result in more creative entrepreneurs. On the contrary, they may hamper the
development of entrepreneurial and creative activities.

True knowledge begins with a moment of confusion and puzzlement –
puzzlement that needs to be honored, cultivated, and built upon. Having a
two-digit number returned as a machine's answer to a student's three- or
five-hour wrestling with a multiple-choice test is not a way to cultivate
puzzlement. Steve Jobs is on record as saying that the California school
system almost broke his curiosity. What kept him engaged with the schools
were (a) his incessant pranks (landing him regularly in suspension), and (b)
the one or two exceptional teachers who recognized his creative energies and
provided him with opportunities to deploy them constructively.

Socrates famously warned against the Sophists who went around
Athens promising to turn inarticulate youngsters into effective rhetoricians –
for a fee. A well-trained Sophist could argue any cause, regardless of its
merits, by framing facts and legitimizing them as incontrovertible evidence,
backed by expert authority. Socrates opposed the Sophists' overconfidence
and arrogance. He may have been the first to oppose the 'sage on the stage'
model of learning, instead opting for learning as *open-ended conversation*. We
will stand in the best tradition of western rationalism if we question the
authority of global assessments, contextualize their meaning, and delineate
their utility, thereby increasing the wisdom of both test-makers and test-
consumers.

### References

Caijing (2010) Li Kaifu: Xiayige pingguo buhui chuxian zai zhongguo [Kai-fu Lee:
the next Apple will not be invented in China].
http://www.caijing.com.cn/2011-09-16/110862857.html (accessed 3 January
2012).

DeBarry, Theodore W. (1991) Confucianism and Civil Society, in K. Michalski (Ed.)
*Europe and Civil Society*. Stuttgart: Klett.

Fairlie, R.W. (2011) *Kauffman Index of Entrepreneurial Activity: 1996-2010.* Kansas City: Kauffman Foundation.

Frager, Robert (1970) Conformity and Anticonformity in Japan, *Journal of Personality and Social Psychology*, 15, 203-210.

Greif, Avner (1994) Cultural Beliefs and the Organization of Society: a historical and theoretical reflection on collectivist and individualist societies, *Journal of Political Economy*, 102, 912-950.

Harris Interactive (2010) *YouthPulseSM 2010: Kauffman Foundation custom report.* Kansas City: Kauffman Foundation.

Hofstede, Geert (2001) *Culture's Consequences: comparing values, behaviors, institutions, and organizations across nations.* Thousand Oaks, CA: Sage.

Isaacson, Walter (2011) *Steve Jobs.* New York: Simon & Schuster.

LeVine, Robert A. (2003) *Childhood Socialization: comparative studies of parenting, learning, and educational change.* Hong Kong: CERC.

Luo, X., Wu, X. & Yan, J. (2011) Ningbo chizi wuqianwan peiyang chuangxin lingjun bajian rencai [Ningbo plans to spend 50 million to cultivate innovate talents], *Ningbo Wanbao [Ningbo Evening News]*, 11 October. http://news.sciencenet.cn/htmlnews/2011/10/253650.shtm

Mahtani, S. & Holmes, S. (2011). Wozniak: Apple couldn't emerge in Singapore. 20 January. http://blogs.wsj.com/searealtime/2011/12/15/wozniak-apple-couldnt-emerge-in-singapore/

Markus, Hazel R. & Kitayama, Sinobu (1991) Culture and the Self: implications for cognition, emotion, and motivation, *Psychological Review*, 98, 224-253.

Meyer, Heinz-Dieter (2002) Tocqueville's Cultural Institutionalism, *Journal of Classical Sociology*, 3, 197-220.

Ong, A. (2012) Singapore Needs to Encourage 'Bad Behavior'. 10 January. http://www.cnngo.com/singapore/life/tell-me-about-it/alexis-ong-singapore-needs-encourage-bad-behavior-718985

Rabbior, G. (1990) Elements of a Successful Entrepreneurship/Economics/Education Program, in C.A. Kent (Ed.) *Entrepreneurship Education: current developments, future directions*, pp. 53-68. New York: Quorum Books.

Ravitch, D. (2012) Schools We Can Envy, *New York Review of Books*, 8 March. http://www.nybooks.com/articles/archives/2012/mar/08/schools-we-can-envy/?pagination=false

Sahlberg, P. (2011) *Finnish Lessons: what can the world learn from educational change in Finland?* New York: Teachers College Press.

Schimmack, Ulrich, Oishi, Shigehiro & Diener, Ed (2005) Individualism: a valid and important dimension of cultural differences between nations, *Personality and Social Psychology Review*, 9, 17-31.

Tobin, Joseph J., Wu, David Y.H. & Davidson, Dana H. (1989) *Pre-school in Three Cultures.* New Haven, CT: Yale University Press.

Triandis, Harry C. (1990) Cross-cultural Studies of Individualism and Collectivism, in J.J. Berman (Ed.) *Nebraska Symposium on Motivation*, vol. 37. Lincoln: University of Nebraska Press.

Tucker, M. (Ed.) (2011a) *Surpassing Shanghai: an agenda for American education built on the world's leading systems.* Boston, MA: Harvard Education Press.

Tucker, M.S. (2011b) *Standing on the Shoulders of Giants: an American agenda for education reform.* Washington, DC: National Center Education and the Economy.

Weber, Max (1988) Die Wirtschaftsethik der Weltreligionen: Konfuzianismus und Taoismus (The conomic ethic of world religions: Confucianism and Taoism], in M. Weber (Ed.) *Gesammelte Aufsaetze zur Religionssoziologie* [Collected writings on sociology of religion], vol. 1. Tuebingen: Mohr Siebeck.

Wee, W. (2011). Apple Co-founder Steve Wozniak Questions Singapore's Creativity. 15 December. http://www.penn-olson.com/2011/12/15/wozniak-questions-singapore-creativity/

Wozniak, S. (2011) Think for Yourself. http://news.bbc.co.uk/today/hi/today/newsid_9661000/9661755.stm

CHAPTER 13

# The International Efficiency of American Education: the bad and the not-so-bad news

## STEPHEN P. HEYNEMAN

ABSTRACT There is ample evidence to suggest that American schools perform worse than schools in many other countries. The United States ranks toward the bottom of the industrialized nations on international tests of academic achievement in science and mathematics. Not only may American schools perform worse, they may do so at the same time as they use more resources than other school systems. In essence, American schools may not only be poor in quality, they may also be less efficient. This chapter will explore some of the evidence on education efficiency. It will suggest that in many ways the assumption is correct – American schools *are* less efficient. It will suggest that the reason for the inefficiency of American schools is the difference in the 'demand to learn' between American and other school children. But the chapter will also explore evidence that suggests that American schools are not less efficient, and in one new way of looking at the problem, it will argue that American schools are more efficient than the schools in the Republic of Korea, one of the world's leading school systems. The chapter will conclude with some advice on the proper role which international comparisons may play in the design of domestic education policy.

### Background

Bad news about American education is a tradition. Often the news emerges from national commissions (Commission on Higher Education, 1947; Committee on Education Beyond High School, 1956; *Saturday Review*, 1961; National Commission on Excellence, 1983; Commission on the Future of Higher Education, 2006; State Scholars Initiative, 2008; Wolk, 2009). In many instances the bad news includes statements that American schools have declined in quality or have been bested by school systems in other countries. International tests of academic achievement have been used to suggest that American school children do not learn as much as children in many other school systems, including the school systems of America's most important trading partners (Lemke et al, 2004; Baldi et al, 2007; Heyneman & Lee, forthcoming).

Sometimes, the school systems which attain first place in the ranking of achievement become a subject of headline news. This was the case, for instance, with the scores of Shanghai on PISA 2009 (*New York Times*, 2010). Attention has turned not only to the rankings of other countries on achievement tests, but also to the comparative efficiency of one system versus another in those rankings (*New York Times*, 2009).[1]

## Efficiency: the bad news

The bad news is not new. Two decades ago the United States spent more money on education yet performed worse on tests of 8th-grade mathematics (Table I).

| Country | Public expenditure on education/capita (A) in dollars | Proportion of students over the international median in 8th-grade mathematics (B) as a percentage | Ratio A/B |
|---|---|---|---|
| Norway | 1111 | 46 | 24 |
| United States | 1040 | 45 | 23 |
| Kuwait | 848 | 3 | 287 |
| Singapore | 724 | 94 | 7 |
| United Kingdom | 649 | 48 | 14 |
| Japan | 602 | 83 | 7 |
| Israel | 584 | 56 | 10 |
| Republic of Korea | 362 | 82 | 4 |
| Hong Kong | 309 | 80 | 4 |
| Czech Republic | 297 | 70 | 4 |
| Hungary | 272 | 60 | 4 |
| Thailand | 206 | 54 | 4 |
| Iran | 183 | 9 | 20 |
| Latvia | 147 | 40 | 3 |
| Lithuania | 71 | 34 | 2 |
| Romania | 55 | 36 | 2 |

Table I. International education efficiency (1991).
Source: Heyneman, 2004.

Table I displays the results of the international test designed by the Educational Testing Service (ETS) used in 1991 prior to PISA. Norway, for instance, spent US$1111 for each adult citizen in the population. A total of 46% of the Norwegian students performed over the international median in

8th-grade mathematics. This would imply that it would cost an additional US$24/adult citizen for an additional one percent of the students to achieve over the international mathematics median. The United States spent US$1040/adult citizen and 45% of the American students performed over the international median. To get an additional 1% over the international median, the United States would need to spend an additional US$23/citizen.

| Country | Total test score | Score ranking | Spending (US$) | Ratio of scores to expenditures | Ratio ranking | Average expenditure for one score point |
|---|---|---|---|---|---|---|
| Finland | 1631 | 1 | 71,385 | 0.023 | 7 | 43.77 |
| Australia | 1589 | 2 | 72,386 | 0.022 | 8 | 45.55 |
| Switzerland | 1552 | 3 | 104,352 | 0.015 | 14 | 67.23 |
| Belgium | 1528 | 4 | 80,145 | 0.019 | 10 | 52.45 |
| Poland | 1503 | 5 | 39,964 | 0.037 | 2 | 26.59 |
| Norway | 1501 | 5 | 101,265 | 0.015 | 14 | 67.47 |
| Denmark | 1497 | 7 | 87,642 | 0.017 | 12 | 58.55 |
| United States | 1496 | 8 | 105,752 | 0.014 | 16 | 70.69 |
| Sweden | 1486 | 9 | 82,753 | 0.017 | 12 | 55.69 |
| Czech Republic | 1471 | 10 | 44,761 | 0.033 | 3 | 30.42 |
| Portugal | 1469 | 11 | 56,803 | 0.026 | 6 | 38.67 |
| Hungary | 1464 | 12 | 44,342 | 0.033 | 3 | 30.29 |
| Germany | 1461 | 13 | 63,296 | 0.023 | 7 | 43.32 |
| Latvia | 1460 | 14 | . | . | . | . |
| Italy | 1458 | 15 | 77,310 | 0.019 | 10 | 53.02 |
| Greece | 1419 | 16 | 48,422 | 0.029 | 5 | 34.12 |
| Russia Federation | 1405 | 17 | 17,499 | 0.080 | 1 | 12.45 |
| OECD average | 1500 | | 69,135 | 0.021 | | 46.09 |

*Notes*:
1. Total test score is the sum of three core subjects, reading, mathematical and scientific literacy.
2. Rankings are based on sample countries examined in this chapter.
3. Cumulative education spending is in equivalent US dollars converted using Purchasing Power Parity (PPP).
4. 'Ratio of scores to expenditure' = test scores achieved when $1 is spent; 'average expenditure for one score point' is an average expenditure to get one test score point. Both of them are calculated by the author.

Table II. Student performance in PISA 2009 and cumulative education spending per student. Source: OECD (2010, 2011).

In other countries, however, the cost would be less. In Singapore and Japan it would only cost US$7 to have an additional 1% of their students perform over the international median; in Korea, Hong Kong, the Czech Republic and Thailand it would only cost US$4. Arguably the most efficient education systems in 1991 were located in Latvia, Lithuania and Romania, where only US$2 or US$3 would be required to have an additional 1% of their students perform over the international median. And the least efficient school system was that of Kuwait, which would require US$287 for an additional 1% of its students to perform over the international median.

Using PISA results from 2009, it appears that the United States has not improved on its level of education efficiency by comparison with other countries (Table II).[2] If one takes the total PISA test score (reading, mathematics and science taken together), the United States ranks 8th out of 17 countries. However, if one incorporates education spending, the United States' ranking drops from 8th to 16th, next to last. The countries with the highest efficiency ranking included Russia, Poland, the Czech Republic and Hungary.

Figure 1 illustrates monetary efficiency in a slightly different way. As one can see, the United States is among the countries which had the highest secondary student expenditures but is positioned lower than many other countries in terms of PISA mathematics performance.

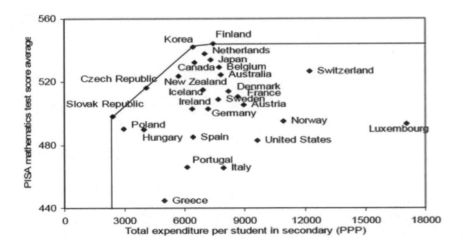

Figure 1. Secondary education spending and average PISA mathematics scores. Sources: OECD Education at Glance 2006; Verhoeven et al, 2007.

Figure 2 illustrates this same issue using cumulative spending for ages 6-15 rather than spending on secondary school students alone. In this case the United States is the highest-spending country in the sample and yet in middle of the sample in terms of total PISA test score performance.

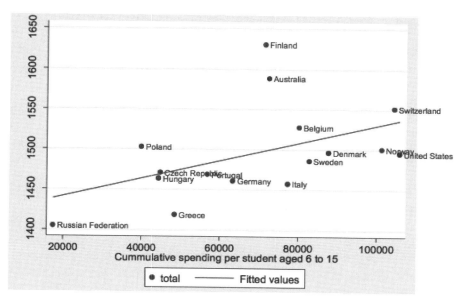

Figure 2. Relationship between student achievement in PISA 2009 and cumulative spending. Source: OECD (2010, 2011).

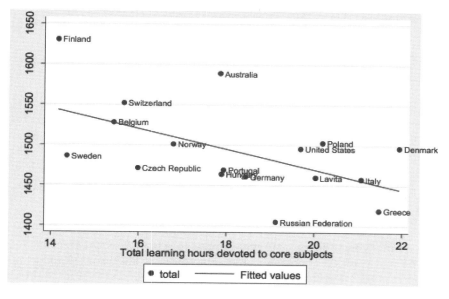

Figure 3. Relationship between student achievement in PISA 2009 and total hours devoted to core subjects. Source: OECD (2010, 2011).

Efficiency can be calculated in many ways; achievement on the basis of pupil expenditure is one. Another is achievement in conjunction with school time. Figure 3 illustrates this principle. American schools devote almost 19 hours/week to core subjects, equivalent to Latvia and Poland, and far more than Sweden, Finland, Belgium and Switzerland. Yet Finland, Switzerland and Australia devote less time to core subjects but have higher PISA achievement scores.

Efficiency can also be calculated in terms of an output indicator, such as the rate at which enrolled students actually graduate. Figure 4 illustrates the connection between secondary school graduation rate and total expenditures per secondary school student. The United States spends more than any other country, with the exception of Switzerland, yet the rate of secondary school graduation is lower than any other country save Spain and New Zealand. The sum of this evidence would suggest that by many different measures the United States is less efficient than other countries and that the record of inefficiency is consistent over at least two decades.

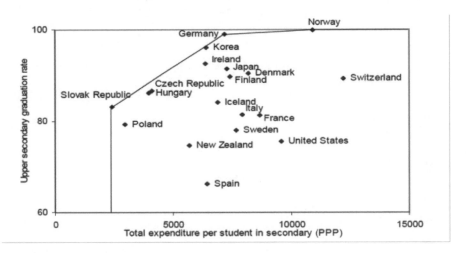

Figure 4. Secondary education spending and upper secondary graduation rates. Source: OECD Education at a Glance 2006, http://www.oecd.org/edu/eag2006; OECD PISA and IMF staff calculations. The line connects countries with the highest observed efficiency and depicts the best practice frontier unadjusted for estimation bias (Verhoeven et al, 2007).

There are many hypotheses as to why American schools are less efficient than those of many other countries. One hypothesis is that American school children express a lower 'demand to learn' than school children in countries with high efficiency in their school systems (Heyneman, 1999). This is sometimes noted as whether 100% of the children want to come to school each day and to try hard each day. In essence, the 'demand to learn' is a culturally shaped attitude or disposition that places the value of education higher or lower on a scale of socially desirable activities. There is, moreover, a gap in the 'demand to learn' between children of different backgrounds in the United States, whereas in high-efficiency school systems there is less of a gap between children of different backgrounds. This suggests that the barrier to student achievement in American schools is not poverty or race but the lack of the demand to learn and the difference in the demand to learn from one social group to another (Heyneman, 2005). This also suggests that better teacher training, a different curriculum or a longer school day will not have the intended effect until the demand to learn is generally augmented and until a high demand to learn is characteristic of all social groups.

| Country | Reading literacy | Mathematical literacy | Scientific literacy | Total test score | Civic knowledge |
|---|---|---|---|---|---|
| Finland | 546 (1) | 536 (4) | 538 (3) | 1620 (3) | 109.3 (2) |
| Australia | 528 (4 ) | 533 (5) | 528 (7) | 1589 (6) | 101.7 (11) |
| Sweden | 516 (9) | 516 (15) | 512 (10) | 1544 (10) | 99.1 (18) |
| Belgium | 507 (10) | 520 (9) | 496 (17) | 1523 (11) | 94.7 (22) |
| Norway | 505 (13) | 499 (17) | 500 (13) | 1504 (15) | 102.9 (9) |
| United States | 504 (15) | 493 (19) | 499 (14) | 1496 (17) | 106.5 (6) |
| Denmark | 497 (16) | 514 (12) | 481 (22) | 1492 (18) | 100.4 (14) |
| Switzerland | 494 (17) | 529 (14) | 496 (17) | 1519 (13) | 98.3 (19) |
| Czech Republic | 492 (19) | 498 (18) | 511 (11) | 1501 (16) | 102.6 (10) |
| Italy | 487 (20) | 457 (26) | 478 (23) | 1422 (24) | 105.4 (7) |
| Germany | 474 (21) | 490 (20) | 487 (20) | 1451 (21) | 99.8 (15) |
| Hungary | 480 (23) | 488 (21) | 296 (15) | 1464 (20) | 101.6 (12) |
| Poland | 479 (24) | 470 (24) | 483 (21) | 1432 (23) | 110.6 (1) |
| Greece | 474 (25) | 447 (28) | 461 (25) | 1382 (27) | 107.9 (4) |
| Portugal | 470 (26) | 470 (24) | 459 (28) | 1399 (26) | 96.2 (21) |
| Russia Federation | 462 (27) | 478 (22) | 460 (26) | 1400 (25) | 99.6 (16) |
| Latvia | 458 (28) | 462 (25) | 460 (27) | 1380 (28) | 91.5 (26) |
| OECD average | 500 | 500 | 500 | 1500 | 100 |

*Notes*:
1. Numbers in parentheses are rankings among all countries participating in PISA and CIVED respectively.
2. Average of civic knowledge is international average, not OECD.

Table III. Student achievement in PISA 2000 and scores from the Civic Education Study (CIVED) 1999 (rankings in parentheses). Sources: OECD (2001) and Schulz and Sibberns (2004).

### Efficiency: the not-so-bad news

*Achievement in Subjects Other Than Math and Science*

Most discussions of achievement concentrate on math and science; some on reading. But the purpose of public schooling and the reasons nations invest in public schooling are broader than skills, jobs and productivity. They include the degree to which schools are able to influence citizenship behavior. On this dimension, American schools may do rather well. Table III illustrates the differences in international ranking using different achievement measures on PISA 2000 and CIVED 1999. The United States was ranked 15th out of 28 countries in reading literacy, 19th in mathematical literacy, and 14th in scientific literacy. However, the United States was ranked 6th in the field of civics education. This could be rather important. Nations which struggle for social cohesion are nations which also struggle economically (Heyneman, 2000). Civil tension reduces trust, and a reduction in trust reduces internal cooperation and trade (Heyneman, 2002/3). One reason why the US economy continues to perform in spite of the low ranking in science and mathematics performance may be associated with the rather good job of the American schools in influencing citizenship.

*Internal Variation in Performance*

The United States is typical of all large and diverse nations in that academic performance is significantly divergent from one region to another. Figure 5 illustrates this divergence in Brazil, where 16% of the students achieved the top levels of mathematics achievement in the south and only 7% in the northeast.

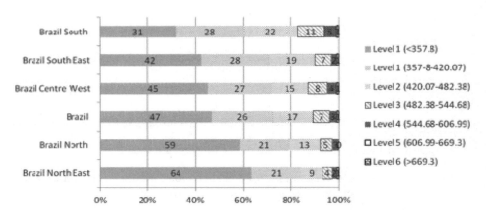

Figure 5. Percentage of students by mathematics proficiency level in regions of Brazil. Source: OECD (2010).

Figure 6 illustrates this divergence in the Russian Federation. The Russian average for PISA 2009 was 475; but this varied from Yakutia at 419 to Moscow at 546. Tables IV and V illustrate this principle in the United States and compare the scores of various states in mathematics (Table IV) and science (Table V) against the scores of various nations. On both measures the top-performing 'nations' in the world – among them Singapore, Hong Kong and Taipei – also include Minnesota and Massachusetts. This suggests that parts of the US school system is as competitive as the best in the world.

| Scale score | Grade 4 | Grade 8 |
|---|---|---|
| 600 | Hong Kong-Ch. (607)<br>Singapore (599) | Ch. Taipei (598)<br>Rep. of Korea (597)<br>Singapore (593) |
| 590 | | |
| 580 | Ch. Taipei (576)<br>*MA-USA (572)* | Hong Kong-Ch. (572) |
| 570 | Japan (568) | Japan (570) |
| 560 | *MN-USA (554)* | |
| 550 | Kazakhstan (549)<br>Russian Fed. (544)<br>England-UK (541) | *MA-USA (547)* |
| 540 | Latvia (537)<br>Netherlands (535) | *MN-USA (532)* |
| 530 | Lithuania (530)<br>*USA (529)*<br>Germany (525)<br>Denmark (523) | Quebec-Ca. (528) |
| 520 | Quebec-Ca. (519)<br>Australia (516)<br>Ontario-Ca. (512) | Ontario-Ca., Hungary (517)<br>England-UK (513)<br>Russian Fed. (512) |
| 510 | Hungary (510)<br>Italy (507)<br>Br. Columbia-Ca., Alberta-Ca.,<br>Austria (505)<br>Sweden (503)<br>Slovenia (502) | Br. Columbia-Ca. (509)<br>*USA (508)*<br>Lithuania (506)<br>Czech Rep. (504)<br>Slovenia (501) |
| 500 | Armenia, *TIMSS Scale Avg. (500)*<br>Slovak Rep. (496)<br>Scotland-UK (494)<br>New Zealand (492) | *TIMSS Scale Avg. (500)*<br>Armenia (499)<br>Basque Country-Sp. (499)<br>Australia (496)<br>Sweden (491) |
| 490 | Czech Rep. (486) | Malta (488), Scotland-UK (487)<br>Serbia (486) |
| 480 | Norway (473) | Italy (480)<br>Malaysia (474) |

| 470 | Ukraine (469) | Norway (469) |
| | Dubai-UAE (444) | Cyprus (465) |
| | Georgia (438) | Bulgaria (464) |
| | Islamic Rep. of Iran (402) | Israel (463) |
| | Algeria (378) | Ukraine (462) |
| | Colombia (355) | Romania, Dubai-UAE (461) |
| | Morocco (341) | Bosnia and Herzegovina (456) |
| | El Salvador (330) | Lebanon (449) |
| | Tunisia (327) | Thailand (441) |
| | Kuwait (316) | Turkey (432) |
| | Qatar (296) | Jordan (427) |
| | Yemen (224) | Tunisia (420) |
| | | Georgia (410) |
| | | Islamic Rep. of Iran (403) |
| | | Bahrain (398) |
| | | Indonesia (397) |
| | | Syrian Arab Rep. (395) |
| | | Egypt (391) |
| | | Algeria (387) |
| | | Morocco (381) |
| | | Colombia (380) |
| | | Oman (372) |
| | | Palestinian Nat'l Auth. (367) |
| | | Botswana (364) |
| | | Kuwait (354) |
| | | El Salvador (340) |
| | | Saudi Arabia (329) |
| | | Ghana (309) |
| | | Qatar (307) |

Scores above 501 are above the international average; scores from 491 to 500 are not measurably different from the international average; scores below 490 are below the international average.

*Note*: Countries are listed by estimated average scores. Figure is not a scaled representation of countries' scores. International/OECD average scores and US scores are presented in italics. While the formulation and construction of assessment scales are the same across the TIMSS, PIRLS, and PISA, the content represented by the scale scores is not the same across different ages within a subject domain.
Source: http://nces.ed.gov/surveys/international/reports/2011-mrs.asp#mathematics

Table IV. Mathematics results by country and US state (International Association for the Evaluation of Educational Achievement [IEA], 2007).

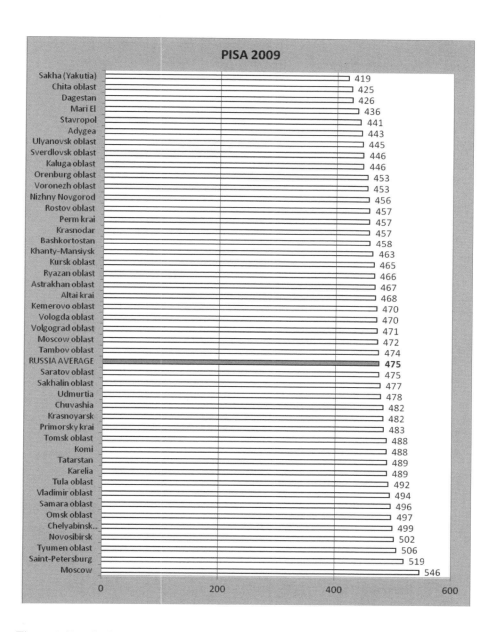

Figure 6. Results by region in Russia (PISA 2009).

| Scale score | Grade 4 | Grade 8 |
|---|---|---|
| 600 | | |
| 590 | Singapore (587) | |
| 580 | *MA-USA (571)* | |
| 570 | | Singapore (567) |
| | | Ch. Taipei (561) |
| 560 | Ch. Taipei (557) | *MA-USA (556)* |
| | Hong Kong-Ch. (554) | Japan (554) |
| | *MN-USA (551)* | Rep. of Korea (553) |
| 550 | Japan (548) | England-UK (542) |
| | Russian Fed. (546) | |
| | Alberta-Ca. (543) | |
| | Latvia, England-UK (542) | |
| 540 | *USA (539)* | Hungary, Czech Rep. (539) |
| | Br. Columbia-Ca. (537) | *MN-USA (539)* |
| | Hungary, Ontario-Ca. (536) | Slovenia (538) |
| | Italy (535) | |
| | Kazakhstan (533) | |
| 530 | Germany (528) | Hong Kong-Ch., Russian Fed. (530) |
| | Australia (527) | Ontario-Ca., Br. Columbia-Ca. (526) |
| | Slovak Rep., Austria (526), | |
| | Sweden (525) | |
| | Netherlands (523) | |
| 520 | Slovenia (518) | *USA (520)* |
| | Denmark, Quebec-Ca. (517) | Lithuania (519) |
| | Czech Rep. (515), Lithuania (514) | Australia (515) |
| | | Sweden (511) |
| 510 | New Zealand (504) | Quebec-Ca. (507) |
| 500 | Scotland-UK, *TIMSS Scale Avg. (500)* | *TIMSS Scale Avg. (500)* |
| | | Basque Country-Sp. (498) |
| | | Scotland-UK (496) |
| | | Italy (495) |
| 490 | Armenia (484) | Dubai-UAE (489) |
| | | Armenia (488) |
| | | Norway (487) |
| | | Ukraine (485) |
| | | Jordan (482) |
| 480 | Norway (477) | Malaysia, Thailand (471) |
| | Ukraine (474) | |
| 470 | Dubai-UAE (460) | Serbia, Bulgaria (470) |
| and | Islamic Rep. of Iran (436) | Israel (468) |
| below | Georgia (418) | Bahrain (467) |
| | Colombia (400) | Bosnia and Herz. (466) |
| | El Salvador (390) | Romania (462) |
| | Algeria (354) | Islamic Rep. of Iran (459) |

| | |
|---|---|
| Kuwait (348) | Malta (457) |
| Tunisia (318) | Turkey (454) |
| Morocco (297) | Syrian Arab Rep., Cyprus (452), |
| Qatar (294) | Tunisia (445) |
| Yemen (197) | Indonesia (427) |
| | Oman (423) |
| | Georgia (421) |
| | Kuwait (418) |
| | Columbia (417) |
| | Lebanon (414) |
| | Egypt, Algeria (408) |
| | Palestinian Nat'l Auth. (404) |
| | Saudi Arabia (403) |
| | Morocco (402) |
| | El Salvador (387) |
| | Botswana (355) |
| | Qatar (319) |
| | Ghana (303) |

Scores above 510 are above the international average; scores from 491 to 509 are not measurably different from the international average; scores below 490 are below the international average.

*Note*: Countries are listed by estimated average scores. Figure is not a scaled representation of countries' scores. International/OECD average scores and US scores are presented in bold font. While the formulation and construction of assessment scales are the same across the TIMSS, PIRLS, and PISA, the content represented by the scale scores is not the same across different ages within a subject domain.

Source: http://nces.ed.gov/surveys/international/reports/2011-mrs.asp#mathematics

Table V. Science results by country and US state (TIMSS 2007).

Table VI illustrates this principle in all the American states. This table shows states' proficiency in mathematics and compares them with nations with the same or similar proficiency levels. For instance, Vermont had a proficiency level similar to Australia, Denmark, Estonia, France and Germany. On the other hand, Tennessee, my own state, had proficiency levels comparable to Croatia, Greece, Israel, Russia and Turkey. The most inefficient school system in the United States, according to this criterion, is the District of Columbia. The Washington, DC level of proficiency was equivalent to that of Mexico, Thailand and Kazakhstan.

| State | Percent proficient | Significantly outperformed by* | Countries with similar percentages of proficient students |
|---|---|---|---|
| 1 Massachusetts | 50.7 | 6 | Canada, Japan, Netherlands, New Zealand, Switzerland |
| 2 Minnesota | 43.1 | 11 | Australia, Belgium, France, Germany, Netherlands |
| 3 Vermont | 41.4 | 14 | Australia, Denmark, Estonia, France, Germany |
| 4 North Dakota | 41.0 | 16 | Denmark, Estonia, France, Iceland |
| 5 New Jersey | 40.4 | 14 | Australia, Austria, Denmark, France, Germany |
| 6 Kansas | 40.2 | 16 | Austria, Denmark, Estonia, France, Slovenia |
| 7 South Dakota | 39.1 | 16 | Austria, Denmark, France, Hungary, Sweden |
| 8 Pennsylvania | 38.3 | 16 | Austria, Denmark, France, Hungary, Sweden |
| 9 New Hampshire | 37.9 | 18 | Austria, Denmark, France, Hungary, Sweden |
| 10 Montana | 37.6 | 18 | Austria, France, Hungary, Poland, Sweden |
| 11 Virginia | 37.5 | 17 | Czech Rep, France, Hungary, Poland, Sweden |
| 12 Colorado | 37.4 | 18 | Czech Rep, France, Hungary, Poland, UK |
| 13 Wisconsin | 37.0 | 18 | Czech Rep, France, Poland, Portugal, UK |
| 14 Maryland | 36.5 | 18 | Czech Rep, France, Hungary, Poland, UK |
| 15 Wyoming | 36.0 | 18 | Czech Rep, France, Poland, Portugal, UK |
| 16 Washington | 35.9 | 19 | Czech Rep, France, Hungary, Poland, UK |
| 17 Ohio | 35.4 | 18 | Czech Rep, France, Poland, Portugal, UK |
| 18 Iowa | 35.2 | 19 | Czech Rep, France, Poland, Portugal, UK |
| 19 Indiana | 35.1 | 19 | Czech Rep, France, Poland, Portugal, UK |
| 20 Oregon | 34.8 | 20 | Czech Rep, Hungary, Poland, Portugal, UK |
| 21 Connecticut | 34.7 | 19 | France, Poland, Portugal, Spain, UK |
| 22 Texas | 34.7 | 21 | Czech Rep, Hungary, Poland, Portugal, UK |

| | | | |
|---|---|---|---|
| 23 Nebraska | 34.6 | 20 | Czech Rep, Hungary, Poland, Portugal, UK |
| 24 North Carolina | 34.5 | 21 | Czech Rep, Hungary, Poland, Portugal, UK |
| 25 Maine | 34.1 | 22 | Czech Rep, Hungary, Poland, Portugal, UK |
| 26 Idaho | 34.1 | 22 | Czech Rep, Hungary, Poland, Portugal, UK |
| 27 Utah | 32.4 | 26 | Italy, Poland, Portugal, Spain, UK |
| 28 Alaska | 32.2 | 26 | Italy, Poland, Portugal, Spain, UK |
| *United States* | *32.2* | *22* | *Italy, Latvia, Poland, Spain, UK* |
| 29 South Carolina | 31.9 | 26 | Italy, Poland, Portugal, Spain, UK |
| 30 Delaware | 31.3 | 28 | Hungary, Italy, Portugal, Spain, UK |
| 31 Illinois | 30.8 | 27 | Czech Rep, Italy, Portugal, Spain, UK |
| 32 New York | 30.2 | 28 | Hungary, Italy, Portugal, Spain, UK |
| 33 Missouri | 29.9 | 28 | Hungary, Italy, Portugal, Spain, UK |
| 34 Michigan | 28.9 | 30 | Ireland, Italy, Lithuania, Portugal, Spain |
| 35 Rhode Island | 27.7 | 34 | Latvia, Lithuania |
| 36 Florida | 27.4 | 34 | Greece, Latvia, Lithuania |
| 37 Kentucky | 27.3 | 34 | Latvia, Lithuania |
| 38 Arizona | 26.3 | 34 | Greece, Latvia, Lithuania |
| 39 Georgia | 24.7 | 35 | Greece, Latvia, Russia |
| 40 Arkansas | 24.4 | 35 | Croatia, Greece, Israel, Latvia, Russia |
| 41 California | 23.9 | 36 | Greece, Russia |
| 42 Tennessee | 23.1 | 36 | Croatia, Greece, Israel, Russia, Turkey |
| 43 Nevada | 23.0 | 36 | Croatia, Greece, Israel, Russia |
| 44 Oklahoma | 21.3 | 36 | Croatia, Greece, Israel, Russia, Turkey |
| 45 Hawaii | 21.2 | 38 | Croatia, Israel, Russia, Turkey |
| 46 Louisiana | 19.0 | 39 | Bulgaria, Croatia, Israel, Serbia, Turkey |
| 47 West Virginia | 18.5 | 41 | Bulgaria, Turkey |
| 48 Alabama | 18.2 | 39 | Bulgaria, Croatia, Israel, Serbia, Turkey |
| 49 New Mexico | 17.4 | 41 | Bulgaria, Serbia, Turkey |
| 50 Mississippi | 13.6 | 43 | Bulgaria, Trinidad and Tobago, Uruguay |

| 51 District of Columbia | 8.0 | 48 | Kazakhstan, Mexico, Thailand |
|---|---|---|---|

*Number of countries whose percentage of proficient students was significantly higher statistically.
*Note*: Lists of countries performing at levels that cannot be distinguished statistically are limited to those five with the largest population.

Table VI. Percentage of students proficient in math by state and countries with similar proficiency levels. Source: Peterson et al (2011).

### Time Devoted to Studying Using Private Tutors

Most studies of education efficiency include time on task within the classroom, hours in the school day, and scheduled school days/year. These are important indicators of effort, but are increasingly inadequate. Their inadequacy is particularly relevant when considering comparisons with countries in south and east Asia.

The typical student in Asia attends several types of schools simultaneously. Such students attend government-run public schools from which the data pertaining to time on task usually derive, but they also attend 'cram schools' on a regular basis. These cram schools are referred to as 'shadow education'. In Japan the cram schools are called 'Juku'; in Korea they are called 'Hogwans'. In general these schools are not managed according to modern styles of teaching; on the contrary, they are there to reinforce rules, principles, formulae and information. They are cram schools in the literal sense. In Korea, for instance, 88% of the elementary students and 61% of the students in general high schools receive private tutoring in cram schools (Kim, 2010, p. 302). A Korean family which earns between US$6000 and 7000/month typically allocates 6.3% (US$440/high school student/month) to private tutoring (Korean Statistical Information Service, 2011). The financial burden on households, the stress on children, and the implications for social inequality have long been recognized and have been subject to considerable research (Heyneman, 2010; Lee & Jang, 2010). In India, approximately 72% of the older primary school students and 52% of the secondary school students receive private tutoring (Ngai & Cheung, 2010). Although it is difficult to research effectively, the portion of students in China who receive private tutoring in math was 28.8% and in English, 29.3% (Zhang, 2011). Other estimates have been made for South America (Mattos, 2007), Europe (Ireson, 2004, Bray, 2011) and the United States (Mattos, 2007). Private tutoring is so common that economists have begun to estimate its fiscal impact. By one estimate, for instance, private tutoring in South Korea increased from 0.34% of gross domestic product (GDP) in 1977 to 2.3% of GDP in 2003, an amount equivalent to 50% of the public expenditure on education (Kim, 2007). The Korean Education Development Institute (KEDI) reports that 84% of the parents in Korea state that private tutoring is a significant economic burden (KEDI, 2003). Some have commented that private tutoring relegates South Korea, among other countries, to a low level of efficiency within the OECD member states (Gundlach & Woessmann, 2001; Kim, 2002). Others have commented on the distortions to higher education selection (Park, 1996), and the fact that memorization of material has a low impact on productivity (Paik, 2000).

We were interested in the degree to which private tutoring might affect Korea's PISA efficiency. The PISA questionnaire asked students about time/week spent in private tutoring. We have added this time to the amount of time in formal school and have compared Korea with the United States.

Table VII illustrates this comparison between the United States and Korea by showing the learning time devoted to studying math in both countries. Korean students report spending 86% more time studying math out of school than American students (2.1 hours/ week as opposed to 0.3 hours/week). While the ratio of time in formal schooling to the PISA score is very close between the two countries (3.54 vs. 3.78), when one adds the time spent studying mathematics outside of formal schooling, the differences are pronounced. The ratio of time/PISA score is 2.46 for Korean vs. 3.27 for American students. In essence, the American school system is one third more efficient than the Korean school system.

| | Math | In-school instructional time for math (hours per week) | Instructional weeks in years | Total hours | Ratio of score to time |
|---|---|---|---|---|---|
| Korea | 552 | 4.1 | 35.6 | 145.9 | 3.78 |
| United States | 472 | 3.7 | 36.0 | 133.2 | 3.54 |
| | Math | Out-of-school instruction time for math (hours per week) | In-school + out-of-school instruction | Total hours | Ratio of score to time |
| Korea | 552 | 2.1 | 6.3 | 224.3 | 2.46 |
| United States | 472 | 0.3 | 4.0 | 144.0 | 3.27 |

*Note*: Math scores are from PISA 2003. Out-of-school activities include working with a tutor and attending out-of-school classes.

Table VII. Mathematical literacy and time studying math.
Source: OECD Programme for International Student Assessment, 2004, Table 5.14.

Table VIII continues this same illustration using the total time studying across all subjects, not only mathematics. The total time Korean students spend studying is about one third more than in the United States. The level of their PISA scores is indeed higher, but the ratio of time/PISA score is considerably different. The ratio for Korea is 0.44, and for the United States it is 0.57. By this account – that is, by comparison with the total time spent studying in private tutoring as well as in school – the American system is about 30% more efficient than the Korean system.

| | Math | In-school instructional time for all subjects (hours per week) | Instructional weeks in years | Total hours | Ratio of score to time |
|---|---|---|---|---|---|
| Korea | 552 | 30.3 | 35.6 | 1078.7 | 0.51 |
| United States | 472 | 22.2 | 36.0 | 799.2 | 0.59 |
| | Math | Out-of-school instructional time for all subjects (hours per week) | In-school + out of school instruction | Total hours | Ratio of score to time |
| Korea | 552 | 5.1 | 35.4 | 1260.4 | 0.44 |
| United States | 472 | 0.7 | 22.9 | 824.4 | 0.57 |

*Note*: Math scores are from PISA 2003. Out-of-school activities include working with a tutor and attending out-of-school classes.

Table VIII. Mathematical literacy and total time studying.
Source: OECD Programme for International Student Assessment, 2004, Table 5.14.

## Implications

For twenty years a common refrain about American education has been that it is inferior to the public school systems in Asia (Stevenson & Stigler, 1992; Stigler & Hiebert, 1999). The problem is that this has ignored the fact that the typical youth in Asia receives only a portion of his or her achievement from the public school system and that test scores in particular are influenced by the quality and intensity of the cram schools. But the refrain of inferiority to school systems in Asia is not only inaccurate scientifically; it is pernicious in another way too. It ignores the fact that the image of their school systems held by local citizens in Japan, Korea and parts of China is one of low quality, not high quality. Instead of crowing about international superiority on international tests of academic achievement, local authorities, parents and the academic community adamantly condemn the quality of their systems.

Adolescence in Asia typically involves cramming scientific and mathematical facts. Studying is treated as a full-time profession in which students are asked to study 80-100 hours/week at home, in school, with tutors and in cram schools. The process has generated problems of depression, suicide, bullying and personality disorder (Lee & Larsen, 2000,

Stankov, 2010; Kong, 2011). High exposure to private tutoring is associated with lower confidence and a dislike of academic work (Kong, 2011). Choi suggests that there 'is a negative influence of shadow education on the way of learning and creativity among high school students' (Choi, 2012). Yun suggests that in Korea, 'overheated shadow education drops the interests of learners and therefore decreases learners' self learning ability' (Yun, 2006, p. 198). Yang agrees and points out that 'as stress from shadow education increases academic motivation decreases. And as the burden on time and mentality among factors of stress from shadow education increases, internal satisfaction decreases ... and problem behavior increases' (Yang, 2011, p. 2). An article in *Yonhapnews* reports on a study which shows that students in cram schools or with private tutors depend on their tutors for what and how to learn, and cannot plan their own study in detail. They accept learning contents meaninglessly and passively and become other-person-led learners without explicit learning goals (*Yonhapnews*, 2007).

Even for those who successfully pass their examinations and enter a university, depression and meaninglessness continue. Unlike the United States, Britain or Canada, scores on university selection examinations in Asia determine not only which university they are allowed to enter, but also which program of study they can take. This is detrimental to their higher education experience. Cho points out the following:

> Most of the [students] are dissatisfied with their universities or departments since they have not chosen them according to their desires but according to their scores ... the years of preparing for the examination under extreme tension and stress also make the winners extremely passive and dull. Many of them have difficulties adjusting to university life ... Courses in liberal arts and social sciences that require analytical and critical thinking confuse and frustrate them endlessly. They are particularly annoyed by questions which do not have definite answers. (Cho, 1995, p. 155)

As Tucker (2011, 2012) has explained, performance among Asian school children stems from a culturally narrow concentration on simplistic indicators of math and science as indicators of success. So damaging has this process become that people in these countries are searching for a way to escape and often look to the United States as having a more balanced way to raise children and adolescents.

They are probably right. While Asians look longingly at the educational and personal effects of a typical American adolescence, Americans are rarely aware of the negative effects on personality development of an adolescence narrowly devoted to math and science scores. Were Americans more aware of these effects, they might look with less jealousy at the success of Asia's PISA scores.

While it is true that many American school systems are in desperate need of repair, it is also true that some school systems in the United States are superb. Furthermore, many Americans emerge from the process of adolescence with deep labor-market experience and a sense of autonomy and personal independence which the typical youth in Asian countries do not have.

## Summary

In comparing ourselves with other countries, we must keep in mind that the indicators of our envy – high scores in math and science – were not acquired in a vacuum, but rather through a different culture with many faults obvious to local populations but not to outsiders. American schools systems are not uniformly poor or inefficient. American students tend to perform better on some types of tests than others; some American states perform well on all tests; and in terms of time spent studying, school systems in the United States may be considerably more efficient than they are made out to be. Americans need to be more careful not to import the 'terror' of a shadow-education adolescence typical of Asia. Americans need to be more circumspect when criticizing their own education policies as if the deficits were so uniform and the virtues so insignificant.

## Acknowledgement

Support of the George W. Bush Institute is gratefully acknowledged; however the views and opinions in this chapter are those of the author alone.

## Notes

[1] Efficiency of a school system is defined here in a straightforward way, as output (e.g. test scores) per unit of input (e.g. per pupil expenditure). While such indicators do not tell the whole story of the quality of a nation's school system, they can highlight discrepancies and problems in need of attention.

[2] Data and tables have drawn on unpublished papers from three graduate students: Bommi Lee (2012) 'Efficiency and Effectiveness in Education Across Countries: what should be measured?'; Yunkuyung Min (2012) 'States' Variation in International Students' Assessment: case of the US and Brazil'; and Jeongwoo Lee (2012) 'An Attempt to reinterpret student learning outcomes: a cross-national comparison'.

## References

Baldi, S., Jin, Y., Skemer, M., Green, P.J. & Herget, D. (2007) *Highlights from PISA 2006: Performance of U.S. 15-year-olds in Science and Mathematics Literacy in an International Context.* Washington, DC: US National Center for Education Statistics, Department of Education.

Bray, M. (2011) *The Challenge of Shadow Education: private tutoring and its implications for policy makers in the European Union.* Brussels: European Commission.

Cho, Hae-Jong (1995) Children in the Examination War in South Korea: a cultural analysis, in S. Stevens, S. (Ed.) *Children and the Politics of Culture*, pp. 141-168. Princeton, NJ: Princeton University Press.

Choi, Jaesung (2012) Unequal Access to Shadow Education and Its Impacts on Academic Outcomes: evidence from Korea. Paper presented at Spring 2012 meeting of ISA RC 28 'Economic Transformation and Social Stratification in Comparative Perspectives', 10-13 May, in Hong Kong.

Commission on Higher Education (1947) *Higher Education for American Democracy* (Truman Report). Washington, DC: US Government Printing Office.

Commission on the Future of Higher Education (Spellings Commission) (2006) *A Test of Leadership: charting the future of US higher education.* Washington, DC: US Department of Education.

Committee on Education Beyond High School (1956) First Interim Report to the President (Eisenhower Report). Washington, DC: US Department of Health, Education and Welfare.

Gundlach, E. & Woessmann, L. (2001) The Fading Productivity of Schooling in East Asia, *Journal of Asian Economics*, 12, 401-417.

Heyneman, S.P. (1999) American Education: a view from the outside, *International Journal of Leadership in Education*, 2(1), 31-34.

Heyneman, S.P. (2000) From the Party/State to Multi-ethnic Democracy: education and social cohesion in the Europe and Central Asia region, *Educational Evaluation and Policy Analysis*, 21(4) (Summer), 173-191.

Heyneman, S.P. (2002/3) Defining the Influence of Education on Social Cohesion, *International Journal of Educational Policy, Research and Practice*, 3(4) (Winter), 73-97.

Heyneman, S.P. (2004) International Education Quality, *Economics of Education Review*, 23, 441-452.

Heyneman, S.P. (2005) Student Background and Student Achievement: what is the right question? *American Journal of Education*, 112(1) (November), 1-9.

Heyneman, S.P. (2010) Private Tutoring and Social Cohesion, *Peabody Journal of Education*, 86(2), 183-188.

Heyneman, S.P. & Lee, B. (forthcoming) Impact of International Studies of Academic Achievement on Policy and Research, in Leslie Ann Rutkowski, Matthias von Davier & David Rutkowski (Eds) *Handbook of International Large Scale Assessment: background, technical issues, and methods of data analysis.* London: Chapman and Hall.

International Association for the Evaluation of Educational Achievement (IEA) (2007) Trends in International Mathematics and Science Study.

Ireson, J. (2004) Private Tutoring: how prevalent and effective is it? *London Review of Education*, 2(2), 183-188.

Kim, Ji-Ha (2007) The Determinants of Demand for Private Tutoring. Unpublished manuscript prepared for Professors Henry Levin and Mun Tsang, Columbia Teachers College (July).

Kim, K.K. (2010) Educational Quality, in C.J. Lee, S.Y. Kim & D. Adams (Eds) *Sixty Years of Korean Education*, pp. 285-325. Seoul: Seoul National University Press.

Kim, K.S. (2002) Educational Investment and Efficiency in South Korea from the Standpoint of International Comparison, *LG Economics*, 22-25.

Kong, J.S. (2011) The Effects of Parent–Child Dysfunctional Communication and Academic Stress on Adolescents' Suicide Ideation, Focusing on the Mediating Effects of Depression and Gender Differences. Master's thesis, Graduate School of Social Welfare, Yonsei University (in Korean).

Korean Education Development Institute (KEDI) (2003) Monitoring Private Tutoring and Analyzing the Cost of Private Tutoring. CR 2003-19. Seoul: KEDI.

Korean Statistical Information Service (2011) *Spending on Shadow Education by School Level and Type/Month, 2007-2011*. Seoul: Korea Education Development Institute.

Lee C.J. & Jang, H.M. (2010) The History of Policy Responses to Shadow Education in Korea: implications for the next cycle of policy responses, in C.J. Lee, S.Y. Kim & D. Adams (Eds) *Sixty Years of Korean Education*, pp. 512-545. Seoul: Seoul National University Press.

Lee, C.J. & Larson, R. (2000) The Korean 'Examination Hell': long hours of studying, distress, and depression, *Journal of Youth and Adolescence*, 29(2), 249-271.

Lemke, M., Sen, A., Pahlke, E., Partelow, L., Miller, D., Williams, T., Kastberg, D. & Jocelyn, L. (2004) *International Outcomes of Learning Mathematics Literacy and Problem-solving: PISA 2003. Results from the US Perspective*. Washington, DC: US National Center for Education Statistics, Department of Education.

Mattos, L.O.N. (2007) Explicadores do Rio de Janeiro: Encontros e desencontros em trajectorias professionais singulars, *Revista Brasileira de Estudos Pedagogicos*, 88(218), 140-156.

National Commission on Excellence (1983) *A Nation At Risk: the imperative for education reform*. Report to the Secretary of Education (May). Washington, DC: US Department of Health Education and Welfare.

*New York Times* (2009) Overpaying for Educational Underachievement. http://economix.blogs.nytimes.com/2009/04/22/overpaying-for-educational-underachievement/

*New York Times* (2010) Top Test Scores from Shanghai Stun Educators. http://www.nytimes.com/2010/12/07/education/07education.html?pagewanted=al l

Ngai, A. & Cheung, S. (2010) *Students' Participation in Private Tuition*. Youth Poll Series No. 188. Hong Kong: Hong Kong Federation of Youth Groups.

Organization for Economic Cooperation and Development (OECD) (2001) *Knowledge and Skills for Life: first results from the OCED Programme for International Student Assessment (PISA) 2000*. Paris: OECD Publishing.

OECD Programme for International Student Assessment (2004) *PISA Learning for Tomorrow's World: first results from PISA 2003*, vol. 659. Paris: OECD.

Organization for Economic Cooperation and Development (OECD) (2006) *Education at a Glance*. Paris: OECD.

Organization for Economic Cooperation and Development (OECD) (2010) *PISA 2009 Results: what makes a school successful? Resources, Policies, and Practices*, vol. IV). Paris: OECD Publishing.

Organization for Economic Cooperation and Development (OECD) (2011) *Quality Time for Students: learning in and out of school*. Paris: OECD Publishing.

Paik, I.W. (2000) *Economics of Education*. Seoul: Hakjisa.

Park, J.S. (1996) The Expansion of Private Tutoring and the Equity of Educational Opportunity in South Korea, *Journal of Economics and Finance of Education*, 5(2), 515-538.

Peterson, P.E., Woessmann, Ludger, Hanushek, Eric A. & Lastra-Anadon, Carlos X. (2011) *Globally Challenged: are U.S. students ready to compete?*, Harvard's Program on Education Policy and Governance & Education.

*Saturday Review* (1961) President Kennedy's Task Force on Education Makes Its Report, *Saturday Review*, 21 January, p. 94.

Schulz, W. & Sibberns, H. (2004) *IEZ Civic Education Study Technical Report*. Amsterdam: International Association for the Evaluation of Educational Achievement (IEA).

Stankov, I. (2010) Unforgiving Confucian Culture: a breeding ground for high academic achievement, test anxiety, and self doubt? *Learning and Individual Differences*, 20(6), 555-563.

State Scholars Initiative (2008) *No Longer At Risk: a nation in peril*. Boulder, CO: Western Interstate Commission for Higher Education.

Stevenson, Harold W. & Stigler, James (1992) *The Learning Gap: why our schools are failing and what we can learn from Japanese and Chinese education*. New York: Summit Books.

Stigler, James & Hiebert, James (1999) *The Teaching Gap: best ideas from the world's teachers for improving education in the classroom*. New York: Free Press.

Tucker, M. (2011) *Strong Performers and Successful Reformers in Education*. Paris: Organisation for Economic Co-operation and Development (OECD).

Tucker, M. (2012) *Surpassing Shanghai: an agenda for American education built on the world's leading systems*. Cambridge, MA: Harvard Education Press.

Verhoeven, M., Gunnarsson, V. & Carcillo, S. (2007) Education and Health in G7 Countries: achieving better outcomes with less spending. IMF Working Paper. Washington, DC: International Monetary Fund.

Wolk, Ronald A. (2009) Why We are Still at Risk, *Education Week*, 29 April.

Yang, E.Y. (2011) The Effects of Shadow Education Stress on Middle School Students' Academic Motivation and Behavior Problems. Master's thesis, Graduate School of Education, Chonnam National University (in Korean).

*Yonhapnews* (2007) *Hangukyuigyoyukryuk, edaerojoeunga?* [Is current Korean education okay?]. http://app.yonhapnews.co.kr/YNA/Basic/article/Press/YIBW_showPress.aspx?contents_id=RPR20070517010800353 (in Korean).

Yun, Young-Ran (2006) Motivation, Interest and Self-learning Ability, *Inha Gyoyukyongu* [Inha Education Study], 12, 181-198 (in Korean).

Zhang Y. (2011) The Determinants of National College Entrance Exam Performance in China – with an Analysis of Private Tutoring. PhD dissertation, Columbia University.

CHAPTER 14

---

# Policy Responses to PISA in Comparative Perspective

## ALEXANDER W. WISEMAN

ABSTRACT Responses to internationally reported PISA results have differed among participating countries. Some governments responded with alarm and a flurry of reform activities, while others responded much more calmly or ignored the results completely. In spite of these differences, the policies implemented in response to PISA have demonstrated remarkable alignment within economic and political subgroups. For example, in some country groups PISA deficits have been associated with a push towards more centralized control, while others have responded with much more focused reforms (e.g. teacher education). This chapter investigates the variety of response patterns across countries, their alignment within national subgroups, and the significant factors that have led some policy responses to differ from to their subgroup's trends.

---

Headline news about large-scale international educational assessments is often more about 'shock' over the assessment results than what assessment information contributes to discussions about educational reform and improvement (Stack, 2007; Waldow, 2009). For example, the Programme for International Student Assessment (PISA) has become synonymous with this 'shock' since PISA 2000 results were released, but 'shock' is only one response to PISA and other large-scale international educational assessments like the Trends in International Mathematics and Science Study (TIMSS). Some countries respond more calmly or ignore their PISA or TIMSS results altogether. These widely varying responses – from shock to ignorance – suggest that the ways that educational policymakers respond to PISA and other international assessments are a product of policy agenda, public opinion and practical application. Using this combination of effects as a foundation, this chapter investigates the kinds of policy responses to PISA that are found in and across participating countries, and how they compare with one another. These various response phenomena may be categorized on a sliding scale of globally convergent versus divergent policy responses. The answer the evidence presented below points toward is somewhere in the middle.

Policy responses are important to discuss because one of the formally stated goals of PISA and other large-scale international assessments is to create an internationally comparative evidence base for educational policy development and implementation. As such, it is not shocking that developing educational (or political or social or economic) policy is an outcome of PISA, TIMSS or any other large-scale international educational assessment, because this is the reason they exist. For example, informing educational policymaking is one of the key reasons that the OECD developed cross-nationally comparative education indicators, and why the OECD's Education at a Glance is a widely recognized source for educational indicators among researchers, policymakers, the general public and the media (Henry et al, 2001). The OECD explicitly states:

> Key features driving the development of PISA have been: its
> policy orientation, with design and reporting methods determined
> by the need of governments to draw policy lessons. (OECD, 2004,
> p. 12)

The OECD's emphasis on drawing policy lessons from PISA suggests that nationally centralized government responses are perhaps intended, but the fallout from PISA, TIMSS and other large-scale assessments is usually much more diverse. One of the most visible responses (i.e. PISA shock) has become institutionalized as the flagship or stereotypical response to PISA and other large-scale international educational assessments – but it is only one response of many. Still, PISA shock serves as the foundation for any discussion of policy responses to PISA because it is so public and popular in the discussions about the impact of large-scale international assessments (Ertl, 2006; Ringarp & Rothland, 2010).

### The PISA 'Shock' Phenomenon

Education policy shock happens when there is a deviation from the norm, often involving mediocre or low performance (i.e. below expectations) (Phillips & Ochs, 2003). The level of shock is defined by the 'industrialized world's educational status quo' (Martens & Leibfried, 2008). The media can play a large role in both creating the normative structures for what is expected as well as highlighting the gaps when expectations are not met. For example, Germany is best known for its PISA 'Schock' following its first participation in 2000 (Waldow, 2009). The flurry of media discussion and public anxiousness about Germany's performance was surprising (Ringarp & Rothland, 2010), especially since comparatively mediocre performance by German students had already been documented by the TIMSS 1995 results to little fanfare (Beaton et al, 1997).

Japan had its own version of PISA shock when it dropped in reading literacy between PISA 2000 and 2003 and then again in math literacy between PISA 2003 and 2006. The drops were comparatively small given the average scores of other participating countries, but the Japanese response was large, perhaps due to the fact that Japan had been promoted worldwide as an educational success story based on its prior TIMSS results (Westbury, 1992; LeTendre, 1999). One interesting anomaly is that the United States has never experienced PISA shock the way that Germany and Japan have, possibly because US educators and policymakers are perpetually pessimistic about the quality of American education (Berliner & Biddle, 1995). For example, US policymakers spent much time during the second half of the twentieth century publicly agonizing about American education in response first to Sputnik and then to *A Nation at Risk*. Some have argued that the 'shock' level never has diminished, but is instead a perpetual characteristic of US education discussions (Rothstein, 1998).

Why is the 'shock' related to PISA and other large-scale international assessments so public and pronounced? Initial reports describing international tests make mainstream media outlets such as newspapers, television news and talk shows, and Internet news and blogs (Koretz, 2009), but are often not nuanced in terms of comparability, mediating factors and specific organizational cultures the way that secondary analyses are. There is rarely fanfare or widespread coverage of secondary analyses using international assessment data, especially in countries where students' average performance is below expectations. In other words, policy responses to large-scale international assessments tend to rely on initial descriptive results instead of on more informative and often more accurate results from the secondary analysis of PISA or TIMSS data (LeTendre et al, 2001).

Is this because secondary analyses are not accessible to the general public and are therefore not a priority among their representatives in government policy positions? Is it because secondary analyses do not target the political agendas or topics that policymakers need or want to address? Is it because secondary analyses are not relevant to practical applications at the school and classroom levels? It is reasonable that all of these are potential reasons why secondary analyses are ignored and initial results are publicly celebrated (or sometimes condemned). But a less complicated and much more obvious explanation is that media coverage of initial results is more complete.

In the educational research community, the importance of media coverage is often overlooked when it comes to thinking about policy responses to secondary analyses of large-scale international assessments like PISA, TIMSS or any other large-scale assessment. However, the importance of the media is not lost on those who organize, plan and disseminate results from these studies. This is evidenced by the media kits, press releases and initial results-announcement events that have become a staple of the PISA dissemination cycle. There are a few, however, in the educational research community who have noticed the impact that the media has (Martens, 2007; Stack, 2007). Martens and Niemann (2010, p. 4) summarize the frequency of newspaper articles related to PISA using one national high-quality daily newspaper with high circulation from 22 countries during the period between December 2001 and November 2008.

Their results show that Germany posts the highest frequency of PISA media coverage with about 250 PISA-related articles, while the US had virtually none that directly referenced PISA during that same time period. It is tempting to draw the conclusion that higher rates of PISA media coverage are associated with higher levels of PISA 'shock', but the interpretation of this data is a bit more complex. For example, Martens and Niemann (2010, p. 5) also looked at the association between the number of PISA-related newspaper articles and a country's PISA ranking. Their data suggest that there is no association between media coverage and average student performance on PISA. Finland ranks very well and has about 110 newspaper articles in the 7-year period covered. The United States ranks near the bottom, but has no PISA-related articles in that same period. But Germany, which ranks above the United States even though it is firmly in the middle of the rankings, has an explosion of media-coverage related to PISA.

If there is an overall trend, then perhaps it is that the worse a country's ranking is, the more differentiated the reactions are. Figure 2 illustrates this in the way that the countries fan out across the article frequency spectrum as the rank drops. But these data do not provide enough evidence to determine whether a country's policy response to PISA is associated with or results from the impact of the media, either directly or exclusively. How then can the differences in policy response to PISA in different countries be explained? And what are the trends in policy response? To examine this requires a deeper understanding of why the 'shock' occurs and how PISA 'shock' influences policy responses.

### PISA 'Shock' Factors

The country that prided itself on its education system, on its contributions to Western science and philosophy – that had produced Einstein, Goethe and Marx – ranked at the lower end of the comparative spectrum. (Martens & Leibfried, 2008, p. 2)

Martens and Leibfried (2008) point out that expectations have a lot to do with why the German public and policymakers responded to PISA the way they did. They suggest that due to normative structures about education and the status quo in Germany and among the German public, 'Germans had always tacitly assumed that they led the world in education' (p. 2). When there is evidence that a nation's educational system and performance is not (or, more specifically, is below) what has been assumed, expected or taken for granted, there is some 'shock' that occurs. And when this evidence is displayed publicly, internationally, and in comparison with other nations' educational systems and performance, the shock is exacerbated. But what specifically is so shocking? What was assumed to have been exposed by the PISA results as untrue or remarkably different from expectations, especially given the fact that Germany's mediocre performance on TIMSS had already been documented at least five years before the PISA results were released?

The expectations that national educational systems worldwide deal with largely revolve around the legitimating myths of 'excellence' and 'equity' (Wiseman, 2005). Legitimating excellence myths assume that students are expected to receive the highest-quality education and perform at the top of whatever scale their performance is measured on. In contrast, legitimating equity myths assume that educational systems are expected to provide equal or at least equitable learning opportunities for all students regardless of their race, ethnicity, socioeconomic class or gender. The reason that excellence and equity are legitimating myths is not because they are untrue or because national education systems do not strive to attain them - they are legitimating myths because it is certain that no educational system has attained or can completely attain system-wide excellence or equity. Yet these constructs guide, inform, and are used to assess educational systems, educators and students in every country worldwide. They represent the global norms and expectations about education worldwide (Wiseman, 2005).

Not surprisingly, the shock factors result from deviations from those globally normed legitimating expectations of excellence and equity. As Figure 3 suggests, excellence is perceived to be lacking in many PISA countries when average literacy levels (in reading, math or science) are low or mediocre compared with other PISA countries and when a high percentage of students are shown to lack basic competency in core subjects (OECD, 2009a). Equity is found to be lacking in many PISA countries as well when large differences are demonstrated between low and high performers and between racial, ethnic and socioeconomic groups (OECD, 2009b). In other words, policy responses to PISA tend to be stronger when PISA results show that students are not achieving expected levels of excellence or equity in their educational systems on average, especially when the results are compared with other higher-achieving or more equitable countries' results.

Although below-average performance and educational inequality exist to some degree in every educational system worldwide, educational excellence and equity expectations are increasingly institutionalized components of formal political, social and economic policies. For example, women have the right to vote in most developed and many developing nations around the world, the civil liberties of women are recognized and even enforced in many nations, and women technically have the opportunity to hold the same positions in the labor market (Ramirez, Soysal & Shanahan, 1997)– although it is well documented that girls and women are often still denied equal access to education even in communities where it is the law (Lewis & Lockheed, 2007). Likewise, standards and expectations are often structurally institutionalized in official national or district policy, but often do not functionally link to education outcomes of achievement or opportunity.

| EXCELLENCE | EQUITY |
|---|---|
| 1. Average literacy levels mediocre compared to other countries | 3. Large differences between lowest and highest performers |
| 2. High proportion of students lack basic competencies in core subjects | 4. Large differences between racial/ethnic and socioeconomic groups |

Figure 1. PISA 'shock' factors.

Much of an organization's, community's or nation's legitimacy within the world system is the result of meeting internationally recognized standards for democratic nations (Takayama, 2008). Having a well-informed and participatory citizenry, having a strong civil society, and having a government that guarantees state-society interactions are all internationally recognized democratic values (Gutmann, 1999). And a key component of each of these democratic values is the guarantee of or opportunity for educational excellence and equity (Berkovitch & Bradley, 1999). Mass schooling is one of the few global institutions that reaches far enough into society to instill these values to the point that the worldwide belief is that excellence and equity is a right and necessary condition in education and society.

The worldwide emphasis on educational excellence and equity can have a double effect because as standards for excellence and equity become institutionalized components of educational policy, the definition and scope of educational failure and inequality expands. This means that more and more differences from the legitimized expectations of excellence and equity are both identified and empirically observed. Increased documentation of education outcomes may provide data which appears to show the condition of education is worse than it is. Often this is a phenomenon associated with increased data, rather than an actual shift in educational quality (Smith & Baker, 2001). There is also the dilemma of unequal and sub-par education in school, higher education and the labor market in spite of the expectations, policies and structures established to support educational excellence and equity (Wiseman & Alromi, 2007).

Given the evidence presented here, it is possible to say that educational excellence and equity expectations may be masking some institutionalized educational failures and inequalities. This mask means that although parity in educational access, achievement and opportunity may exist, current conditions in schools worldwide are still not uniformly equal or excellent. As a result, excellence and egalitarian values lead to widespread parity in many educational contexts even though consistent excellence and sustainable equality may not be firmly within grasp in any educational system around the world. It is, therefore, when the 'cloak of equality' is removed and the inequalities or educational failures that were unexpected are revealed that the 'shock' occurs (Benschop, 1996). How national educational systems and policymakers respond to PISA has more to do with the degree to which educational excellence and equity were 'cloaked' in a particular system than with how they were exposed. The difficulty is in measuring the PISA responses at the national or system level.

## Excellence and Equity Responses to PISA

Comparatively examining policy responses to PISA requires that the elements of the policy responses are identified and operationalized. These responses are typically characterized by several assumptions related to educational excellence and equity expectations. The first assumption is that progress is the result of positive change. This suggests that the way to measure progress towards excellence and equity is through increases in either construct. In terms of excellence, this is ubiquitously defined as increases in or high levels of performance. Progress towards excellence is typically more difficult to define since it means either a reduction in advantage of one group compared with another or no difference in access, achievement or opportunity between groups.

The second assumption is that high levels of excellence and equity measure success in educational systems and the policies that shape them. 'Success' sets the stage for comparison because it emphasizes the demonstration of excellence and equity rather than the value of each set of expectations. The third assumption is that educational systems operate within the boundaries of a meritocracy. This is a strong foundational belief of educational systems worldwide, which suggests that the environment within educational systems (and in schools specifically) creates a zone where individuals can earn or achieve what they have based on their own efforts (i.e. merit) rather than as a result of historical or systemic privilege or some other form of non-merit-based gain. The assumption that success in educational excellence or equity is the product of effort and is somehow deserved creates a dangerous context for policy responses to PISA and other large-scale international assessments. Yet these three assumptions lie behind most policymakers' responses to PISA.

For example, in June 2011, in Tokyo, at the 14th OECD Japan Seminar, titled 'Strong Performers, Successful Reformers in Education', many high-ranking Ministry of Education and National Education Department officials discussed why their countries were either 'strong' performers or 'successful' reformers. These officials' comments are relevant representations of official policy responses both within specific national educational systems and across them. The seminar objectives, agenda and individual presenters' slides were publicly posted online, so the evidence from this seminar is available for widespread analysis.[1] Several of the presentations from these policymakers provide descriptive examples of the kinds of policy responses that PISA engenders.

An example of a performance-driven expectation for education comes from the Japan Seminar. Ken Suzuki (2011), Senior Vice Minister in the Japanese Ministry of Education, Culture, Sports, Science and Technology (MEXT), gave a presentation explaining how Japan constructed an evidence-based improvement cycle using PISA results as its platform. In so doing, Suzuki pointed out the reasons why there was a PISA 'crisis' in Japan using a visual aid to show how Japan's performance levels dropped in reading literacy between PISA 2000 and 2003 and then again in math literacy between PISA 2003 and 2006. While Japan's performance on PISA is enviable from the positions of many other participating PISA countries, the drop from the top group to the group above the mean was not what the officials at MEXT nor the Japanese public expected in terms of 'excellence' (OECD, 2011).

In contrast to the excellence woes of the Japanese were the improvements by the Polish. The Polish example presented at the 2011 OECD Japan Seminar suggested that the key to solving the excellence problem is sometimes to solve the equity problem first. Miroslaw Sielatycki, Undersecretary of State with the Polish Ministry of National Education, gave a presentation explaining the ways that developing the competencies of the lowest-performing students (i.e. narrowing the gap between the high and low performers) and of girls (a group that is frequently marginalized in educational systems worldwide) allowed Poland to be one of the few PISA countries to gain in average reading performance since PISA 2000 (Sielatycki, 2011).

A closer look at gender differences in international student assessment scores across PISA, TIMSS and PIRLS (the Progress in International Reading and Literacy Study) shows that absolute gender equity is still not achieved (Hamano, 2011) in spite of many improvements in gender-equitable education worldwide. Yet the evidence suggests that equity is often a pre-condition for excellence, particularly concerning performance on large-scale international assessments. For example, in studies done using TIMSS data, when countries' national average performance rises on international assessments, the increase is often associated with a significant improvement on the part of marginalized or minority groups (specifically girls and women), coupled with stability or some improvement on the part of majority or dominant groups (specifically boys and men) (Else-Quest et al, 2010).

In other words, excellence significantly improves when equity rises. In these cases, equity is defined as raising the learning and performance of marginalized or minority groups – which decreases performance gaps – rather than raising the performance of the dominant or majority group – which may increase performance gaps (Atweh et al, 2011). The policy lesson is that countries that focus on policy reforms geared towards equity tend to improve overall student performance on international achievement tests like PISA. Yet, equity reforms are not the initial response of most countries facing what they often perceive as an education crisis. The shock response is one of excellence, not equity. It is more often the case that equity reforms precede national performance assessments rather than result from them. This is due in part to the importance of international educational assessment as political soft power.

## PISA as Soft Power

National policies for excellence and equity issues in participating PISA countries as well as the policy responses to large-scale international assessments are the product of shared expectations about what is legitimate and what is 'normal' for a national educational system. This norm-based legitimacy is even more pronounced at the local level of policy implementation, and is a key reason why policies that deviate from the school- and community-level norms are likely to be implemented in classrooms. Yet PISA and other large-scale assessments are more often tools of 'soft power' than they are harbingers of legitimacy-driven needs or meritocratic school- and classroom-based agendas (Bieber & Martens, 2011). For example, the use of education as a policy platform by US president Ronald Reagan at the end of the Cold War and the accompanying report, *A Nation at Risk*, has provided much evidence that internationally comparative educational performance is not so much about making progress in excellence and equity in schools as it is about creating globally competitive participants in the social, political and economic marketplace.

*A Nation at Risk* was released around the same time as the Second International Mathematics Study (SIMS) and the Second International Science Study (SISS), and suggested the development of internationally comparative education indicators as a way to both export the American debate about educational excellence (or lack thereof) and identify how and where US students needed to improve in order to be 'first in the world' (Commission on Excellence in Education, 1983). This push for dominance in the world market is perhaps part of the meritocratic assumptions that hypothetically support educational excellence and equity expectations worldwide (Brown & Tannock, 2009). But there is also the contrasting example of the French, who in the mid-1980s and early 1990s supported the development of the OECD's work to develop education indicators that policymakers expected would provide evidence that an inequitable French system 'fostered poor performance' (Henry et al, 2001). In other words, like the US's *A Nation at Risk*, the OECD's PISA was part of a French political agenda to create an evidence base to support a specific policy position (Dobbins & Martens, 2012). This is not an isolated tactic or unusual use of international achievement studies.

In short, participation in PISA and all international educational assessments is a political tool that educational policymakers use for gaining and exercising soft power. By participating in international assessments, countries legitimize their educational systems to a degree by belonging to the group of nations that visibly places emphasis on (i.e. that values) public education, and creates a 'culture' of education that establishes mass schooling as a foundation for economic, political and social development for individuals as well as the country as a whole (Boli & Ramirez, 1986; Smith & Baker, 2001). The policy response to PISA among those countries that participate is, therefore, also a form of soft power. The policy responses to PISA come in many forms, but follow two basic patterns as a result of attraction, borrowing, mimicry or coercion; they are convergence and isomorphism.

## Convergence vs. Isomorphism

Although differences in local adaptations of national educational policy are relatively common, it is difficult to find evidence of truly divergent policy responses to PISA. Instead, it is much more likely to find some policy responses that converge, and even more likely to find policy responses to PISA that closely resemble 'isomorphism' (Wiseman et al, 2010). Policy convergence as a response to PISA occurs when different countries produce similar policy responses with similar implementation of those policies (Bieber & Martens, 2011). Literally, the policies in different systems, which were developed in response to PISA results, sometimes closely resemble convergence by tending towards a common result or conclusion. An example is the extension of school hours or days of instruction in poor-performing educational systems to match the average hours or days common in high-performing systems (e.g. OECD, 2011). Policy isomorphism, on the other hand, is when policy responses to PISA across participating countries correspond or are similar, but do not actually converge (Wells & Henkin, 2005). An example is when poor-performing educational systems revise their national curriculum to address the same content that higher-performing educational systems' curriculum covers, but without implementing the exact same curriculum (e.g. Bulut, 2007). The evidence suggests that policy isomorphism as a response to PISA is much more likely than either divergence or convergence.

The process of policy isomorphism, while not identical from country to country, does follow some general paths, which include: immediate large-scale policy-driven reforms as a response to low performance on summary reports (e.g. Germany) (Ertl, 2006; Neumann et al, 2010); research-driven national model development to understand the link between student learning and performance (e.g. Japan) (Bransford et al, 2009; Takayama, 2010); and a regional comparison approach looking at contextual factors that impact school effectiveness and academic achievement (e.g. the United States) (Willms, 2010; Peterson et al, 2011). Each of these response patterns follows the logic of 'evidence-based' policymaking, which looks at the crisis or situation and determines 'what works' best in order to either fix poor performance, develop national models for improvement, or identify contextual factors that drive school effectiveness (Wiseman, 2010).

In some instances, policy responses are driven by PISA performance rankings – perhaps more often than not, because these comprise the initial and widely disseminated evidence in many countries that excellence or equity expectations are not being met (LeTendre et al, 2001). Whichever approach policymakers take, the fact that PISA data is quantifiable and standardized across countries leads many policymakers to assume it is a legitimized evidence base for educational policy reform and agenda-setting (Smith & Baker, 2001; Smith, 2002), often regardless of whether national means and international comparisons do adequately represent the most pressing issues and problems in a nation's educational system.

## Comparative Policy Responses

While there are certainly many different policy responses to PISA, the ones that receive much attention from policymakers, the public and the media are related to improving teacher quality, developing accountability systems around standards, and creating opportunities for equitable education. These policy responses do not 'converge' across countries as much as they isomorphically correspond among countries. The 14th OECD Japan Seminar on 'Strong Performers and Successful Reformers' mentioned above provides examples of each. At least ten representatives from different countries participated in this 2011 seminar, and they are a purposeful sample to select because they all were identified and invited to participate because of their strong performance or improvement on PISA. These are countries where, if convergence were to be observed, it would most likely occur. Yet that does not happen. Neither do these participating countries show signs of policy divergence. Instead, there is an isomorphism that occurs among these ten countries' educational systems and their policy responses to PISA that is rationally bounded into shared categories of expectations for reform, but which varies within the boundaries set by the legitimate expectations for each country's context and history.

### The Importance of Teachers

Given that Finnish and Singaporean students performed very well on PISA, it is not surprising that there is little doubt about or constructive criticism of the Finnish and Singaporean teachers among policymakers responding to PISA in other countries. This is one more example of how the policy responses vary. But as an example of strong performers, both Finland and Singapore are pored over by policymakers interested in reforming teacher preparation or raising teacher quality in response to PISA results (Sahlberg, 2011b). As Grek (2009) points out, Finnish educators and policymakers were surprised by the ways that PISA launched them into the spotlight. For example, she quotes Finnish educational researchers as saying, 'At a single stroke, PISA has transformed our conceptions of the quality of the work done at our comprehensive school and of the foundations it has laid for Finland's future civilization and development of knowledge' (Valijarvi et al, 2002, p. 3).

The policy responses of average or below-average performing countries to Finland's success have been to elevate the discourse about teacher quality (Darling-Hammond & Rothman, 2011). For example, the importance of Finland's teachers in their comprehensive school system has become a model for other countries in terms of the individualization teachers provide to students, teachers' autonomy in evaluating student performance and selecting textbooks, and the high status of teachers in Finnish society in general (Sahlberg, 2011b). Likewise, Singapore's teachers are promoted as a key model for countries whose educational expectations for excellence were not met, especially related to the training and standards Singaporean teachers are required to meet (Choo & Darling-Hammond, 2011; Keat, 2011).

While the training and preparation of teachers contributes to policy responses to PISA, the professional respect and status of teachers necessarily follows and is a frequently discussed topic related to teacher education and teaching policy reform (Sahlberg, 2011b,c). For example, PISA director Andreas Schleicher has emphasized in highly visible media outlets that the highest-performing countries like Finland and Singapore 'recruit only high-performing college graduates for teaching positions, support them with mentoring and other help in the classroom, and take steps to raise respect for the profession' (Dillon, 2011). As a result of this type of widely held and publicly affirmed causal assumption, the teacher-quality discourse among many countries' educational policymakers has taken a turn towards higher standards for teacher recruitment and selection (Beese & Liang, 2010). And this assumed connection between teacher characteristics and student performance has a long history within large-scale international assessments like PISA (Huber & Gordel, 2006), even though the exact characteristics of teacher quality and their importance to student learning take decidedly different tracks in Finland and Singapore.

*Educational Equity*

Another frequent policy response to PISA concerns the opportunity for, availability of, and implementation of educational equity. As the Director General for the Center for International Mobility in Finland, Pasi Sahlberg (2011b) pointed out at the 2011 OECD Japan Seminar that PISA results show that the strongest performers have the least variation between schools, but relatively high levels of student variation within schools. This is due to the policy practices of inclusion and attempts to ensure system-wide equity in education. The ways that countries respond to issues of educational equity as a response to PISA can vary, however, even though they correspond in their attempts to address the same equity issues.

For example, Burhanuddin Tola (2011), from Indonesia's Ministry of National Education, provides evidence that Indonesia is approaching educational equity issues using vocational and polytechnic education as its policy response. This response from the Indonesian perspective involves creating an educated and prepared future workforce to serve Indonesia's many economic developments. Indonesia, therefore, provides an example of a research-driven national policy response to PISA, which was developed to understand the practical link between student learning and performance, but which also responds to and generates soft power among nations and policymakers. The Indonesian response is also a completely different approach to achieving educational equity even though the Indonesian and Finnish approaches are both based on shared assumptions about the legitimacy and importance of educational equity.

### Standards-driven Accountability

In the case of both teacher quality and educational equity, the national policy approach is to first develop national standards, which are then developed into national educational policy, and then implemented within local school and community contexts. And standards-driven accountability is often the way that national educational systems then monitor the link between policy and practice. National and international assessments are often used as accountability tools even though large-scale assessments such as these provide only one way of looking at performance and identifying problems to target for reform. The accountability processes also support and legitimate soft-power agendas, used by educational policymakers and others. Yet, even within a standards-driven accountability system, which rationally bounds the educational policy and practice in many educational systems (and in all of the systems that participated in the 14th OECD Japan Seminar), there is neither convergence nor distinct divergence.

For example, the efforts of the Japanese educational system and educational policymakers, who used a survey in addition to the PISA results to identify problems with their educational sector that they thought they should address with new educational policies and reforms, show how one educational system acts within shared global expectations, but also locally adapts the process (Suzuki, 2011). Japanese policy responses to PISA came in two areas: (1) improvement of learning content; and (2) improvement of the educational system. Both of these responses to PISA took place within the shared set of expectations about the perceived validity of large-scale assessment and evidence-based decision-making. And both types of response also fit broadly into reform trends shared by other OECD participating countries. Improvement of learning content included revised courses of study through national standards, systematic content revision and improved government screening of textbooks (Takayama, 2008, 2010). Improvement of the educational system included reduced class sizes, increases in the number of new teachers, enhancement of continuing education and professional development for teachers, revision of the school management model to create more involvement and empowerment of the community, and developing an accountability system from the national level to local levels (Suzuki, 2011).

These three comparative policy responses (teacher quality, educational equity and standards-driven accountability) provide an isomorphically constructed approach to globally legitimized yet locally adaptable responses to PISA and other international educational assessments. Through these comparative policy responses it is possible also to see the process of legitimate response within contexts and phenomena of both PISA shock and norms regarding both excellence and equity in national educational systems.

## Policy Response Trends

If creating education indicators and evidence to encourage and support the development of policy or at least policy lessons is a key purpose of PISA, there is ample evidence that PISA has been a success (Anderson et al, 2010; Milford et al, 2010). Policy responses to PISA may be incorporated into pre-existing 'soft power' agendas or as a response to evidence-based policymaking. These responses are more likely to correspond broadly across nations than they are to converge, and within nations the emphasis is more on legitimization of reform efforts even if the legitimate policy is to push responsibility to the local schools and districts. Finally, there are trends in the ways that educational policy responses form using PISA as the base, which consistently include (although in various formats) the three areas of (1) teacher quality; (2) educational equity; and (3) accountability and standards.

Countries like Germany, whose normative expectations for education are most egregiously contradicted by the PISA results and publicly documented in the media, are more likely to respond with 'shock' and immediate large-scale policy-driven reforms. Countries like Japan, whose normative expectations are contradicted, but whose policy response is more research- or evidence-based, tend to engage in research-driven national model development to understand the link between student learning and performance. And countries like the USA, whose expectations are not necessarily challenged by PISA results (even when those results show high levels of poor performance), tend to engage in regional comparison by looking at contextual factors that impact school effectiveness and academic achievement.

There is, however, a further policy lesson to be learned from this investigation of policy responses to PISA in comparative perspective. Internationally comparative education assessments influence educational policy and practice independently from the organizations that develop and administer them as well as from the national policymakers and educational systems that promote and participate in them. This is due to PISA and other large-scale assessments becoming incorporated into a shared culture of education worldwide. While the role of power and coercion is always relevant – especially at the beginning of change movements – the phenomenon of cultural incorporation is less explicit and much more implicit in terms of the significance that assumptions and shared norms about the value and relevancy that assessments like PISA have in different educational systems worldwide.

This perspective is not without its critics. There are those in academia, in particular, who argue that PISA participation and resulting uses of PISA data are forced on subordinate – often seemingly passive – systems and individuals, especially in developing countries (Chung, 2010). There are others who argue that countries, communities and individuals are agents of resistance leading to the development of uniquely different and contextualized educational systems and practices. While examples of these scenarios exist, they are not the norm. Instead, there is a remarkable degree of agency among international organizations, national education systems and policymakers and the local public regarding PISA participation, internationally legitimized educational reforms, and in particular the development and implementation of teacher quality, educational equity and standards-based accountability systems. This agency and resulting participation reflect local adaptation as one form of resistance or contextualization, but it rarely involves complete rejection or divergence from either PISA or PISA-referencing policy responses. In fact, local agency or resistance in local communities, especially in those that are already part of an educational system that participates in PISA, is often directed more towards rationalizing and contextualizing participation, as the examples of Finland, Singapore, Indonesia and Japan have shown, than towards not participating or breaking the connection to the legitimacy that PISA provides in the global community.

There are, of course, examples of educational systems that have stopped participating in international educational assessments. One of the most discussed examples is South Africa and TIMSS. The Republic of South Africa participated in TIMSS from 1995 to 2003, and then announced that it was no longer going to participate. South Africa was consistently a bottom performer in TIMSS and the decision to stop participating in TIMSS was partly due to a desire to focus more specifically on reducing variation within South Africa's educational system than on international comparisons. However, a large reason for not participating further was to maintain some legitimacy in the international educational community rather than continue to post the lowest recorded performance in cycle after cycle. It is also important to note that South Africa turned its attention more fully to its own national large-scale educational assessments as an alternative. In other words, resistance to TIMSS was not a rejection of or drastic divergence from the globally legitimized and shared norms about educational assessment, but was instead a contextualized close adaptation of the legitimate model represented by TIMSS. This is further evidenced by South Africa's re-entry into TIMSS in 2011.

Finally, from a policymaker's perspective, there are several general points. First, it is beneficial to recognize the location of a particular educational system within the larger culture of education by taking a meta-perspective and identifying the legitimate norms and assumptions about PISA at each level and for each group of stakeholders. Second, it is important to recognize and articulate where local or contextualized norms, traditions and assumptions and international educational assessment overlap and where they diverge from the cross-nationally legitimized assumptions. Lastly, a policymaker's role is to balance the shared and the unique norms and assumptions about PISA or other large-scale assessments in order to maximize the benefit an educational system receives from either global or local adaptation, while also minimizing the consequences or missed opportunities that result from those adaptations.

In summary, this discussion of policy responses to PISA does not point towards convergence nor does it point towards divergence. Instead it points to both explicit and implicit evidence that policy responses to PISA are incorporated into a broader culture of education characterized by shared norms, traditions and assumptions about assessment and policy, local context and community, and both conformity and resistance. These many cultures weave together to create a complex tapestry of policy responses to PISA. Recognizing this complexity creates a framework to understand the responses of shock, resistance and accommodation that often accompany PISA.

### Note

[1] http://www.oecd.org/document/12/0,3746,en_32252351_32235731_4775022
0_1_1_1_1,00.html

### References

Anderson, J.O., Chiu, M.-H. & Yore, L.D. (2010) First Cycle of PISA (2000-2006) – International Perspectives on Successes and Challenges: research and policy direction, *International Journal of Science and Mathematics Education*, 8, 373-388.

Atweh, B., Graven, M., Secada, W. & Valero, P. (2011) *Mapping Equity and Quality in Mathematics Education*. Dordrecht: Springer.

Beaton, A.E., Mullis, I.V.S., Martin, M.O., Gonzalez, E.J., Kelly, D.L. & Smith, T.A. (1997) *Mathematics Achievement in the Middle School Years: IEA's Third International Mathematics and Science Report*. Boston: International Study Center, Boston College.

Beese, J. & Liang, X. (2010) Do Resources Matter? PISA Science Achievement Comparisons between Students in the United States, Canada, and Finland, *Improving Schools*, 13(3), 266-279.

Benschop, Y.W.M. (1996) *De Mantel Der Gelijkheid, Gender in Organisaties.* Assen: Van Gorcum.

Berkovitch, N. & Bradley, K. (1999) The Globalization of Women's Status: consensus/dissensus in the world polity, *Sociological Perspectives*, 481-498.

Berliner, D.C. & Biddle, B.J. (1995) *The Manufactured Crisis: myths, fraud, and the attack on America's public schools.* Cambridge, MA: Perseus.

Bieber, T. & Martens, K. (2011) The OECD PISA Study as a Soft Power in Education? Lessons from Switzerland and the US. *European Journal of Education*, 46(1), 101-116.

Boli, J. & Ramirez, F.O. (1986) World Culture and the Institutional Development of Mass Education, in J.G. Richardson (Ed.) *Handbook of Theory and Research for the Sociology of Education*, pp. 65-90. New York: Greenwood Press.

Bransford, J.D., Stipek, D.J., Vye, N.J., Gomez, L.M. & Lam, D. (Eds) (2009) *The Role of Research in Educational Improvement.* Cambridge, MA: Harvard Education Press.

Brown, P. & Tannock, S. (2009) Education, Meritocracy and the Global War for Talent, *Journal of Education Policy*, 24(4), 377-392.

Bulut, M. (2007) Curriculum Reform in Turkey: a case of primary school mathematics curriculum, *Eurasia Journal of Mathematics, Science & Technology Education*, 2(3), 203-212.

Choo, T.L. & Darling-Hammond, L. (2011) Creating Effective Teachers and Leaders in Singapore, in L. Darling-Hammond & R. Rothman (Eds) *Teacher and Leader Effectiveness in High-performing Education Systems*, pp. 33-42. Washington, DC and Stanford, CA: Alliance for Excellent Education and Stanford Center for Opportunity Policy in Education.

Chung, J.H. (2010) Finland, PISA, and the Implications of International Achievement Studies on Education Policy, in A.W. Wiseman (Ed.) *The Impact of International Achievement Studies on National Education Policymaking*, vol. 13, pp. 267-294. Bingley: Emerald Group Publishing.

Commission on Excellence in Education. (1983) *A Nation at Risk.* Washington, DC: Government Printing Office.

Darling-Hammond, L. & Rothman, R. (Eds) (2011) *Teacher and Leader Effectiveness in High-performing Education Systems.* Washington, DC and Stanford, CA: Alliance for Excellent Education and Stanford Center for Opportunity Policy in Education.

Dillon, S. (2011) US is Urged to Raise Teachers' Status, *New York Times*, 16 March, p. A22.

Dobbins, M. & Martens, K. (2012) Towards an Education Approach a La 'Finlandaise'? French Education Policy after PISA, *Journal of Education Policy*, 27(1), 23-43.

Else-Quest, N.M., Hyde, J.S. & Linn, M.C. (2010) Cross-national Patterns of Gender Differences in Mathematics: a meta-analysis, *Psychological Bulletin*, 136(1), 103-127.

Ertl, H. (2006) Educational Standards and the Changing Discourse on Education: the reception and consequences of the PISA study in Germany, *Oxford Review of Education*, 32(5), 619-634.

Grek, S. (2009) Governing by Numbers: the PISA 'effect' in Europe, *Journal of Education Policy*, 24(1), 23-37.

Gutmann, A. (1999) *Democratic Education*. Princeton, NJ: Princeton University Press.

Hamano, T. (2011) The Globalization of Student Assessments and Its Impact on Educational Policy, *Proceedings*, 13, 1-11.

Henry, M., Lingard, B., Rizvi, F. & Taylor, S. (2001) *The OECD, Globalisation and Education Policy*. Oxford: IAU Press/Pergamon Press.

Huber, S.G. & Gordel, B. (2006) Quality Assurance in the German School System, *European Educational Research Journal*, 5(3-4), 196-209.

Keat, H.S. (2011) Singapore Education Reform Journey. Paper presented at the 14th OECD Japan Seminar 'Strong Performers, Successful Reformers in Education'. http://www.oecd.org/dataoecd/45/37/48357652.ppt (accessed 30 November 2011).

Koretz, D. (2009) How Do American Students Measure Up? Making Sense of International Comparisons, *The Future of Children*, 19(1), 37-51.

LeTendre, G.K. (1999) *Competitor or Ally? Japan's Role in American Educational Debates*. New York: RoutledgeFalmer.

LeTendre, G.K., Baker, D.P., Akiba, M. & Wiseman, A.W. (2001) The Policy Trap: national educational policy and the Third International Math and Science Study, *International Journal of Educational Policy, Research and Practice*, 2(1), 45-64.

Lewis, M. & Lockheed, M. (2007) *Inexcusable Absence: why 60 million girls still aren't in school and what to do about it*. Washington, DC: Center for Global Development.

Martens, K. (2007) How to Become an Influential Actor: the 'comparative turn' in OECD education policy, in K. Martens, A. Rusconi & K. Leuze (Eds) *New Arenas of Education Governance: the impact of international organizations and markets on educational policy making*, pp. 40-56. New York: Palgrave Macmillan.

Martens, K. & Leibfried, S. (2008) How Educational Policy Went International: a lesson in politics beyond the nation-state [electronic version], *The German Times Online*, January. http://www.atlantic-times.com/archive_detail.php?recordID=1132 (accessed 28 November 2011).

Martens, K. & Niemann, D. (2010) *Governance by Comparison: how ratings & rankings impact national policy-making in education*. Transtate Working Papers, 139. Bremen: Sfb 597, Staatlichkeit im Wandel.

Milford, T., Ross, S.P. & Anderson, J.O. (2010) An Opportunity to Better Understand Schooling: the growing presence of PISA in the Americas, *International Journal of Science and Mathematics Education*, 8, 453-473.

Neumann, K., Fischer, H.E. & Kauertz, A. (2010) From PISA to Educational Standards: the impact of large-scale assessments on science education in Germany, *International Journal of Science and Mathematics Education*, 8, 545-563.

Organisation for Economic Co-operation and Development (OECD) (2004) *Problem Solving for Tomorrow's World: first measures of cross-curricular competencies from PISA 2003*. Paris: OECD.

Organisation for Economic Co-operation and Development (OECD) (2009a) *Education at a Glance 2009: OECD indicators*. Paris: OECD.

Organisation for Economic Co-operation and Development (OECD) (2009b) *Equally Prepared for Life? How 15-year-old Boys and Girls Performed in School*. Paris: OECD.

Organisation for Economic Co-operation and Development (OECD) (2011) *Strong Performers and Successful Reformers in Education: lessons from PISA for the United States*. Paris: OECD.

Peterson, P.E., Woessmann, L., Hanushek, E.A. & Lastra-Anadon, C.X. (2011) Globally Challenged: are US students ready to compete? The latest on each state's international standing, *Education Next*, Fall, 51-59.

Phillips, D. & Ochs, K. (2003) Processes of Policy Borrowing in Education: Some Explanatory and Analytical Devices, *Comparative Education*, 39(4), 451-461.

Ramirez, F.O., Soysal, Y. & Shanahan, S. (1997) The Changing Logic of Political Citizenship: cross-national acquisition of women's suffrage rights, 1890 to 1990, *American Sociological Review*, 735-745.

Ringarp, J. & Rothland, M. (2010) Is the Grass Always Greener? The Effect of the PISA Results on Education Debates in Sweden and Germany, *European Educational Research Journal*, 9(3), 422-430.

Rothstein, R. (1998) *The Way We Were? The Myths and Realities of America's Student Achievement*. New York: Century Foundation Press.

Sahlberg, P. (2011b) The Finnish Advantage: good teachers. Paper presented at the 14th OECD Japan Seminar 'Strong Performers, Successful Reformers in Education'. http://www.oecd.org/dataoecd/33/43/48358184.ppt (accessed 30 November 2011).

Sahlberg, P. (2011c) The Professional Educator: lessons from Finland, *American Educator*, 35(2), 34-38.

Sielatycki, M. (2011) Poland: successes and challenged educational reforms. Paper presented at the 14th OECD Japan Seminar 'Strong Performers, Successful Reformers in Education'. http://www.oecd.org/dataoecd/45/39/48357781.ppt (accessed 30 November 2011).

Smith, M.C. (2002) Drawing Inferences for National Policy from Large-scale Cross-national Education Surveys, in A.C. Porter & A. Gamoran (Eds) *Methodological Advances in Cross-national Surveys of Educational Achievement*, pp. 295-317. Washington, DC: National Academy Press.

Smith, T.M. & Baker, D.P. (2001) Worldwide Growth and Institutionalization of Statistical Indicators for Education Policy-making, *Peabody Journal of Education*, 76(3/4), 141-152.

Stack, M. (2007) Representing School Success and Failure: media coverage of international tests, *Policy Futures in Education*, 5(1), 100-110.

Suzuki, K. (2011) PISA Survey and Education Reform in Japan: construction of an evidence-based improvement cycle. Paper presented at the 14th OECD Japan

Seminar 'Strong Performers, Successful Reformers in Education'. http://www.oecd.org/dataoecd/45/41/48358140.ppt (accessed 30 November 2011).

Takayama, K. (2008) The Politics of International League Tables: PISA in Japan's achievement crisis debate, *Comparative Education*, 44(4), 387-407.

Takayama, K. (2010) Politics of Externalization in Reflexive Times: reinventing Japanese education reform discourses through 'Finnish PISA success', *Comparative Education Review*, 54(1), 51-75.

Tola, B. (2011) Indonesia Reading Proficiency and Influencing Factors. Paper presented at the 14th OECD Japan Seminar 'Strong Performers, Successful Reformers in Education'. http://www.oecd.org/dataoecd/33/49/48360434.ppt (accessed 30 November 2011).

Välijärvi, J., Linnakylä, P., Kupari, P., Reinikainen, P. & Arffman, I. (2002) *The Finnish Success in PISA—and some reasons behind it.* Jyväskylä: Institute for Educational Research.

Waldow, F. (2009) What PISA Did and Did Not Do: Germany after the 'PISA-shock', *European Educational Research Journal*, 8(3), 476-483.

Wells, R. & Henkin, A.B. (2005) Exploring the Trend toward Isomorphism in International Education, *International Journal of Educational Reform*, 14(3), 268-281.

Westbury, I. (1992) Comparing American and Japanese Achievement: is the United States really a low achiever? *Educational Researcher*, 21(5), 18-24.

Willms, J.D. (2010) School Composition and Contextual Effects on Student Outcomes, *Teachers College Record*, 112(4), 1008-1037.

Wiseman, A.W. (2005) *Principals under Pressure: the growing crisis.* Lanham, MD: Scarecrow Press.

Wiseman, A.W. (2010) The Uses of Evidence for Educational Policymaking: global contexts and international trends, in A. Luke, G.J. Kelly & J. Green (Eds) *Review of Research in Education*, vol. 34, pp. 1-24. Washington, DC: American Educational Research Association.

Wiseman, A.W. & Alromi, N.H. (2007) *The Employability Imperative: schooling for work as a national project.* Hauppage, NY: Nova Science Publishers.

Wiseman, A.W., Pilton, J. & Lowe, J.C. (2010) International Educational Governance Models and National Policy Convergence, in S.K. Amos (Ed.) *International Educational Governance*, vol. 12, pp. 3-19. Bingley: Emerald Publishing.

# Notes on Contributors

**PAUL ROBERT ANDREWS**, PhD, Manchester Metropolitan University, is Professor of Mathematics Education at the University of Stockholm, Sweden. He has written extensively on cross-cultural analyses of mathematics teaching and the impact of teacher beliefs on classroom practice. His most recent publications include a chapter in the edited volume *Mathematical Knowledge in Teaching* and articles in the *Journal of Mathematical Behavior*, *Comparative Education Review* and *ZDM*. A recent (2011-2012) President of the Mathematical Association, he is also a member of the editorial boards of *Research in Mathematics Education* and the *Cambridge Journal of Education*.

**AARON BENAVOT**, PhD, Stanford University, is a Professor in the Department of Educational Administration and Policy Studies at SUNY-Albany, USA, with interests in global education policy and comparative education research. Previously, he served for four years as a senior policy analyst on the Education for All Global Monitoring Report team at UNESCO headquarters in Paris. As part of UNESCO's education sector, he focused on the areas of literacy, education for sustainable development, quality learning enhancement and lifelong learning. He is currently the editor or co-editor of five professional journals. His publications list includes three books, two edited volumes, 14 book chapters, five published reports, and more than 25 journal articles.

**MANON DE HEUS** has a Master's degree from the University of Tilburg, Netherlands and is now a freelance writer and journalist. Her prior experience includes serving as a researcher and teacher at Tilburg University, where she taught courses on Inequality and Family Relationships.

**JAAP DRONKERS**, PhD, Free University of Amsterdam, is currently Professor of International Comparative Research at Maastricht University, Netherlands and previously occupied chairs at the University of Amsterdam and the European University Institute (EUI) in Florence. His publications focus on a wide range of topics, including the causes and consequences of unequal educational and occupational attainment, changes in educational opportunities, effect differences between public and religious schools, the educational and occupational achievement of migrants, the linkages between school and the labor market, and the effects of parental divorce on children.

He edited *Quality and Inequality of Education: cross-national perspectives* (Springer, 2010).

**STEPHEN P. HEYNEMAN** served the World Bank for 22 years. Between 1976 and 1984 he helped research education quality and design policies to support educational effectiveness. Between 1984 and 1989 he was in charge of external training for senior officials worldwide in education policy and between 1989 and 1998 he was responsible for education policy and lending strategy, first for the Middle East and North Africa and later for the 27 countries of Europe and Central Asia. In 1998 he was appointed vice-president in charge of international operations of an education consultant firm in Alexandria, Virginia. In September 2000 he was appointed Professor of International Education Policy at Vanderbilt University in Nashville, USA. He received his BA in Political Science from the University of California at Berkeley, his MA in African Area Studies from UCLA in 1965, and his PhD in Comparative Education from the University of Chicago in 1976.

**CINDY JONG**, PhD, Boston College, is an Assistant Professor of Mathematics Education in the STEM Education Department at the University of Kentucky, USA. Her research interests include measuring teachers' conceptions of mathematics teaching and learning along with examining teachers' conception of teaching mathematics for social justice. She is a developer of the Mathematics Experiences and Conceptions Surveys (MECS), designed to longitudinally examine teachers' conceptions.

**DAVID HUNT KAMENS**, PhD, Columbia University, is Emeritus Professor of Sociology at Northern Illinois University, USA and was a research professor at George Mason University, Fairfax, USA, from 2006 to 2009, studying women in science. He is the author of numerous papers on the topics of sociology of education and political sociology. His publications include a forthcoming book, *Knowledge for the Masses* (co-authored with John Meyer and Aaron Benevot), *Beyond the Nation State: the reconstruction of nationhood and citizenship* (Emerald Press, 2012), and *The Evolution of the American State and Polity, 1950-2005* (co-authored with R. Jepperson).

**BOB LINGARD**, PhD, University of Queensland, is a professorial research fellow in the School of Education and the Institute for Social Science Research at the University of Queensland, Australia. He previously held the Andrew Bell Chair in Education at the University of Edinburgh. Bob has published widely in sociology of education. His recent books include *Changing Schools* (with Terry Wrigley and Pat Thomson; Routledge, 2012); *Globalizing Education Policy* (with Fazal Rizvi; Routledge, 2010); and *Educating Boys* (with Wayne Martino and Martin Mills; Palgrave, 2009). He is editor of the journal *Discourse: studies in the cultural politics of education*. Bob is a former president of the Australian Association for Research in Education and is a fellow of the Academy of Social Sciences, Australia.

**MARLAINE E. LOCKHEED**, PhD, Stanford University, served at the World Bank for 19 years, initially as a research sociologist with interests in education effectiveness, equity and quality and later holding senior management positions with responsibilities for education policy and lending for the 14 countries of the Middle East and North Africa and for the evaluation of the World Bank's training programs for senior officials worldwide. She was previously a principal research sociologist at Educational Testing Service in Princeton, NJ, where she directed research on gender and education. She has been a visiting fellow at the Center for Global Development, a visiting professor at Harvard, Stanford, Princeton and the University of Texas, and a member of various journal and advisory boards. She is author or editor of 80 chapters and journal articles, four journal special issues and seven books, including *Improving Primary Education in Developing Countries* and *Exclusion, Gender and Education: Case Studies from the Developing World*.

**XIN MA**, PhD, University of British Columbia, is a Full Professor in the College of Education at the University of Kentucky, USA and a Spencer Fellow of the United States Academy of Education. His research interests include the psychology of mathematics education, school effectiveness and improvement, and program evaluation. He is the author of two books and seven book chapters, and he has authored or co-authored more than eighty articles in a variety of academic journals. His recent publications focus on technology in the mathematics classroom (*Educational Psychology Review*) and within-school gender gaps in reading, mathematics, and science literacy (*Comparative Education Review*).

**HEINZ-DIETER MEYER**, PhD, Cornell University, is Associate Professor of Education and Organization, State University of New York (SUNY) Albany, USA. His more than forty articles, book chapters and edited volumes focus on organizations, new institutionalism and education governance. He has been a Harman Fellow at Harvard University and a Visiting Scholar at Peking University, Penn State, and the East-West Institute in Honolulu, among others. Recent publications include articles on institutional design in *Comparative Sociology* (2012), on colonization of public education in *Educational Philosophy and Theory* (2010), and on dilemmas of decentralization in *American Journal of Education* (2009). He is also the editor, with Brian-Rowan, of *The New Institutionalism in Education* (SUNY Press).

**TAYA L. OWENS**, doctoral candidate, University at Albany, SUNY, USA, currently works as a research assistant at the Rockefeller Institute of

Government in Albany. Prior to beginning her doctoral studies, she worked as a research and planning analyst for the Tennessee Higher Education Commission and as a legislative assistant to the Tennessee General Assembly. She began her career in educational policy in the classroom, as an English instructor at the Zaporozhsky Institute of Economics and Information Technologies in Ukraine and Ferghana State University in Uzbekistan.

**RISTO RINNE** is a professor of education and director in the Department of Education at the University of Turku, Finland. He is also the director of the Centre for Research on Lifelong Learning and Education (CELE) in the University of Turku as well as the director of the Finnish Graduate School in Education and Learning (FiGSEL). His main interests and publications include sociology of education, international comparative education, educational policy, citizenship and learning in the knowledge society, and history of education. He has also published many articles and books in the field of transmission and building the educational knowledge base in Europe.

**KATHRYN SCHILLER**, PhD, is Associate Professor in the Department of Educational Administration & Policy Studies at the University at Albany, USA. She is also affiliated with the Department of Sociology, the Center for Social & Demographic Analysis, and the Nelson A. Rockefeller College of Public Affairs & Policy. A sociologist trained at the University of Chicago, her research explores the role of schooling in the development of human capital, focusing on how organizational structures and social networks shape individuals' developmental trajectories. An article in the *Journal of Marriage & Family* found that the academic advantages of living with both parents are greater in more affluent countries using the Third International Mathematics and Science Study.

**SAM SELLAR**, PhD, University of South Australia, is a postdoctoral research fellow in the School of Education at the University of Queensland, Australia. Sam has also been a Postdoctoral Research Fellow in the Australian National Centre for Student Equity in Higher Education, hosted by the University of South Australia. His research focuses on contemporary developments in schooling and higher education policy. He has recent publications in the the *Journal of Education Policy, Comparative Education* and *Discourse: Studies in the cultural politics of education*. He is an associate editor of the journal *Critical Studies in Education*.

**TIINA SILANDER** is the Head of the Teacher Education Department at the University of Jyväskylä, Finland. She has worked at the Department of Teacher Education as a Senior Assistant of Science Pedagogy since 2006. Prior to that, she worked in the Institute for Educational Research in the research group for Assessing Learning Outcomes. Within teacher education

Dr Silander is responsible for planning and development of both primary teacher and subject teacher education.

**HANNU JAAKKO SIMOLA**, PhD, University of Helsinki, is a professor of sociology at Helsinki University, Finland. He is a member of the board of the Doctoral Programme of Comparative Research on Educational Policy, Economy and Assessment and of the Finnish Graduate School in Education and Learning and serves as head of the research group focusing on new policy, politics, and the governance of education. His recent publications include *The Finnish Miracle of PISA: historical and sociological remarks on teaching and teacher education* and *Trans-national Technologies, National Techniques, and Local Mechanisms in Finnish University Governance.*

**DANIEL TRÖHLER**, PhD, University of Zurich, is Professor of Education and director of the research unit for socio-cultural research on learning and development titled Languages, Culture, Media, and Identities, and of the Doctoral School in Educational Sciences at the University of Luxembourg. He is also a visiting professor of comparative education at the University of Granada, Spain. His latest publications include the AERA Outstanding Book of the Year, *Languages of Education: Protestant legacies, national identities, and global aspirations* (Routledge, 2011), and *Schooling and the Making of Citizens in the Long Nineteenth Century: comparative visions* (with Thomas S. Popkewitz and David F. Labaree; Routledge, 2011). He served as guest editor of the journal *Studies in Philosophy and Education* for the 2012 Special Issue (volume 31, no. 5), *Historicising Jean-Jacques Rousseau: four ways to commemorate his 300th anniversary.*

**JOUNI ENSIO VÄLIJÄRVI**, PhD, University of Jyväskylä, is a professor of educational research and Docent at the University of Oulu, Finland and Director of the Institute for Educational Research. As an expert in the evaluation of educational systems, he serves as National Project Manager in the OECD's Programme for International Student Assessment (PISA). He publishes extensively in journals related to Finnish education and research-based teacher education. His most recent journal article, 'Teachers' Professional Skills and Research-based Teacher Education for the Future', appears in the *Korean Journal of Teacher Education.*

**JANNE VARJO**, PhD, University of Helsinki, is a post-doctoral researcher working at the University of Helsinki, Finalnd, and more particularly within the New Politics, Governance and Interaction in Education research unit (KUPOLI) at the Institute of Behavioural Sciences. His current research interests are in applying the ideas of governance of compulsory education at the sub-national level and the political economy of education. He is currently working on a three-year post-doctoral project, 'Travelling Policies and

Embedded Politics – an Analysis of Dynamics of Local Education Politics', funded by the University of Helsinki.

**ALEXANDER W. WISEMAN**, PhD, Pennsylvania State University, is Associate Professor of Comparative and International Education in the College of Education at Lehigh University, USA. His research and publications focus on internationally comparative analyses of national educational systems, technology use in schools worldwide, the transition from school to work, gender and education, and institutional approaches to comparative education. His work has appeared in *Compare*, *Prospects*, *Educational Researcher*, *Research in Comparative and International Education*, and the *Comparative Education Review*. He is the editor of the *Annual Review of Comparative and International Education* (Emerald Publishing, 2013) and senior editor of the online journal *FIRE: Forum for International Education in Research* (http://preserve.lehigh.edu/fire/).

**JING YUAN** is a doctoral student at the Department of Educational, School, and Counseling Psychology at the University of Kentucky. Prior to her doctoral studies, she worked as a research assistant for a large-scale project on Students' Academic Achievement Evaluation (SAAE) sponsored by the Ministry of Education, P.R. China. Her research interests include psychology of science education, school effectiveness, and advanced data analysis of large-scale surveys.

**YONG ZHAO**, PhD, University of Illinois, currently serves as Chair and Associate Dean for Global Education in the College of Education, University of Oregon, where he is also Weinman Professor of Technology and Professor in the Department of Educational Measurement, Policy, and Leadership. His works focus on the implications of globalization and technology on education. He has published over 100 articles and 20 books, including *Catching Up or Leading the Way: American education in the age of globalization* and *World Class Learners: educating creative and entrepreneurial students*.

# Index